CIRCLE OF STARS

CIRCLE OF STARS

A History of the EU – and
the People Who Made It

DERMOT HODSON

YALE UNIVERSITY PRESS
NEW HAVEN AND LONDON

All reasonable efforts have been made to provide accurate sources for all images that
appear in this book. Any discrepancies or omissions will be rectified in future editions.

For information about this and other Yale University Press publications, please contact:
U.S. Office: sales.press@yale.edu   yalebooks.com
Europe Office: sales@yaleup.co.uk   yalebooks.co.uk

Set in Minion Pro by IDSUK (DataConnection) Ltd
Printed in Great Britain by TJ Books, Padstow, Cornwall

Library of Congress Control Number: 2023941188

ISBN 978-0-300-26769-3

A catalogue record for this book is available from the British Library.

10 9 8 7 6 5 4 3 2 1

To Emma, William and Hugh

Against the background of blue sky, twelve golden stars form a circle, representing the union of the peoples of Europe. The number of stars is fixed, twelve being the symbol of perfection and unity.

The Council of Europe and the European Council (1996)

Contents

CONTENTS

PART IV 'Do Not Be Late'

Illustrations

1. Danes vote 'yes' to the Maastricht Treaty, May 1993. Gamma-Rapho via Getty Images.
2. European Commission President Jacques Delors addresses MEPs, February 1993. © Communautés européennes 1993 – EP.
3. Sir James Goldsmith campaigns for a public vote on whether the UK should remain in the EU, January 1997. Shutterstock / AP Photo / Alastair Grant.
4. Viviane Reding attends the Cannes Film Festival, May 2001. © European Communities, 2001.
5. Václav Havel meets Jacques Delors, March 1991. © European Communities, 1991.
6. Signing of Poland's Treaty of Accession, April 2003. © European Communities, 2003.
7. Dutch 'no' voters celebrate the defeat of the European Constitution, June 2005. Shutterstock / AP Photo / Bas Czerwinski.
8. Michael O'Leary campaigns for a 'yes' vote in Ireland's second referendum on the Lisbon Treaty, October 2009. Shutterstock / AP Photo / Peter Morrison.
9. Wim Kok welcomes Tony Blair to Amsterdam, June 1997. © European Communities, 1997.
10. Soldiers on patrol outside the European Commission's Berlaymont headquarters, February 2015. Shutterstock / AP Photo / Virginia Mayo.

Prologue
Hopes and Fears

The Trap

On 10 February 1993, Jacques Delors delivered a speech to the European Parliament in Strasbourg to mark the beginning of his third term as president of the European Commission. It should have been a hopeful occasion. The French socialist former finance minister, the European Community's best-known official, had brought a measure of ambition to Brussels not seen since the days of Walter Hallstein. Whereas Hallstein had been cut down to size by French President Charles de Gaulle for wearing 'the insignia of sovereignty', Delors had won the confidence of Helmut Kohl, François Mitterrand and Margaret Thatcher, three Heads of State or Government who agreed on little else, with a bold economic plan.[1] The Single Market Programme had sought to remove all remaining barriers to the free movement of goods, services, capital and people between the twelve member states of the European Community – Belgium, Denmark, France, Germany, Greece, Ireland, Italy, Luxembourg, the Netherlands, Portugal, Spain and the United Kingdom – by the last day of 1992.[2] By promising lower prices for consumers, new opportunities for businesses and up to 2 million new jobs, the plan had not only revived popular support for European integration in the Twelve but encouraged a host of other countries, including the new democracies of Central and Eastern Europe, to seek membership.[3] As the Single Market Programme drew to a close, member states had agreed to transform the European Community into a bold, new European Union, complete with the single currency that

1

Delors had argued for. Despite these and other achievements, the Commission President offered not so much an encomium for Europe as a counsel of despair. 'The economy is in crisis, society is in crisis, democracy is foundering,' Delors told Members of the European Parliament (MEPs). 'Victims abound, beginning with the unemployed and the dispossessed. And if the trend continues there are other potential losers. The very idea of a united Europe could be in peril.'[4]

When Sir James Goldsmith published his book, *Le Piège*, in September 1993, he couldn't have hoped for much.[5] The Anglo-French billionaire was ostensibly retired by this point and little known outside business circles and the pages of *Private Eye*, a satirical magazine which he repeatedly sued for libel.[6] Born into wealth, Goldsmith's ambitions of following his father into the House of Commons had long since faded. Instead, he built a sprawling, successful empire in pharmaceuticals, retail and finance on both sides of the Atlantic. He had a talent for building up businesses, including Mothercare and Bovril, and an even greater one for selling them. Although Goldsmith strenuously denied being a corporate raider, he reportedly served as an inspiration for the unscrupulous Sir Lawrence Wildman in Oliver Stone's *Wall Street* (1987). A risk-taker who challenged the prevailing consensus, Goldsmith sold his assets before the United States stock market crash of 1987 and moved to Mexico with his fortune intact to build a vast nature reserve.

In retirement, the entrepreneur planned to devote more time to public commentary on his eclectic political interests, which were informed by his brother Teddy's environmentalism and a taste for the apocalyptic. In *Le Piège*, Goldsmith warned of pandemics, environmental catastrophes and the threat of 'forty Chernobyls'.[7] His main focus was the General Agreement on Tariffs and Trade, which he saw as ushering in a new era of globalism that would disadvantage industrial and developing countries alike. Goldsmith's interventions on these topics had hitherto sunk without trace, but *Le Piège* quickly became a bestseller in France. *The Trap*, an English-language update of Goldsmith's book published in November 1994, had a new target.

'European ruling elites,' he warned, were 'seeking to destroy the identity of every European nation.'[8]

Goldsmith's animus towards European officials was new. He had supported the United Kingdom's accession to the European Communities in 1973 and backed the Britain in Europe campaign in the country's referendum two years later. Now in the fourteen months between the publication of *Le Piège* and *The Trap*, he distilled a new brand of right-wing populism whereby he alone could protect the people against 'a supranational, centralized, bureaucratic state.'[9]

Euroscepticism was as old as the European Communities and right-wing populism was older still, but Goldsmith fused these 'thin-centred' ideologies in new ways.[10] He portrayed the EU not simply as a capitalist club, as earlier generations of Eurosceptics had done, or as a dirigiste threat to the free market, as Thatcher had said in her speech at the College of Europe in Bruges in September 1988, but as the conduit for a new and destructive form of 'globalism'.[11] The post-war economic order prospered, Goldsmith argued, because it allowed regional trading organisations such as the European Community to protect member states' interests. Global free trade was now stripping away such protections, he contended, in favour of a 'worldwide market' that pitted industrialised countries against developing countries for the first time. By embracing globalism, Goldsmith warned, Europe was vulnerable to low-wage competition and joblessness, as well as religious wars and an 'uncontrolled invasion' of immigrants.[12]

Maastricht (1992)

Delors' and Goldsmith's fears for the future of Europe had a common stimulus: the Maastricht Treaty. Named after the Dutch city in which it was signed in February 1992, Maastricht envisaged a new stage in the process of European integration started four decades earlier with the creation of the European Community.[13] One of several international organisations launched in the post-war period to advance European integration, the European Community was the most dynamic; its concerted approach to the coal and steel sector paved the way for a customs union, a common market and common policies in areas such as agriculture, trade and transport. The European Community also stood out for the significant powers it transferred to European officials. The exemplar of this institutional choice was the European Commission, an independent administrative body comprised of seventeen Commissioners and a permanent staff of around 15,000 officials as of 1992, which was given a virtual monopoly over proposing new policy and legislation.[14]

The Maastricht Treaty didn't dismantle these policies or institutions; instead, it built three new 'pillars' on top of the European Community. The EU formally referred to two of these legal constructs but, in practice, soon came to refer to all three. The first pillar extended the European Community's reach to areas such as culture, public health and the environment and committed member states to economic and monetary union, an ambitious project to replace national currencies with a single currency, which would eventually be known as the euro. The second pillar was the common foreign and security policy, through which the EU would 'promote peace, security and progress in Europe and in the world'.[15] Foreign policy had been largely off limits to the European Community, whereas the Maastricht Treaty raised the possibility of an EU defence policy. The third pillar concerned justice and home affairs, including a common approach to immigration and asylum designed to protect the safety and security of EU citizens. Unlike the 1986 Single European Act, Maastricht conferred comparatively few new powers on the Commission, with responsibility for monetary policy to be delegated in due course to a new body of European officials: the European Central Bank (ECB). By contrast, the treaty gave the European Parliament significant new policy-making powers. Although MEPs had been directly elected by European voters since 1979, the Council of Ministers – in which ministers from each member state government met – decided whether Commission proposals should become law. Under Maastricht, MEPs were finally given the power to co-decide proposals in certain policy areas, turning the European Parliament into the world's first transnational legislature.

The founding treaties of the European Community had been approved by national parliaments with ease. The ratification of the Maastricht Treaty, in contrast, set off a political firestorm. In June 1992, Danish voters rejected the treaty by a margin of less than 50,000. The EU would launch with or without Denmark, insisted the eleven other member states, but France's wafer thin referendum vote for Maastricht in September 1992 and a brewing rebellion against the treaty on the backbenches of the British Conservative Party confirmed that the political discontent witnessed in Denmark was no isolated case.

Although Maastricht is remembered as a 'milestone' of the 'Delors era', the Commission President was actually deeply ambivalent about the treaty.[16] François Mitterrand and Helmut Kohl were its real driving forces, albeit for different reasons.[17] The French president had come to power in 1981 promising to defend the French franc from speculation.[18] But, having been forced to abandon his programme of public works, jobs and investment when speculators sold the French franc with abandon, he turned to the idea of a single currency to restore French and European influence in the international monetary system.[19] In the twilight of a presidency marked by fluctuating popularity and a private battle with prostate cancer, Mitterrand also saw Maastricht as an opportunity to secure his legacy as a European statesman. A towering figure, both politically and physically, Kohl was reticent about giving up the Deutsche Mark, which symbolised West Germany's remarkable track record of economic growth and stability. However, the chancellor put his weight behind the project when Mitterrand agreed to a monetary union modelled on Germany's own. From its firm commitment to price stability, to its strong support for central bank independence and requirements that participating member states demonstrate their economic convergence, the Maastricht Treaty sought to make the single currency a facsimile of the Deutsche Mark.[20] Kohl also saw Maastricht as a means to embed the newly united Germany and the continent's new democracies in, what he called, 'pan-European processes'.[21] The chancellor's vision of political union was not a federal one which sought to centralise decision-making in Brussels, but a practical one aimed at safeguarding Germany and Europe's place in a rapidly changing global order. Fears that his country would receive a disproportionate share of migrants and refugees from Central and Eastern Europe were uppermost in his mind.[22] Just as Mitterrand had won Kohl around to monetary union, Kohl won Mitterrand over to a common approach to immigration and asylum and other areas of justice and home affairs.

Margaret Thatcher was aghast at the idea of ceding sovereignty in such sensitive policy domains. At the peak of her formidable powers, she had been a pragmatic pro-European who campaigned for the UK to remain in the European Community and inspired the Single Market Programme. But as her influence waned at home and abroad, she became increasingly disillusioned with, and confrontational towards, the European Community. Thatcher's resignation in November 1990, in part because senior members of her cabinet sought a more constructive approach to negotiations over Maastricht, cleared the way for John Major to become prime minister. Major was determined to put the UK at 'the heart of Europe' and to build an EU that was responsive to international events and 'open to the outside world'.[23] But he led a party that was deeply divided between members who shared his pro-Europeanism and those who embraced Thatcher's belated Euroscepticism as a mark of respect for their fallen leader.

Had Delors been asked to sign the Maastricht Treaty, he would likely have done so through gritted teeth. Although he supported economic and monetary union, and had been closely involved in its design, the Commission President worried that the treaty's strict limits on government borrowing once the single currency came into effect would be economically and politically unworkable. However, his preferred approach of creating an EU budget instrument to help member states adjust to economic shocks enjoyed next to no support. Most member states were willing to consider a single monetary policy for the sake of achieving low inflation and exchange rate stability, but none relished giving up their powers to tax and spend.

Delors was also uneasy about political union. Having failed to win support for a high-level committee on this concept – which jarred with his pragmatic, piecemeal vision of European integration – the Frenchman badly miscalculated by backing a plan to do away with the EU's proposed three pillar structure and so strengthen the Commission's powers. The brainchild of Dutch Foreign Minister Piet Dankert, a federalist former president of the European Parliament, this proposal was greeted with consternation by other member states. Foreign ministers overcame this diplomatic impasse by giving governments control over the EU's common foreign and security policy and justice and home affairs. Delors was dismayed, fearing that the Commission would be sidelined within the new EU.

Speaking at the Maastricht Treaty's signing ceremony in February 1992, the Commission President struggled to summon up the sense of optimism that this solemn occasion demanded. The treaty had been achieved at the 'cost of compromise' and 'the expense of a certain institutional logic', he told his fellow dignitaries, while doing little to disguise his doubts that the EU would be less 'dynamic and responsive to our legitimate concerns' than the European Community had been of late.[24]

By the time Delors stood to address the European Parliament eleven months later, his confidence in the Maastricht Treaty had been further shaken. Denmark's 'no' vote against the treaty spoke to his worst fears about the EU, as did the European Community's failure to prevent war in Bosnia-Herzegovina. The exchange rate mechanism crisis, meanwhile, cast doubt on member states' commitment to fixed exchange rates, and by extension the single currency, after speculators forced the UK and Italy to break their peg to the European Currency Unit, a forerunner to the euro. 'The euphoria of 1990, in the wake of the liberation of Central and Eastern Europe, has given way to a period of depression, with the Yugoslavian tragedy looming in the background,' Delors told MEPs, continuing: 'To be frank, routine cooperation between our twelve member states has weakened in the face of these developments.'[25]

The origin of Goldsmith's fears over Maastricht was more nebulous. His initial response when Communism collapsed in Central and Eastern Europe was to champion European federalism. In 1990, he called for a European Constitution, a common European currency and a European Senate, ideas which resurfaced in *Le Piège* but went missing in *The Trap*.[26] That Goldsmith went in a matter of months from chiding the Commission for being 'too bureaucratic' to accusing European officials of 'acting by stealth' to overthrow national democratic structures – just as he once did of the Soviet Union and its sympathisers – suggested a degree of discombobulation at the Cold War's abrupt end.[27] There was also a strong hint of opportunism surrounding Goldsmith's sudden conversion to Euroscepticism. Maastricht was built on a sustained process of deliberation and consensus-seeking between governments, officials and experts, which the businessman found it politically profitable to challenge.[28]

Whatever his true motivations, Goldsmith found in Maastricht one last opportunity to realise his political ambitions. A mesmeric public speaker, he lectured to business audiences in the 1970s and 1980s on topics ranging from Third World debt to the British class system. But he remained a political outsider. The Conservative Party, while content to take his money, rarely sought his counsel. When Goldsmith gave testimony to the United States Senate on corporate takeovers, he was surprised by the warm reception he received. 'It was one of the first times in my life that I was not counter-culture,' he later remembered.[29] As a businessman with interests in oil and mining, Goldsmith struggled to speak with credibility on environmentalism. As a businessman with interests on both sides of the Channel, he was the ideal commentator on the new EU. Even the pro-EU *Observer* looked to Goldsmith as a European Ross Perot, an anti-politician willing to speak truth to traditional purveyors of power.[30] Goldsmith's wealth helped too. In July, he backed efforts by William Rees-Mogg, former editor of *The Times* and a fellow Europhile turned Eurosceptic, to seek a judicial review of Maastricht in the English courts.

On 1 November 1993, the Maastricht Treaty entered into force without ceremony. Rees-Mogg's legal challenge had failed, as expected. Eurosceptic rebels in the British Conservative Party had embarked upon a course of action with profound long-term consequences, but, in the short term, they merely delayed ratification. Danish voters had changed their mind in a second referendum held after the government secured opt-outs from the treaty's most sensitive provisions.[31] Brussels was unusually quiet that All Saints' Day and not only because of the public holiday. 'No one is in the mood for this kind of thing. We have urgent problems to tackle, which we can only tackle by sharing power and sovereignty in a Union,' reported one official.[32] There was uncertainty too over what the new endeavour should be called. UK Prime Minister John Major made a last-ditch attempt to retain European Community, which made legal sense in so far as the term European Union referred only to new areas of cooperation under the Maastricht Treaty.[33] Other national leaders had little time for such diplomatic circumlocution and soon settled on European Union.[34]

'We Have Changed, the World Has Changed More'

Delors' third term as Commission President – approved by the European Parliament with only a few grumbles – was a low-key affair. He invested most of his energies in a pioneering and remarkably pessimistic report on the state of the EU economy. The White Paper on Growth, Competitiveness and Employment started with a puzzle: the EU had completed the Single Market Programme on schedule, created 9 million jobs in the second half of the 1980s and added a half percentage point to annual growth rates; but 17 million Europeans were out of work and the rate of unemployment seemed to be 'steadily rising from cycle to cycle'.[35] The Commission's explanation was simple and stark: the world had entered an era of 'unavoidable globalisation' and the EU was lagging behind.[36] 'The truth is that although we have changed, the world has changed more,' the report concluded.[37]

9

Meanwhile, James Goldsmith had formed a new right-wing party, Movement for France, with Philippe de Villiers, a politician who broke with the centre-right over his opposition to the Maastricht Treaty. Goldsmith was duly elected as a French MEP in June 1994. Joining forces with Danish and Dutch MEPs, the billionaire established Europe of Nations, the EU's first Eurosceptic political group. The European Parliament had often disappointed those who believed in the promise of transnational democracy. In the hands of Goldsmith, it became a powerful megaphone for communicating a simple political message across borders, challenging the idea of European integration while, in its own contrary way, embodying it. Although Europe of Nations survived for only two years, it showed that right-wing populism was a potent force in post-Maastricht politics and inspired future Eurosceptic groupings in the European Parliament.[38]

In June 1994, the European Commission embarked on a new economic agenda, which sought to boost growth, jobs and international competitiveness through labour market reforms and policies designed to exploit 'the possibilities and opportunities offered by the information society'.[39] However, member states had baulked at the White Paper's calls to invest 574 billion European Currency Units (around US$683 billion in 1994 prices) in European transport and energy networks, telecommunication and environmental programmes by the end of the decade.[40] A frustrated Delors finished his term of office as Commission President six months later. Opinion polls suggested that he had a good chance of winning the French presidential election, but he decided not to stand, perhaps because of concerns over his own health, perhaps out of deference to his daughter, Martine Aubrey, a rising star in the French Socialist Party who harboured presidential ambitions of her own.[41] Delors' time on the European stage was essentially over.

In November 1994, Goldsmith appeared on British television to rail against the Maastricht Treaty, Delors and the German government for championing 'one state, one parliament, one government'.[42] He promised to put up a candidate in each constituency in the UK's next general election. If he won a majority, he would form a government that would introduce a single piece of legislation for a referendum on the nature of the United Kingdom's EU membership. Goldsmith would resign the premiership after 30 days and trigger fresh elections. The Referendum Party gained less than 3 per cent of the vote in May 1997, but Goldsmith declared victory. 'We were a pressure group,' he concluded on election night. 'All the parties that refused referendums, to begin with, have become referendum parties.'[43] Six weeks later, he died of a heart attack brought on by pancreatic cancer.

Despite their political differences, Delors and Goldsmith both believed that European integration had been utterly transformed by Maastricht. For Delors, 'the people of Europe came to life when the Treaty on European Union was signed and the ratification process began.'[44] Henceforth, the task of EU policy-makers was to 'explain, again and again, what we are doing and why'.[45] For Goldsmith, European political leaders were running scared of the people. The 'real reason' why the British government hadn't held a referendum, he argued, was that 'Maastricht would be resoundingly rejected by the British people'.[46] The two men's predictions about where this change would lead the EU proved to be inaccurate. The nation state didn't disappear, as Goldsmith warned, although numerous right-wing populists would mimic his warnings to powerful effect. Nor did national governments turn away from Europe, as Delors predicted. Instead, they stuck with the EU in the three turbulent decades that followed. This book tells the story of why.

There is no single way to write a contemporary history of the EU, which is arguably the most powerful and contentious international organisation ever created. A political system with its own parliament, currency and laws, not only does the EU impact the daily lives of nearly 500 million Europeans, but its policies also resonate for good and ill worldwide. There are many excellent histories of European integration, with the best known focusing on social forces, summitry and the power of economic ideas.[47] This book doesn't dismiss such factors, but it does place greater emphasis on the people who shaped the EU's evolution since Maastricht. What follows is not a 'Great Man' theory of history; for one thing, as is shown, many of the EU's most important achievements were brought about by women once they had an opportunity to lead. Nor is it, to borrow the historian Alan Milward's phrase, about 'the lives and teachings of European saints'.[48] There is no shortage of sinners for those who come looking for a morality tale, even if it is not written with this purpose in mind. By focusing on people, this book aims to show that the EU is not a faceless bureaucracy but a vibrant polity in which impassioned individuals contest their countries' place in Europe and Europe's place in the world.

It is tempting to recount the history of the EU through a small cast of characters, whose personal differences embody distinct visions of Europe. This book seeks instead to capture the transnational chorus that has spurred the EU's development. For example, Tony Blair's impact on the European Union during his decade as UK prime minister cannot be understood without considering his rise and fall alongside other Third Way leaders, such as António Guterres in Portugal, Wim Kok in the Netherlands and Gerhard Schröder in Germany. A key theme in what follows is the fluidity of EU politics, which sees presidents and prime ministers come and go, while providing proponents and opponents of European integration with multiple venues in which to make their voices heard.

The book's ensemble includes citizens, cultural figures, parliamentarians and business and labour representatives, but it is chiefly comprised of the presidents or prime ministers of EU member states – the Heads of State or Government, as these national leaders are collectively known – European officials and right-wing populists.[49] The history of the EU is written by all three groups, yet it is the Heads of State or Government, this book argues, who penned the most important moments in European integration since Maastricht. That national leaders were the locus of power in the EU does not mean that European officials were peripheral. Without institutions such as the European Commission and European Central Bank, the consensus that prevailed among member states wouldn't have been translated into concrete policies, credible commitments and a tangible presence on the world stage. However, the claim that the EU is controlled by Eurocrats is not only misleading; it provides political cover for national leaders, who agree to work together but too often blame Brussels when the results prove unpopular. It also suits right-wing populists, who thrive on claims that national democracy is being overrun by foreign elites, while they themselves undermine fundamental values.

The central thesis of this book is that national leaders stuck with the EU after Maastricht not because they shared an ideological commitment to ever closer union but because they believed that their countries could manage global crises more effectively by working together. This shared understanding was both powerful and problematic. During its first three decades, the Heads of State or Government created a common asylum policy, launched the euro and showed global leadership on issues ranging from climate change to the Covid-19 pandemic. They also welcomed sixteen new member states, mostly from Central and Eastern Europe. Despite these achievements, national leaders' naïve embrace of globalisation as a force for good opened the door to right-wing populists who portrayed the EU as a threat to national sovereignty, identity and standards of living. The resulting tensions came to a head over the United Kingdom's referendum vote to leave the EU in June 2016, but they did not come to an end.

The EU is often viewed through a monochrome filter, which reduces European integration to a project thriving in adversity or, more commonly, close to collapse. Predictions of the single currency's imminent demise were ever-present during the euro crisis, and the EU was portrayed as being in mortal danger during the 2015 global refugee crisis. This book does not downplay the severity of these or other crises or the toll taken by the Union's response to them. Nor does it suggest that the EU has always lived up to the circle of stars on the European flag, a symbol of unity, solidarity and harmony.[50] And yet, by telling the EU's story over thirty turbulent years, it s hows that the Union has endured in ways that defied Delors' and Goldsmith's predictions.

13

PART I
'THE PEOPLE OF EUROPE CAME TO LIFE'

1

Maastricht to Amsterdam

'No Reasons to Get Back'

In the spring of 1993, Steve Averill and Shaughn McGrath were commissioned to produce artwork for a hastily recorded album.[1] They started with a graffiti baby, created by the Northern Irish painter Charlie Whisker, and turned the child into a cosmonaut floating in space. The graphic artists' initial concept was to put their stranded explorer at the centre of a circle of stars in homage to the European flag. However, Carter the Unstoppable Sex Machine, a band from South London, had used a similar image the previous year. So Averill and McGrath's colleague Brian Williams pixilated the flag and photoshopped it onto digitally distorted images of three notorious European Heads of State, Nicolae Ceauşescu, Vladimir Lenin and Benito Mussolini, and the Brandenburg Gate, a symbol of European division and, later, unity. The artists named their young cosmonaut Zoo Europa. Their clients liked the design and the moniker, which they reworked into the album's title: *Zooropa*.

U2 had originally looked to the United States for inspiration. But, having mined this seam until it was spent, the band relocated to Berlin in 1990, where they channelled Walter Benjamin, Jean Baudrillard and David Bowie. One track recorded during this period was 'Zoo Station'. Named after Bahnhof Zoo, an S-Bahn stop on Hardenbergplatz, the song's lyrics elliptically compared Berlin's creative energy with American paralysis under the presidency of George H.W. Bush.[2] Each evening on its 1992 American tour, the band's politically charged singer, Bono, would prank-call the president, as Bush fell further and further behind in the polls to self-proclaimed U2 fan Bill Clinton. When the tour reached Europe, its political focus changed. Previously, Bono would open the show by jerkily dancing before a snow pattern of static on a giant video wall. Now he appeared to the final movement of Beethoven's Ninth Symphony, the European anthem, flashing a mock-fascist salute before an animated European flag which lost one star after another. Rather than calling the White House, the singer now heckled right-wing populists such as MEP Jean-Marie Le Pen and spoke nightly to journalists in Sarajevo, a city under siege.

Europe was in the cultural ether that summer. The recently completed Single Market Programme had created a seemingly border-less space between the twelve member states of the European Community, promising new economic opportunities for their 370 million citizens. The Maastricht Treaty turned this Community into an ambitious new European Union, which, having survived its brush with Danish voters, agreed that Central and Eastern Europe's new democracies would become members. By their own admission, U2 were too busy having fun to follow the fine detail of such events, but they were struck by the rise of right-wing populists and troubled by the disconnect between European politicians 'pontificating about the single market and single currency' while responding to the Yugoslav Wars with 'uncertainty and prevarication'.[3]

'Zooropa', the title track of the band's 1993 album, turned these concerns into a 'manifesto' for a new Europe and a new world.[4] Beginning with a white noise of global voices, the singer intones advertising slogans from European and US multinational companies, including Audi ('Vorsprung durch Technik'), Zanussi ('Better by Design') and American Airlines ('Fly the Friendly Skies'). But this soulless single market gives way to a hopeful determination. However difficult it might be to navigate this new Europe with 'no compass' and 'no map', there were 'no reasons to get back'.[5]

European Union 1976–92

Maastricht wasn't written on a blank page. As the historian Kiran Klaus Patel shows, the treaty's three signature projects – the single currency, the common foreign and security policy and cooperation in the field of justice and home affairs – had been on the European Community's agenda since the 1970s.[6] However, cooperation in these fields had either stalled or taken place outside the European Community's decision-making structures. The 1970 Werner Plan to establish an economic and monetary union by the end of the decade was soon abandoned amid the international economic crisis that followed the collapse of Bretton Woods and the first oil shock. Although member states endorsed a new plan for economic and monetary union in Madrid in June 1989, they concluded at the same summit that a single currency couldn't be realised without, what eventually became, the Maastricht Treaty.[7] The European Political Cooperation, which was created in 1970, allowed foreign ministers to produce joint declarations on questions of international peace and security, issues which the European Community had hitherto steered clear of. However, such efforts had next to no impact on world affairs, as Patel acknowledges.[8] It was not until the Maastricht Treaty entered into force that the EU had a fully fledged foreign and security policy which sought to protect 'the common values, fundamental interests and independence of the Union' or seriously considered a common defence policy.[9] Member states, meanwhile, initiated cooperation on drug policy in 1971 and counter-terrorism in 1975, but discussions in these and other areas of justice and home affairs remained on an ad hoc footing until the EU was created. However, Maastricht was not just about the formalisation of the hitherto informal. It was also about the realisation of a political project that had been flown as a trial balloon two decades earlier and burst.

In October 1972, the Heads of State or Government of Belgium, Denmark, France, West Germany, Ireland, Italy, Luxembourg, the Netherlands and the United Kingdom met in Paris, where they invited the European Commission, the European Parliament and the European Court of Justice to prepare a report on transforming 'the whole complex of the relations' between members of the European Community into a European Union.[10] It was twenty years by this point since the establishment of the European Coal and Steel Community and fourteen since the founding of the European Economic Community and the European Atomic Energy Community. The European Community, as these entities were collectively known, had enjoyed early success, most noticeably in the creation of a customs union, common market and common agricultural policy. But the project had lost its way in the mid-1960s after Charles de Gaulle recalled French diplomats and ministers from Brussels after a row over qualified majority voting. This empty chair crisis was resolved by a compromise which ensured no member state could be outvoted on matters of 'vital national interest'.[11] The downside of this arrangement was that it slowed down Community decision-making at a time of growing international instability.

Although he had been a close ally of his predecessor Charles de Gaulle, French President Georges Pompidou sought to revive the European Community rather than keep it in check. Pompidou's first major foreign policy decision as president was to drop his country's veto on UK accession to the European Community. His second was to call a referendum not only on whether Denmark, Ireland, Norway and the UK should be allowed to join the European Community but on whether France should embrace 'the new opportunities opening up in Europe'.[12] Two-thirds of voters supported Pompidou, who in turn convinced his fellow Heads of State or Government to support his plans for 'European Union' in Paris in October 1972.[13] Growing frustrated with the European institutions' slow deliberation on this subject, national leaders soon took matters into their own hands.[14]

Belgian Prime Minister Leo Tindemans accepted the invitation to study what form European union should take with energy, enthusiasm and a heavy heart. A European federalist marked by his teenage experience of Nazi occupation, Tindemans saw European unity as vital for his own country's security. He was also a European pragmatist, who cut his political teeth on plans to decentralise power among Belgium's fractious French- and Flemish-speaking communities. He understood from the outset that a federal Europe enjoyed next to no political support among other leaders.

After touring nine national capitals to meet with political leaders and civil society, Tindemans' message was direct: public opinion was favourable towards the European project and frustrated with political leaders' lack of commitment to it. 'Almost all the people to whom I spoke,' the Belgian prime minister told his fellow Heads of State or Government, 'could not imagine a better future for their country than that offered by the building of Europe.'[15] But the public was sceptical of national leaders' willingness 'to establish a genuine European Union and solve the real problems of the day at European level'. In a television address marking the publication of his report in December 1975, the Belgian prime minister cut a professorial figure, clutching a pen and making notes, as if writing his recommendations in real time. Preferring to disappoint federalists rather than alarm other Heads of State or Government, Tindemans eschewed calls for a European Constitution or even a treaty revision in favour of practical steps to give meaning to the idea of European Union. Member states, he argued, needed to speak on the world stage with one voice, even on questions of security and defence, to develop a common economic and monetary policy, if necessary among a subset of member states, and to serve European citizens rather than the 'pleasure of the technocrats', including through the protection of rights.

The European Council, as the Heads of State or Government now christened their regular summits, greeted the Tindemans Report with polite indifference. The Belgian prime minister may have diluted his proposals to suit their tastes, but his recommendations remained, as the historian Mark Gilbert memorably put it, 'strong beer . . . which nobody had the courage to gulp'.[16] French President Valéry Giscard d'Estaing's abstemiousness was particularly damaging. France's youthful president had promised to continue efforts to rejuvenate European integration after Pompidou's untimely death, but the liberal leader was enfeebled by France's troubled economy and, what Michael Leigh called, 'a network of political constraints at home'.[17] Lacking a stable parliamentary majority, Giscard depended on the support of Jacques Chirac's Rally for the Republic, but Chirac resigned as prime minister after two years and moved further to the right in his effort to retain control of his party from Gaullists. In December 1978, while recuperating from a car crash, Chirac launched a veiled attack from his hospital bed against Giscard's 'party of foreigners', further limiting the president's ability to lead on European issues.[18] Political support for Tindemans' ideas was no greater in other member states. Faced with rising inflation, increasing unemployment and energy shortages, national leaders turned inwards.

For Tindemans, the EU's establishment in November 1993 'confirmed' what he had tried to achieve in his report almost two decades earlier.[19] But this claim downplayed key differences between his vision of a European Union and the one codified by the Maastricht Treaty. The European Commission should 'reassert its freedom of action' and 'add its own brand of dynamism to the building of the European Union', Tindemans had argued. Maastricht gave the European Commission limited say over new and sensitive areas of cooperation. The European Parliament should be given the right to propose legislation like a regular parliament, Tindemans had suggested. Maastricht conferred no such right, allowing the European Parliament instead to co-decide on European Commission proposals in some policy areas, this power having hitherto rested solely with national representatives in the Council of Ministers. The biggest difference between the Tindemans Report and Maastricht, however, concerned how the idea of European union was received. In writing his report, the Belgian prime minister was supremely confident that public opinion favoured deeper European integration. The first Eurobarometer published in 1974 had, after all, shown that three-quarters of Europeans viewed progress towards European unity to be insufficient.[20] Just how divisive the EU would be with the general public became apparent from the moment that Maastricht was signed.

The Post-Maastricht Period

In 1991, 72 per cent of respondents surveyed by the Eurobarometer agreed that their country's membership of the European Community was a good thing.[21] By 1996, this figure had fallen to 48 per cent, its lowest level since 1981.[22] The EU's economic problems partly explained this trend. While Europeans awaited the growth and jobs promised when the single market was completed, the EU followed other industrialised economies into a sharp downturn in the early 1990s. The resulting recession was short-lived, but unemployment in the EU-15 remained above 10 per cent of the civilian labour force until the end of the decade.[23] And yet, the economic situation couldn't entirely explain popular discontent with the EU. In Tindemans' time, people had looked to the European Community for respite from an unfolding international economic crisis. That the recession of the early 1990s had the opposite effect was due in no small measure to the efforts of right-wing populists. When George Pompidou announced his referendum in March 1972, the result was never in doubt. When UK Prime Minister Harold Wilson called a referendum three years later on whether the UK should remain a member of the European Community, he was equally optimistic. However divided Wilson's Labour Party may have been over European integration, British voters backed Remain as expected. From the moment they sought popular approval for the Maastricht Treaty, Danish Prime Minister Poul Schlüter and French President François Mitterrand could see that things had changed.

A solid supporter of European integration, Schlüter didn't choose to hold Denmark's referendum on Maastricht; the treaty had failed to win a five-sixths majority in the Danish Parliament and so had to be put to a public vote. An experienced campaigner, Schlüter enjoyed the support of most of his country's biggest political parties, key trade unions and business groups, and large sections of the national media. But he struggled against an insurgent 'no' campaign led by the left-wing Socialist People's Party and right-wing populist Progress Party.

The Progress Party had performed poorly in the 1990 general election, yet its warnings over the EU's threat to sovereignty struck a chord with Danish voters, who narrowly rejected the treaty. Eighty per cent of those who voted 'no' expressed a preference for 'political freedom' over the economic benefits of European integration.[24]

Mitterrand was under no obligation to hold a referendum on Maastricht, which could have easily won approval in the French parliament. With polls predicting a decisive 'yes', he saw an opportunity to boost his flagging presidency, which had been damaged by the worsening economic outlook and a decade in power.[25] Although he could count on the support of his principal political opponents, Valéry Giscard d'Estaing and Jacques Chirac, Mitterrand faced a vociferous 'no' campaign led by three rebels: Philippe Séguin, Charles Pasqua and Philippe de Villiers. Coming from the Gaullist wing of Chirac's party, Séguin and Pasqua rehearsed familiar arguments about European officials having too much power.[26] De Villiers broke from Giscard's centrist Union for French Democracy in an altogether less predictable manner. An aristocratic businessman who opened a hugely popular historical theme park in Pays de la Loire, he criticised Maastricht, by turns, as not integrationist enough and for eroding French sovereignty and encouraging immigration. On the second of these points, de Villiers echoed Jean-Marie Le Pen, who had once supported European unity as a means to renew the continent's past glory but now denounced Maastricht for opening the door to uncontrolled migration.[27] Although the 'yes' side narrowly won, it was a moral victory for the 'no' campaign and a personal one for de Villiers and Le Pen, who became national figures.

Denmark's second referendum on the Maastricht Treaty resulted in a comfortable win for the 'yes' campaign, which benefited from the decision of the Socialist People's Party to switch sides. The experience nevertheless emboldened Europe's right-wing populists, who stepped up their criticisms of the EU and the politicians who built and continued to defend it. The nineteen seats secured by Sir James Goldsmith and Philippe de Villiers' Eurosceptic grouping in the 1994 European Parliament election showed how politicians who presented themselves as outsiders could inflame popular distrust in the EU to win power in the post-Maastricht period.[28]

Goldsmith took little practical interest in the European Parliament. His real aim was to win a seat at Westminster by sowing Eurosceptic discontent in the UK. 'As you know, just about the only good thing in Maastricht was the fact that it states that in 1996 we must look at the whole thing again,' he told a fringe event at the 1994 Conservative conference in Bournemouth.[29] Unusually for a European treaty, Maastricht listed several unresolved issues that member states agreed to revisit in a fresh intergovernmental conference. The so-called leftovers were arcane, concerning the classification and hierarchy of Community acts, the relationship between the Western European Union, a defence pact, and EU security and defence policy and the general effectiveness of new 'policies and forms of cooperation'. These matters could and should have been dealt with in short order.[30] Instead, the 1996 conference became a focal point for hopes and fears about the future of the EU.

Leftovers

Luxembourg Prime Minister Jacques Santer was indirectly to blame for this turn of events. An acolyte of Pierre Werner, architect of the ill-fated plan for economic and monetary union, Santer had sought to make his mark during negotiations over the Maastricht Treaty by tabling an early draft of the agreement. The Luxembourg draft was faithful to the political compromise sought by member states, most noticeably in its determination to keep the Commission at arm's length from the common foreign and security policy and justice and home affairs. But the text added a federalist flourish to this compromise by referring to the EU as 'a new stage in the gradual process leading to a federal Union' and setting 1996 as a deadline for an intergovernmental conference to 'strengthen the federal character of the Union'. Although he was not an ardent federalist, Santer was keen to assuage those, like Belgian Prime Minister Jean-Luc Dehaene, who wanted much deeper integration. But in so doing, Santer either failed to appreciate, or discounted, the difficulties that such language would create for John Major, as he battled against Eurosceptic sentiment in the UK Conservative Party. Since the text required the unanimous approval of all national leaders, the 'F' word was inevitably excised from Maastricht's final draft, which referred instead to the EU as 'a new stage in the process of European integration' and reduced the planned conference to a tidying up exercise. Some Eurosceptics still saw a federalist plot or an opportunity to stoke up fears over one.

A month before Goldsmith spoke in Bournemouth, Wolfgang Schäuble, leader of the largest centre-right group in the Bundestag, and Karl Lamers, the group's foreign policy spokesperson, had co-authored a position paper calling for closer cooperation among a hardcore of member states. Schäuble laboured under no illusions that the UK would be part of this vanguard group, which would be restricted to those countries that would participate in economic and monetary union. His real target was Southern European member states such as Greece, Italy, Portugal and Spain, who he believed couldn't and shouldn't be part of a single currency given their track record of economic instability. For Schäuble, it would be better for France, Germany and the Benelux to forge ahead. But Goldsmith misrepresented Schäuble and Lamers' paper as an attempt by Germany's ruling parties to create a federal state in which the EU would eradicate national identity. If this plan received approval, he warned the Conservative Party, the European Parliament would eclipse national parliaments and the European Commission would take on the task of a 'European government'. Prefiguring questions about why he had turned on a project that he had so recently supported, Goldsmith described himself as a 'true European' who would save the European Community from the 'far right' forces that Maastricht looked set to unleash. And yet, with his warnings over sovereignty and migration, the business tycoon's politics took on an increasingly populist tone.

The Heads of State or Government, who had become the most important actors in EU treaty revision by the 1990s, didn't so much dream of 'ever closer union' in the early years after Maastricht entered into force, as lie awake thinking about enlargement. Four countries – Austria, Finland, Sweden and Norway – were poised to join the EU in 1995. Norway changed its mind after a referendum, but the others joined as planned, by which point the European Council had already decided that the 'associated' countries of Central and Eastern Europe would become EU members if they so desired. Moral obligation and market opportunities drove the EU to enlarge after the Cold War, leaving national leaders with two major questions. Would the EU still function with so many new member states? Would its oldest, largest member states still wield the same influence?

After de Gaulle's empty chair crisis, member states kept the politics of qualified majority voting out of the public eye as much as possible. Voting weights were quietly recalculated after Greece, Portugal and Spain joined the Communities in the 1980s, but neither the Single European Act nor Maastricht challenged the status quo. However, warnings by Goldsmith and others that national vetoes were at risk forced this issue into the open. Enlargement added to these worries because of the prospect that small- and medium-sized member states queuing to join the EU could outvote older, larger member states.

That John Major voiced strong concerns over proposed changes to the EU's voting weights during accession negotiations with Austria, Finland, Norway and Sweden was predictable. The UK's domestic discourse on Europe had grown so febrile by this point that even Paddy Ashdown, the urbane leader of the Liberal Democrats, sounded like a hardliner; 'No amount of clever words or verbal gymnastics can hide the fact that the Government have made a fool of Britain in Europe,' Ashdown argued when the prime minister brokered a temporary solution to the issue.[31] More unusual was the fact that Major made common cause with Spanish Prime Minister Felipe González. Spain was altogether more comfortable with EU membership, yet González chaffed at the fact that his country had fewer votes than France, Germany, Italy and the UK. Under the so-called Ioannina Compromise, EU foreign ministers agreed to keep one eye on the old voting weights to make sure that countries such as the UK and Spain weren't disadvantaged under the new ones. This formula convinced few, so the Heads of State or Government agreed that the 1996 inter-governmental conference should consider not just the Maastricht leftovers, but the 'effective operation' of EU institutions in an enlarged EU. To this list, the EU added the need to consider 'other possible improvements in a spirit of democracy and openness'. What began as a check-up now looked more like invasive surgery to treat the problems of legitimacy facing the EU's body politic.

Amsterdam (1997)

Negotiations over political union at Maastricht had been disorganised and divisive. Seeking to avoid a repeat in 1996, the Heads of State or Government convened a high-level preparatory group led by Carlos Westendorp, a Spanish diplomat with extensive experience in European matters. The group's membership included Michel Barnier, a rising star of the French right, and David Davis, a British Eurosceptic who had whipped MPs to vote for Maastricht despite his personal views. Barnier had high hopes for 1996, which he saw as an opportunity not only to prepare for enlargement, but also to 'rediscover Europe's popular legitimacy'.[32] Davis was more interested in protecting his government's red lines. The UK would not, he told the House of Commons, give up any opt-outs or relinquish a veto over 'industrial policy, social policy, regional policy and environmental policy'.[33]

Unusually for an exercise of this kind, the Westendorp Report made no pretence of consensus. 'Many of us think it is important that the Treaty should clearly proclaim such European values as equality between men and women, non-discrimination on grounds of race, religion, sexual orientation, age or disability and that it should include an express condemnation of racism and xenophobia and a procedure for its enforcement,' the report concluded, while noting that 'One of us believes that the rights and responsibilities we have as citizens are a matter for our nation states'. It didn't take a detective to know who the 'one' was, but, despite such differences, the group concurred that a limited treaty revision was warranted to make Europe more relevant to its citizens.

A more creative – if unsolicited – contribution to the 1996 conference came from former Belgian Prime Minister Leo Tindemans, who chaired a forty-eight strong group of MEPs, MPs, officials and experts to consider 'tomorrow's Europe'.[34] Included in this group were Jens-Peter Bonde, a leader of the 'no' campaign in Denmark's referendums on the Maastricht Treaty, and Bill Cash, a British Conservative MP and noted Maastricht rebel. Such balance was reflected in the group's final report, which acknowledged the 'fear of excessive centralization, bureaucracy, loss of democracy and loss of independence' felt by some members while acknowledging that others viewed member states as having limited independence to begin with because of 'market forces or political reality'. Rather than present one set of recommendations, the group presented various scenarios, ranging from the status quo to the empowerment of either the Commission or the Council of Ministers as the EU's primary policy-making bodies. That Bonde and Cash didn't demand the dissolution of the Union was striking, as was their tacit acceptance that the EU was far from being a superstate as things stood. Euroscepticism, for the time being, was about preserving member states' influence over European integration rather than embracing disintegration.

The treaty signed by the Heads of State or Government in Amsterdam's Burgerzaal in October 1997 acted on areas identified in opinion polls as top priorities for the EU. A belief that the EU could help member states to navigate global challenges was the common theme. To those who wanted action on the environment, it elevated sustainable development to one of the Union's fundamental objectives. To those who sought efforts to combat unemployment, it stepped up the coordination of national employment policies. To those who wanted more to be done on organised crime, drug trafficking and immigration, the Amsterdam Treaty allowed the EU to legislate on visas, asylum, immigration and judicial cooperation in civil matters. Under the Maastricht Treaty, these issues had been decided by member state governments under an intergovernmental pillar. Now EU institutions were allowed to decide on justice and home affairs policy through traditional decision-making channels. The decision to create a High Representative for Foreign and Security Policy provided the EU with a clearer international presence. New policy commitments on peacekeeping and humanitarian intervention also sought to learn lessons from the Yugoslav Wars.

Amsterdam was simultaneously sensitive to public opinion and too abstract for most Europeans. The Irish government, which chaired the opening rounds of the 1996 intergovernmental conference, had hoped to produce a text that could explain the EU's delicate balance of power to citizens. After long meetings and late nights, the final text remained 'disappointingly impenetrable', concluded Bobby McDonagh, an Irish diplomat with a ringside seat from the reflection group to the signature ceremony.[35] The treaty's loquaciousness might have been excusable if it had produced decisive institutional changes, but its drafters dissembled. The Commission was not radically resized in the name of greater efficiency. An attempt to rotate smaller states' rights to nominate a Commissioner was seen off. Large member states agreed to nominate one rather than two Commissioners only when a deal was done on qualified majority voting. Under pressure from Spanish Prime Minister José María Aznar, González's successor, to find 'a solution for the special case of Spain', the Heads of State or Government agreed to convene yet another intergovernmental conference at least one year before the number of member states reached twenty.[36] Before this conference was launched in February 2000, the EU's legitimacy crisis went from bad to worse after European Commission President Jacques Santer and his team of Commissioners resigned over allegations of financial mismanagement.

Santer's Fall (1999)

Few post-war political theorists studied democracy in more depth than the 'Dean of American political science', Robert A. Dahl; none were more damning of the EU's democratic credentials. That MEPs had been directly elected by European voters since 1979 – making the European Parliament the world's first truly transnational parliament – didn't alter his view. The Union was not, and probably never would be, democratic, he argued, four decades after his ground-breaking study of democracy in New Haven, Connecticut. 'Swedish citizens may now have more influence on the policy decisions of the EU than Norwegians,' he accepted, 'but would anyone contend that they exercise as much influence in the European Parliament as they do in their own?'[37]

The ability of elected representatives to hold executives to account on behalf of the people or demos was, for Dahl, a crucial characteristic of democracies. His scepticism about the European Parliament's capacity to play this role was understandable. Although it was empowered to force the resignation of the Commission, the two-thirds majority required to approve this motion of censure frustrated MEPs' attempts to use it. However, this changed in March 1999, when Commission President Jacques Santer and his College of Commissioners – having survived two motions of censure from the European Parliament – quit before they could face a third.

Jacques Delors had arrived in Brussels in search of a *grand projet*, which he found in the Single Market Programme. Santer, who succeeded Delors in 1995 after a decade as Luxembourg prime minister, settled instead on 'doing less and doing it better'.[38] This slogan disappointed those who wanted a more entrepreneurial Commission, but the Luxembourger's declaration was a clever response to those who saw European officials as intent only on the pursuit of ever closer union. The new president also dedicated himself to a degree that Delors never had to streamlining the internal workings of the Commission. This agenda included, somewhat ironically, promoting value for money and more effective financial management.[39]

The scandals that brought down Santer were, in some respects, a storm in a plastic spit cup. To the *Daily Telegraph*'s polemical Brussels correspondent Boris Johnson, the Commission was 'haemorrhaging money in fraud', but an independent body found no evidence of financial impropriety by any Commissioner and only one clear-cut incident of favouritism in Commission appointments. That one notable exception was European Commissioner for Science and Technology Edith Cresson. The European Court of Justice found that the former French prime minister had hired a dentist 'acquaintance' to do a research job for which he was unqualified for six months longer than he was contractually allowed.[40] Serious though this offence was, financial rule-breaking was not peculiar to the EU. Eight months after Santer resigned, Germany's Christian Democratic Union was engulfed by a scandal over undisclosed donations from arms dealers. The affair soured Helmut Kohl's legacy as chancellor and forced the resignation of his heir apparent, Wolfgang Schäuble.[41]

Santer's fall showed that the European Parliament could hold EU executives to account, despite Dahl's prediction. This point went largely unnoticed outside Brussels and Strasbourg. In the rest of Europe, the incident weighed heavily on the EU's image as a troubled and crisis-ridden organisation. As negotiations over what would become the Nice Treaty loomed, the Heads of State or Government came under renewed pressure to bring the EU closer to its citizens.[42] The changes triggered by Maastricht had begun as an attempt to tie up loose ends, but national leaders were now tying themselves in ever tighter knots.

2

Return to Europe

'An Ingenious Machine'

'[W]hat does Europe mean to a Hungarian, a Czech, a Pole?' asked the novelist Milan Kundera in the *New York Review of Books* in April 1984.[1] His answer, in short, was almost everything. 'For them, the word "Europe" does not represent a phenomenon of geography but a spiritual notion synonymous with the word "West",' Kundera argued of his compatriots and Central European neighbours. 'The moment Hungary is no longer European – that is, no longer Western – it is driven from its own destiny, beyond its own history: it loses the essence of its identity.' Widely read at the time of its publication, Kundera's essay captured the ideological pull of Western European capitalism and democracy to many in Central and Eastern Europe.[2] It had lasting influence too in reimagining Communism's collapse as an act of European integration which it fell to the EU to consecrate.[3]

In fact, the dissidents who overthrew Communist rule in Central and Eastern Europe hadn't given much prior thought to the European Community, which was much less visible and contentious than NATO in the Eastern Bloc. When the Polish trade unionist Lech Wałęsa visited Rome in January 1981, he met with Italian labour leaders and Pope John Paul II.[4] Solidarity, in so far as it engaged with the idea of Europe before 1989, focused on transnational ties with trade unions and the Catholic Church rather than international organisations. When Victor Orbán spoke in Budapest's Heroes' Square in June 1989 on behalf of 'young people who today are fighting for European bourgeois democracy', the Fidez (*Fiatal Demokraták Szövetsége*) leader envisaged Hungary resuming the 'path of Western development' rather than joining the road to ever closer union.[5] When Civic Forum's Václav Havel called for a 'return to Europe' before a crowd of 500,000 protesters at Prague's Wenceslas Square in November 1989, he meant that Czechoslovakia should, once again, take its place among Europe's 'free, democratic and prosperous' nation states.[6] He spoke before a sea of red, white and blue, not blue and gold.

For Havel, the logical site from which to return to Europe after the Cold War was not the EU but the Conference for Security and Cooperation in Europe. Tracing its origins to the 1975 Helsinki Accords, the conference brought together countries from Eastern and Western Europe, including the Soviet Union, in an ongoing dialogue concerning economic, political and security issues. Although this dialogue delivered mixed results, the Helsinki Accords' commitment to human rights gave hope to Havel and other Czech intellectuals who defied their country's communist government by signing Charter 77, a powerful manifesto for civic freedom. Speaking in Strasbourg in May 1990 as Czechoslovakia's democratically elected president, Havel called for the Conference on Security and Cooperation in Europe to serve as the basis for a new European Confederation through which the continent could 'achieve political integration as a democratic community of democratic states'.[7] The Organisation for Security and Co-operation in Europe, as the conference was renamed in 1995, fell well short of these aims, but it showed that a pan-European security architecture could be designed, if not easily built. A veteran of the Prague Spring, who had seen Soviet tanks on the streets of the Czechoslovak capital, Havel remained fearful of Moscow's intentions and so sought to bind Russia to pan-European bodies. He was wary too of the United States, at first, and called for NATO's ' "Northern" security zone' to be replaced by a new ' "Helsinki" zone' which would, in time, allow the last American soldier to leave Europe.[8]

Havel's radical vision of pan-European cooperation was tempered by clear-eyed pragmatism. He could see how little support his plan for a European Confederation enjoyed among NATO leaders, who remained more committed than ever to the transatlantic alliance as the Cold War came to an end. The chief exception was French President François Mitterrand, who had used his New Year's address in December 1989 to propose a new pan-European body committed to dialogue, peace and security among all European states.[9] As a junior minister, Mitterrand had attended the 1948 Congress of Europe and he remained committed four decades later to its ideal of creating an economic and political union 'open to all European nations democratically governed'.[10] The French president also saw an opportunity to bolster France's position in the new European order and partly for this reason found little international support for his ideas. This left NATO as the only credible guarantor of European security, concluded Havel, who met with Polish President Lech Wałęsa and Hungarian Prime Minister József Antall in Krakow in October 1991, when the three leaders issued a joint call for closer cooperation with the alliance. By the end of the decade, their countries were NATO members. Bulgaria, Estonia, Latvia, Lithuania, Romania, Slovakia and Slovenia followed in 2004.

NATO enlargement remained a sensitive subject even after the Soviet Union's dissolution in December 1991, but there was no such taboo over seeking EU membership, which Havel, Wałęsa and Antall put at the centre of their foreign policies from 1990. Why had EU membership suddenly become so attractive? Trade was the most pressing reason. COMECON, the economic agreement linking the Soviet Union and its satellite states, had long struggled to achieve self-sufficiency, leaving its members to seek closer ties with the European Community even before Communism's collapse. By February 1989, the European Commission had concluded a trade and cooperation agreement with Czechoslovakia and opened talks with Bulgaria, Poland and Romania.[11] COMECON's collapse two years later made it more urgent to seek new trade opportunities with EU member states.

The Europe Agreements, which sought to upgrade these trade and cooperation ties, provided tariff-free access to the EU for industrial goods only.[12] Agriculture, which accounted for as much as one-fifth of total exports for some Central and Eastern European countries, still faced significant restrictions and the EU remained quick to use defensive trade instruments where its interests were threatened.[13] By 1996, the Czech Republic – which split from Slovakia three years earlier – had a trade deficit close to 5 per cent of gross domestic product (GDP).[14] To some economists, trade deficits of this size were a by-product of economic recovery, but to others they were a warning sign of unsustainable external imbalances.[15] Trade deficits were higher still in Estonia, Latvia and Lithuania, which had gained their political independence from the Soviet Union while remaining economically vulnerable to its collapse.[16] Joining the single market was the surest way for Central and Eastern European economies to boost exports and attract inward investment, and applying for EU membership was the most credible way to achieve such access.

As with earlier enlargements, joining the EU was as much about politics as economics. Havel put this most succinctly in a speech to the European Parliament in December 1994 in which he rejected claims that the EU was 'a monstrous superstate', describing it instead as 'a space that allows the autonomous components of Europe to develop freely and in their own way in an environment of lasting security and mutually beneficial cooperation based on principles of democracy, respect for human rights, civil society, and an open market economy'.[17] These words were offered not as a summary of what the EU stood for, but of what it might become. The Maastricht Treaty, Havel confessed, had seemed to him to be 'an ingenious modern machine' which lacked a 'spiritual or moral or emotional dimension'. It had addressed his 'reason', but not his 'heart'. In March 1994, Hungary applied to join the EU. Bulgaria, the Czech Republic, Estonia, Latvia, Lithuania, Poland, Romania, Slovakia and Slovenia did likewise over the next three years. Hitherto, the EU had seen at most two or three members join at once. Now, it was preparing for its first Big Bang enlargement.[18]

The Big Bang (2004, 2007)

That twelve countries joined the EU in the 2000s is heralded as one of the Commission's most significant achievements in the post-Maastricht period.[19] And yet, successive Commission Presidents blew hot and cold on this issue. Fearful that the pace of European integration would be slowed, or even reversed, by welcoming too many new members too quickly, Jacques Delors sought alternatives to enlargement. The Community's 'internal development must take precedent over enlargement', he told MEPs in January 1989, while suggesting that closer cooperation between the Twelve and other European countries should take place in different institutional settings.[20] Under this system of 'concentric circles', as Delors' proposal came to be known, a larger outer circle of countries would be given a chance to join organisations such as the European Free Trade Area and the soon-to-be-created European Economic Area, while the EU remained a smaller inner circle of tightly integrated member states.[21] Delors' ever-cautious successor, Jacques Santer, also saw grave risks from the Big Bang enlargement, which he warned in March 1995 could create 'an impotent and as it were invertebrate area' rather than the 'world power' that member states had envisaged at Maastricht.[22] The Luxembourger was not only concerned about Central and Eastern European countries' readiness to join the EU but also about the Union's ability to function with so many additional members.

The Big Bang ultimately happened because EU Heads of State or Government wanted it to, albeit with varying degrees of enthusiasm.[23] This conviction stemmed not from a shared ideological commitment to the uniting of Europe but from a slow burning consensus that the EU could most effectively respond to the Cold War's end by taking in new members. Helmut Kohl was an early and vocal proponent of enlargement. The 'attraction and appeal of the European Community is, and shall remain, a decisive constant of the pan-European development', the West German chancellor argued in November 1989 with a speed and a sense of purpose that took the British and French by surprise.[24] European integration, for Kohl, was a way of embedding a reunited Germany in a political union which promoted peace and stability in Central and Eastern Europe. The anticipated economic gains to Germany from enlargement were also considerable.[25] Between 1989 and 1991, West Germany's exports to Poland alone increased by 120 per cent. Were Poland to join the single market, they could increase ninefold, one economist predicted in 1992.[26]

Margaret Thatcher also supported EU enlargement once the single market had been completed, but the UK prime minister lacked credibility on the issue given her increasing antipathy towards the Community. Her successor, John Major, was seen as advocating enlargement to distract from, and perhaps even slow, deeper integration. François Mitterrand, meanwhile, feared a loss of French influence in an enlarged European Community. Having failed, like Havel, to win support for a European Confederation stretching from the Atlantic to the Urals, the French president sided with Kohl on the need for EU enlargement.

At the European Council in Copenhagen in June 1993, the Heads of State or Government finally agreed that Central and Eastern European countries would become EU members if they so wished, but only once they were 'able to assume the obligations of membership by satisfying the economic and political conditions required'.[27] At this summit, national leaders also agreed to assess Cyprus and Malta's membership applications, which had gone unanswered for three years. The two Mediterranean island nations had asked to join the European Community in July 1990 after rethinking their future in the non-aligned movement. Cypriot President George Vassiliou also saw European integration as a catalyst for reuniting the island, which had been divided since Turkish troops invaded in 1974 in response to a Greek-backed military coup.

The Preamble to the Maastricht Treaty confirmed EU member states' respect for the 'principles of liberty, democracy, respect for human rights and fundamental freedoms, and the rule of law', but national leaders went further at Copenhagen by requiring future candidates to establish stable institutions to give effect to these and other values, and to create robust market economies.[28] The Copenhagen criteria, as they came to be known, rightly recognised the sizeable economic, social and political challenges still facing this region, while at the same time reassuring wavering member states that accession would foster reform in candidate countries.

The EU launched accession negotiations with Cyprus, the Czech Republic, Estonia, Hungary, Poland and Slovenia in March 1998. Santer's resignation ten months later removed the last obstacle to the Big Bang enlargement. The Luxembourger had initially sought to limit eastern enlargement to the Czech Republic, Hungary and Poland, but his successor, Romano Prodi, believed that enlarging the EU 'from 15 to 20 to 25 to 30 Member States' was possible with a 'comprehensive strategy'.[29] While this strategy remained vague, Prodi convinced the College of Commissioners to support the opening of accession negotiations with Bulgaria, Latvia, Lithuania, Malta, Romania and Slovakia. Günter Verheugen, the Commissioner for Enlargement, was an astute choice to lead these negotiations. As a former foreign policy adviser to German Chancellor Gerhard Schröder, Verheugen kept one ear to the ground in Berlin, as he talked with candidate countries.[30] Schröder was less evangelical than Kohl about enlargement, but the new chancellor supported the EU's 'historic mission' in Central and Eastern Europe, providing the budgetary burden for Germany could be minimised. Seizing the opportunity created by his country's six-month presidency of the EU in the first half of 1999, Schröder toured member states and worked with the Commission to secure support for strict limits on agriculture spending and regional aid in the EU budget over the period 2000–6.[31]

The EU budget was also a sore spot for Major's successor as UK prime minister, Tony Blair. Under a deal negotiated by Margaret Thatcher, the EU returned around €4 billion to the UK each year, but this deal became harder and harder to defend in Brussels as the country went from being the 'Sick Man of Europe' to one of its strongest economic performers and the EU looked to progressively admit poorer member states. Although he faced pressure from other members to end the UK's rebate after enlargement, Blair actively called for Central and Eastern European countries to be offered EU membership. Enlargement seemed to be one of the few European issues that he could lead on without apparent fear of retribution from British Eurosceptics.[32]

The Big Bang enlargement would not have happened without the European Commission's determination to close one negotiating chapter after another, as enlargement jostled for attention with other issues on the Heads of State or Government's agenda.[33] Nor would it have been possible without the determination of Central and Eastern Europe's politicians to remould their economies, legal systems and societies to join the EU and voters' support for such efforts. A cross-party consensus on EU membership prevailed in accession countries, ensuring that the constitutional and legislative changes sought by the EU were adopted with a minimum of delay. In Poland, the premiership passed from Jerzy Buzek, a veteran of Solidarity, to Leszek Miller, the last secretary-general of Poland's Communist Party, but preparations to join the EU continued apace.[34] In a period marked by the hardships of economic transition and fragmenting political parties, politicians remade their societies in the hope of a better future inside the EU.

By far the poorest of the candidate countries, Bulgaria and Romania were never likely to make the first wave of enlargement. They were determined, however, to make the second. In 1997, Prime Minister Ivan Kostov inherited a Bulgarian economy in free fall, but he got a grip on hyperinflation with a currency board which tied the lev to the Deutsch Mark and pushed through extensive reforms with the help of the International Monetary Fund (IMF) and World Bank. Kostov's tough economic policy choices convinced the EU to open accession negotiations, yet Bulgarian voters demanded greater resolve in tackling corruption and looked to Simeon Saxe-Coburg-Gotha, who returned from exile to the country he once ruled as a child tsar with a promise of 'economic and social renewal' within 800 days. Saxe-Coburg-Gotha's pledges were never entirely credible, but he carried on Kostov's reform agenda and maintained momentum in accession negotiations with the Commission. Romania's road to EU membership followed a more circuitous route, as Ion Iliescu, who helped overthrow Nicolae Ceauşescu without convincing as a democrat, won, lost and regained the presidency. Reformers such as Emil Constantinescu, a geology professor turned liberal politician, and Traian Băsescu, a merchant seaman who made his name as mayor of Bucharest, did just enough to open and advance accession negotiations with the EU.

Slovakia was most in danger of being left behind in the race to join the EU. Following the dissolution of Czechoslovakia in 1993, commentators saw the Czech Republic as being the stronger candidate for EU membership. Poorer and with an economy orientated towards communist-era heavy industry and trade with former COMECON members, Slovakia was still some distance from becoming a robust market economy. Its economic problems were compounded by the autocratic tendencies of its three-term prime minister, Vladimír Mečiar. A lawyer who rose to prominence in anti-communist demonstrations in 1989, Mečiar created a plainspoken persona that contrasted with Havel's intellectualism. Beginning as an economic reformer, Mečiar had drifted towards right-wing populism by his third term, in which he challenged the freedom of universities and the press and called for the repatriation of Slovakia's Hungarian minority. The European Commission's assessment in 1997 that Slovakia had failed to meet the political conditions for membership produced few concessions from Mečiar, but it emboldened opposition parties who formed a coalition government in the 1999 legislative election.[35] Led by Mikuláš Dzurinda, a centre-right politician who trained for marathons in between meetings, the government pushed through ambitious economic and political reforms, helping to unlock accession negotiations with the EU.

'The historic process launched in Copenhagen in 1993 to overcome the divisions throughout our continent is about to bear fruit,' concluded the European Council in December 2002.[36] The Czech Republic,

Estonia, Hungary, Latvia, Lithuania, Poland, the Slovak Republic and Slovenia, it was decided, would join the EU two years later along with Cyprus and Malta. Bulgaria and Romania would follow soon afterwards. In April 2003, a little over a year before he and nine other Heads of State or Government took their seats at the European Council, Slovak Prime Minister Mikuláš Dzurinda finished the London marathon in 3 hours, 56 minutes and 3 seconds, 20 minutes ahead of Tony Blair's director of communications, Alastair Campbell.[37]

The European Union and Western Balkans (1989–2019)

In 1991, Yugoslavia applied to join the European Communities, achieving this goal at the turn of the millennium and helping to limit the secessionist ambitions of its states through constitutional means. Cornelius Adebahr's alternative history of Yugoslavia as a 'big Belgium' was offered as a fictitious thought experiment about how the EU might have prevented Europe's bloodiest conflict since the Second World War.[38] In reality, the break-up of Yugoslavia created challenges in the face of which the EU floundered, even if the states that emerged from this conflict sought and, in some cases, secured EU membership.

The European Community had a long history of economic cooperation with Yugoslavia, which by 1989 had become its second most important trading partner in the Mediterranean region.[39] Building on this cooperation, the Commission called for an association agreement with Yugoslavia just before Slovenia and Croatia declared their independence in June 1991.[40] At first, European Community foreign ministers sought to preserve Yugoslavia's territorial integrity, but Germany controversially broke from this consensus by rapidly recognising the two breakaway republics. Whether Germany did so because its political leaders believed in states' right to self-determination or to increase their country's influence in Central and Eastern Europe was hotly debated. Regardless, the incident ensured that the Maastricht Treaty's common and foreign security policy got off to an inauspicious start.[41] The

EU-sponsored Brioni Agreement struggled under the weight of member states' divergent views by encouraging Slovenia and Croatia to pause plans for independence while a peaceful settlement could be sought. The agreement suited Slovenia, which achieved its independence without further bloodshed, but it failed to prevent Croatia from sliding into war. By the end of 1991, the European Community recognised that the situation was spiralling out of control and sought external support. United Nations (UN) Peacekeepers were deployed too late and sparingly to prevent multiple instances of ethnic cleansing and genocide. In one of the worst episodes, the Bosnian Serb army killed 8,372 Muslim men and boys in the Bosnian town of Srebrenica despite the presence of a Dutch battalion under UN command.

However much the break-up of Yugoslavia exposed the EU's shortcomings, it also demonstrated its magnetism for Europe's new democracies. Having struggled to convince the EU of its statehood, Slovenia encountered few difficulties in becoming a member state in May 2004. One month later, the Heads of State or Government recognised Croatia as a candidate country, the death of its wartime leader, Franjo Tudjman, having paved the way for a more progressive generation of leaders, beginning with Stjepan Mesić. All countries that joined the EU in the post-Maastricht period took unpopular decisions to reap the economic and political benefits of membership, but few were more controversial than the Croatian secret service's involvement in pan-European efforts to apprehend Lieutenant General Ante Gotovina for war crimes and crimes against humanity during the Croatian War for Independence. Gotovina had been indicted by the International Criminal Court for involvement in the killing of 324 Krajina Serb civilians and prisoners of war and forcibly displacing 90,000 Serb civilians. Hailed as a national hero for his role in winning the war, Gotovina's arrest in the Canary Islands and subsequent trial in The Hague was deeply unpopular among the Croatian public, but it helped to unfreeze accession negotiations with the EU and secure membership in 2013. Gotovina overturned his conviction on appeal and returned home to a hero's welcome, although not before he had made the case for his country to join the EU.

Serbia's application in 2009 to become an EU member, a decade after Belgrade had been rocked by NATO airstrikes, marked an extraordinary turn of events. Slobodan Milošević's genocidal campaign in Kosovo had branded the Federal Republic of Yugoslavia as a European pariah. The prime minister's overthrow by a patchwork of pro-EU opposition groups, and subsequent transfer to the International Criminal Tribunal for the former Yugoslavia, allowed Serbia to become a democratic state. Once crippled by economic sanctions, Serbia now rebranded itself as a high-tech hub. Nordeus, a mobile gaming company developed by Branko Milutinović, Ivan Stojisavljević and Milan Jovović, three alumni of Belgrade University and Microsoft, epitomised this success story, even if it distracted from the wider challenges facing the Serbian economy, including its high levels of inequality compared to other candidate countries.[42]

The most serious obstacle to Serbia's membership of the EU was political rather than economic, as the presidency passed from Boris Tadić, a pro-European pragmatist, to Tomislav Nikolić and, later, Aleksandar Vučić, both members of the right-wing populist Serbian Progressive Party.[43] Vučić nudged his party in a more pro-EU direction, allowing talks on EU membership to advance, although his refusal to recognise Kosovo as an independent state remained a stumbling block. That five member states refused to do the same blunted the EU's calls for reconciliation in this region, as well as blocking Kosovo's ambitions to join the Union.

When the former Yugoslav Republic of Macedonia, Montenegro, and Bosnia and Herzegovina applied, in turn, to join the EU, Cornelius Adebahr's thought experiment seemed less and less far-fetched.[44] But the chances of the former Yugoslavia's constituent republics reuniting under a European flag remained slim. Although the EU opened negotiations with the Republic of North Macedonia, Montenegro and Albania, these talks were making slow progress even before the French president announced a moratorium in 2019 on further enlargements, citing the EU's lack of progress on its own internal reforms. Meanwhile, the Heads of State or Government's acceptance of Bosnia and Herzegovina as a potential candidate, yet not an actual one, left the country in a liminal state.[45]

Turkey

In December 2004, Recep Tayyip Erdoğan landed at Ankara's Esenboğa Airport to a rapturous welcome from supporters waving Turkish and European flags. The prime minister had just returned home from Brussels, where EU Heads of State or Government signalled their willingness to begin accession negotiations, subject to the implementation of specific reforms concerning fundamental freedoms and human rights. Turkey had enjoyed on-off relations with the European Community since 1963, when it signed an association agreement that established a customs union and raised the possibility of future membership. Following Turkey's partial return to democracy in 1983 after a military coup, Prime Minister Turgut Özal submitted the country's application to join the European Community. Taking two years to respond, the Commission ruled out membership in 1989, but it left the door ajar for future talks if Turkey continued its economic and political development. A cautious decision, it nonetheless boosted the prime minister's pro-market and, to a lesser extent pro-democratic, agenda.

Whereas Özal embodied the pro-Western tradition among Turkish political elites, Erdoğan stood for populist Islamist politics. But both shared a commitment to joining the EU. As prime minister, Erdoğan backed the United Nations' Annan Plan, which sought to end the division of Cyprus, and promised EU leaders that he would recognise the Mediterranean island state even after Greek Cypriots voted down the deal. From overturning laws on the death penalty to strengthening minority rights, he secured wholesale changes to Turkey's constitutional, political and administrative system.[46] Fêted in Brussels, he was named European of the Year in 2004, an award previously bestowed by the European Voice, an EU news organisation, on activists such as U2's politically engaged lead singer, Bono.

Accession negotiations began in 2005 and soon ran aground. Part of the problem was that Turkey still refused to recognise Cyprus as a sovereign state even though it needed its support as an EU member state to advance accession negotiations. Cyprus, meanwhile, sought every opportunity to secure diplomatic recognition from Ankara, while sowing doubt about whether it would ultimately accept Turkey as an EU member state. These contradictions quickly unravelled when Erdoğan agreed to extend the EU–Turkey Customs Union to all new EU member states but then refused to open up Turkish ports to Cypriot vessels. The EU responded by freezing negotiations over eight chapters before Cyprus blocked six more. The sense of relief among some EU leaders was palpable, amid growing pressure from right-wing populists to block the accession of a Muslim-majority country.

In the Netherlands, Pim Fortuyn's insistence that the EU's borders 'shouldn't cross the Bosporus' went hand in hand with his description of Islam as a 'backward culture' and criticism of Muslim migrants for failing to integrate themselves into Dutch society. A former left-wing sociology professor at Erasmus University Rotterdam and prolific writer, Fortuyn made a name for himself by saying the unsayable in a country known for its liberal consensus. With his shocking statements, sharp suits and pet King Charles Spaniels, the openly gay politician became a media star, who leveraged his newfound fame by starting his own eponymous, right-wing populist political party. Nine days before the 2002 Dutch general election, Fortuyn was shot and killed in the car park of a Hilversum radio station by an animal rights activist who sought to protect minority groups from the politician's 'stigmatising political ideas'.[47] The election went ahead despite the profound sense of anxiety that gripped the Netherlands, with the Pim Fortuyn List coming second and joining a coalition government led by the centre-right Christian Democratic Appeal.

The government fell after just eighty-seven days amid infighting between members of the Pim Fortuyn List, which struggled without its founder. By this point, the centre-right People's Party for Freedom and Democracy had appointed a charismatic freshman parliamentarian as party spokesperson. With his bouffant peroxide hair and increasingly critical remarks about Islam and multiculturalism, Geert Wilders parted ways with his parliamentary colleagues in 2004 after publishing a manifesto calling for a permanent ban on Turkish membership of the EU.[48] Within six years, Wilders' Freedom Party would hold the balance of power in the Netherlands, just as the Pim Fortuyn List had done before it.

The right-wing populist backlash against EU enlargement was not limited to the low countries. In France, Philippe de Villiers won more than a million votes in the first round of the 1995 presidential election after voicing strong opposition to Turkish membership of the EU.[49] By the 2000s, de Villiers' controversial pledge had been appropriated by mainstream politicians, including former president Valéry Giscard d'Estaing, who insisted that Turkey was 'a different culture, a different approach, a different way of life' which had no place in the EU, and Nicolas Sarkozy, who won the presidency in 2007 on a pledge to block Turkish membership.[50] As France's interior minister, Sarkozy had won plaudits from progressives for promoting dialogue between the state and Muslim groups before his harsh words about young, mainly Muslim, men rioting in Parisian banlieue endeared him to the populist right.[51]

Erdoğan's frustrations with the EU were apparent long before this point. Speaking at St Antony's College, Oxford in 2004, he contrasted the ease with which Greece had been welcomed into the European Community, with the onus placed on Turkey 'to prove why it was European, and defend the contributions it could make to the EU'.[52] By the time that protesters gathered in Istanbul's Gezi Park in May 2013 to oppose plans for the space's redevelopment and demand political freedoms, Turkey's negotiations with the EU had ground to a halt. Whether a genuine offer of EU membership would have made

Turkish authorities think twice about their heavy-handed response to Gezi Park protesters, which left twenty-two dead, or the political purges that followed the 15 July 2016 coup d'état attempt is moot. But the effective end of Turkey's EU dream made it easier for Erdoğan to start to undo three decades of democratic reform, as he sought to preserve his grip on power.

The European Neighbourhood

'The "return to Europe", the great slogan of opponents of communism and reformers of post-communist states, was always an oxymoron. The Europe which preceded the imposition of communism in Eastern Europe was dead by 1989.'[53] These words by Timothy Snyder, one of the preeminent historians of this region, capture well the secondary role that the EU played in the political imaginations of those who brought four decades of Communist rule to an abrupt end. The revolutions of this period were fought over fundamental values such as freedom of expression and the rule of law and the belief that Western European models of democracy and capitalism offered a better life. And yet, as Snyder notes, returning to Europe rapidly acquired a different meaning after 1989 as Central and Eastern Europe's nascent democracies made joining the EU the overarching aim of their foreign policies. It was EU Heads of State or Government, above all, who answered this call, not just as an act of solidarity or economic self-interest, but because they believed that enlargement would encourage political reforms and economic regeneration in aspiring member states. Faced with geopolitical upheaval after the Cold War, national leaders looked, once again, to the EU to forge a collective response.

Whether the EU could foster reform and regional stability without continuously taking in new members remained one of the defining foreign policy questions of the post-Maastricht period. The European Neighbourhood Policy was Romano Prodi's attempt at an answer. Having arrived in Brussels in bullish mood about the Big Bang, the

Commission President came to the view that the Union could not 'go on enlarging forever'. So he unveiled an approach – reminiscent of Jacques Delors' concentric circles – which offered states on the EU's eastern and Mediterranean borders aid, access to the EU's single market and cooperation on policies ranging from the environment to crime, terrorism and illegal migration. Faced with rising anti-globalisation and Eurosceptic sentiment, the Heads of State or Government embraced Prodi's European Neighbourhood Policy. However, neither he nor they could say why countries which aspired to EU membership would settle for something that fell well short, and what would become of those whose future lay beyond the European Union's limits.

Endorsed by the European Council in October 2003, the European Neighbourhood Policy suffered from three serious contradictions.[54] First, it championed democracy, human rights and the rule of law, a paired down version of the Copenhagen criteria, in a region where such values were contested. Second, it excluded Russia, yet included countries that had historically been within its sphere of influence. Third, it left open the possibility that the 'silver carrot' of cooperation might one day turn gold.[55] The European Neighbourhood Policy is 'distinct from the process of enlargement', the Commission insisted, but 'this does not prejudge how relations between neighbouring countries and the EU may develop in the future'.

The European Neighbourhood Policy's shortcomings were apparent from the outset in Ukraine. In 1994, Leonid Kuchma, an aerospace engineer turned politician, was elected president with a reputation as an impatient reformer who would complete the ex-Soviet republic's stalled economic transition and consolidate democratic rule. But Kuchma's privatisation scheme, in which every Ukrainian adult was given a voucher to buy shares in state-owned companies, empowered a small coterie of wealthy individuals who swept up these coupons on the black market.[56] Georgiy Gongadze, a journalist and political activist, shone a light on Ukrainian oligarchs' growing political influence via an online news site, which evaded

Kuchma's restrictions on opposition parties and the freedom of the press. In September 2000, Gongadze was kidnapped.[57] Two months later, the journalist's decapitated body was found in a forest outside Kyiv. Although the EU expressed concern over Gongadze's murder, EU–Ukraine summits continued uninterrupted under the European Neighbourhood Policy. By the early 2000s, Kuchma's reformist zeal had long since been extinguished, but this didn't deter the president from talking up Ukraine's chances of joining the EU, even as he sought closer trade ties with Russia. The contradictions underpinning EU–Ukraine relations came to a head in late 2004, as pro-EU Viktor Yushchenko stood against pro-Russian Viktor Yanukovych in a disputed election to succeed Kuchma.

The European Neighbourhood Policy's weak impetus for reform could also be seen in Belarus. By the mid-2000s, the country received €10 million in aid from the EU each year, despite being ruled by Alexander Lukashenko, a Soviet-era strongman who resisted free and fair elections and maintained an economy that was, for all intents and purposes, centrally planned.[58] In 2008, the leader of the Belarusian Social Democratic Party, Mikola Statkevich, was jailed for ten days for waving a European flag, but financial assistance from the Union continued to flow. Few European flags were visible twelve years later when Lukashenko secured a sixth consecutive term, despite the largest pro-democracy protests in the country's history and concerted opposition from independent candidate Svetlana Tsikhanouskaya. During this turbulent period, Russian news showed two protesters arguing: 'Tomorrow no one will come here under this flag. Don't use the blue flag.' 'I won't', replied the other.[59] Although the video's authenticity was questionable, it conveyed no less clearly the gap between protesters' political hopes and promises that the EU would 'stand with the people of Belarus'.[60] The EU had served as a beacon for reform in Central and Eastern Europe after the Cold War, but its light was flickering.

3

Nice to Lisbon

'We Can't Go On Like This' (2000)

An estimated 80,000 protesters gathered in Nice in December 2000 to form a human chain around the Palais des Congrès Acropolis.[1] Their signs read 'No, No, No to a federal Europe – Yes, Yes, Yes to a social Europe'. And 'A social Europe does not belong to the bosses'. A violent fringe, including Spanish anarchists and Basque nationalists, threw stones and Molotov cocktails at French police, who replied with rubber bullets, baton charges and teargas. Tensions also ran high inside the conference venue, where the Heads of State or Government had gathered to agree on the second treaty revision since Maastricht. The leaders weren't only preparing the EU for its Big Bang enlargement; they were also jockeying for position before the countries of Central and Eastern Europe and island states of Cyprus and Malta entered the race. Germany sought influence commensurate with its position as the EU's most populous member state and its principal paymaster. France saw parity with Germany as sacrosanct. The Netherlands wanted more votes than its smaller neighbour Belgium. All governments worried what fate would await them at home if they returned to accusations that they had sacrificed their national vetoes.

It fell to Jacques Chirac, whose dalliance with Euroscepticism had given way to a pro-European pragmatism and a successful run for the French presidency, to square these circles. After ninety hours of ill-tempered negotiations, the Nice Treaty was unveiled. Chirac had convinced other Heads of State or Government to back a new system of Council voting, whereby EU legislation would be adopted if it enjoyed a qualified majority of votes cast by a simple majority of member states representing at least 62 per cent of the EU's population. A clear, if cumbersome, formula, it allowed smaller member states to save face while making it more difficult for larger ones to be outvoted. The compromise also unlocked a deal to reduce the number of Commissioners to less than one per member state once twenty-seven countries had joined the EU. Small member states feared a loss of influence from this arrangement, but Commission President Romano Prodi had warned that his institution could be paralysed if it had to keep creating portfolios for Commissioners from new member states.

Chirac deserved credit for securing a deal on issues that had been too difficult to resolve in Amsterdam three years earlier. But the French president received little gratitude from fellow leaders. 'We can't go on like this,' the sleep-deprived UK Prime Minister Tony Blair told reporters.[2] Haggling over votes made him 'sick', German Chancellor Gerhard Schröder confided.[3] The protesters outside the building need not have feared a federal Europe, which was never on the agenda, but their pleas for a Social Europe to protect workers' rights and the Union's most vulnerable citizens went unanswered. The summit's most significant breakthrough on policy was on security and defence, where national leaders endorsed Blair and Chirac's plan to equip the EU with the means to deploy military forces independently of NATO. The EU would have no troops of its own, but member states would, for the first time, be able to deploy military personnel under a European flag on peacekeeping and humanitarian missions.

The Nice Treaty's biggest problem was that it had been overtaken by events even before it was signed. In May 2000, German Vice-Chancellor and Foreign Minister Joschka Fischer gave a speech at the Humboldt University in Berlin on the future course of European integration. His assessment was damning. The EU risked becoming 'stranger' and more 'incomprehensive' to citizens as it enlarged, he warned; something needed to be done before popular support for the EU hit 'rock bottom'.[4] The solution, Fischer argued, lay in the creation of a 'European federation', which would not supersede nation states, but draw a clearer line between the sovereign responsibilities of the EU and individual members. To achieve this division, the vice-chancellor concluded, Europe needed a constitution.

This intervention was remarkable for both personal and political reasons. Fischer was no European federalist. As a young man, he had swapped radical left-wing politics for environmentalism and dedicated his career to making the German Green Party electable. As leader, he helped to rebrand the Greens as a pro-European party, but this move was born of pragmatism rather than a deeply held belief in ever closer union. Even now, Fischer remained agnostic about whether the EU needed a strong executive or collective government via the European Council. His proposals sprang, above all, from a profound sense of frustration with the status quo. Fischer's vision of a European Constitution also looked curiously like the German political institutions that he had railed against as a militant member of parliament. In 1984, Fischer had been excluded from the Bundestag for calling its vice-president 'ein Arschloch [an asshole]'.[5] Now he advocated a bicameral European Parliament, which bore a striking resemblance to Germany's parliamentary system, and a European Constitution which looked a lot like Germany's Basic Law. Most extraordinary was the timing of the Humboldt speech, which undercut negotiations on the Nice Treaty, despite Fischer's insistence that he was speaking in a personal capacity about issues that lay in the more distant future.

After a matter of weeks, Jacques Chirac appeared before the Bundestag to propose that the new treaty should be followed by a more open-ended period of reflection, perhaps in the form of a convention, to prepare a European Constitution.[6] As the political reverberations from Fischer's speech continued, even Tony Blair expressed his approval for a 'charter of competences' for the EU and national governments.[7] The Nice Treaty duly included a Declaration on the Future of the Union, which committed member states to yet another round of treaty revision. Echoing Fischer, it called for a debate on the 'delimitation of powers between the European Union and the Member States' and the 'simplification of the Treaties'.[8] EU leaders, it was agreed, would meet at Laeken in December 2001 to begin a 'deeper and wider debate about the future of the European Union', as a prelude to a further round of treaty revision.[9] Before they could do so, however, member states still needed to ratify Nice.

The Irish government had routinely put all major treaty revisions to a referendum ever since it lost a legal challenge by Raymond Crotty, an agricultural economist at Trinity College Dublin, who had opposed Ireland's membership of the European Community from the outset.[10] The Irish Supreme Court's ruling in the 1987 *Crotty* case didn't require a referendum on all future treaty revisions, but successive Irish governments feared further cases if they sought consent via parliament alone. Besides, Irish voters' resounding 'yes' to the Single European Act, Maastricht and Amsterdam gave them little reason to fear a public vote against Nice. But such complacency opened the door to Crotty's academic colleague and co-campaigner, Anthony Coughlan, who found a new and receptive audience for his arguments against European integration.

Coughlan, like Crotty, began as a left-wing nationalist, who saw Ireland's accession to the European Community in 1973 as incompatible with his country's hard-won independence from the UK. Although he remained committed to these views, Coughlan's increasingly strident warnings about a European superstate in the 1990s endeared him to British right-wing Eurosceptics.[11] He also found a new ally in Justin Barrett, an Irish anti-abortion campaigner whose opposition to the Nice Treaty flowed from his wider critique of the EU, refugees, politicians, liberalism, the Good Friday Agreement and homosexuals or, as he put it, 'the whole rotten cabal of the left'.[12]

Ireland's voters weren't so much seduced by Coughlan and Barrett, as confused by their claims and counterclaims as to what purpose the Nice Treaty really served. Just 35 per cent of eligible voters went to the polls, with 54 per cent of those who did opposing the treaty.

Coming from a country which seemed at ease with EU membership, the result sent shock waves through Brussels. However, instead of pausing to consider the causes of popular disenchantment, not only in Ireland but elsewhere in the EU, the Heads of State or Government pressed on with plans for treaty revision, leaving it to Irish Taoiseach (Prime Minister) Bertie Ahern to deal with his government's own goal. Ahern eventually did so by securing a declaration from EU partners reaffirming Irish neutrality, which had never really been under threat, and announcing a second referendum.[13] This time, Coughlan's National Platform and Barrett's No to Nice campaign faced a well-drilled civil society campaign, which encouraged voters to approve the Nice Treaty by 63 per cent to 37 per cent in October 2002.[14] A victory for pro-Europeans, the result was seized upon by Eurosceptics as further evidence that the EU was hard of hearing when confronted with voters who asked difficult questions about European integration.[15] By the time Nice entered into force five months later, plans for the next treaty were already underway.[16]

The European Constitution (2004)

Wim Kok was a popular choice to become President of the Convention on the Future of Europe. As a trade union leader, he had played a key role in the Wassenaar Agreement, a pioneering form of social partnership between workers and employers that helped to turn the ailing Dutch economy around. As prime minister, his socially progressive, economically liberal policies influenced European thinking on the Third Way, every bit as much as Bill Clinton. A veteran of EU treaty negotiations, Kok was the perfect candidate to steer a debate on how to bring the Union closer to its citizens and whether a European Constitution was the best means to achieve this. But under pressure from Jacques Chirac – who insisted that the job must go to a Frenchman even if it meant empowering his one-time political rival – the Heads of State or Government switched their support at the eleventh hour to Valéry Giscard d'Estaing.

In the quarter-century since Giscard lost the French presidency he had repeatedly, but unsuccessfully, tried to regain the political limelight. His ambitions of becoming prime minister under the presidencies of François Mitterrand and Jacques Chirac were thwarted, as was his attempt to resume the role of finance minister. Europe provided an alternative arena for Giscard, who served one term in the European Parliament, where he made the case for the European Council to have a president elected by universal suffrage, all the while refusing to rule himself out for such a job. He also made a concerted effort to become the first president of the European Central Bank, even though he had no experience in central banking, and dismissed Wim Duisenberg's eventual appointment to this role as 'a casting mistake'.[17] Aged 74 when the Nice Treaty's declaration on the future of Europe was signed, Giscard saw the Convention as his last opportunity to lead.

The Convention was an innovative attempt to open up the process of EU treaty-making. Having hitherto negotiated treaties behind closed doors and failed to bring Europe closer to the people, national leaders invited representatives of the European Commission, European Parliament, national parliaments and observers from various European bodies and civil society to meet for one year in public in Brussels to prepare the ground for the next intergovernmental conference. Candidate countries would be represented in the same way as current member states and civil society observers would be invited to attend and feed into discussions. Concerned to keep Giscard in check, the Heads of State or Government sent their own personal representatives to the Convention, and appointed two former prime ministers, Giuliano Amato of Italy and Jean-Luc Dehaene of Belgium, as the Convention's vice-presidents. A twelve-person praesidium was included to manage the Convention's day-to-day work. Its members included Michel Barnier, a veteran of the Westendorp Group and by now a Commissioner, and Gisela Stuart, a member of the UK House of Commons.

The Convention worked better than expected, but it was not as participatory as had been hoped. Too many delegates were drawn from a narrow group of EU insiders who sought change but shied away from asking difficult questions about why so many Europeans had grown disillusioned with the Union. The most striking exception was Gisela Stuart, a Bavarian who had moved to the UK to study before joining the British Labour Party and becoming an MP. Her constituency, Edgbaston, had been a Conservative stronghold, but Stuart won voters over in May 1997 with her critical stance towards the EU, which helped to deflect recurring criticism of her nationality from political opponents.[18] Blair described Stuart as 'very New Labour'; however, it is more probable that he used her as a barometer to gauge how Eurosceptic voters might view the work of the Convention.[19] If so, he should have paid closer attention to Stuart, as she felt marginalised and belittled by other members of the praesidium, who had, in her view, refused to engage in serious debate over the future of Europe. 'Any representative who took issue with the fundamental goal of deeper integration was side-lined,' she later told the Fabian Society.[20]

Whether Stuart came with an axe to grind – or left with one – is not entirely clear. But other, more engaged Eurosceptics, like Danish MEP Jens-Peter Bonde, fared no better in the Convention. Whereas Stuart remained unconvinced that the EU needed a constitution and so was reluctant to engage with the work of the Convention, Bonde fought line by line over the draft treaty, pushing his own points, while suggesting that a majority of citizens would be 'indifferent to or even happy with a dissolution of the EU'.[21] 'Since it is difficult to change the citizens, it might be easier to change the way we make the decisions in Europe,' he declared in a submission to the Convention that stretched to more than one hundred pages. To Bonde, the Convention could be saved if it presented Europeans with a genuine choice between a federal Europe organised along the lines of the United States and a slimmed-down Union that would limit the powers of the Commission to a focus only on cross-border issues.

European officials found the European Convention nearly as uncomfortable as Eurosceptics. Michel Barnier got himself in hot water after he and António Vitorino, the Commission's other delegate to the Convention, worked in secret to prepare a draft constitution. Commission President Romano Prodi had approved the project, but he failed to inform the College of Commissioners, who had been presented with an alternative official draft treaty.[22] The secret draft was merely a feasibility study, Prodi insisted; and yet, the fact that it was code-named Penelope merely added to concerns about Barnier and Vitorino's clandestine activities. The affair undermined Prodi's credibility and with it the Commission's standing within the Convention. Having fun at Prodi's expense and the project's Homeric name, Giscard compared the Convention to Odysseus and insisted the text it produced would not be spurned.[23]

When they met at Laeken in December 2001, the Heads of State or Government had left open the question of whether the group's final document should include 'different options' or specific 'recommendations' and even what the status of that document should be.[24] Giscard made clear in the Convention's opening ceremony that he would seek 'a broad consensus on a single proposal' that would be nothing less than a constitution.[25] Delivered two years later, the Convention's final text didn't quite live up to this billing; it remained a treaty between states, albeit one couched in constitutional language. But the Convention produced much more than a tidying-up exercise. Its draft European Constitution sought to re-establish the EU, redefine its values and objectives and reform its institutions. Its proposals included a detailed description of the EU's competences, an EU Charter of Fundamental Rights that would be binding not just on EU institutions but on member states, the creation of a full-time president of the European Council, the transformation of the High Representative role into that of EU Minister for Foreign Affairs, a simplified allocation of voting rights in the Council of Ministers and a new ordinary legislative procedure which made the Council and European Parliament equal partners in most policy areas. Achieving consensus on these points took guile, initiative and flexibility. Giscard demonstrated all three qualities from the moment he circulated a skeleton draft of the text to the painstaking process of redrafting that followed. In the hands of a different president, the draft Constitution could have suffered the same lonely fate as the Tindemans Report three decades earlier.

National leaders accepted Giscard's draft constitutional treaty without fundamental amendments.[26] But he and they badly underestimated the ability of right-wing populists to tap into voter frustration over globalisation, immigration and other dimensions of the global order and direct it at the EU. The Convention had discussed the possibility of referendums, with Giscard briefly mooting the idea of an EU-wide referendum. However, it wasn't entirely certain how this would work in member states that usually relied on parliamentary approval of EU treaties. The intergovernmental conference on the European Constitution which followed could plead no such ignorance. Soon after this body began its work, the Czech Republic, Denmark, Luxembourg, the Netherlands, Poland and Portugal signalled their intention to hold referendums on the final agreement. In the UK, Tony Blair insisted that no referendum was necessary before relenting in the final few months of the intergovernmental conference. In France, Jacques Chirac begrudgingly followed suit before José Luis Rodríguez Zapatero, a surprise winner in the 2004 Spanish general election, was obliged to carry out a manifesto pledge to hold a public vote.

Four-fifths of Spanish voters who went to the polls answered Zapatero's plea to be 'the first in Europe' to endorse the European Constitution, but less than half of those who could vote did.[27] This followed a lacklustre 'yes' campaign, a dearth of information about the issues at stake and mixed messages from the opposition People's Party. Zapatero's conservative predecessor as Spanish prime minister, José María Aznar, who had opened the European Convention by citing the great Spanish federalist, José Ortega y Gasset, now criticised the European Constitution's new rules on Council voting as 'diabolical' for Spain. 'Spain had a place among the big nations, but it is now at a table with the small players,' he told journalists after his election defeat to Zapatero.[28]

In France, the referendum was not so much a re-run of the 1992 vote on the Maastricht Treaty as a sign of how fractured the country's political system had become since then. Having faced Jean-Marie Le Pen in the second round of the 2002 presidential election, Chirac should have seen the writing on the wall. The president found himself outflanked on the right by Le Pen, who railed against the EU's impact on French jobs and promised that a 'no' vote would 'explode like a bomb' aimed at the country's political leaders,[29] and on the left by Laurent Fabius, who insisted that a 'no' vote would force member states back to the negotiating table to beef up the treaty's social policy provisions.[30] Most saw Fabius' move as an opportunistic one designed to differentiate himself from his Socialist Party rival, François Hollande, a protégé of former Commission President Jacques Delors. But Delors' insistence that the European Constitution, which he supported, could be renegotiated, captured the French left's ambivalence over the EU's reform plans.[31] On 29 May 2005, French voters resoundingly rejected the European Constitution. Three days later, Dutch voters delivered another blow to the project.

That the Netherlands held this referendum despite its long history of parliamentary democracy was due, in no small measure, to the efforts of Frans Timmermans, a rising star in the opposition Labour Party and one of two representatives of the Dutch Parliament on the European Convention. Timmermans cut a low profile in Brussels, with his most significant contribution addressing the future of the European statistical system.[32] But he harboured more fundamental doubts about the final agreement and saw an opportunity to inflict defeat on Prime Minister Jan Peter Balkenende's centre-right coalition. Working with other parties on the left, Timmermans secured a consultative referendum on the European Constitution, the first nationwide Dutch referendum on any issue since 1805.[33] Having done so, Timmermans watched Geert Wilders re-enter the public domain after anonymous death threats over his remarks about Muslims had forced the populist politician into hiding.[34] Risking his life in a political environment that had grown no less febrile three years after Pim Fortuyn's murder, Wilders dominated the referendum campaign by framing it as a vote about 'sovereignty and immigration' and drawing tenuous links between Turkey's future membership of the EU and the European Constitution.[35] Because the referendum was consultative, the Dutch Parliament had yet to scrutinise or properly debate the European Constitution before it was put to the people, a majority of whom felt ill-informed about its text. Close to 62 per cent of voters rejected the treaty, leaving the European Constitution in tatters, and Timmermans on the verge of quitting politics.[36]

Lisbon (2007)

Inevitably, it fell to the Heads of State or Government to find a way out of the EU's constitutional crisis. Meeting in Brussels in June 2005, the European Council took note of the referendum results in France and the Netherlands, while incongruously suggesting that citizens in these countries remained no less attached to 'the construction of Europe'.[37] In truth, national leaders were short of ideas, and so they played for time by announcing a 'period of reflection'. The ratification of the European Constitution, they insisted, shouldn't be abandoned during this period. However, of the six other member states that were due to hold referendums, only Luxembourg pressed ahead. Prime Minister Jean-Claude Juncker, a veteran of the Maastricht negotiations, secured a comfortable majority in support of the Constitution, but his counterparts in the Czech Republic, Denmark, Ireland, Poland, Portugal and the UK couldn't be so sure and called off their votes. None were more relieved to cancel their referendum than Tony Blair, who would have struggled to make the case for a constitutional treaty in a country without a codified constitution, even before his political powers had started to wane.

The European Commission broke the vow of silence during this period with Plan for Democracy, a pioneering attempt to create a virtual European public sphere which showed just how polarising online political exchanges could be. Although the plan's 'Debate

Europe' website attracted more than one million visitors in its first four months, 90 per cent of comments were left by men aged between 18 and 44 and 56 per cent were in English.[38] Brussels insiders and British Eurosceptics dominated the debate, which produced no shortage of name-calling yet few new political ideas. Margot Wallström, the European Commissioner behind this forum, also launched a blog to share her thoughts on European issues and demystify the work of EU decision-makers, but she received a torrent of Eurosceptic and misogynist abuse for her efforts. While Wallström looked to new technology to find a way forward, Austria's Chancellor Wolfgang Schüssel looked to the past by inviting European politicians, intellectuals and artists to Salzburg to mark Mozart's 250th birthday. Organised around musical themes – 'The European crisis. A sad sound?', 'What now? A new sound?', 'Muses und Sirens' – the Sound of Europe conference sounded like a requiem for the EU's constitutional dream, try as the participants did to sound a note of optimism.[39] Old and new visions of Europe collided when Wallström's attempt to broadcast live vox-pops with citizens in Salzburg failed. 'Don't do that to me, that is a nightmare,' sighed Wallström, as giant video screens remained blank.[40]

Angela Merkel, Germany's new chancellor, used her first set-piece speech on Europe to suggest an alternative way forward. Although she was portrayed in the media as 'inexperienced and largely untested', this assessment overlooked the battles she had fought to become the first woman leader of her party and country.[41] Having grown up in East Germany and served as press secretary to the German Democratic Republic's first and last democratically elected leader, Merkel had also seen far greater political turmoil than the EU had in the post-Maastricht period. She used her first major address on Europe as chancellor to insist that the European Constitution was absolutely necessary and promised to find a way forward during Germany's six-month presidency of the EU in the first half of 2007.[42] True to her word, Merkel signed the Berlin Declaration to mark the 50th anniversary of the Treaties of Rome along with Hans-Gert Pöttering and José Manuel Barroso, the presidents of the European Parliament and European Commission respectively. A bland birthday-card-to-self, the Declaration praised the EU's unique contribution to 'peace and understanding, while identifying 'growth, employment and social cohesion' and the fight against 'terrorism, illegal migration and organised crime' as paramount.[43] The text's true purpose lay in its final paragraph, which promised to place the EU 'on a renewed common basis before the European Parliament elections in 2009'. Precisely how became apparent in June 2007, when national leaders announced a new intergovernmental conference. The European Constitution was dead, but its contents would be salvaged in yet another treaty.

Negotiations over what would become the Lisbon Treaty were short, although at times, acrimonious. Merkel had done the heavy lifting during the German presidency by getting national leaders to agree on the overall approach. The substance of the European Constitution would be preserved as much as possible, but the text would be defanged of its 'constitutional character': the existing treaties would be amended rather than replaced with a single new legal text; the position of EU Minister for Foreign Affairs would be changed to High Representative of the Union for Foreign Affairs and Security Policy; references to the European flag, anthem and motto as symbols of the Union would be jettisoned; otherwise the text was indistinguishable from the European Constitution. Other issues were up for negotiation, especially the issue of voting rights. Lech and Jarosław Kaczyński – identical twins who had gone from being child actors to right-wing populist president and prime minister of Poland respectively – raised the temperature by insisting that the rules for calculating a qualified majority take account of their country's war dead.[44] But Merkel kept her cool while the Kaczyńskis captured the headlines they had sought and accepted small-scale concessions.

The Lisbon Treaty, as it came to be called, was signed by national leaders in a lavish ceremony in the Manueline Jerónimos Monastery. The Heads of State or Government sat in chevron formation on a stage as each took turns to sign the treaty before a giant screen showing their national flag. Try as Portuguese Prime Minister José

Sócrates did to convey the historical importance of the day, the mood was better captured by the mournful Fado music that brought the ceremony to a close. Under pressure from opposition leader, David Cameron, for not holding a referendum, UK Prime Minister Gordon Brown cited a prior engagement with a parliamentary select committee and arrived late. As Chancellor of the Exchequer, Brown had cut an isolated figure while eurozone finance ministers met to discuss a project that the Scot had no intention of joining. As prime minister, he breached diplomatic etiquette by distancing himself from a treaty that he had negotiated two months earlier. Arriving late in Lisbon, Brown signed the treaty in the National Coach Museum of Portugal, to which the other leaders had travelled by tram for lunch.

In Lisbon, Sócrates spoke passionately about the need for a stronger EU that could 'respond to the longings of European citizens'.[45] He had also promised a referendum on the European Constitution but ruled out holding one on the Lisbon Treaty on the dubious grounds that it would undermine the legitimacy of the treaty's approval by national parliaments elsewhere. This left Ireland as the only member state to hold a referendum. Learning little from the Nice Treaty, Irish Taoiseach Brian Cowen campaigned without energy, in contrast to Declan Ganley, a Gatsbyesque businessman who made his fortune in timber and telecommunications in Russia, Central and Eastern Europe and the United States before buying Moyne Park mansion in Abbeyknockmoy, a village in Galway.[46] A supporter of Cowen's party, Fianna Fáil, Ganley was little known outside business circles and had shown no interest in politics until he founded the Libertas Institute in October 2006. Billed as a right-of-centre think tank, Libertas morphed into a right-wing populist pressure group, as Ganley's campaign against the Lisbon Treaty gathered momentum and media attention.[47] Ganley had supported Nice, but he saw Lisbon as the last stand for democracy, which he alone could save on behalf of the people of Europe. Likening himself to Leonidas I in the Battle of Thermopylae, the Libertas leader took his stand against Ireland's band of pro-EU elites with half-truths and hyperbole.[48] Were Lisbon to be ratified,

Ganley warned, it would interfere with the country's laws on abortion and allow children to be detained for educational purposes.[49] The 'yes' campaign proved powerless in the face of such alarmest claims, which spoke to popular concerns about the treaty's impact on Irish identity and influence. On 12 June 2008, 53 per cent of Irish voters rejected the Lisbon Treaty.

The Irish 'will have to vote again', Nicolas Sarkozy reportedly said before travelling to Dublin to meet with 'yes' and 'no' campaigners.[50] Brian Cowen prevaricated before convincing EU leaders to backtrack on their plans to reduce the number of Commissioners and to provide legal guarantees on tax, neutrality and abortion, paving the way for a second referendum. This time, Ganley joined the 'no' campaign late, having previously declared that he would step aside from politics after failing to secure a seat in the European Parliament. He also faced stiff competition from a revived 'yes' campaign, which put civil society groups, entrepreneurs and sportspeople out front and kept Ireland's political leaders in the background and warned of the risks to the Irish economy, as the global financial crisis gathered force.

In spite, or perhaps because, of his long track record of animosity towards the European Commission, Ryanair's CEO Michael O'Leary was the breakout star of Ireland's second referendum on Lisbon. Asked whether he had read the treaty, he insisted that he had and 'nearly died of boredom', but he proved more than a match for Ganley, whom he accused of self-promotion.[51] Coming from the man who flew a Ryanair plane to the airline's new hub in Porto for a pro-Lisbon photo opportunity with Portuguese Prime Minister José Sócrates, O'Leary's claim was rich. The airline chief's willingness to enter the political foray nevertheless undercut Ganley's claim to speak for business and brought an energy that the first referendum campaign lacked. On 2 October 2009, Irish voters backed Lisbon by 67 per cent. One month later, Czech President Václav Klaus became the last EU leader to sign the treaty. A staunch Eurosceptic, he refused to put pen to paper until the Czech government agreed to seek an opt-out from the EU Charter of Fundamental Rights. The Czech government reluctantly agreed, leaving the Lisbon Treaty to enter into force in December 2009.[52]

The Heads of State or Government had spent sixteen years digesting Maastricht's leftovers. The results hadn't brought the EU closer to its citizens, but rather revealed the gulf between the people and policy-makers, while giving right-wing populists opportunities to sow discontent over European integration. And yet, reports that the EU was doomed after the French and Dutch 'no' votes against the European Constitution were proven wrong. Although it made heavy weather of its 'long constitutional crisis', as the political scientist Mark Pollack calls it, the Union salvaged most of the reforms contained in the European Constitution and survived Ireland's ratification crises over the Lisbon Treaty.[53] These reforms were far from perfect, but they ensured that the EU could function after enlargement and gave the Union a more coherent presence on the international stage. The experience nevertheless dulled national leaders' appetite for major treaty reforms, with Gordon Brown, in particular, urging other Heads of State or Government to 'stop looking at constitutions or semi-constitutions or institutions for a long time ahead and for the fore-seeable future concentrate on the big issues ahead of us'.[54] Eight years later in 2017, France's youthful new president Emmanuel Macron delivered a speech at the Pnyx in Athens, where he called for a new debate on the future of Europe.[55] The UK, meanwhile, found itself negotiating a treaty of a different sort.

4

Fundamental Values

The Haider Affair (2000)

In 1986, a small, liberal, centrist party in Austria found itself close to collapse. Fearing electoral devastation, the Austrian Freedom Party turned to Jörg Haider, a political outsider who dressed smart-casually, described Third Reich employment policies as 'orderly' and favoured a complete ban on immigration.[1] Haider's pan-Germanism led him to support Austria's membership of the EU at first, but the country's accession referendum provided a rare opportunity to challenge the prevailing consensus between the left-wing Social Democratic Party of Austria and its conservative rival, the Austrian People's Party. Although voters ultimately backed EU membership, Haider's anti-globalist critique of the EU attracted considerable media attention and helped to differentiate the Austrian Freedom Party from the political mainstream. In 1999, Haider caused a political earthquake by taking his party to second place in Austria's legislative election. When the first-placed Social Democratic Party of Austria failed to form a coalition, it fell to the Austrian Freedom Party and the Austrian People's Party to strike a deal. Right-wing populists had held local and regional offices in post-war Europe and, on occasion, propped up governments, but the Austrian Freedom Party was the first right-wing populist grouping to enter a governing coalition as the largest party.

Austria's government-in-waiting sought to lessen the political back-lash against their coalition by nominating Wolfgang Schüssel of the

Austrian People's Party as chancellor and keeping Haider outside the cabinet. But the nomination of Susanne Riess-Passer, a Haider loyalist, as deputy chancellor created the impression that the Austrian Freedom Party leader would wield influence behind the scenes. The Amsterdam Treaty included a new provision to strip member states of their voting rights if they breached the EU's values, which Schüssel, as foreign minister, had pushed hard for over concerns about democracy and the rule of law in Central and Eastern Europe. Now as premier, he faced calls for this provision to be used against his own government, which the Heads of State or Government of the fourteen other EU member states feared could normalise right-wing populism throughout the Union.

As Portugal occupied the EU's rotating presidency, it fell to this country's prime minister, António Guterres, to find a way forward. To Guterres, who grew up under the *Estado Novo* dictatorship and represented his country in negotiations to join the European Community, the Austrian People's Party had breached 'the essential values of the European family' through its choice of coalition partner.[2] 'Nothing will be as before,' he warned.[3] Since the government hadn't yet taken office, it was difficult to show, as the treaty required, that Austria had committed a serious and persistent breach of EU fundamental values. So, encouraged by French President Jacques Chirac and German Chancellor Gerhard Schröder, Guterres prepared a statement on behalf of the Fourteen, which promised to break off bilateral political contacts with Austria if the coalition went ahead.[4] While Heads of State or Government occasionally formed caucuses of this sort, they had never challenged the internal affairs of a member state to this degree. It was a remarkable public defence of EU values, as well as a provocative one. Austrian Chancellor Schüssel responded by blocking EU legislation and threatened to do the same for future treaty changes and enlargement.[5] He also hinted at a referendum, confident that the Austrian public, whatever its views on Haider, resented EU interference on a matter of national sovereignty.[6]

Commission President Romano Prodi was blindsided by the Haider affair. Guterres didn't consult the Italian, who was reluctant to operate outside the treaties and characteristically slow to build consensus among Commissioners.[7] The Commission's response was to keep a watching brief on the Austrian government to ensure that its policies were compatible with the EU treaties, but confidence in such measures quickly drained. So Guterres turned instead to Luzius Wildhaber, President of the European Court of Human Rights, who convened a Wise Persons Group comprised of eminent politicians and lawyers to examine the new Austrian government's commitment to EU values. When the group visited Vienna, Haider offered them CDs, videos and teddy bears in his own likeness. The Wise Persons refused these peculiar presents on point of principle yet bestowed a gift of their own when in their final report they called for an end to sanctions against Austria.

The Austrian Freedom Party could be accurately described as a 'right-wing populist party', the report accepted.[8] Its members, more-over, had a long track record of 'ambiguous language' that could be interpreted as 'xenophobic or even racist'.[9] And yet, the Wise Persons could find no evidence that Austrian Freedom Party ministers had acted on 'past statements and behaviour' or otherwise threatened the rights of immigrants, refugees or members of minority groups. Even if they had, the report implied, the sanctions imposed by other EU member states risked becoming 'counterproductive and therefore should be ended'.[10] Having rushed to defend EU values, the Union now found how difficult it was to confront a member state on a matter of national sovereignty and leaders restored political contacts with Austria. The short-term winner was the Austrian People's Party, which not only clung on to power despite its poor showing in the 1999 election, but also boosted its standing at home through its defiance of the EU. Haider fared less well. His resignation as party leader in February 2000 was widely seen as a tactical move designed to distance himself from the coalition; however, it set in motion a slow but destructive power struggle in the Austrian Freedom Party, which returned as a coalition partner in 2002 after an early general election, with far fewer seats.[11]

The EU was both humbled and emboldened by this episode. As with the empty chair crisis three decades earlier, EU institutions had learned how difficult it was to challenge a recalcitrant member state on a point of national sovereignty. In this sense, Prodi was a keener student of European history than the Heads of State or Government. Unlike the empty chair crisis, which led to a long and costly compromise over Council voting, member states sought new ways to defend EU values in response to the Haider affair. Timing, for once, was on the EU's side, with Austria's coalition government coming to power not long after national leaders had agreed to create a new EU Charter of Fundamental Rights.

An older organisation with a distinct legal basis and larger membership, the Council of Europe was a much weaker engine of European integration than the EU. But the Strasbourg-based organisation broke new ground in 1953 when its then fourteen members signed the European Convention on Human Rights and agreed to establish a European Court of Human Rights. The European Community's founding treaties, in contrast, largely steered clear of codifying its values. Maastricht went much further by requiring the EU to respect fundamental rights, as guaranteed by the European Convention on Human Rights and resulting from national constitutional traditions.[12] The rise of right-wing populists suggested that neither the European Convention nor national constitutional traditions were as secure as they had looked in 1992 and encouraged the Heads of State or Government to codify the EU's fundamental values, rather than deferring to Strasbourg and member states on such matters.

In June 1999, four months before Austrian voters went to the polls, the European Council invited Roman Herzog, a former president of Germany, and before that head of his country's Federal Constitutional Court, to chair a convention tasked with drafting an EU Charter of Fundamental Rights. Under strict instructions not to write a constitution, Herzog instead produced what was, for all intents and purposes, a European bill of rights.[13] In twelve tersely written pages, the EU Charter declared the Union to be founded on the values of human dignity, freedom, equality and solidarity and the principles of democracy and the rule of law. Among the rights enumerated were the right to non-discrimination on grounds of race, colour or ethnicity, the right to asylum, freedom of expression, including media pluralism, academic freedom and the right to a fair and public hearing from an impartial tribunal. To politicians who sought to sow racial discord, stifle democracy or restrict the rule of law, these words offered a powerful rebuke. The catch was that they applied only to the EU and its decision-making processes. A citizen couldn't, in other words, hold national authorities to account for breaching the EU Charter of Fundamental Rights in the normal course of domestic decisions. The Charter – which became legally binding when the Lisbon Treaty entered into force in December 2009 – was nevertheless a major step for the EU and a defiant, if belated, response to right-wing populists' electoral success in Austria.

National leaders went a step further in the Nice Treaty by allowing the Council of Ministers to declare a member state to be at risk of breaching the EU's values rather than waiting for such a violation to occur. However, thanks to Schüssel, among others, the so-called Article 7 procedure could be triggered only if a four-fifths majority agreed. Even if this threshold could be reached, the country in question would face no more than a recommendation to change its ways in the first instance. The Nice Treaty allowed tougher sanctions, including the removal of voting rights in the Council of Ministers, only if member states unanimously agreed that the country in question had engaged in a serious and persistent breach of EU values. The Convention on the Future of Europe debated the thermonuclear option of requiring member states that persistently breached EU values to leave the Union, but this was dismissed as impractical and replaced in the European Constitution with a provision to allow a country to withdraw from the EU of its own accord.[14] Still, the EU ended the 2000s with greater leverage over its values than it had begun with, and it was not long before such provisions were put to the test.

Forward and Back: Lithuania and Italy

Central and Eastern Europe is sometimes portrayed as a region in which political leaders' commitment to EU fundamental values withered once the golden apple of membership had been plucked. But such accounts do little justice to new member states that cultivated such values and old member states that didn't. Valdas Adamkus' tenure as president of Lithuania exemplified the consolidation of democracy and the rule of law in the newly enlarged EU. Silvio Berlusconi's four terms as prime minister of Italy illustrated the political decay facing some of the Union's founding members.

Having joined the resistance against German and Soviet invasion during the Second World War, Adamkus claimed asylum in the United States, where he trained as a civil engineer, rose through the ranks of the Environmental Protection Agency and remained active in the Lithuanian American community. In 1997, he moved home and, within a year, won the presidency on a promise to restore trust in public service.[15] A popular leader with a reputation for probity, Adamkus championed democracy and the rule of law and stood up to right-wing populists, such as Vytautas Šustauskas, a politician with a track record of anti-Semitic remarks who became mayor of Kaunas.[16] The president fared less well against Rolandas Paksas, a populist former stunt pilot, who beat the odds to win the second round of the 2003 presidential election. But Paksas' removal from office a year later on corruption charges demonstrated the robustness of Lithuania's fledgling constitution and cleared the way for Adamkus to contest and regain the presidency. Although his second term was a turbulent one, not least because of the global financial crisis, Adamkus battled corruption and Russian interference and championed democracy at home and in Ukraine. Like other member states, Lithuania faced systemic problems in the post-Maastricht period, including high levels of distrust in political institutions, but it exemplified the Union's values in other ways.[17]

Silvio Berlusconi shattered 'Italy's political norms and heralded a new era of populism. The Milanese businessman started out in real estate before diversifying into television, where he built the country's largest media company. Having done so, Berlusconi used the flattering coverage he received on Canale 5 and other channels he owned to propel his political career. Four months after forming Forza Italia in December 1993, Berlusconi became prime minister in a coalition with the National Alliance, a party with neo-fascist roots, and the Northern League, a separatist party which sought independence for northern Italy.[18] European socialists bristled at Italy's new government, with Commission President Jacques Delors decrying the 'hideous beast' that Berlusconi had brought to life, but the centre right proved more forgiving.[19]

The Socialists and Democrats had come first in every European Parliament election since 1979. Wilfried Martens, chair of the European People's Party, saw a high-stakes opportunity to end his rival's winning streak. Helmut Kohl's Christian Democratic Union, John Major's Conservative Party and Wolfgang Schüssel's Austrian People's Party were mainstays of the European People's Party, but declining support for Mino Martinazzoli's Italian People's Party didn't bode well. Although its political values were populist rather than Christian democratic, Berlusconi's Forza Italia had three times as many seats in the European Parliament as Martinazzoli and a palpable sense of political momentum. So Mertens flew to Milan to begin talks with the Forza Italia leader, who saw European People's Party membership as a stamp of approval.[20] In 1999, the European People's Party, with Forza Italia as its newest member, won more seats than the Socialists and Democrats for the first time, a political feat that Martens' successors were determined to match.

Berlusconi's first stint as prime minister lasted less than a year after tensions over his media holdings caused the Northern League to quit the government. But the billionaire regained the premiership on three further occasions over the next two decades, with each term marked by populist promises and corruption scandals. In 2013,

Berlusconi was convicted for tax fraud, for which he was sentenced to community service and temporarily barred from holding public office.[21] While the Italian Senate supported this ban, Berlusconi remained a prominent member of the European People's Party, which he urged to end its tradition of grand coalitions with the Socialists and Democrats and form an alliance with right-wing populists instead.[22]

When Matteo Renzi's ruling Democratic Party suffered a heavy defeat in Italy's parliamentary election in May 2018, Forza Italia was unable to capitalise, in part because Berlusconi was still banned from public office. A technocratic government followed by fresh elections seemed probable before Matteo Salvini's right-wing populist Northern League and Luigi Di Maio's left-wing populist Five Star Movement entered into negotiations. Despite their differences, the two leaders hammered out a programme for government which promised to deport up to half a million migrants and to regulate Islamic associations and mosques.[23] Italy, in which a pro-European consensus once seemed impermeable, was about to get its first Eurosceptic government.

Twelve years earlier, Salvini had cheered for Germany rather than his native Italy in the World Cup Final.[24] A right-wing regional separatist, he championed the break-up of the Italian Republic before rebranding the Northern League as a populist-nationalist party which promised to protect Italy from external threats posed by migration, globalisation and the EU. Five years earlier, the Five Star Movement's Luigi Di Maio was selling drinks in Naples' Stadio San Paolo. Like so many of Italy's economically disadvantaged twenty-somethings, he still lived with his parents. Di Maio was drawn to Beppe Grillo, a charismatic comedian who railed against Italy's ruling class after years of economic stagnation, and promised instead action on public water, transport, sustainable development, internet access and the environment. Grillo was unkempt, openly Eurosceptic, prone to racist provocations and, having been convicted for manslaughter following a car accident in which three people lost their lives, barred from holding elected office.[25] Telegenic, well-groomed and the youngest-ever vice-president of the Chamber of Deputies, Di Maio softened his party's rhetoric on migration and Europe while maintaining alliances with right wing Eurosceptics in the European Parliament. When Grillo stood aside in 2017, Di Maio won the resulting leadership contest by a landslide.

In June 2018, three weeks after Italy's new coalition government took office, Emmanuel Macron compared the rise of populism in the EU to a form of 'leprosy'.[26] What's worse, the French president added, is that 'nobody is horrified by that'. Macron's remarks caused an immediate rift between Paris and Rome; they also revealed a sense of helplessness among many national leaders about how to handle a government that openly contested the Union's fundamental values. During the Haider affair, the perceived gap between the Austrian Freedom Party's campaign rhetoric and policies had helped to de-escalate tensions between Austria and other EU member states. But there was no such ambiguity from Italy's new interior minister, Matteo Salvini, who closed Italian ports to irregular migrants and talked openly of saving Europe from becoming an 'Islamic caliphate'.[27] Fearing a backlash from Italian voters, who had grown steadily more sceptical about the benefits of European integration, neither national leaders, the Commission, nor MEPs seriously considered citing Italy for a serious breach of EU values. The collapse of Italy's coalition government after fourteen months granted the EU a reprieve, but it would soon be facing a right-wing populist government led by Giorgia Meloni, a politician who stoked fears over refugees and rekindled Benito Mussolini's commitment to 'God, the homeland and the family'.[28] Meanwhile, the challenge to the Union's fundamental values in Poland and Hungary was gathering momentum.

Illiberal Democracy

Lech Kaczyński and his twin brother Jarosław had served as advisors to Lech Wałęsa, but they forged separate paths as Solidarity splintered. After early success, Jarosław's Christian democratic Centre

Agreement suffered a heavy electoral defeat and thereafter moved to the right. In his brief spells as security minister and, later, attorney general in governments of the left and right, Lech took a hard line against former communists, the security services and corruption. The fusion of these political themes with a celebration of Poland's glorious past and Christian conservatism came together in the Law and Justice party, a new right-wing populist party founded by the brothers in 2001. It soon struck a chord with voters who had grown tired of waiting for EU membership and living with double-digit unemployment rates. Within four years of the party's launch, Lech held the Polish presidency. Jarosław was prime minister within five.

In power, the Kaczyńskis presented themselves as scourges of the elites. In foreign policy, this meant scoring points against the EU, as when Lech threatened not to sign the Lisbon Treaty, even if compromise typically followed once Polish headlines had been secured. At home, the brothers stepped up their attacks on those associated with Communist rule. This populist message took on a harder edge after Poland's Constitutional Tribunal challenged new lustration legislation, which required individuals working in law, the media, universities and a range of other professions to sign an affidavit about their dealings with the security services before 1989. Previous lustration laws concerned around 36,000 individuals, but this now covered between 400,000 and 700,000 people, leading to concerns that the Kaczyńskis were targeting their political opponents rather than coming to terms with the country's communist past.[29] When Poland's Constitutional Tribunal declared key elements of this legislation to be unconstitutional and warned against using lustration to exact political revenge, the Law and Justice party deepened its attack on 'communist era judges' and, with that, the rule of law.[30]

Following his speech as a student leader in Budapest's Heroes' Square in 1989, Viktor Orbán studied political science at the University of Oxford on a scholarship funded by George Soros, the Hungarian fund manager turned philanthropist who later founded the Central European University in Budapest. Orbán quickly returned home to frontline politics with Fidesz, which transformed itself from a protest movement to a political party and mounted a radical liberal challenge to Hungary's Catholic conservatives and former communists. With their long hair, unshaven faces and casual attire, Fidesz's youthful members shook up Hungarian politics, but they were crowded out by left-wing parties at the polls. So Orbán smartened up his image and took his party to the political right in search of electoral success.

Hungary started its economic transition much earlier than the rest of Central and Eastern Europe. Its experiment in gradualism helped to attract foreign investment and spur private sector activity, but it also delayed economic recovery and resulted in high public debt and unemployment. As hopes for a more prosperous future crashed on the rocks of economic reality, voters took Fidesz's newfound nationalism, faith and family values at face value and propelled Orbán to the premiership. Whereas Law and Justice gave free rein to their populist instincts, Orbán governed as a Christian democrat. Having joined the Liberal International in 1992, Fidesz defected to the centre-right European People's Party eight years later. Groomed by centre-right grandees Wilfried Martens, Hans-Gert Pöttering and Joseph Daul, Orbán quickly became the party's vice-president. But signs of populism were discernible in the Hungarian prime minister's reluctance to ensure political balance on the boards of public service broadcasters and his failure to protect the rights of his country's Roma community.[31]

Voters grew tired of such politics, but not for long. In Hungary, Orbán lost the premiership after voters installed a left-liberal coalition, which promised to tackle corruption and restore freedom of expression. In Poland, Civic Platform's Donald Tusk brought Jarosław Kaczyński's time as prime minister to an end and won plaudits for his pro-European outlook and cautious championing of civil liberties.[32] When Lech was killed in a plane crash in April 2010, along with his wife and a large delegation of Polish dignitaries, and Jarosław lost the ensuing presidential election to Civic Platform's Bronisław Komorowski, it looked like the Law and Justice party's time had passed.[33] But Tusk's appointment as president of the European Council provided a second chance after Civic Forum failed to unite behind Ewa Kopacz and lost the presidency and premiership to the Law and Justice party. Poland's new president, Andrzej Duda, and new prime minister, Beata Szydło, were presented as the new moderate faces of the Law and Justice party, even though Jarosław Kaczyński remained as party leader and continued to exercise considerable influence behind the scenes. By this point, Viktor Orbán had returned to power, having capitalised on Hungarian voters' frustration with the country's socialist prime minister, Ferenc Gyurcsány, who was surreptitiously recorded telling his party they had 'fucked it up and lied' after the global financial crisis.[34]

Right-wing populists such as Sir James Goldsmith and Jean-Marie Le Pen presented themselves as the genuine representatives of the people against the EU's sinister supranational elite. The same was true of the Kaczyńskis and Orbán and yet these leaders, as the political scientist Stefan Auer notes, did not seek to quit the EU but to oppose it from within.[35] A key difference, of course, was that Law and Justice and Fidesz were not just challenger parties like Goldsmith's Referendum Party and Le Pen's Front National; they headed challenger governments with the power to act on their Eurosceptic manifestos.[36] Opinion polls in Poland and Hungary showed little appetite among voters for leaving the EU, so their ruling right-wing populists sustained themselves instead on a diet of confrontation with the Union over policies and political principles.[37]

Fidesz's coalition, formed with the like-minded Christian Democratic People's Party after the April 2010 parliamentary elections, gave it a supermajority in the National Assembly, which it used to replace Hungary's constitution with a new Fundamental Law. Joseph Daul, leader of the European People's Party in the European Parliament, praised the Fundamental Law for incorporating the EU Charter, but the Council of Europe's legal watchdog, the Venice

Commission, was less sure. Having raised eyebrows over the initial document, the Venice Commission sounded the alarm over subsequent amendments. By weakening the powers of parliament, increasing political control over the constitutional court, the media, the central bank and universities and failing to give explicit protection of minority rights, the new constitution had become, the Venice Commission concluded in 2013, 'a political means of the governmental majority'.[38] The EU's response showed how much had changed in a decade. In 2000, the Heads of State or Government had taken Austria to task, while the Commission urged caution. Now national leaders waited for the Commission to take the lead. The reasons for this role reversal were partly procedural but above all political. By allowing the Commission and European Parliament to initiate action against a member state at risk of breaching EU values, rather than leaving this issue to the European Council, the onus was no longer on member states to act. This suited the Heads of State or Government, especially those who belonged to the European People's Party. With European Parliament elections fast approaching, the centre-right grouping could ill afford to lose Fidesz's eleven MEPs. So it fell instead to Commission President José Manuel Barroso and Commissioner for Justice, Fundamental Rights and Citizenship Viviane Reding to devise a response to Orbán's actions.

Like António Guterres, José Manuel Barroso had come of age during Portugal's *Estado Novo*. Although he quit the far left of Portuguese student politics for the centre-right Social Democratic Party – which like Fidesz switched from the Liberal International to the European People's Party – Barroso consistently looked to the EU as a buttress of democracy in his own country and Europe more generally.[39] After Orbán returned as prime minister and took over the EU's rotating presidency, Barroso reminded him to act 'in a European manner'.[40]

Viviane Reding, by then in her third term as Commissioner, after spells in charge of education and culture and information society and the media, brought considerable experience to the role. But she found herself in uncharted territory when she likened the French government's deportation of Roma migrants to practices not seen since the Second World War and launched an infringement procedure against France before the European Court of Justice. Orbán was already watching closely. 'You cannot insult France without consequences and Ms Reding has insulted her,' the Hungarian prime minister told EU reporters.[41] Barroso backed Reding, who soon switched her attention from Paris to Budapest.

As a former leader of the European People's Party in the European Parliament, Reding might have joined Joseph Daul in accommodating the Hungarian government. Instead, she gave Orbán one month to address concerns that Hungary's new constitution violated EU law. When these concerns weren't fully addressed, she launched infringement proceedings before the European Court of Justice.[42] This move was a partial success. Whereas Reding had bowed to pressure from Paris to drop similar proceedings over the deportation of Roma citizens, she maintained the pressure on the Orbán administration and extracted concessions on some constitutional reforms. A high-blown debate over EU values this was not. Rather than challenging plans to retire judges early as an attempt to remove political opponents, Reding argued instead that such measures ran contrary to EU law on age discrimination.

Reding's strategy worked, but only as a stopgap. Although Orbán was willing to make concessions on specific points of EU law, the Hungarian prime minister pressed ahead with his constitutional reforms and grew more outspoken about his real intentions. Each year he gave a talk at a summer school for young right-wing conservatives in Băile Tuşnad, a Romanian spa town with a majority population of Székely Hungarians. His theme in 2014 was 'regime change'.[43] Like the events of 1989, the 'Western financial crisis' had created a 'different world overnight', he argued, yet this time the challenge was not to defeat Communism but to address the failure of liberal democracy to win the 'great world race' to find 'the most competitive way of organising state and society'. China, India, Russia, Singapore and

Turkey understood this, the prime minister argued, as did Hungary. It was an extraordinary intervention from a one-time liberal leader. More incredible still was Orbán's confident prediction that it was possible 'to build an illiberal nation state within the EU'.

Why had Reding not triggered Article 7 before things had reached this point? Because, she told a Brussels think tank, the requirement of a two-thirds majority in the European Parliament and unanimity in the European Council before a member state could face sanctions made it 'heavy to handle'.[44] Her solution, and that of Barroso, was a rule of law mechanism, which served as a sort of precursor to Article 7. Engaging member states in a constructive discussion about EU fundamental values, it was hoped, would encourage practical solutions to rule of law concerns rather than stalemate or a stand-off.

Jean-Claude Juncker, Barroso's successor as Commission President and yet another member of the European People's Party, had little faith in this approach. Having chaired meetings of eurozone finance ministers for a decade, Juncker had dealt with no shortage of recalcitrant states. He also understood that member states were unlikely to grant the Commission stronger powers if they baulked at non-binding recommendations to begin with. 'The dictator's coming,' he remarked to Latvian Prime Minister Laimdota Straujuma, as the Hungarian prime minister approached for a pre-summit press photo. 'Dictator!' exclaimed Juncker, as he shook Orbán's hand and playfully, yet forcefully, slapped his cheek.[45]

When it regained the premiership in November 2015, the Law and Justice party lacked the parliamentary majority required to amend the Polish constitution, so it engineered a constitutional crisis instead.[46] In her final months in office, Ewa Kopacz, who succeeded Tusk as prime minister, had controversially appointed five new judges to Poland's Constitutional Tribunal. While three justices had been due to retire, Kopacz's appointment of the other two looked like a blatant attempt by the Civic Platform to pre-empt the Law and Justice party's nominees. Andrzej Duda, Poland's right-wing populist president refused to accept the five judges' oaths, in response to which his

Law and Justice colleague Beata Szydło, the country's new prime minister, pushed through five nominees of her own. When the Tribunal declared this move to be unconstitutional, the court was forced to accept the decision by parliament, which then passed a series of laws that effectively ended the tribunal's judicial independence. As a result of these changes, the Venice Commission concluded, the Tribunal bore similarities to, and in some cases was much worse than, its Soviet-era predecessor.[47]

The Heads of State or Government came under increasing pressure to act but to little effect. As the Law and Justice party sat with the UK Conservative Party in the European Parliament, UK Prime Minister David Cameron was reluctant to challenge or draw attention to his populist bedfellows. Having borne the brunt of the Kaczyńskis' uncompromising foreign policy a decade earlier, Angela Merkel saw Duda's presidency as an opportunity to reset relations with Poland rather than ratchet up tensions. Once again, it fell to the Commission to fill this void.

Frans Timmermans – who had returned from the political wilderness after triggering the Netherland's referendum vote against the European Constitution to become Dutch foreign minister and then Reding's successor at the European Commission – brought energy and experience to this role, if little optimism. A keen student of Central and Eastern Europe, he had watched the collapse of Communism as a Dutch diplomat in Moscow, before serving as an advisor to Max van der Stoel, a leading voice for fundamental rights in the Organization for Security and Co-operation in Europe. As a member of the Party of European Socialists, Timmermans was also under pressure to act. The head of this group in the European Parliament, Martin Schulz, had already compared Poland's constitutional crisis to a coup.[48] Timmermans couldn't hope to keep his job if he used such language; nor could he afford to remain silent. After calling on the Polish justice minister to reconsider the reform, and receiving short shrift, Timmermans triggered the Commission's rule of law mechanism for the first time.

Polish Prime Minister Beata Szydło was happy to play along, seeing dialogue with the Commission as a way to buy time and reduce media pressure, while pressing on with judicial reforms. But Timmermans was no fool; shining a light on the Law and Justice party was about the limit of what he could achieve without greater support from member states. The inconclusive, in-camera discussions that followed when the Commission finally triggered Article 7 in December 2017, merely underlined such limits. Unless the Heads of State or Government agreed that Poland was in breach of the EU's values and that disciplinary action was warranted, the country's constitutional crisis would continue. But Viktor Orbán had no intention of supporting such action while his own stand-off with the EU continued.

The Hungarian prime minister's real target in his Băile Tuşnad speech in 2014 was not the EU; it was non-governmental organisations (NGOs). The illiberal state should be governed by 'elected and professional statesmen and lawmakers,' he told his student audience, not 'political activists attempting to promote foreign interests'.[49] While he name-checked Norwegian NGOs in this speech, Orbán's real target was his old benefactor, George Soros. Soros' Open Society Foundation was not a prolific player in Hungarian politics; it provided relatively small grants to civil society groups and spoke out occasionally against government policies. But the Central European University had a bigger footprint, as a centre of research excellence and one of Europe's top graduate schools. When the Hungarian government presented draft legislation to the National Assembly, imposing costly new requirements on NGOs and foreign universities, it made no secret about who the intended target was. Minister for Human Capacities Zoltan Balog promised 'to use all legal means at our disposal to stop pseudo-civil society spy groups, such as the ones funded by George Soros'.[50] A month earlier, Orbán stood accused of anti-Semitism when he compared Soros to 'a predator swimming in Hungarian waters'.[51]

The Central European University's (CEU) students and its rector Michael Ignatieff mobilised quickly against the government's proposed higher education law. 'I stand with CEU' was aimed less at Orbán than the European People's Party, which continued to treat the Hungarian prime minister as a likeable rogue rather than a threat to EU values.[52] Manfred Weber, the group's leader in the European Parliament and a key target of this campaign, promised to defend freedom of speech, thought and research 'at any cost'[53] and then stood by as the Central European University relocated to Vienna. Weber declared himself 'extremely disappointed' with the news, while rejecting calls for Fidesz to be expelled from the European People's Party.[54] A suspension followed on the eve of the 2019 European Parliament elections, but it took another two years before Orbán finally quit. When he did, Weber declared himself regretful at losing a member of the 'family'.[55] By this point, MEPs had already passed a resolution to trigger Article 7 against Hungary. Two hearings in the Council followed in 2019, but they proved no more conclusive than the Polish case. Without strong and unanimous support from the Heads of State or Government, the disciplinary measures envisaged under Article 7 would never be triggered. No such support was forthcoming because national leaders, however much some wished to see more progressive governments win power in Hungary and Poland, were not willing to risk EU cooperation by taking a principled stance over the Union's values.[56]

Austria Redux (2018)

In December 2018, the Austrian Freedom Party returned to government in Austria, once again in a coalition with the Austrian People's Party. Haider had quit the party twelve years earlier, but it found a suitable replacement in Heinz-Christian Strache, a dental mechanic with alleged links to far-right groups.[57] A right-wing populist for the social media age, he connected with voters through ring tones and xenophobic rap songs.[58] Having come close to winning the presidential election in 2016, the Austrian Freedom Party came second in parliamentary elections a year later and opened coalition negotiations with the Austrian People's Party's leader Sebastian Kurz.

When he struck a deal with Jörg Haider's party in 2000, Wolfgang Schüssel was fifty-five years old and probably facing his last chance to become prime minister. Kurz was just thirty-one, having risen to prominence as a hardline minister in his early twenties. By borrowing the Austrian Freedom Party's policies, as in his promise to close Islamic kindergartens, Kurz improved the Austrian People's Party electoral performance.[59] He also ensured that coalition talks between the two parties were straightforward.[60] The main stumbling block was over Europe, but Strache agreed not to pursue Austria's exit from the EU in exchange for becoming the country's vice-chancellor and securing senior cabinet positions for his party colleagues. Schüssel had been shunned by fellow Heads of State or Government in 2000. Kurz was congratulated. Péter Szijjártó, Hungary's foreign minister, expressed his 'joy' at the arrival of a government that shared a similar view on migration and praised Austrian voters for embracing 'value-based policies that guarantee security and stability'.[61] 'One more @EPP prime minister,' boasted Irish Taoiseach Leo Varadkar. 'Am no longer the youngest of the bunch!'[62]

The EU's willingness to challenge Austria in 2000 had proved to be a high watermark for the defence of EU values in the post-Maastricht period. The Austrian government's refusal to back down in the face of sanctions, sapped national leaders' willingness to confront one another over breaches of EU fundamental rights even as they sought to codify such rights in EU law. European officials struggled to fill this void without stronger backing from the Heads of State or Government, allowing right-wing populists to thrive in new and old member states alike. The EU survived such confrontations, but its commitment 'to the principles of liberty, democracy and respect for human rights and fundamental freedoms and of the rule of law' in the Maastricht Treaty was greatly diminished as a result.

5

European Culture

Europa

You will now listen to my voice.
My voice will help you and guide
you still deeper into Europa.
Every time you hear my voice,
with every word and every number,
you will enter a still deeper layer,
open, relaxed and receptive.
I shall now count from one to ten.
On the count of ten,
you will be in Europa.

This hypnotic induction, spoken by the iconic Swedish actor Max von Sydow, opens Lars von Trier's *Europa* (1992). The film was supported by Eurimages, a fund created not by the EU but by the Council of Europe, an older pan-European organisation, to encourage cross-border film productions. Whereas the Council of Europe's cultural policy attracted little comment, the EU's growing involvement in this domain in the 1990s drew accusations of 'federalist thought control'.[1] For Gerard Delanty, a sociologist, the EU's efforts to create a 'European cultural identity' were mostly 'pathetic exercises in cultural engineering' that fell well short of their stated aims.[2] For the social anthropologist Cris Shore, the EU's attempt to construct a European identity, however well-intentioned, smacked of 'nation-building' and the appropriation of national cultures into a 'unitary "European" history'.[3] However, such accounts overstate the influence of European officials, who entered the cultural domain guardedly and used the limited resources at their disposal to support cultural industries facing fierce global competition rather than a federalist agenda.

The real puzzle is not why the EU would seek to involve itself in cultural policy, but why it took so long. The Council of Europe saw culture as safe ground compared to other areas of cooperation and adopted a European Cultural Convention in 1954 at a time when its members remained reluctant to build on their early commitments to human rights. Two years later, the European Broadcasting Union, an association of public sector broadcasters, started the Eurovision Grand Prix, later renamed the Eurovision Song Contest, to foster European solidarity and experiment with live television link-ups. Few accused the Council of Europe of cultural hegemony. The Eurovision, as it came to be known, revelled in pop pastiche and regional rivalries rather than the subversion of nation states. Becoming the world's most watched live non-sporting television event, the Eurovision became a symbol of European unity, albeit one that the EU played no part in.[4] A report that the Union itself was planning to enter the 2021 Eurovision Song Contest was quite obviously an April Fool's joke even before it suggested that a Commissioner would sing the song.[5]

Carlo Ripa di Meana was a guiding force behind EU cultural policy. As president of the Venice Biennale, Ripa di Meana had transformed one of Europe's oldest cultural institutes into a more politically and socially minded body following violent student protests at its eponymous art exhibition in May 1968. As the first European Commissioner to hold a brief for culture, he floated various ideas, including a tongue in cheek suggestion that Italy cede sovereignty of Venice to the European Community, before settling on more modest calls to support the circulation of 'European cultural products'.[6] Ripa di Meana made no secret, however, of his desire to foster 'a European cultural identity'.[7] His vision of cultural policy was an expansive one, which encompassed Community support for theatre, television and, through the European Capital of Culture, the curation of events designed to celebrate European cities' cultural diversity and development. It also included support for cinema, which Ripa di Meana saw as 'a cultural factor of crucial importance'. In 1987, he convinced EU culture ministers to support Mesures pour encourager le développement de l'industrie audiovisuelle (MEDIA), a pilot project designed to support the cross-border distribution of European films.[8] A full-scale programme of the same name was launched in 1991, a year before Maastricht gave the EU explicit authority to act in the cultural domain. The treaty walked a precarious line between cultural unity and diversity. The Community should not only bring Europe's 'common cultural heritage to the fore', it insisted, but also 'contribute to the flowering of the cultures of the Member States'.[9]

If anyone was engaged in cultural engineering during the post-Maastricht period, it was not in Brussels but Hollywood. American film studios' interest in European history – or, more commonly, sentimental reimaginings thereof – can be seen in Mel Gibson's *Braveheart* (1995), Ridley Scott's *Gladiator* (2000) and Oliver Stone's *Alexander* (2004). Ron Howard's *Da Vinci Code* (2005) brought new cinematic meaning to 'doing Europe', as the film's protagonists hurtled between heritage sites in Paris, London, Lincolnshire and Midlothian in search of the Holy Grail. Only Studio Canal Plus was able to match Hollywood's productive capacity and tightly integrated international distribution and marketing networks.[10] The Parisian company used its position to finance some of the most successful French-language films of the 1990s and 2000s, including Jean-Pierre Jeunet's *Le Fabuleux Destin d'Amélie Poulain* (2001), and Hollywood blockbusters of its own, such as James Cameron's *Terminator 2: Judgment Day* (1991) and Paul Verhoeven's *Basic Instinct* (1992). The French studio was also behind some of the most successful British films of this period, including Stephen Daldry's *Billy Elliot* (2000), Sharon Maguire's *Bridget Jones's Diary* (2001) and Richard Curtis' *Love Actually* (2003).

MEDIA's aim was not to create European champions like Studio Canal Plus but to support the Union's predominately small- and medium-sized production and distribution companies.[11] In 1995, the EU-15 made 325 full-length, nationally produced feature films, compared to 510 in 1980.[12] The United States was making twice as many films per year by the mid-1990s and enjoying considerably greater commercial success. The 'discrepancy' between European and US films was, Ripa di Meana argued, 'appalling'.[13] Even in France, which had Europe's most advanced motion picture industry, US films accounted for 57.4 per cent of gross box office receipts in 1995.[14] The corresponding figures for Germany and the UK were 87.1 per cent and 83.7 per cent respectively. Distribution was another major challenge, with most nationally produced films in the EU not shown outside their home countries.[15] With an initial budget of €200 million for a five-year period, MEDIA was small compared to the sums spent by many national governments on audiovisual policies, but the Commission used its limited resources wisely by providing seed money for film development and funds to promote and show films in other countries, thus bringing films to a bigger audience.

Although it was no panacea, MEDIA played its part in the revival of European cinema. In 2018, the EU-15 produced nearly 1,300 films, compared to 560 a decade earlier.[16] EU member states didn't benefit equally from this boom, but nor was it concentrated in countries with comparatively bigger film industries. The Netherlands, for instance, went from making thirteen films a year in 1997 to 86 by 2018.[17] A significant share of this increased production came from films co-financed by European partners, as in Dorota Kobiela and Hugh Welchman's *Loving Vincent* (2017). An experimental, animated biography of Vincent van Gogh produced by companies from the Netherlands, Poland, Switzerland and the UK, the film was one of the highest-grossing European films of 2018. With the support of MEDIA, cross-border co-productions became commonplace; they accounted for a fifth of European films produced between 2007 and 2016 and around half of box office receipts for European films. The growing popularity of EU productions meant a declining market share for US films, which accounted for 62.6 per cent of EU box office receipts in 2018 compared to 71.2 per cent in 2002.[18]

Fears that European officials might support films with a federalist agenda were misplaced. Of the thousands of productions funded by the EU between 1991 and 2018, few dealt explicitly with Europe as a political project, even in passing. Those that did were rarely sympathetic to the EU, as in Phyllida Lloyd's *The Iron Lady* (2012), which depicted a heroic Margaret Thatcher fighting 'to retain British sovereignty of Britain' and 'the integrity of the pound', and Costa-Gavras' *The Adults in the Room* (2012), a fictionalised account of Greek Finance Minister Yanis Varoufakis' rough treatment by EU partners during the euro crisis. A sense of identity formation can be found in Christian Carion's *Joyeux Noël* (2005), which tells the story of the Christmas truce, a series of ceasefires on the Western Front in December 1914, from the perspective of Danish, French, German and Scottish protagonists. But the film's attempt to remember the First World War as European history, as the film scholar Mariana Liz argues, merely drew attention to divisions over the European Constitution at the time of the film's release.[19]

Not all films backed by MEDIA won critical acclaim. Oliver Hirschbiegel's *Diana* (2012) was dismissed by the *Daily Mail* as 'Squirmingly embarrassing, atrocious and fabulously awful'.[20] However, a significant number won accolades at film festivals in Europe and beyond. The nine nominations received by Yorgos Lanthimos' *The Favourite* (2018) at the 91st Academy Awards showed MEDIA not only at its most critically and commercially successful but also at its most ambivalent. Lanthimos achieved international recognition for *Kinetta* (2005), a deadpan, macabre story in which three people in an out-of-season Greek resort make a violent film. Domestic financing for Greek films dried up during the global financial crisis, leading Lanthimos to look abroad for funding. MEDIA supported *Dogtooth* (2009) and *The Alps* (2011), with the former becoming the first Greek-language film to be nominated for an Academy Award in thirty-two years.

Dogtooth's recognition was not only an extraordinary achievement for Greece; it epitomised the EU's belief that homegrown productions could reach a global audience with the right investment in marketing and distribution. It also revealed Lanthimos' transition from being a Greek filmmaker to a more nebulous sort of European one. Produced by Element Pictures, an Irish company, in collaboration with filmmakers from France, Greece, the Netherlands and the UK, Lanthimos' *The Lobster* (2015) was shot on location in Kerry and Devon with British, Greek, Irish and French actors. Taking more than US$18 million at the box office on a budget of US$4 million, the film won the Jury Prize at the Cannes Film Festival and an Academy Award nomination for Best Original Screenplay. Element Pictures worked again with Lanthimos on *The Killing of a Sacred Deer* (2017) before securing a third instalment of EU funding for *The Favourite* (2018).

Although Lanthimos' success was celebrated in Greece, his films became less rooted in Greek culture. The *Killing of a Sacred Deer* was loosely based on the Greek tragedy Iphigenia and – like *The Lobster* – set in an unidentified, amorphous Europe in which characters audibly come from different parts of the Continent but without explanations of why they came to be in one place. This choice is partly creative. Lanthimos is not interested in making films about politics. Even *The Favourite* relegates the War of Spanish Succession to something which happens off-screen. Lanthimos' non-depiction of Europe also had a practical dimension. His films lacked the budget to shoot in multiple locations. It was simply easier to set the action in, what film critic Mark Kermode refers to as, a 'Euro Netherworld' comprised of two unidentified locations: 'the town' and 'the woods'.[21]

Nordic Noir

However successful Lanthimos may have been as a filmmaker, his work reinforced the idea of EU cultural policy as highbrow and elitist. Nordic noir showed that European popular culture was possible. This cultural turn began – or, more accurately, was revived – in 1993 with the publication of Peter Høeg's novel *Miss Smilla's Feeling for Snow* (1992). Maj Sjöwall and Per Wahlöö had already transposed the figure of the hardboiled detective from American pulp fiction to a Nordic setting in the *Martin Beck* series (1965–75), an idea updated in Henning Mankell's *Faceless Killers* (1991), the first of thirteen novels about a misanthropic Swedish detective, Kurt Wallander. Høeg shared Mankell's interest in detective fiction as a vehicle for discussing Nordic society's place in Europe and the wider world; but the former broke new ground, and established a key characteristic of Nordic noir, by making his protagonist a hardboiled heroine. Smilla Qaaviqaaq Jaspersen, an unemployed loner with a background in the scientific study of glaciers, travels from Copenhagen to Nuuk in Greenland to investigate the death of a neighbour's son. Greenland's dark winter days bring atmosphere to Høeg's story as well as an opportunity to reflect on the relationship between Denmark and its autonomous territory. Greenlanders refer to Danes in the novel as 'Europeans', a label that alludes both to the island's Inuit heritage and its departure from the European Communities following a referendum vote in 1982.[22]

Miss Smilla's Feeling for Snow found a readership not only because of the sharpness of Høeg's storytelling but also because the book subverted the Nordic miracle. In the 1990s, economists had started to doubt the ability of GDP to measure a society's progress and turned instead to measures like the World Bank's annual Human Development Index to capture other variables like life expectancy and educational attainment and opportunities. Scoring at the very top of such indices, Denmark, Norway and Sweden became objects of interest and envy among European politicians who sought to emulate their economic policies.[23] And yet, the 1990s was a difficult time for Nordic countries; financial deregulation paved the way for a banking crisis, exposing nefarious dealings between the worlds of industry, finance and politics. Although government intervention helped to stem this crisis, it provided fertile ground for far-right parties, as did rising levels of immigration and asylum from Central and Eastern Europe. Nordic noir captured these economic, political and social upheavals and showed that the image of the region's 'Almost Nearly Perfect People', as the journalist Michael Booth called it, was a myth.[24]

Peter Høeg's success inspired a new generation of hugely popular detective fiction, including Stieg Larsson's *Millennium Trilogy* and Jo Nesbø's 'Harry Hole' series. It was on the screen, however, that Nordic noir had its biggest cultural impact. The European Commission was quick to spot this potential and provided financial backing for Bille August's *Smilla's Sense of Snow* (1997). Although this film received mixed reviews, perhaps because it substituted Høeg's ambivalent ending with a half-baked Hollywood one, Niels Arden Oplev and Daniel Alfredson's *Millennium Trilogy* (2009) was a critical and commercial success. Television was even more suited than cinema to this character-driven drama, with *Forbrydelsen* (*The Killing*, 2007), a joint production by Danish and German public broadcasters, becoming a pan-European hit. European television had traditionally included a high share of foreign programming but, with *Forbrydelsen*, Europeans started to watch television made partly or wholly in other EU member states. MEDIA encouraged this cultural shift by financing a new wave of cross-border productions aimed at international audiences. The most successful example was *Bron|Broen* (2011), a Nordic noir produced by Sweden's Sveriges Television and Denmark's Danmarks Radio, which ran for four seasons, and was broadcast in 188 countries worldwide.[25] Named after the Danish and Swedish words for bridge, *Bron|Broen* is a bilingual police procedural set on – and around – the eponymous Øresund Bridge, a real-life rail–road bridge connecting Copenhagen in Denmark with Malmö in Sweden. Built with support from the EU, this bridge embodied the Maastricht Treaty's commitment to link European regions through trans-European networks. In Hans Rosenfeldt's *Bron|Broen*, the Øresund Bridge serves as a conduit for criminality and police cooperation. The first episode begins with the discovery of human remains at the precise point on the bridge marking the border between Denmark and

Sweden. A joint investigation led by Saga Norén from the Malmö County Police and Martin Rohde, her counterpart from Copenhagen, follows, taking the viewer back and forth across the Øresund Bridge in search of a 'Truth Terrorist' who uses violence to draw attention to society's shortcomings.

The Europe depicted in *Bron|Broen* was borderless, much more so, in fact, than the EU in the 2010s. Although the Amsterdam Treaty introduced cross-border cooperation between national police forces, joint investigations of the kind undertaken by Norén and Rohde remained rare. Legal and operational differences, including those concerning the admissibility of evidence and the disclosure of information, posed significant barriers to pan-European police work.[26] Nor were relations between Denmark and Sweden quite so harmonious. In 2015, as the third season of *Bron|Broen* went to air, Danish voters rejected plans to end the country's opt-out from EU justice and home affairs, a result that led to the country's withdrawal from Europol, the EU's agency for law enforcement cooperation. In the same year, Sweden introduced identity checks on people crossing the Øresund Bridge in response to the global refugee crisis of 2015. These anachronisms made little difference to the show's European viewers, who watched in their millions. *Bron|Broen* became, Ib Bondebjerg argues, a 'mediated cultural encounter between Europeans' through which they could understand their differences as well as what they had in common.[27]

Bron|Broen inspired several re-makes, including *The Tunnel* (2013), a British-French drama in which the action switched from Kent to Nord-Pas-de-Calais via the Channel Tunnel and the *Bridge* (2013) set on the US-Mexican border, yet none worked as well without the Nordic noir backdrop. Such was the power of this European genre that television producers sought to reimagine far-flung film locations as Nordic. Ann Cleeves' *Shetland* (2013) could, at least, draw on the Scottish archipelago's distant Scandinavian past, but Ken Bruen's *Jack Taylor* (2011) struggled to do the same for Galway, a city with Celtic and Norman roots.

Nordic noir showed that a European culture was possible. What of the EU's wider efforts to promote European television? As with cinema, the small screen faced a wave of imports from the 1970s onwards. One study of selected European television markets suggested that 56.8 per cent of fiction broadcast in 1997 originated from the United States.[28] The EU's Audiovisual Media Services Directive (2010) – and before that the Television Without Frontiers Directive (1989) – provided a degree of protection to European television producers by requiring broadcasters to devote a majority of transmission time to 'European works', that is, work originating from EU member states or certain other European countries.[29] However, the implementation of this legislation was patchy and skewed towards homegrown productions rather than EU imports. In a survey of European television channels, conducted by the Commission in 2007, European works accounted for 64 per cent of transmission time, but non-domestic works accounted for only 8.1 per cent.[30] Jimmy Perry's *Dad's Army* (1968), a BBC comedy about an ageing Home Guard platoon during the Second World War, remained a Saturday night staple in the UK, the country which recorded the joint lowest transmission time for European works.[31] The Television Without Frontiers Directive may have increased the prevalence of must-see American shows on European screens, the historian and political theorist Luuk van Middelaar argues, by fostering the EU's image as one big advertising market.[32]

Netflix's arrival in Europe in 2012, five years after it started streaming video-on-demand in the United States, was heralded as a boon for independent European producers and yet it was anything but that at first. A study of all EU member states in 2015 revealed that European works accounted for just 21 per cent of video-on-demand catalogues.[33] Anticipating revisions to the Audiovisual Media Services Directive which required streaming services to dedicate at least 30 per cent of their catalogues to European works, Netflix began diversifying its purchases and productions. One beneficiary was *Occupied* (2015), a political thriller co-created by Nordic noir writer Jo Nesbø. Produced by Norwegian, French and Swedish television companies with support from MEDIA, *Occupied* tells the story of Jesper Berg, a Green prime minister of Norway, who responds to a deadly hurricane by turning off the country's fossil fuel production. Facing an energy crisis of its own, the EU conspires with Russia to seize control of Norway's oil and gas fields, leaving Berg in charge of a government with ever-decreasing autonomy. The EU depicted in this drama is a regional hegemon prepared to use force to protect the shared interests of its member states. 'I demand to talk to a national leader,' cries Berg, as he speaks to fictional Commissioner Pierre Anselme, via video link while being held at gunpoint. The Swedish prime minister appears on screen, showing an EU that is at last capable of speaking with one voice, its mask as a normative actor having finally slipped. EU policy-makers didn't comment on the series, but Russia's ambassador to Norway expressed regret over the television series' attempt to scare viewers 'with a non-existent threat from the East'.[34]

'That's TV Kids, Broadcast Live As It Happens'

As well as supporting cross-border productions, the European Commission had long aspired to see a pan-European television channel. As European Commissioner for cultural affairs, Carlo Ripa di Meana backed Europa-TV, a multilingual channel launched by five members of the European Broadcasting Union hailing it, rather anachronistically, as an opportunity for cultural unity not seen 'since the Roman Empire'.[35] The Italian had one eye on the past and another on the future, in particular, the launch of CNN International in 1985. Should he really have learned about the United States' bombing of Libya from a news channel broadcast from Atlanta, Ripa di Meana asked.[36] Simultaneous translation into English, Dutch, German and Portuguese proved prohibitively costly for Europa-TV, which exhausted its three-year budget in a little over twelve months. The experiment had worked in theory, if not in practice, insisted Ripa di Meana, who blamed member states for their failure to support the project. The European Broadcasting Union tried instead with

Euronews, which offered a European perspective on international events in multiple languages. Member states, once again, showed no interest, but the European Commission provided funding in exchange for programming dedicated specifically to EU affairs.[37]

A study of Euronews' first decade by Iñaki Garcia-Blanco and Stephen Cushion showed a news channel that – although it offered more in-depth treatment of European issues than its national counterparts – fell well short of creating a European public sphere.[38] National governments dominated its news stories; EU institutions and citizens were largely absent. Anchors and reporters, so crucial to the image and reputation of regular news channels were unseen; voiceovers helped to keep the costs of multilingual broadcasts down. The launch of *Good Morning Europe* in 2018, a breakfast show broadcast from *La Confluence* in Lyon, created space for breaking news and down-the-barrel interviews with EU policy-makers from a dedicated studio in the European Parliament. In 2021, a Portuguese venture-capital firm run by the son of a senior advisor to Hungarian Prime Minister Viktor Orbán acquired a controlling stake in the channel, which by now boasted a monthly viewership of 64 million and reached 440 million homes in 160 countries.[39] The channel retained its independence, insisted its CEO, while Orbán laughed off claims that he was seeking to suppress media freedom in Europe, despite his efforts to do just that in Hungary.[40]

The launch of MTV Europe in 1987 began a more radical experiment in pan-European broadcasting. Although it primarily played music videos by English-speaking artists, the channel was no facsimile of its older, American counterpart. Based in London's Camden Town, MTV Europe compiled its own music chart, hosted the annual European Music Awards and produced original programming aimed at, and presented by, young Europeans. Germany's Kristiane Backer, the UK's Paul King and the Netherlands' Simone Angel became emissaries of a new European youth culture, yet none matched the star power of Ray Cokes, a francophone Briton who joined the station after hosting a music show on Belgium's RTBF.

Cokes' *MTV Most Wanted* premiered in 1992, offering a chaotic mix of sketches, phone-ins, live performances and backchat between presenter and crew. The show attracted 60 million viewers in 38 countries, making Europe feel, argues media scholar Alida Hujić, 'like one big country' four nights per week.[41]

Although it couldn't claim direct credit for this television revolution, the EU was not slow to seize the opportunities to speak to the channel's young European viewers. Keen to burnish its socially conscious image, MTV Europe was happy to reciprocate. 'The European elections may not appear particularly sexy, but it's very important that people be informed', declared Brent Hansen, MTV's Europe director of programming in 1994, shortly before Jacques Delors – incongruously joined by ex-Soviet president Mikhail Gorbachev – participated in an MTV Vote Europe debate.[42] Despite such initiatives, the EU remained protective of national broadcasters and slow to uphold MTV Europe's complaints about restrictive practices by video performance rights companies and major record labels. Although the channel eventually resolved this issue, the high price it paid to broadcast music videos across European borders hit its profitability.

Losing market share to national broadcasters like VIVA, a German-language music channel, MTV Europe had also become a target for the anti-globalisation movement.[43] To Brent Hansen, by now head of MTV Europe, Denmark's 'no' vote against the Maastricht Treaty suggested that nationalism was on the rise, prompting a rethink of the channel's original vision of a single programming schedule for the Continent.[44] In 1997, MTV Europe launched national and regional variants, including MTV Central, MTV UK and Ireland and MTV Italia, a profitable move but one that fragmented its content and reach. By this point, Cokes had parted company with the channel after being pelted with beer bottles in a raucous outside broadcast in Hamburg. 'That's TV kids, broadcast live as it happens', insisted Cokes, as he signed off on his show and, as it turned out, his time at MTV Europe.[45]

The cultural influence of music television was waning by the late 1990s, yet the idea of a pan-European music space had already found new life in Europe's burgeoning music festival scene. In Central and Eastern Europe, Hungary's Sziget Festival and Poland's Pol'and'Rock Festival exemplified these trends. Each began as a relatively small festival in the early 1990s attracting local visitors in the tens of thousands to watch local bands. By 2019, they were drawing crowds of half a million from all over Europe to watch an international roster of artists. The Sziget Festival was started in 1993 by Müller Péter Sziámi, an underground poet and musician during the communist period, and Károly Gerendai, an entrepreneur. Held on Óbudai-sziget, an islet in the Danube, the event championed freedom of expression and modelled itself as 'a New Woodstock on the Danube'.⁴⁶ Indeed, Jethro Tull and other performers from the original Woodstock appeared at the second Sziget Festival. Originally known as Woodstock Festival Poland, the Pol'and'Rock Festival was started by Jurek Owsiak, a broadcaster and member of the Polish punk scene who sought to raise money for children's health care through an event dedicated to the themes of love, friendship and music.

As they grew in scale, attracting international bands and global brands, the Sziget Festival and Pol'and'Rock left less room for local artists and attendees. But the events retained their commitment to progressive politics, even as the Hungarian and Polish governments embraced right-wing populism.⁴⁷ The Sziget Festival's NGO island became a focal point for annual debate on Europe, the environment, anti-racism and LGBTQ rights to the obvious frustration of Viktor Orbán's party, Fidesz, which had long since abandoned its roots in young liberal activism. Pol'and'Rock Festival hit a nerve in 2019 when Poland's Commissioner for Human Rights participated in a roundtable at the festival on hate speech and Polish judges staged a mock trial to highlight concerns over threats to the rule of law.⁴⁸

The House of European History

The 1990s marked the beginning of a new phase of growth and uncertainty for European museums. Although the continent experienced a museum boom, the idea of such institutions as repositories of culture faced a fierce backlash. When work on a new Guggenheim museum in Bilbao's down-at-heel Abandoibarra district began in October 1993, Spanish authorities were criticised for diverting public money away from alleviating high unemployment and other social problems. But, by attracting more than one million visitors per year to see Frank Gehry's twisted titanium structure and its extraordinary collection of contemporary art, the Bilbao effect inspired a wave of museum-led urban regeneration from Arles to Dundee. In stark contrast, Brussels' AfricaMuseum found itself at the centre of controversy over European museums' colonial legacies. When it re-opened in 2018 after a five-year hiatus, the museum gave greater prominence to Congolese artists such as Aimé Mpane, but it faced continued criticism for the racist imagery and words that adorned the museum building and for displaying items that had been obtained illegally during Belgian rule in the Congo.[49]

Amid these seismic shifts, tentative signs of what Bjarne Rogan refers to as a 'European museology' emerged.[50] A pioneering step was the opening of Berlin's Museum of European Cultures in 1999. Dedicated to the collection and display of everyday cultural encounters in Europe since the eighteenth century, the museum served less as a marker of post-war Germany's commitment to European integration than as a means of reuniting old collections in a historically sensitive way. Established in 1873 to mark the unification of the German state, the Museum of Folklore had been decimated by the Nazis, who separated German and European folklore and destroyed much of both. After the war, the museum's collections were divided between East and West Berlin, leaving difficult questions about how to remember German folklore after reunification. Borrowing the EU's cultural policy of unity in diversity 'helped purify [the collection] of its hyper-nationalistic, Nazi connotation', argues Chiara De Cesari, an anthropologist, even if its conception of Europe was noticeably Christian.[51]

The Musée des Civilisations de l'Europe et de la Méditerranée in Marseille embraced Europe for more pecuniary reasons. Founded in

1937, the National Museum of Popular Arts and Traditions in Paris faced falling visitor numbers in the 2010s and accusations of cultural obsolescence. Moving the collection to Rudy Ricciotti's latticework construction in Marseille in 2013 helped to seal the city's bid to become the European capital of culture, which in turn helped to channel nearly €6 billion in new investment in the country's second city. The museum's focus on the Europe of the Mediterranean reflected the city's geography, but also French President Nicolas Sarkozy's project for a Union for the Mediterranean, which sought closer cooperation between EU member states and neighbouring countries from North Africa, the Middle East and Southern Europe.

The UK, although it experienced its own curatorial renaissance during this period, stood apart. Seemingly impervious to public debate about decolonising British history, the Imperial War Museum retained its name and opened a shiny new branch in Manchester in 2002. The British Museum, meanwhile, dedicated more rooms to the Middle East than pan European history and continued to display around half of the surviving sculptures from the Parthenon, which had been removed from Athens by Lord Elgin in the early 1800s. The museum's trustees continued to defend its unique display of world heritage, but this argument was significantly weakened by the opening of the Acropolis Museum in Athens in 2009, its glass-walled hall ready to display the temple's surviving sculptures against the backdrop of their original location. As the Vatican Museums and the Antonino Salinas Regional Archaeological Museum in Palermo returned fragments of the Parthenon frieze to Greece, pressure mounted on the British Museum to do the same.[52]

Wary of this treacherous cultural terrain, the European Commission limited itself to providing modest financial support to exhibitions and encouraging the cross-border exchange of collections. The European Parliament was far bolder. In his inaugural speech as president of the EU legislature, Hans-Gert Pöttering appealed to a 'shared European culture' rooted in 'Greek philosophy, Roman law, the Judeo-Christian heritage, the Enlightenment' and called for efforts to 'rediscover the things that are common to us all'.[53] To this end, Pöttering proposed the creation of a 'House of European History' to cultivate a collective memory of European history and unification.[54] Ten years and an estimated €56 million later, a museum dedicated to the interpretation of history from a European perspective opened in Parc Leopold, a stone's throw from the European Parliament in Brussels.[55]

Pöttering's didactic vision of a museum which would show 'people, especially the younger ones, how not to stray from the path to European unification' spoke to concerns by Gerard Delanty, Cris Shore and other scholars about the EU harnessing culture to advance European federalism.[56] However, such didacticism was quickly dispensed with, as Pöttering sought to build and maintain support for his proposal within the European Parliament both during and after his tenure as president. Some MEPs still criticised the project, with Front National's Dominique Bilde, for one, arguing that a museum of national histories would be preferable to a 'propaganda tool for European integration'.[57] 'As Europe is losing competitiveness and geopolitical weight, it is becoming a museum anyway,' quipped Lajos Bokros, a Hungarian politician.

It's Our History, an EU-funded exhibition housed in the Tour & Taxis building in Brussels to mark fifty years since the Treaty of Rome, won plaudits for recounting the EU's history through the lives of '27 ordinary Europeans – one per member state', but it was criticised for its heroic depiction of post-war European integration and its treatment of 1945 as 'year zero'.[58] The Parlamentarium, a €15 million visitor centre launched in 2011, also drew fire from the Eurosceptic press as a 'temple' to MEPs. Keen to circumvent such criticisms, Pöttering deferred to the historians and curators who made up the House of European History's Academic Board and management team.[59] The most important voice in this regard was the project's creative director, Taja Vovk van Gaal.

A former director of the City Museum of Ljubljana, Vovk van Gaal had grown up listening to stories about her grandfather's time in the

Slovene resistance and her father's conscription to the Eastern front.[60] The ill-treatment of both men after the war encouraged Vovk van Gaal to question official accounts of Josip Tito's wartime heroics and benevolent leadership and led her to become a historian and curator, as Yugoslavia succumbed to economic collapse and ethnic division. This lived experience discouraged Vovk van Gaal from presenting a unified vision of European history; instead, she sought to represent the multiple meanings and memories surrounding the idea of Europe and to provoke debate about the EU's origins and evolution. The House of European History must, she insisted, speak to an 80-year-old in Latvia as well as a 20-year-old in Portugal.

Vovk van Gaal was determined to avoid a 'too Western' account of European history. This meant speaking of Stalinism alongside Nazism and acknowledging the differing memories and interpretations of Communism's legacy. It meant recognising the toll taken on Central and Eastern Europe by the transition from central planning to market capitalism and the uncertain future of those countries to which the offer of EU membership was not extended. It meant, above all, rejecting a singular account of European history in favour of a multi-perspectival approach. To the historian Wolfram Kaiser, the House of European History's kaleidoscopic vision was not just a personal choice by Vovk van Gaal and others.[61] It was a political necessity born of the need to maintain political support for the museum among Central and Eastern European MEPs. A key voice here was Pöttering's successor as European Parliament president, Jerzy Buzek.

In June 2008, Buzek – a former Polish prime minister and veteran of Solidarity – had joined Václav Havel, among other ex-dissidents, in signing the Prague Declaration. An early marker of Central and Eastern Europe's political and intellectual influence on the EU after the Big Bang enlargement, this document called for an 'all-European' understanding of Communism.[62] Although this declaration didn't equate Nazism and Stalinism, it treated them as distinct sides of the same totalitarian coin and called for Communism's wrongdoings to be recognised as crimes against humanity, just as Nazi atrocities had been after the Second World War. National leaders had no stomach for such historical debates, but the European Parliament, which by now had nearly two hundred MEPs from Central and Eastern Europe, adopted a series of declarations which sought to forge a common understanding of Europe's past.[63] These declarations were largely symbolic, but such symbolism seeped into the House of European History.

'It is a house which, by showing us the dynamics of European history, enables us to better understand recent history, as well as the present,' declared Hans-Gert Pöttering as he cut the blue tape on the renovated Eastman Building in May 2017.[64] 'Those looking for a temple to EU propaganda will be disappointed,' concluded a British journalist, who noted that a visitor had 'to climb to the fourth floor before seeing the blue and gold EU insignia'.[65] The permanent exhibition was constructed instead around a series of European objects. A piece of pottery used as a voting ballot in the ancient Agora of Athens. A Cooke and Wheatstone telegraph. A pistol used in the plot to assassinate Archduke Ferdinand. An early edition of James Joyce's *Ulysses*. A testimonial artwork created from the coat of Joseph Fränkel, a Holocaust survivor. A faded mural of Nicolae Ceauşescu. A baby's shoe found on a beach. These and other items were accompanied by sparse text, which offered pointed questions and few conclusive answers.

Although it provoked the reflection and debate that Vovk van Gaal had sought, few commentators praised the House of European History. Some argued that the museum devoted too much attention to Central and Eastern Europe, while others suggested it didn't go far enough.[66] The Platform of European Memory and Conscience, an advocacy group created after the Prague Declaration, published a damning report on the museum for downplaying 'the criminal nature of Communist rule' and for its inadequate presentation of the Holocaust, which was represented not in a single space in the museum, but different parts of the permanent exhibition.[67] Piotr Gliński, Minister for Culture in Poland's right-wing populist government, criticised the museum for presenting his country as complicit in the Holocaust and for ignoring Europe's Christian roots. Four months later, the Polish Senate passed a law against accusing the Polish state or nation of carrying out crimes committed during the Nazi occupation. We have a right 'to defend historical truth', insisted President Andrzej Duda, but his party's critics decried attempts to turn Poland into 'the only blameless nation in Europe'.[68]

Much the most interesting commentary on the project came from Thomas Bellinck, a Belgian artist who opened the House of European History in Exile in 2013. Set in 2063, the imaginary museum looked back on the EU's collapse in 2018 after reaching thirty-three members, excluding the UK but including Montenegro, the Former Yugoslav Republic of Macedonia, Serbia and an independent Scotland. 'Europe dwindled to what it had always been,' the exhibition recounted, 'a politically divided continent.'[69]

Vovk van Gaal continued to defend the House of European History, as did the museum's backers in the European Parliament, whose status as elected representatives gave them licence, as they saw it, to debate such sensitive subjects in public.[70] European officials rarely claimed such authority, which explains why they approached culture so gingerly. The most successful cultural policy of the post-Maastricht period, the European Commission's MEDIA programme sidestepped grand debates about European identity and instead approached culture as an industry in need of support from fierce global competition. Judged in these terms, the EU made an important and often overlooked contribution to European culture in the post-Maastricht period, to the benefit of artists and audiences rather than federalist hypnotists.

PART II
'SORRY, BUT THERE IS NO WAY YOU'RE LEAVING THIS ROOM UNTIL YOU AGREE'

6

The Frankenstein Directive

Roam Sweet Roam

On 31 December 1992, ten months after the Maastricht Treaty was signed, the embryonic EU concluded a seven-year plan to complete the single market. Jacques Delors' most significant achievement as Commission President had been to win national governments' support for nearly three hundred pieces of legislation designed to remove the remaining barriers to the free movement of goods, services, people and capital between member states. And yet, six and a half years later, in the summer of 1999, Iayn Dobsyn, an IT worker from Salford, discovered first-hand just how significant national borders still were in this apparently borderless Europe. Holidaying in Portugal, Dobsyn downloaded an episode of Fox TV's drama *Prison Break* and several songs using his British mobile broadband card.[1] He returned home to a bill of £31,500. Dobsyn's service provider, Yes Telecom, was a subsidiary of Vodafone, a British telecom company operating across Europe, including in Portugal. Vodafone was not unusual in this regard; by the late 2000s, Germany's T-Mobile, Sweden's TeliaSonera and Spain's Telefonica were all operating on a pan-European scale. But telecom markets remained divided along national lines. Whereas Americans paid a flat rate for using their devices anywhere in the United States, Europeans travelling to other member states switched from home to foreign networks and paid a premium for calls, texts and data.

The Single Market Programme had made only passing reference to telecoms, and even then, it focused largely on the search for a common standard. It conveyed limited concern for the high costs of telephony for European consumers or awareness of how a 120-year-old Finnish company which had recently diversified from paper, rubber and cables into electronics had already started a technological revolution.[2] Although the American company Motorola had demonstrated the first handheld mobile phone in 1973, Nokia's Mobira Cityman 900 was the first to be widely used on 1G, the first-generation wireless cellular technology. The EU's role in the eventual liberalisation of the European telecoms sector is seen as a post-Maastricht success story, but it was a sector in which national borders remained unsurmountable.

Until the early 1990s, state-owned telephone companies charged high and seemingly arbitrary prices, especially for calls between EU member states. The cost of calling Copenhagen from Madrid, for example, was twice the cost of calling Madrid from Copenhagen.[3] Spurred on by the privatisation of British Telecom, which was completed in 1993, and the more modest separation of postal and telecommunications services in France and Germany, the European Commission stepped up its efforts after Maastricht to end public monopolies in this sector. In 1996, it finally convinced member states to end the protection of voice telephony, paving the way for new market entrants and significantly greater competition. In the eighteen months after this decision took effect, more than 1,000 licenses were issued to new telecommunications providers and call tariffs fell by 35 per cent on average.[4]

Despite these benefits, the EU had a single market for telecoms in name only. Competition increased within member states, but incumbents retained sizeable market shares and, in many cases, control of network infrastructures. The EU continued to define the geographic scope of markets in national terms, allowing prices to be set and spectrums to be allocated member state by member state.[5] Cross-border telecom mergers were rare and by no means encouraged.[6] Cross-country differences in tariffs and the quality of service reflected this state of affairs. In 2005, the cost of a ten-minute local call ranged from 16 cents in Bulgaria to 75 cents in Slovakia.[7]

Five years after the Mobira Cityman 900 was released, Nokia sold the first mobile phone to use the Global System for Mobile Communications (GSM), which thanks to quick thinking by European and national officials became a global standard for the fledgling mobile sector. And yet, EU policy-makers still worried about being left in the slow lane. Under the Telecommunications Act 1996, the Clinton Administration exposed telecom providers to much greater competition and encouraged incumbents to share existing networks and their competitors to build new ones. The EU not only lacked telecoms giants that could invest on the scale of Verizon and AT&T; it also encouraged new entrants to lease networks from incumbents. An EU regulation which required incumbents to unbundle the loop between telephone local exchanges and customers encouraged market entry while discouraging investment in new infrastructure.[8]

The United States also raced ahead of the EU on the information superhighway. Although the World Wide Web had been developed in Europe by Tim Berners-Lee, a British scientist working at CERN in Geneva, internet usage initially grew much faster in America than in Europe. By 1994, 22 per cent of Americans had used the internet in the last three months. The corresponding figure for the EU was less than 5 per cent.[9] By 2005, the number of fixed broadband subscriptions per 100 people stood at 17 in the United States and 12 in the EU.[10] That broadband prices were significantly higher in the EU than in the United States partly explained this difference, one consequence of which was that Europeans were slower to engage in electronic commerce and other opportunities created by the new technology.[11]

This transatlantic trend was reversed when it came to mobile phone usage. By 2006, there were 121 mobile cellular subscriptions for every 100 people in the EU, compared to 86 in the United States.[12] Nokia played a major part in this boom with its must-have handsets, which featured in Hollywood films such as the Wachowskis' *The Matrix* (1999). Competition within member states made a difference too, as incumbents and new entrants raced to sign up customers. But this race stopped at national borders, where telecom companies and national regulators stood guard. Member states, although they stood by the single market after 1992, remained wary about extending its frontiers.

The European Commission's efforts in the 2000s to create a single market for telecoms underlined not only the pivotal role played by European officials in EU policy-making, but also the limits of their powers. An important and often overlooked actor was Viviane Reding, who became European Commissioner for Information Society and Media in November 2004, having previously held the culture portfolio. Reding had a lifelong passion for communications. She studied at the Sorbonne under Roland Barthes and Umberto Eco, two giants of semi-otics, the study of sign processes, before working as a journalist for the *Luxemburger Wort*. With her bouffant hair and keen eye for photo opportunities, Reding defied lazy stereotypes about faceless Eurocrats. A red-carpet regular at the Cannes Film Festival during her time as European Commissioner for Education and Culture, where she rubbed shoulders with Quentin Tarantino and other Hollywood luminaries, she gained a reputation as a powerful advocate for the European film and television industry. This attention won Reding a second term under Commission President José Manuel Barroso, who put her in charge of telecoms and other aspects of the EU's emerging digital agenda.

Reding seemed reluctant to challenge public broadcasters, who used concerns over cultural and linguistic diversity to shield them-selves against the single market. But she showed no such caution with telecom providers. A month into her new role, the Commissioner backed an investigation into the high costs faced by EU citizens for using their mobile phones in other member states and followed up with a scoreboard for international roaming charges. When this exer-cise showed that charges had remained high for a year or more, Reding seized her chance to call for the regulation of wholesale and retail roaming prices as part of a wider reorganisation of European telecoms. The backlash by industry representatives was predictable, but the fiercest battle was in Brussels, where Reding fought a rear-guard action against Commissioners Peter Mandelson and Günter Verheugen, who voiced concerns over the competitiveness of telecoms providers. Reding conceded on plans to end charges for receiving mobile calls abroad but won Commission backing for a cap on roaming costs before securing support from wavering national governments and a more enthusiastic European Parliament.

Under a regulation enacted in 2007, the EU imposed a maximum price on voice calls made in other member states and reduced the scope for 'bill shock' by ensuring that travellers received a text on mobile usage in other parts of the Union.[13] The extension of this cap to the cost of text messages and data roaming came too late for Iayn Dobsyn to enjoy *Prison Break* at a reasonable price, but it reduced the cost of roaming by up to 42 per cent over four years, saving consumers an estimated €15 billion.[14] Having progressively reduced roaming prices, the EU eliminated them altogether in 2017. Under the Roam Like Home reform, mobile users paid the same prices for using their devices in other member states as they did domestically.

Reding's roaming reforms were no accident. As the political scientists Michelle Cini and Marián Šuplata observe, the Commissioner had deliberately sought out a high-profile issue that could demonstrate the single market's value for consumers as well as businesses.[15] Suggestions that Martin Selmayr, Reding's tenacious spokesperson, was the true driving force behind this project are open to question. True, Selmayr ran a canny media campaign, timing press releases on roaming to coincide with peak seasons for European tourism and patiently building the case for European regulation. But it was Reding who bet her considerable political capital on roaming, who stood up to telecoms providers and members of the College of Commissioners and who used her three decades of experience in European politics to build a coalition for change. Her political instincts were correct. A survey in 2018 indicated that 82 per cent of people who travelled to another member state felt they had benefited from the EU's new roaming rules.[16] Even Rupert Murdoch's *Sun* approved. Under the headline 'Roam Sweet Roam', the tabloid reported that 'Brits travelling abroad will no longer face sky-high roaming charges when using their phone'.[17]

Truer to form, the article made no mention of the Commission's role in this process, attributing the law instead to the European Parliament.

Significant though the European Commission's intervention on roaming was, its impact on European telecoms shouldn't be over-stated. The end of roaming charges benefited only those Europeans who travelled abroad. It didn't end the high costs of terminating mobile calls or the surcharges on international landline calls between member states. Although the EU slowly addressed these issues, the telecom sector remained characterised by limited cross-border competition. British mobile phone users on the Kent coast, for instance, continued to receive 'welcome to France' messages but they were unable to sign up for deals by French telecom providers.[18] Although voice over internet protocol services cut across national borders, they didn't supplant traditional telecom companies. The creation of Skype in 2003 by a team of Nordic entrepreneurs and Estonian program-mers was a European success story before its hasty acquisition by Microsoft, but it made no more than a dent in numbers using fixed-line or mobile voice telephony. Text message providers were harder hit by WhatsApp, although this messaging service remained a comple-ment rather than an alternative to mobile phone services.

Launched by Commission President Jean-Claude Juncker in May 2015, the digital single market sought to build on the abolition of roaming charges with a wide-ranging reform agenda designed to allow EU consumers and businesses seamless access to online activi-ties. By harmonising e-commerce laws, encouraging cross-border parcel delivery, updating the EU's copyright framework and reducing VAT burdens for cross-border sales, Juncker promised to add €416 billion to the Union's GDP.[19] However, such promises proved difficult to keep. A new EU geo-blocking law, which took effect in 2019, sought to end cross-border restrictions on online content; however, popular streaming services such as Netflix were exempt.[20] The special pleading came not from Netflix in this case but the European film industry, which found it more profitable to sell rights for their works on a country-by-country basis rather than the continent as a whole.[21]

The Copyright Directive, another key strand of Juncker's Digital Single Market strategy, triggered a fierce debate between big tech and big-name artists. The directive was necessary, the Commission insisted, to allow digital content to be shared across borders while protecting the rights of content creators.[22] Google representatives disagreed, warning that journalists, musicians and academics would be prevented from sharing their work under the proposed rules.[23] Sir Paul McCartney, no less, countered in an open letter to the European Parliament. To read the man who wrote 'Eleanor Rigby' preaching in dissonant Eurospeak about 'User upload content providers' and the benefits of Article 13 for Europe's 'music ecosystem' was disconcerting.[24] And yet, there was no doubting the former Beatle's conviction that the proposed law provided a fairer deal to artists. The law passed in 2019 but battles between big tech and national authorities slowed its implementation.[25]

The Polish Plumber (2005)

The EU's piecemeal efforts to integrate European telecoms and digital services were symptomatic of a wider problem. However impressive efforts to complete the single market by 31 December 1992 had been, the project's completion coincided with a profound transformation in the European economy. This shift created new trade opportunities but exposed new fissures in the single market, which proved far less integrated than some hoped for, and others feared.

The services sector accounted for 56 per cent of total employment in the EU-15 in 1980. Ten years later, it was 64 per cent and rising.[26] The splintering of services from goods, as the economist Jagdish Bhagwati called it, was a key driver behind this shift, as businesses contracted out activities that were previously carried out in house. So too was the internet, which was tailormade for e-commerce in a way that earlier Videotex systems such as Minitel prefigured. In *The Competitive Advantage of Nations*, one of the bestselling business books of the 1990s, the economist Michael Porter heralded 'a new era of international services competition' as businesses and consumers looked beyond national borders for good deals on an astonishing array of services.[27]

Jacques Delors' 1994 White Paper on Growth, Competitiveness and Employment spoke of a 'second industrial revolution' on services, yet its ideas on liberalising specific sectors, from transport to telecommunications, were modest and no less popular with member states for this.[28] His successor as Commission President, Jacques Santer, sought a general strategy for opening EU services to competition, but the Heads of State or Government were unconvinced. Part of the problem, as the political scientist Mitchell Smith shows, was that preferences varied from sector to sector as well as member state to member state: While French President Jacques Chirac sought bigger markets for France's highly competitive banks, he was protective of his country's state monopoly over gas and electricity; German Chancellor Gerhard Schröder didn't dare open his country's publicly owned savings banks to European competition, but he was willing to liberalise postal services; UK Prime Minister Tony Blair embraced a single market for gas and electricity since these sectors had already been liberalised in the UK, yet he drew the line at postal services, which even his free-market predecessor Margaret Thatcher had baulked at privatising.[29] Frustrated by the EU's falling productivity growth, the Heads of State or Government finally agreed in March 2000 that the Commission should prepare a strategy for the removal of barriers to services.[30] But Romano Prodi was Commission President by then and he shared little of Santer's enthusiasm for this task.

Prodi had come to Brussels with a reputation as an economic reformer. A politically engaged professor of industrial policy at the University of Bologna, he oversaw the privatisation of state assets as president of Italy's Institute for Industrial Reconstruction before becoming prime minister in a centre-left government which defied expectations by meeting the Maastricht Treaty's convergence criteria for joining the euro. As a mainstream economist, Prodi believed in the liberalisation of services as a means to boost growth and productivity in the EU. As a politician, he had seen up close how contentious the liberalisation of Italian sectors such as energy and telecoms could be and saw similar rumblings in France.[31] That the Commission finally proposed a new EU services directive in 2004 owed less to Prodi than his Commissioner for the single market, Frits Bolkestein.

Bolkestein was an old man in a hurry. The Dutch liberal entered the Berlaymont at sixty-six, one of the oldest Commissioners to take office, after a career in business and politics. Two decades earlier, as Dutch minister of international trade, he had published a book of interviews with Europe's leading liberal politicians. Bolkestein's questions were brief, but they betrayed a deep frustration with the direction of economic policy in the Netherlands, and Europe more generally.[32] 'Do you share the opinion of others that unions have become too powerful?' he asked the then president of the European Commission, Gaston Thorn. 'Do you think that the welfare state, because it is so nationally determined and bound up in national rules and regulations, has inhibited the process of integration of Europe?' he asked Jean Rey, a founding father of the European Coal and Steel Community and former Commission President. 'France liberalised her economy rather late. One wonders if that is the reason why large French companies are smaller in size than those in Great Britain, Germany or The Netherlands,' he asked Jean-François Deniau, a French diplomat and former European Commissioner.

Such views cannot have endeared Bolkestein to Prodi, who had already encountered the Dutchman's attempts, as liberal leader in the Dutch 'rainbow coalition', to block Italy's membership of the euro. Initial reports suggested that Bolkestein would be denied the single-market portfolio he coveted before the Commission's president-elect relented. Bolkestein wasted no time in calling for the single market to be extended to areas such as postal services, occupational pensions and corporate takeovers. Bolkestein's Postal Services Directive exposed deep divisions between member states. Germany led the charge for liberalisation, confident that Deutsche Post was primed for European competition, but France and the UK were protective of La Poste and the Royal Mail's national monopolies. The resulting compromise saw the Commission abandon its plans for the full liberalisation of the sector, with competition restricted to letters and packages weighing more than 50 grams, more than double the industry average. The Commission's takeover directive suffered a similar fate, with Germany switching from leader to laggard, in its efforts to protect companies from hostile takeovers. Bolkestein was bitterly disappointed, telling the Brussels press corps that he couldn't, on this occasion, countenance the 'diplomatic delusion that any result is better than none'.[33]

Faced with political headwinds, Bolkestein changed tack rather than course. The Commission's single market strategy was bogged down in sector-specific detail, he suggested; what was needed was an overarching approach to the service-driven economy. So emerged the services directive, one of the European Commission's great own goals of the post-Maastricht period. A grand bargain on EU services – of the kind achieved for goods in 1985 – only ever stood a limited chance of success. The directive would have added €33 billion to the value of the services sector and generated 600,000 new jobs, by one estimate.[34] But the same study suggested that member states with large, competitive service sectors, including the UK and the Netherlands, stood to gain considerably more than those that lacked comparative advantage, including France and Germany. The liberalisation of services, where successful, had tended to proceed on a sector-by-sector, country-by-country basis rather than through multilateral deals. The Uruguay Round of global trade talks had produced a General Agreement on Trade in Services in 1993, but it provided little or no impetus for liberalisation.[35] The Doha Development Round, launched eight years later, foundered in part on opposition to opening up services.

Whereas financial products could be bought and sold on electronic trading platforms with relative ease, sectors such as construction still required providers to deliver services in person. The free movement of services thus became inextricably linked to the free movement of workers and attendant concerns over social dumping. In this regard, the country-of-origin principle was the most controversial aspect of the Commission's draft services proposal, tabled by Bolkestein in March 2004. This principle sought to ensure the free movement of services by stipulating that a business providing a service in another member state would be subject to the laws in which this business was established rather than those in which it was operating. This provision would not lead to social dumping, the Commission insisted, because host country rules on employment and working conditions would apply to such businesses in line with the EU's earlier directive on posted workers.[36] Consequently, the Commission saw no reason why an increase in posted workers as a result of the service directive would cost jobs in host countries.[37] Such reassurances provided little consolation to trade unions, which had long criticised the posted workers directive as providing insufficient protection.

Belgium's regional elections in June 2004 offered an early sign of the pressures facing member states from interest groups and anti-globalisation activists to limit the single market's reach in services.[38] At a time when regional divisions in this country were widening, socialists, greens and Christian democrats from both the Flemish- and French-speaking communities united in a 5,000 strong march against what was by then known as the Bolkestein Directive. This identification of the draft law with Bolkestein wasn't entirely fair. He had spent two years discussing the services directive with member states and the signals had been broadly positive. The College of Commissioners had also unanimously endorsed the proposal despite grumblings from Germany's Günter Verheugen. But Bolkestein was the proposal's staunchest advocate, arguing that the removal of 'archaic, overly burdensome' rules would be a historic step for the single market. Bolkestein also provided an easy target for the left, given his pious praise for 'the tougher conditions and colder climate of the Anglo-Saxon form of capitalism'.[39] His successor as Commissioner with responsibility for the single market, Charlie McCreevy, was no less liberal economically;

however, the Irishman was shrewder and quickly saw that the services directive would not fly. Bowing to criticism from some sections of the European Parliament, the Commission gutted the proposal's reference to the country-of-origin principle. This climbdown came too late. By this point, the EU's services directive had become embroiled in France's referendum on the European Constitution.

In December 2004, Philippe Val published an article in the satirical magazine *Charlie Hebdo* mocking the idea of 'a Polish plumber or an Estonian architect' moving to France for work.[40] Running with this idea, Philippe de Villiers, a right-wing populist with a reputation for anti-immigrant statements, warned in *Le Figaro* that one million French jobs were at risk because 'the Bolkestein Directive allows a Polish plumber or an Estonian architect to offer their services in France with the wages and social security rules of their country of origin.'[41] Though he had left Brussels at that point, Bolkestein insisted on a right of reply and did few favours to McCreevy. Ever the critic of France's economic model, the Dutchman told reporters that he hoped to hire Polish workers at his holiday house in Ramousies in northern France because of the difficulties of finding French electricians or plumbers.[42] A group of local electricians responded by cutting the power supply to Bolkestein's holiday home.[43] This act of protest energised opposition to the services directive, which French trade unions – reflecting their fears for a free-market Prometheus – renamed the Frankenstein Directive. Among the majority of voters who rejected the European Constitution, only a small share cited their opposition to the Bolkestein Directive as a motivation. But concerns over outsourcing, economic liberalism and a lack of social protection were uppermost.[44]

The diluted EU services directive was approved by the Council of Ministers and European Parliament in 2006, but its implementation by member states remained patchy. A high-level report by former single market Commissioner Mario Monti, published in 2010, bemoaned the EU's 'strongly fragmented' services market, the fact that one-fifth of services had a cross-border dimension and the EU's productivity gap with the United States.[45] Monti called not only for the implementation of the services directive to be stepped up but also for liberalisation in areas not covered by this law, including the cross-border provision of services. José Manuel Barroso's 2011 Single Market Act endorsed Monti's message and included services among its twelve priority areas for boosting growth and strengthening confidence following the global financial crisis. But this nod to the Single European Act's silver jubilee underscored the Commission's continued tentativeness over the single market for services. The European Parliament and Council were less enthusiastic still and services received scant mention in the Single Market Act, a Barroso initiative that quickly fizzled out. Elżbieta Bieńkowska, the single market Commissioner during Jean-Claude Juncker's presidency, captured the sense of frustration among European officials surrounding this once-coveted portfolio. After a speech at the European Parliament in 2018 on the regulation of animal testing, microphones heard her complain: 'Fuck how I hate this!' 'Only six months and you can come home,' responded the Polish tabloid *Fakt24*.[46]

The Ryanair Generation (1992–2022)

The boom in budget airlines is a striking exception – arguably, the only major one – to the single market's struggles after Maastricht. It counted as a major victory for European officials, albeit one that saw the Commission work with, rather than against, member states to liberalise air travel. Entrepreneurs ensured that such reforms benefited European consumers, although this new era of low-cost air travel laid bare the social and environmental downsides of European integration and did little to reassure workers that the EU would protect them from global competition.

By the beginning of the 1990s, Europe's aviation sector had become a byword for inefficiency, as state-owned flag carriers shunned competition over prices, schedules and even the quality of sandwiches.[47] The result was high prices, poor service and a flight map focused on national capitals to the detriment of Europe's regions. By the end of this decade, low-cost carriers had entered the European market in droves, driving prices down and capturing market share from incumbents. In 1992, it cost a family of four €1,600 to fly from Paris to Milan. By 2017, this figure had fallen to €100.[48] The number of routes in the EU increased by 300 per cent over roughly the same period, with regional airports recording millions more passengers.[49]

Too often the EU appeared remote to Europeans and as something that principally benefited big business. Not so the single market for aviation, which reached many, if by no means all, sections of European society. For little more than the cost of taxes, service charges and duties – or less than the price of a pair of jeans, as one easyJet ad put it – Europeans could fly to two hundred airports daily.[50] Customers complained about poor service, cancellations and lost luggage, but they still flew in record numbers. A majority still holidayed in their own country, yet most of those who vacationed abroad did so in another EU member state. Holidaymakers became more adventurous too in their choice of destination: Croatia's Adriatic coast became the new Italy, Bulgaria's Black Sea coast the new Magaluf. In 1972, Interrail's new student pass encouraged young Europeans to spend a month crisscrossing the continent.[51] Forty years later, easyJet encouraged their children to discover Europe one weekend at a time.

Cheap flights also made a difference to the European workplace. Super-commuting between countries, once the reserve of wealthy elites like Sir James Goldsmith, became a rite of passage for young professionals in sectors such as law and higher education. Airlines also provided new options for 'commuter couples' by making it easier for partners to be together on weekends after working in different countries mid-week.[52] Such arrangements were often a matter of necessity rather than choice, as employment opportunities at home became more precarious and, in the era of two-income households, more complicated. Previous generations of emigrants left family and friends behind. For what the novelist Joseph O'Connor christened the 'Ryanair generation', it meant living between two worlds.[53]

Although the 1957 Treaty of Rome had envisaged a common transport policy for the fledgling European Economic Community,[54] member states stubbornly resisted efforts to move towards this goal. No other sector seemed more suited to European cooperation in theory and yet so immune from it in practice.[55] A breakthrough came in June 1992, four months after Maastricht was signed, when the Council of Ministers agreed on a package of reforms designed to encourage market entry by new airlines and free pricing for tickets. If national governments had the final word on such reforms, they were encouraged to find their voice by the Belgian socialist Karel Van Miert, Commissioner for Transport and Consumer Affairs in Delors' second administration. Whereas most commissioners arrived in Brussels after a career in national politics, Van Miert had extensive experience of the Commission and European politics more generally. In the 1960s, the Belgian worked as a trainee under Sicco Mansholt, founding father of the Common Agricultural Policy, before returning as special advisor to the Commission's reform-minded vice-president, Henri Simonet. Elected to the European Parliament in 1979, Van Miert sat with Jacques Delors in the socialist group, the two men sharing a vision of social democracy tempered by market reforms. Such experience was used to the full when Van Miert returned to Brussels and sought to unlock the politics of EU transport policy.

Van Miert recognised that European integration was a physical as well as a political project and he saw competition policy as the bridge between the two.[56] At his instigation, the Commission gave notice to member states that the rules of the single market applied to aviation and promised to take action against all forms of discrimination on grounds of nationality.[57] Making common cause with Leon Brittan, the Competition Commissioner, he won support for a package of reforms in 1989 that was too liberal for Delors before making the case for more ambitious changes still. Van Miert also successfully navigated a sharp downturn in the aviation sector due to the Gulf War, which had caused a spike in fuel prices and a sharp fall in demand. Although he drew criticism from Brittan, among others, for approving state aid to Iberia, Air France and Alitalia, such approval was offered on the condition that these airlines open themselves up to competition.[58] By the end of the decade, a single market for aviation was in operation, allowing EU airlines to fly between any two member states. The privatisation of Iberia and Air France was also underway and Alitalia, having been denied further state aid by Van Miert when he took over as Competition Commissioner, was on the slow path to bankruptcy, something that would have been inconceivable in the heyday of protectionism.

European officials, as was so often the case, took their cue from member states. In this case, the Commission looked to the United Kingdom, which not untypically had one eye on the United States. In 1978, the Carter Administration deregulated the airline industry, fostering fierce competition and falling prices. Margaret Thatcher mirrored this policy not only for ideological reasons but also material ones; she feared that a new generation of American mega-airlines would outcompete British Airways on the lucrative transatlantic market.[59] With European level reform beyond her reach, Thatcher negotiated a new bilateral agreement with the Netherlands in 1984. By the end of the decade, discount fares on the London to Amsterdam route had fallen by 25 per cent and the number of weekly flights had increased by 60 per cent.[60] In a deliberate attempt to spur change in Europe, the British government followed up with an agreement between the UK and Ireland to allow an additional operator on flights between Dublin and London. Having successfully bid to be this new entrant, Ryanair began its transformation from a small, regional airline into Europe's largest carrier.

Despite the British experience, it was by no means preordained that EU reforms would favour low-cost carriers. At the time, economists saw the Dublin–London route as a special case that reflected the unusually strong economic and social ties between the UK and Ireland.[61] The power of incumbents and the pull of national politics was simply too strong for serious cross-border competition, it seemed. For aviation expert Brian Graham, the Commission's reform proposals were 'likely to be terminally compromised' because of the desire of Europe's largest airlines to amass more market power.[62] Such warnings were only partly correct. Europe's largest airlines did use the single market as an opportunity to consolidate their position, in ways that weren't always noticed by passengers. While flag carriers such as Spain's Iberia and British Airways remained in name, they were taken over by large, and largely invisible, multinationals such as the International Airlines Group. Yet such mergers were arguably unavoidable in a sector plagued by profitability problems. Germany's Lufthansa had just 14 days' cash in hand left in 1992 when it began a radical restructuring programme that led to alliances with other airlines and, eventually, the takeover of Brussels Airlines, Austrian Airlines, Eurowings and SWISS.[63] By 2018, the Lufthansa Group was the world's third-largest airline and Europe's biggest. The resurgence of incumbents didn't preclude market entry, however. Eighty new airline companies entered the EU market between 1993 and 1996 alone.[64]

The boom in budget airlines was driven not only by the Commission and member states working in tandem but also by an entrepreneurial spirit too little acknowledged by Europe watchers.[65] None were more entrepreneurial than Michael O'Leary, who joined Ryanair in 1988 after working as a tax advisor to one of the airline's founders. His initial, roving brief was to stem the company's losses, which were escalating amid spiralling costs and fierce competition with the state-owned Aer Lingus.[66] This role brought O'Leary to Dallas to meet Herb Kelleher, co-founder of Southwest Airlines, who pioneered a low-cost, short-haul business model that thrived after Carter's deregulation.[67] Whereas Kelleher's business model saw a well-treated workforce as the best way to win customer loyalty, O'Leary offered low fares and tough love.[68] The airline, as the economist Sean D. Barrett put it, provided:

No sweets, newspapers, free food or beverage service. No seat allocation. No business class service. More seats per aircraft and a higher load factor . . . No interlining or connecting journey tickets are issued . . . No airport lounge service . . . no company retail ticket outlets; no frequent flyer programme; stricter penalties for 'no show' passengers.[69]

Ryanair launched its first flights to Continental Europe in 1997, with connections to Paris, Brussels and Stockholm. The Brussels route was significant, not only because it transplanted Southwest's practice of flying to secondary airports, in this case, Charleroi, an underused aerodrome sixty kilometres outside Brussels; it also reflected O'Leary's preoccupation with the EU. Airport transfers to Charleroi even left from outside the Wild Geese pub in the heart of Brussels' EU Quarter, servicing European officials travelling to and from their countries of origin. O'Leary himself became a familiar face in Brussels and an outspoken champion for the liberalisation of aviation.

'Brussels is full of monuments to the "builders of Europe". There is the Schuman district, the Monnet circle, the Spinelli building,' noted *The Economist* in 2005.[70] Perhaps it was now time for 'Boulevard O'Leary'. The newspaper had a point. Between 1995 and 2004, low-cost carriers increased the supply of flights in Europe by 90 million seats, benefiting not only large cities but also regions that had previously lacked scheduled air services.[71] Ryanair and easyJet led the way, operating more than 350 routes between them by 2004. These airlines survived while many others perished amid fierce competition from flag carriers and one another. Debonair, Flywest, Go, V Bird and Virgin Express were just some of the low-cost carriers that came and went or were subsumed during this boom. Of the forty-three airlines that entered this sector between 1992 and 2012, all but ten survived.[72] By 2016, Ryanair was Europe's largest airline group by passenger numbers.[73]

Despite this success story, relations between the Commission and low-cost airlines remained strained. O'Leary praised the single market for aviation as 'the stand-out achievement for the EU' since Maastricht, but he earned a reputation as its *enfant terrible*. A flashpoint occurred in 2004 over the question of unfair state aid to Charleroi Airport. Three years earlier, O'Leary told reporters that

Belgium's Walloon government had allowed Ryanair to land 'practically for free', in an attempt, perhaps, to seek similar deals from public authorities elsewhere in Europe.[74] When the Commission ruled that some aspects of this deal were incompatible with the single market and ordered Belgium to recoup up to €4.5 million from the airline, O'Leary dismissed the EU as 'the evil empire'.[75] 'You cannot have civil servants trying to design rules that make everything a level playing field,' argued O'Leary. 'That's fucking North Korea, and everyone's starving there.'[76] The EU's Court of First Instance overturned this decision on appeal – a victory not only for Ryanair but also low-cost carriers more generally.[77] In the decade that followed, the Commission fought a rear-guard action, limiting without eradicating the sweeteners to which Ryanair and other low-cost airlines had grown accustomed. The budget airline boom survived, but in so doing revealed the contours of the single market to be continuously shifting. In the 1990s, O'Leary had railed against the Commission's refusal to address 'unjustified' subsidies for flag carriers.[78] By the 2020s, his airline routinely defended subsidies of a different sort as vital to its business model.[79]

The contentious politics of the EU's single market for aviation can be seen in the tale of Lübeck Airport, a small regional hub in northern Germany. Lübeck reaped the benefits of low-cost aviation in the 2000s when Ryanair and Wizz Air launched flights to the UK, Italy, Sweden and Poland, among other destinations. Buoyed by passenger numbers, Ryanair announced plans in 2005 for a new base in Lübeck, but the airline quickly backtracked after the Administrative Court of Schleswig-Holstein ruled against plans to upgrade the airport's infrastructure.[80] Protracted legal challenges and investigations followed over whether the fees paid by budget airlines for using the airport gave them an unfair advantage over competitors, but before this issue was resolved, Ryanair shifted its operations to nearby Hamburg.[81] Wizz Air continued to operate out of Lübeck until 2016, leaving the airport without any commercial airlines. While Ryanair continued to seek out secondary airports, it also began to compete directly with flag carriers at Europe's largest hubs, including Charles de Gaulle in Paris and Schiphol Airport in Amsterdam. A radical departure from its original business model, this reflected a concerted effort to attract more business travellers as well as Ryanair's transition into a more conventional airline.

If concerns over financial inducements for low-cost airlines spoke to the dark side of the single market, so too did the erosion of workers' rights in the aviation sector. Staffing is one of the few costs that airlines can control, and Europe's budget airlines took this logic to its limits. A 2016 study reported that agency work, self-employment and zero-hours contracts were increasingly prevalent among low-cost carriers and that salaries of junior pilots were frozen or falling.[82] A Ryanair cabin crew member, writing anonymously in the *Irish Times*, reported having no base salary, being paid only for flying time, facing difficult-to-reach targets for inflight sales, which were not paid by Ryanair but by their suppliers, and being prevented from joining a union.[83] Loopholes in EU employment regulations made such practices possible, with many Ryanair workers employed under Irish law even though they lived in other EU member states.[84] Far from hiding controversial employment practices, O'Leary used them to drum up publicity, as when he banned staff from charging their mobile phones at work.[85] Although Ryanair began to recognise non-pilot unions in some member states in 2018, this came too late to prevent industrial action that caused the cancellation of hundreds of flights across Europe. Occasional strikes were a price worth paying for low-cost flights, replied O'Leary, while threatening to move operations to member states with more liberal industrial relations.[86] The European Court of Justice began to chip away at such practices, as in its 2017 rulings that Ryanair employees weren't bound to take disputes to Irish courts, but progress was piecemeal.[87] Concerns that market forces came first in 1992 and the European social model second were born out in this case, at least.[88]

Whether the boom in budget airlines would continue was by no means certain by the 2020s. The Ryanair generation continued to explore Europe in record numbers, but a new, more environmentally conscious generation questioned such choices. In Sweden, Björn Ferry, an Olympic winning biathlete and television personality, inspired the #jagstannarpåmarken (I'll stay on the ground) movement after he gave up flying and started navigating Europe by night train. Although this trend and similar ones such as #flygskam (flight shaming) and #tagskryt (train bragging) made train journeys fashionable once again, they had little discernible impact on air travel.[89] But Ryanair faced criticism after becoming the first airline to enter the top ten carbon emitters in Europe.[90] The airline's claim that it was 'Europe's greenest/ cleanest airline' failed to convince campaigners[91] and prompted the Commission to consider an EU-wide kerosene tax.[92]

The Hoover Affair (1993)

In April 1993, the leader of Europe's largest trade union organisation pushed a vacuum cleaner through the streets of Brussels.[93] Flanked by colleagues from the European Trade Union Confederation (ETUC), Emilio Gabaglio was protesting against Hoover's decision to move hundreds of jobs from Dijon-Longvic to Cambuslang in Scotland. Respectfully received at the European Commission's Berlaymont building by Jacques Delors, the demonstrators marched on to nearby Avenue de Cortenbergh. There they presented the vacuum cleaner to Zygmunt Tyszkiewicz, head of Europe's biggest business association, the Union of Industrial and Employers' Confederations of Europe (UNICE). Tish, as the Polish-born, British-educated Tyszkiewicz was better known, greeted the party coolly but thereafter displayed the appliance in his office as one of his 'favourite trophies'.[94]

Gabaglio and Tish were, by this point, familiar players on the European scene. This was due in no small part to Delors. A committed trade unionist long before he joined the French Socialist Party, the Commission President saw the Single Market Programme as necessary to deal with Europe's economic malaise as well as the only realistic focal point for deeper integration. But he saw the single market as neither fully achievable nor desirable without measures to preserve Europe's social models, including social protection, working and living conditions and collective bargaining. Social dialogue was another indispensable part of this vision; without it, Commission President Jacques Delors told an audience in Brussels in 1986, 'my friends from the European Trade Union Confederation will look the other way when they pass me in the street; business will lose interest in Europe and confine its attention to the market.'[95] The Frenchman's intentions were sincere, but his warning proved prescient.

In the first month of his presidency, Delors invited ETUC and UNICE, and representatives of Europe's public employers, to the château de Val Duchesse in Brussels to explore shared interests on macroeconomic policy and technological change. The Single European Act formalised this social dialogue and paved the way for the Social Charter, a solemn declaration of workers' rights adopted by all Heads of State or Government in 1989, except for Margaret Thatcher. 'The Socialist Delors' Socialist Charter', she would call the agreement after leaving office.[96] All member states, except the UK, signed up to closer cooperation on social policies at Maastricht while looking to 'management and labour' not only to find common ground but also to play a role in the implementation of EU legislation.[97] The resulting negotiations were acrimonious at times. However, they produced agreements on parental leave and part-time work and established Gabaglio and Tish as voices for, if not quite of, European workers and business respectively.

The Hoover affair, as ETUC's Jean Lapeyre called it, embodied not only hopes for Social Europe but fears for its demise.[98] Gabaglio's efforts to forge a united front between Scottish and French trade unions failed, as did exploratory talks led by Delors. Hoover chose Cambuslang over Dijon-Longvic after the AEEU agreed to a pay freeze, more precarious working conditions and the use of their pension pot as collateral to fund factory investments.[99] The Scottish union faced criticisms for these concessions, but it was clear to all concerned that talks with Dijon-Longvic would continue if discussions with Cambuslang broke down.[100] Far from gloating, Tish understood that ETUC and the European Commission would seek amends. Having previously resisted moves to enshrine workers' rights to consultation on corporate restructuring, the UNICE director-general entered into a social dialogue with ETUC on this issue and maintained informal channels of communication with Gabaglio even after the Confederation for British Industry had walked out. When the Commission eventually won support for a new directive on European Working Councils, this was seen as a defeat for UNICE. But Tish had worked behind the scenes to find a compromise. The resulting law was far from perfect, yet it provided European workers with rights to information and consultation that some had hitherto lacked while limiting exposure to larger enterprises operating in two or more member states.

Although ETUC and UNICE were at odds on this issue, as on so many others, their leaders maintained a healthy respect for one another. 'When he goes, I will miss him not only as a partner but also as a friend,' said Gabaglio of Tish in 1997.[101] 'There are some very well thought-out strategies behind all the arm-waving,' replied Tish of his Italian counterpart a year later. There was no such chemistry between John Monks and Philippe de Buck. Monks came to Brussels with a reputation as a 'consummate politician and a pro-European' after a decade in charge of Britain's Trades Union Congress.[102] De Buck was an experienced lobbyist with extensive experience in Belgian industrial relations. Well-qualified though these men were, they failed to advance the social dialogue beyond broad, non-binding agreements on work-related stress, harassment and violence at work and inclusive labour markets. Sectoral dialogues produced agreements on issues ranging from health care to hairdressing but precious little legislation. The overarching problem was that the dynamics of social Europe had shifted. Under Delors, the Commission's close working relationship with ETUC served as a useful disciplining device; if the social dialogue failed to reach an agreement, there was a reasonable chance that the Commission would step in with legislative proposals of its own. After Delors, the Commission moved closer to UNICE, putting the onus on ETUC to accept soft agreements or no agreement at all. José Manuel Barroso's arrival at the Berlaymont, in particular, provoked deep concerns in ETUC.[103]

A surprise choice to lead the Commission, Barroso had been centre-right prime minister of Portugal for a little over two years when the Heads of State or Government agreed on his candidacy. He had started his political career as a member of an underground Maoist-Leninist group, but he switched his allegiance to the new centre-right Social Democratic Party after Portugal's right-wing dictatorship fell.[104] Rising through the ranks of this party over the next two decades, Barroso made peace with market capitalism and forged a reputation as a fiscal conservative, an able communicator and a staunch Atlanticist. He became prime minister aged 46.

Poul Nyrup Rasmussen, the president of the European Socialists, expressed grave doubts about Barroso's commitment to 'the European project' and the principles of 'social responsibility and security'.[105] But UK Prime Minister Tony Blair preferred the pro-market Portuguese to Guy Verhofstadt, the federalist Belgian prime minister backed by French President Jacques Chirac and German Chancellor Gerhard Schröder. That Barroso had supported the US-led invasion of Iraq, while Verhofstadt hadn't, may also have influenced Blair, who rallied enough support from like-minded Heads of State or Government to overrule Chirac and Schröder.

The European Commission would 'consult and listen' with social partners, promised Barroso in a speech to the European Parliament in October 2004.[106] However, his determination to prioritise the economy over environmental and social concerns indicated otherwise. All three goals were his children, he told MEPs. 'Like any modern father, if one of my children is sick, I am ready to drop everything and focus on him until he is back to health . . . but it does not mean I love the others any less.'[107] Barroso was 'certainly not the extreme free-market liberal he is often made out to be in the media', declared ETUC Secretary John Monks after meeting the new Commission President for the first time, but the two found little common ground.[108]

Speaking in London in 2015, after Barroso's two terms as Commission President had come to an end, ETUC General Secretary Bernadette Ségol praised the 'decades of vision, commitment and hard work' that had gone into building Social Europe, while expressing deep frustration at the time spent 'fighting merely to defend what we have already achieved'.[109] By this point, the Hoover plant at Cambuslang had long since closed. In 2002, workers had to bid for their jobs once again after the firm considered moving the production of a new cylinder vacuum cleaner to its lower-cost plant in Lisbon.[110] This scenario was averted after Scottish trade unions agreed to shorter breaks and faster production.[111] Eighteen months later, the plant was closed and most of its production moved to China. 'Despite improvements in efficiency made over many years, continued production is proving uneconomic and unviable in today's market conditions', a spokesperson announced.[112] The trade unions had been duly consulted on the decision in accordance with EU law. The European Commission made no public comment.

7

The Third Way

'Europe's New Hope' (1999)

In April 1999, US President Bill Clinton hosted a roundtable broadcast live on C-SPAN. He was flanked by four leading European social democrats: UK Prime Minister Tony Blair, Italian Prime Minister Massimo D'Alema, Dutch Prime Minister Wim Kok and German Chancellor Gerhard Schröder. The politicians were in Washington DC not to address a world crisis or to announce a diplomatic breakthrough, but to discuss a theory: the Third Way. No ordinary political event, it had the look and feel of an academic panel for which some participants had prepared more thoroughly than others. Blair seemed nervous and Schröder bemused. D'Alema came laden with papers and jotted down additional thoughts while Clinton celebrated the European left's seemingly inexorable rise. Kok, who looked most comfortable with the format, acknowledged that the Third Way was a 'very broad Third Avenue', but he defended it as a political approach that had helped his country to adapt to globalisation while maintaining its high social standards.[1] Like his fellow panellists, the Dutch prime minister identified 'opportunity' and 'responsibility' as the watchwords of the Third Way, as expressed through welfare policies that required unemployed people to seek work and economic policies that embraced the possibilities of new technologies. He also added a word of caution: 'We must know that there are not only winners . . . We only have a Community if the winners feel responsible for the losers.' For two hours, the politicians outlined a shared vision of the future. It seemed, as one British journalist later put it, that 'social democrats were on the cusp of a new era of fertile cooperation'.[2]

When the Maastricht Treaty was signed seven years earlier, the left seemed to be a spent force. Of the twelve governments that founded the EU, just two were led by social democrats. France's François Mitterrand had been president for over a decade, but his early experiment in socialist Keynesianism – which responded to the country's rapidly rising unemployment rate by increasing the minimum wage and social security benefits – had failed to revive the country's economic fortunes and was quickly abandoned. Whether fairly or not, Mitterrand's U-turn in 1983 had discredited not only 'the French left's old ideological outlook', as the political scientist Ronald Tiersky argues, but also that of West European social democrats more generally.[3] This left Spanish Prime Minister Felipe González clutching the red rose. Although González had a reputation as a moderniser, he presided over one of the EU's poorest economies. With the notable exception of the European Parliament, where the Socialists and Democrats remained the largest party for the time being, the left had seen its electoral fortunes and economic credibility badly damaged by the economic crises of the 1970s. The decline of manufacturing jobs and a diminished role for trade unions in the 1980s amplified the left's problems. From the end of the Cold War to what the economist Ted Levitt called 'the sweeping gale of globalization', the 1990s seemingly belonged to the right.[4]

Early signs that politics would not go to plan occurred in Denmark in January 1993, when Prime Minister Poul Schlüter's centre-right coalition collapsed. Initially, it looked like the Conservative People's Party and Danish Social Liberal Party would stick with Schlüter, but they switched support to the Social Democrats, whose modernising, media-savvy leader, Poul Nyrup Rasmussen, formed the first centre-left government in Denmark in a decade. The country's last social democratic prime minister had presided over a two-fold increase in unemployment and double-digit inflation.[5] With a little over a year left before elections, Rasmussen sought to claw back his party's economic credibility by demonstrating that he could create jobs while keeping inflation and government borrowing in check. To the consternation of the Social Democrat's left wing, which sought higher government expenditure on education and infrastructure, Rasmussen cut the marginal rate of income tax and made unemployment benefit less generous and conditional on participating in training. His gamble paid off. In 1993, Denmark's unemployment rate was 10.3 per cent.[6] Within a year, it had fallen to 8.3 per cent, helping the Social Democrats to an election victory. Within five years, Denmark's unemployment rate was 5.4 per cent, one of the lowest in the EU.

The Danish Social Democrats' revival was not an isolated case. In the Netherlands, Wim Kok's Labour Party went from being a junior coalition partner in 1989 to head of a left-liberal coalition five years later. Keen to show that this was not the Labour Party of Joop den Uyl – whose Keynesian response to the 1973 oil shock was blamed for wage inflation and rising joblessness and put the left out of office for a decade – Kok proposed more flexible rules for hiring and firing workers and mimicked the active labour market policies being tried in Denmark. Unemployment was already falling by the time a 1997 law put this so-called flexicurity approach into practice, but further falls consolidated Kok's reputation as a reformer and added to the renewed sense of political momentum surrounding European social democracy. Election victories for the left in Finland and Sweden added to this red wave, which reached its crest with wins for Romano Prodi's Olive Tree in Italy, Tony Blair's New Labour in the UK and Gerhard Schröder's Social Democrats in Germany.

By 1999, eleven out of the EU's fifteen member states had social democratic governments. France might have been in the vanguard of this movement had Jacques Delors run for president four years earlier, but the Socialist Party instead chose Lionel Jospin, a serious-minded but soporific former education minister who came a distant second to his right-wing rival Jacques Chirac. Such was the momentum behind Europe's social democrats, however, that Jospin became prime minister in June 1997.

Europe's resurgent social democrats were a political phenomenon in search of a name, which British sociologist Anthony Giddens duly provided.[7] Giddens had written extensively about socialism, but it was his 1998 book, *The Third Way*, which crystallised his thinking and connected with lay readers.[8] The only way for social democracy to survive the discrediting of socialism since the 1970s, he argued, was to 'transcend' the 'old left' and the 'new right'.[9] By old left, Giddens meant Keynesianism, a comprehensive welfare state and the pervasive presence of government in the economy and society.[10] By new right, he meant neo-liberal beliefs in 'free markets' and 'minimal government'.[11] Classic social democracy was no longer viable, Giddens argued, because the economic, political and societal underpinnings of this ideology had disintegrated. The Third Way could overcome these contradictions, he insisted, by helping citizens to navigate globalisation and by linking social rights to individual responsibilities. Active labour market policies epitomised this approach, he suggested, by supporting unemployed people, in accordance with social democratic values, while incentivising them to seek work.[12]

The Third Way offered a remarkably positive vision of globalisation. To Giddens, the increased depth and coverage of global trade compared to earlier periods, the expanded role of financial markets, the diffusion of new information and communication technologies and the capacity of 'distant events' to shape our daily lives as never before, and vice versa, had transformative potential that went well beyond the economic sphere.[13] Globalisation could also unleash destructive forces, he accepted, but it was better to manage such risks than embrace protectionism, which would lead to 'a world of selfish and probably warring economic blocs'.[14]

Giddens' ideas were also remarkably influential. In June 1998, Tony Blair and Gerhard Schröder co-authored *Europe: The Third Way / Die Neue Mitte*, a pamphlet which declared their 'common destiny' within the EU and called on fellow social democrats 'to meet the challenge of the global economy while maintaining social cohesion'.[15] Building a knowledge-based economy by investing in human capital should, they insisted, be the top priority.[16] 'Let us together build social democracy's success for the new century,' the two leaders declared. 'Let the politics of the Third Way and the Neue Mitte be Europe's new hope.'[17]

In reality, the Third Way took limited interest in cooperation beyond the nation state. It was, at heart, a theory about national politics. While Giddens recognised the shared challenges facing social democratic parties, he appeared to be more interested in what each could do in national settings than what they could do together. This is suggested, for instance, in his discussion of ecological modernisation, which focused less on the United Nations Framework Convention on Climate Change than on how social democrats could borrow ideas from green parties when it came to national environmental legislation.[18] Cosmopolitan national democracies would find it easier to build a new system of transnational governance, Giddens argued.[19] But the corollary of the Third Way was that states would have less need for such systems if all embraced the same economic and political philosophy. The two sides of this argument can be seen in Gidden's apparent ambivalence towards Europe. Although he presented the EU as a rebuke to those who doubted the possibility of transnational governance, he asked little of the Union beyond further efforts to address its own democratic deficit.[20] Social democracy, it would seem, was best left to national politicians and parties.[21]

The Lisbon Strategy (2000)

As more and more social democratic parties won power in Europe, Third Way thinking made its mark on the EU. This change was most visible in the European Council, where centre-left Heads of State or Government worked together with a sense of determination and common purpose rarely seen in the Union before or since, leaving right-wing counterparts in their wake. At an EU summit in Amsterdam in June 1997, Wim Kok invited fellow Heads of State or Government for a pre-summit bike ride; the UK's youthful prime minister, Tony

Blair, gamely accepted, while an ageing German Chancellor Helmut Kohl, French President Jacques Chirac and Commission President Jacques Santer walked awkwardly behind.[22] This photo opportunity captured the summit's political dynamics, as the Dutch presidency won backing for a Third Way-inspired Resolution on Growth and Employment, which committed member states to modernise social protection systems and exchange best practice regarding national employment policies.[23] At a follow-up summit in Cardiff, Tony Blair secured agreement for a 'light procedure' to monitor national reforms of product and capital markets. At the European Council in Cologne, Schröder convinced other leaders to create an informal dialogue over macroeconomic policy between EU institutions and social partners.[24]

Third Way reforms seemed to be working, with the unemployment rate in the EU falling from 11 per cent in 1997 to 8 per cent in 2000.[25] But unemployment was half this rate in the United States, which continued its long boom.[26] Since 1995, US start-ups had seized upon rising internet usage among households to sell everything from airline seats to pet food online, attracting venture capital in record amounts and fuelling a 400 per cent increase in the stock market's value by the decade's end. The EU seemed, as one official of the Organisation of Economic Co-operation and Development put it, 'to be lagging behind in most aspects' of the race.[27] When it came to readiness for electronic commerce, for example, the Union trailed the United States on virtually every conventional indicator, from the availability of internet hosts and secure web servers to expenditure on ICT.[28]

Portugal was no high tech hub, but its socialist prime minister, António Guterres, had a strong personal interest in technology, having taught telecommunications and signal processing theory at Lisbon's Instituto Superior Técnico before entering politics. His real passion, however, was education, drawing on his experience of Social Catholic literacy programmes in Portugal's poorest communities. A proponent of the Third Way – in deeds, if not always in words – Guterres led a minority government focused on reducing the country's budget deficit to meet the Maastricht Treaty's criteria for euro membership. But he maintained government expenditure on education, used Expo '98 to showcase Lisbon to tech entrepreneurs, such as Microsoft CEO Bill Gates, and championed the importance of 'technological innovations, the new information and knowledge-based society' for social democracy.[29] Portugal's EU presidency in the first half of 2000 presented the perfect opportunity to continue this conversation.

Guterres provided the political impetus for the Lisbon Strategy, as this exercise came to be known, but it was his sherpa, Maria João Rodrigues, who had led the way. An industrial economist and former employment minister, Rodrigues spent two years touring national capitals preparing for the Portuguese presidency. A prolific thinker, talker and writer, she found little resistance to her ideas, but rather broad agreement among mainstream economists and Third Way politicians about the ends and means of economic policy. This consensus, which she sketched for the European Council, rested on four fundamental points.[30] First, macroeconomic policy's role was to keep inflation low and otherwise fine-tune the economy in the short run. Second, a short-run macroeconomic policy was no substitute for a long-run growth policy, which in the era of globalisation and new technologies, increasingly centred on knowledge, be it human capital, research and development, or the internet. Third, a knowledge economy required new institutions and social rules, not only to foster innovation but also to renew Europe's social models. Fourth, the EU should use its policy instruments to support a knowledge economy, but its most important role was to encourage national governments' reform efforts.

Rodrigues' submission to the European Council in Lisbon in March 2000 offered a cacophonous mix of contemporary economic, social and political theories. It was music to the ears of Third Way leaders, who set the EU a new strategic goal of becoming 'the most competitive and dynamic knowledge-based economy in the world' within ten years.[31] Concretely, the Heads of State or Government committed themselves to raising the average employment rate in the

EU from 61 per cent in 2000 to 70 per cent by the decade's end, increasing the female employment rate from 51 per cent to 60 per cent over the same period and boosting the number of 18- to 24-year-olds in further education and training.[32]

The Lisbon Strategy committed member states to new EU legislation on issues ranging from electronic commerce to the single market for services alongside efforts to promote cross-border integration in financial services. But Lisbon was not a *grand projet* in the way that Delors' 1985 White Paper on Completing the Internal Market had been. Whereas the latter envisaged a raft of European legislation to unlock the free movement of goods, services, workers and capital, the former accepted that the regulation of labour markets was a matter for member states, and a highly sensitive one to boot. 'No new process was needed' to achieve the EU's new headline goal, national leaders insisted in March 2000.[33] Instead, the Union would rely on a new 'open method of coordination', which set broad guidelines for the EU that member states would translate into national policies tailored to their own specific needs.

With its concern for the 'quantum shift resulting from globalisation and the challenges of a new knowledge-driven economy', the Lisbon Strategy was closer in spirit to Delors' 1994 White Paper on Growth, Competitiveness and Employment.[34] And yet, there was a fundamental difference between the two initiatives. Delors had sought, however tentatively, to harness the combined resources of the EU and its member states to boost Europe's international competitiveness.[35] The Lisbon Strategy, although it called for investment in 'knowledge infrastructures', accepted that achieving the Union's aims would 'rely primarily on the private sector, as well as on public–private partnerships'.[36] The EU's role was to provide a catalyst for such investment where it could.

In a Eurobarometer survey published in 2000, 90 per cent of respondents saw tackling unemployment as a top priority for the EU, but only 54 per cent believed that the fight against unemployment should be the subject of joint EU decision-making, as opposed to a purely national competence.[37] Had the EU kept quiet about the economic challenges it faced, it would have been criticised as being out of touch. Had it spoken up more forcefully about the need for common policies, it would have been accused of over-reach. The open method steered between the Scylla of inaction and the Charybdis of interference by seeking consensus and best practice.[38] In effect, Lisbon codified what Third Way politicians had done throughout the 1990s while signalling to citizens that the EU heard both their concerns and their ambivalence.

A wide-ranging agenda to begin with, the Lisbon Strategy grew ever wider. By 2003, EU member states had adopted over one hundred policy guidelines, covering not only macroeconomic policies and employment reforms but also a panoply of issues ranging from expenditure on health care and transport taxes to the development of Galileo, the EU's satellite navigation system.[39] The breadth of these guidelines was the product of a continuous dialogue between national governments over their economic policies and priorities and genuine policy learning. But the Commission and member states also disguised differences by adding more and more priorities. The Lisbon Strategy had become, as European Commissioner for Enterprise and Industry Günter Verheugen put it, a 'Christmas tree' creaking under the weight of ever shinier baubles.[40]

The real problem with Lisbon lay in politics rather than process. Third Way leaders, determined to offer a positive vision of globalisation, failed to heed warnings about its uneven gains. Gøsta Esping-Andersen, an influential Danish sociologist, sounded the alarm loudest in a background paper commissioned for the Portuguese presidency, which warned against creating 'a smattering of "knowledge islands" in a great sea of marginalised outsiders'.[41] The outsiders had already begun to organise. In the months before the European Council in Lisbon, anti-globalisation activists demonstrated at the G-8 summit in Cologne and the World Trade Organization (WTO) ministerial meeting in Seattle. In the months that followed, the annual meetings of the IMF and World Bank in Washington DC and the G-8 summit in Genoa saw larger and more violent protests. The Lisbon Strategy's promise of 'sustainable economic growth with more and better jobs and greater social cohesion' rang hollow for such protesters, who saw labour market reforms, a deeper internal market and integrated financial markets as key tenets of neo-liberalism.[42] At the European Council in Gothenburg in Sweden in June 2001, 20,000 people gathered, as the Heads of State or Government reaffirmed their commitment to such goals, adding sustainable development to the Lisbon Strategy's aims for good measure. Anti-globalisation protests prefigured deeper shifts in public opinion. In the EU, 39 per cent of people viewed globalisation as a threat in 2003.[43] By 2006, this figure had risen to 47 per cent.[44]

The Lisbon Strategy had been warmly embraced by the EU's centre-right and liberal governments. The labour market reforms favoured by Luxembourg's Christian democratic Prime Minister Jean-Claude Juncker during his country's presidency of the EU in 1997 were indistinguishable from those championed by Dutch Prime Minister Wim Kok and his Danish counterpart Poul Nyrup Rasmussen, who in turn had mimicked the employment policies of centre-right parties in their countries.[45] This consensus served as a powerful engine for European integration, but it overlooked new societal cleavages over globalisation, which political outsiders moved rapidly to exploit. In France, Jean-Marie Le Pen transformed the Front National from a party of free trade to the champion of 'un nouveau protectionnisme' and pushed Lionel Jospin into third place in the opening round of the 2002 presidential election.[46] Although Chirac easily defeated Le Pen in the run-off, the Socialist Party suffered further humiliation when it lost 115 seats in that year's legislative elections. The Front National didn't win power in either the presidential or legislative elections, but it exploited popular frustration with the prevailing economic and political consensus and demonstrated the power of political outsiders to damage, if not yet supplant, mainstream parties. One by one, António Guterres, Wim Kok and Poul Nyrup Rasmussen lost power. German Chancellor

Gerhard Schröder secured a second term and then ended his chances of a third with the Hartz reforms, which introduced means-tested unemployment benefits with stringent requirements to accept employment.

The EU paid a price too for its failure to address popular concerns over globalisation. Of those who voted against the European Constitution in France, only 4 per cent declared themselves to be against European integration.[47] The most prevalent reasons for voting 'no' were economic, including the belief that the European Constitution would have negative effects on the employment situation in France and that the treaty was too liberal.[48] In fact, economic policies were conspicuous by their absence from the European Constitution. The referendum was a proxy vote for the Lisbon Strategy. 'What's wrong with them?' a companion asked Tony Blair as news of the French vote came in. 'I'm afraid the question is "what's wrong with us?"' replied the UK prime minister.[49]

Hampton Court (2005)

Tony Blair was a politician who thrived when his back was against the wall. He outmanoeuvred Gordon Brown to secure his party's leadership when the incumbent, John Smith, died suddenly. As Labour leader, Blair challenged his colleagues to relinquish their constitutional commitment to the common ownership of the means of production and won.[50] As prime minister, he brokered the Belfast/Good Friday Agreement, which established a new power-sharing assembly in Northern Ireland and brought a tentative end to the Troubles. After al-Qaeda attacked the United States on 11 September 2001, he stood 'shoulder to shoulder' with US President George W. Bush, committed British troops to Afghanistan and faced down parliamentarians and protesters who opposed military intervention in Iraq.[51]

Blair's back was against the wall once again after the failure of the European Constitution. Although the French and Dutch 'no' votes provided a welcome pretext for cancelling the UK referendum, the prime minister risked becoming the fall guy for the EU's constitutional crisis. At the European Council in June 2005, Jacques Chirac sought to deflect from his own lacklustre performance in this referendum campaign by demanding an end to the UK's £3 billion rebate from the EU budget. Chirac knew that he was making life difficult for Blair, who returned the favour by calling for cuts to European subsidies for French farmers. The European Council ended acrimoniously, fuelling concerns that the EU's constitutional problems foreshadowed a wider political crisis for European integration.

Blair regrouped before the European Parliament, where he declared his commitment to European integration despite his own party's ambivalence towards the EU. He also delivered a blunt message about the Union's future:

> If Europe defaulted to Euroscepticism, or if European nations, faced with this immense challenge, decide to huddle together, hoping we can avoid globalisation, shrink away from confronting the changes around us, take refuge in the present policies of Europe as if by constantly repeating them we would, by the very act of repetition, make them more relevant, then we risk failure. Failure on a grand, strategic scale.[52]

Blair's real audience was his fellow Heads of State or Government, who he feared would turn inwards after the failure of the European Constitution and reject the global vision of the EU that Third Way leaders had championed for nearly a decade.

It fell to Blair, by virtue of the United Kingdom's six-month presidency of the EU, to organise an informal summit in October 2005. Playing for time on the EU budget – and bereft of solutions to the Union's constitutional crisis – he invited other national leaders 'to step back from the usual pressures of European business' to explore how the Union could address the issues that Europeans 'really care about'.[53] The prime minister picked as his theme: 'the opportunities and challenges of globalisation'.[54] The summit was supposed to take place in Leeds Castle, but this venue was booked for a wedding and the happy couple demanded a hefty fee to reschedule.[55] So the Heads of State or Government gathered instead in Hampton Court, which, with its historical ties to Henry VIII, didn't quite convey the sense of European harmony that Blair had sought. But it was no less grand a location for this reason.

Hopes that Blair's 'fireside chat' on globalisation – as some commentators dismissed it – might shed new light on this familiar challenge were low.[56] Third Way tropes were evident in a study prepared for the UK presidency by Belgian economist André Sapir, who criticised the EU for being 'stuck in a system of mass production, large firms, existing technology and long-term employment patterns that is no longer suitable in today's world characterised by rapid technological change and strong global competition'.[57] But Sapir also said something new. Categorising national welfare systems into Nordic, Anglo-Saxon, Continental and Mediterranean varieties, he showed that Nordic and Anglo-Saxon member states alone had delivered high rates of employment and strong support for globalisation. By failing to reform, Continental and Mediterranean countries weren't only lagging economically, Sapir concluded, they were growing more sceptical about the new global order.

The Hampton Court Summit also revealed Blair's growing concern about the destructive forces unleashed by globalisation. The prime minister's letter of invitation to this meeting asked other Heads of State or Government how the EU could meet not only the 'competitive challenge' of globalisation but also 'maintain the security of . . . [its] citizens in a world of unprecedented movement of goods, capital and people'.[58] Having downplayed the risks from globalisation in the late 1990s, issues such as immigration and job losses were now playing on Blair's mind. In many countries, the 'Pandora's box' of social anxieties and political frustrations was rapidly opening; 'neo-populist and extreme left formations will not hesitate to incite these anxieties and frustrations against the EU, forcing other parties in a corner', warned the Italian political scientist Maurizio Ferrera in a background paper prepared for the summit.[59] 'An increasing number of people consider themselves as losers, potential or imaginary losers as well; and they, of course, resist change. They are also the ones who are now turning against European integration [which is] perceived by them as a vehicle of change and the dreaded globalisation,' warned the Greek economist Loukas Tsoukalis in another submission.[60]

Cathartic though this discussion was, it had the look and feel of an inconclusive corporate away day. National leaders enjoyed a change of scene, good food and fine wine and stimulating conversation, but the summit made little difference to the real business of running the EU.[61] None present seriously questioned the Lisbon Strategy, which had been re-launched earlier that year after a mid-term review authored by former Dutch Prime Minister Wim Kok, who had reaffirmed the EU's economic agenda as being more relevant than ever, while criticising member states' failure to implement it. The most significant policy commitment arising from Hampton Court was the creation of a new European Globalisation Adjustment Fund 'to provide support for workers made redundant as a result of major structural changes by world trade patterns due to globalisation.'[62] The fund's significance lay less in its size, which was limited to €500 million, than in EU leaders' acknowledgement that they must do more to protect Europeans from the downsides of globalisation. Between 2007 and 2013, the fund covered training, career advice and other active labour market policies for 106,000 individuals who lost their jobs.[63] In Ireland, for instance, the government successfully applied for €15 million in support for 2,400 workers made redundant by Dell Computers as a result of international competition.[64] One study found several instances where UK workers would have been eligible for compensation under the European Globalisation Adjustment Fund. But Blair's successors as prime minister, Gordon Brown and David Cameron, refused to participate in the scheme, citing 'unaffordably high costs to the UK and to UK taxpayers', among other concerns.[65]

The Global Financial Crisis (2007–8)

The Third Way was premised on a relatively simple formula: social democratic parties sought to regain the credibility that they had lost after the international economic crises of the 1970s so that they could win political office and further their goals of equality and social justice. Achieving these goals was impossible without economic growth, but growth had to be achieved without triggering inflation or losing control of government borrowing. So social democratic governments favoured macroeconomic policies committed to low inflation, sound public finances and market-friendly policies to encourage entrepreneurship, research and development and other sources of long-term growth.

Third Way economic policy was enormously successful, or so it seemed. By 2007, the EU economy had finally shrugged off the effects of the dot.com crash and grown by 3.2 per cent, exceeding the target set by national leaders at Lisbon.[66] Despite this achievement, consumer price inflation in the EU was moderate and the average budget deficit was close to zero. When the Maastricht Treaty was signed, the EU's unemployment rate was 11 per cent.[67] By 2007, it had fallen to 7.0 per cent. More significantly, the rate of joblessness in the Union had remained relatively low during the slowdown of the early 2000s. Unemployment, it seemed, was no longer rising 'cycle to cycle' as the Commission had feared in its White Paper on Growth, Competitiveness and Employment.[68]

The EU had few remaining Third Way leaders, by this point, but their economic and political ideas lived on. In Denmark, centre-right Prime Minister Anders Fogh Rasmussen kept his Social Democrat namesake's flexicurity approach, as unemployment fell to record lows. The Netherlands was hit hard by the dot.com crash, but Jan Peter Balkenende's centre-right coalition did what Wim Kok would have done by reining in inflation, reducing the budget deficit and persisting with active labour market policies. By 2007, the Dutch economy was, once again, one of the fastest-growing in Europe. Italy's right-wing populist Prime Minister Silvio Berlusconi broke most decisively from the economic policies of his Third Way predecessors, but his promise of tax cuts, pension increases and 1.5 million new jobs sounded too good to be true and so it proved.[69] Although Italy's unemployment rate declined under Berlusconi, GDP stagnated and public finances deteriorated markedly. After five years, voters had enough and turned to Third Way stalwart, Romano Prodi, who having quit the Commission Presidency, became Italian prime minister for a second time.

The United States had always been the jewel in the Third Way's crown. When Bill Clinton was elected president in 1992, he inherited an economy that was recovering from recession, yet still struggling to create jobs and facing a rising budget deficit. At 7.5 per cent, the country's unemployment rate was low by European standards but high by American ones. By 2000, the US economy had recorded twenty-nine consecutive quarters of continuous growth; the government posted a budget surplus, and the country was experiencing its lowest rates of inflation since the 1960s.[70] Thanks to the president's active labour market policies, the rate of unemployment had fallen to 4 per cent.

In his testimony to the United States Senate Committee on Banking, Housing, and Urban Affairs in July 1997, Alan Greenspan, head of the United States Federal Reserve, asked whether new technologies such as fibreoptics, telecommunications, computing and the internet were driving 'a once or twice in a century phenomenon that will carry productivity trends nationally and globally to a new higher track'.[71] The gnomic central banker refused to be drawn on an answer, but the mere fact that he posed the question was interpreted as a vindication of the Third Way. In fact, Greenspan's loose monetary policies and Clinton's permissive approach to financial regulation revealed deep contradictions at the heart of the Third Way, which reified stability while allowing serious imbalances to develop behind a veneer of low consumer price inflation and budget surpluses. Such myopia was not unique to this generation of left-wing governments.

Policy choices made before and after their time in office contributed to the global financial crisis, but proponents of the Third Way could and should have challenged the wishful thinking underpinning their economic paradigm.

In 1993, US domestic credit to the private sector was 121 per cent of GDP. By 2007, it was 206 per cent.[72] Cheap credit, and affordable housing policies that made it easier for subprime borrowers to secure mortgages despite their poor credit rating, caused average house prices to increase by more than 200 per cent between the first quarter of 1992 and the first quarter of 2007, at which point the US housing bubble suddenly burst.[73]

The serious delinquency rate – the percentage of mortgage loans not repaid in 90 days or in the process of foreclosure – increased from 0.75 per cent for US prime mortgages in the second quarter of 2006 to 1.67 per cent by the fourth quarter of 2007.[74] The United States could have weathered this storm, but the rate for subprime mortgages increased from 6.24 per cent to 14.44 per cent over the same period.[75] In April 2007, New Century Financial Corporation, a subprime lender, filed for Chapter 11 bankruptcy protection, as concerns over the exposure of Bear Stearns and other Wall Street giants to subprime mortgages grew. But Europeans called for calm. 'The most likely prospect is that financial system stability will be maintained in the period ahead,' concluded the European Central Bank in June 2007, while acknowledging that some European financial institutions were directly exposed to subprime losses.[76]

European confidence didn't last long. On the early morning of 9 August 2007, BNP Paribas issued a press release suspending trading on two investment funds, citing the 'complete evaporation of liquidity in certain market segments of the US securitisation market'.[77] By lunchtime, the European Central Bank had provided nearly €100 billion in short-term financing to banks so as 'to ensure orderly conditions in the euro area markets'.[78] A little over a month after the BNP Paribas press release, customers of Northern Rock, a British bank, began queuing around the block in their hundreds to withdraw their savings. A relatively small player in the British banking system, Northern Rock had relied heavily on money markets to raise funds for mortgages. But as liquidity concerns spread across the Atlantic, Northern Rock was forced to seek emergency support from the Bank of England. It was the first run on a British bank since 1905 when customers fled the Birkbeck Bank, which served as an inspiration for the ill-fated Fidelity Fiduciary Bank in *Mary Poppins*. As Chancellor of the Exchequer, Gordon Brown had preached the Third Way gospel of 'light touch' financial regulation.[79] Now, as prime minister, he used the heaviest of hands to nationalise Northern Rock.

When the Heads of State or Government gathered in Brussels in June 2008, they were relatively upbeat.[80] The Third Way had always acknowledged that globalisation could be disruptive, and the national leaders were confident that the financial turbulence emanating from the United States would pass. The British bank, Barclays, was sufficiently bullish to open talks with troubled US investment bank Lehmann Brothers about a possible takeover until UK regulators registered their disapproval. Unable to find an American buyer, US Treasury Secretary Hank Paulson allowed Lehmann Brothers to slide into bankruptcy. National leaders' sangfroid over the financial crisis quickly evaporated as shares in European banks plummeted and depositors panicked about their savings. Fortis, Western European bank of the year in 2007, was abruptly broken up after the Belgian, Dutch and Luxembourg governments failed to agree on a coordinated rescue package. In the UK, Bradford and Bingley became the second bank to be nationalised under Gordon Brown's watch. Fearing further bank runs, Brown floated the possibility of raising deposit insurance from £35,000 to £50,000.[81] But before he could do so, his Irish counterpart, Brian Cowen, unilaterally guaranteed all deposits in Irish banks, a move that encouraged British savers to move their deposits across the Irish Sea. 'The Irish way is not the right way,' complained Angela Merkel, shortly before she provided a blanket guarantee for German savers.[82]

As chancellor, Brown had made few friends in Brussels by lecturing other finance ministers about the need for economic reform.[83] He had carried on in a similar vein as prime minister but now reached out to other national leaders to forge a more coordinated approach to the unfolding crisis. Brown was ill at ease as premier, the technocratic style that had served him so well in the Treasury sounding stilted from the Downing Street podium. However, he was made for the global financial crisis, and the global financial crisis was made for him.

When France's centre-right president Nicolas Sarkozy invited eurozone Heads of State or Government to Paris for an emergency summit, Brown was an incongruous addition to the guest list but an influential one, as member states agreed to take forward the UK prime minister's plan for a coordinated bank rescue package. 'United Europe has pledged more than the US', boasted Sarkozy after EU member states had committed around €2 trillion to support, guarantee and, if necessary, recapitalise banks.[84] This was hyperbole. Determined to protect German taxpayers, German Chancellor Angela Merkel had quickly killed off any talk of a common crisis fund. This left national governments to commit their own resources to support national banks, with little regard for whether they had the means to do so and what the consequences would be for their economies and the EU more generally if they didn't. And yet, member states brought Europe's banking system back from the brink of collapse, albeit at considerable cost. As credit and confidence drained away and cuts to government expenditure loomed, the EU economy entered its steepest-ever recession.[85] The very worst of the economic fallout was limited for the time being to Hungary, Latvia and Romania, which were swiftly offered financial support from the EU and the IMF.

Savouring the results of this summitry, the Heads of State or Government saw an opportunity for global leadership. Sarkozy was at his frenetic best, flitting between the United Nations General Assembly in New York, the Asia–Europe meeting in Beijing and the Francophone summit in Quebec to call for a global conference to create a new system of 'regulated capitalism'.[86] Inviting himself to

Camp David, Sarkozy delivered a stark message to US President George W. Bush from the EU that this was a worldwide crisis that required a worldwide solution. José Manuel Barroso came along for the ride, quite literally, when the Commission President squeezed into the back of Golf Cart One, while Sarkozy sat up front next to a bewildered Bush. All the energy flowed from Sarkozy at the Camp David press conference, but the Europeans got what they had come for when Bush invited leaders of developed and developing nations to an international meeting to 'strengthen and modernise their financial systems'.[87] The G-20 leaders' summit in Washington DC the following month – the first time this forum had gathered at the level of Heads of State or Government – sent reassuring messages to financial markets and paved the way for a more consequential meeting at London's Excel Centre in April 2009.

The London Summit produced nothing like the 'new Bretton Woods' that Brown and Sarkozy had talked about beforehand. The modest, temporary stimulus package and reforms to financial regulation agreed upon suggested a reluctance to challenge key tenets of Third Way thinking about macroeconomic stability and the drivers of long-term growth. In spite of its challenges, globalisation remained the best route to global growth and prosperity, the leaders concluded.[88] A similar consensus prevailed among EU leaders, who declared in October 2009 that an economic recovery was imminent, called for a swift withdrawal of fiscal stimulus measures and announced plans for a renewed 'European strategy for jobs and growth as part of an upcoming review of the Lisbon Strategy'.[89] Blair, D'Alema, Schröder and Kok had long since lost power, yet faith in the Third Way endured. Behind their business-as-usual demeanour, the Heads of State or Government watched with growing alarm as Greece's new finance minister, George Papakonstantinou, announced that the country's budget deficit had been seriously and systematically underreported. The global financial crisis was receding, but the euro crisis was just beginning.

8

The Euro Crisis

Whatever It Takes (2012)

In July 2012, Mario Draghi took to the podium at the Global Investment Conference in London.[1] Twenty years earlier, he had played a pivotal role in the single currency's creation, as a member of Italy's delegation to the negotiations which produced the Maastricht Treaty. Now as president of the European Central Bank, Draghi found himself as the European official to which the world looked to save the euro. For two years, the eurozone had been buffeted by a sovereign debt crisis which started in Greece before spreading to Ireland, Portugal and Spain. Financial assistance from the EU and IMF had brought respite but not restored financial market confidence. Without a drastic change in policy direction, it seemed only a matter of time before a member state quit the euro or found itself forced out. Were this to happen, the idea of the euro as a project that irrevocably fixed exchange rates and permanently replaced national currencies would be over.

Draghi seemed to revel in economic and political drama. As director-general of the Italian Treasury, he had steered his country through the 1992 European exchange rate mechanism crisis before helping it to meet the Maastricht Treaty's criteria for euro membership, against the odds. Known for his tailored suits from Sartoria Sabino in Naples and his American-accented English, the Massachusetts Institute of Technology-educated economics professor was dismissed by critics as a 'young yuppie', while being touted by supporters as a future managing director of the IMF.[2] Romano Prodi's appointment as Commission President effectively ruled Draghi out of the running for the Fund, as EU member states were unlikely to endorse two Italians for such senior positions in close succession. So, after a decade in the Italian Treasury, Draghi moved to London as head of Goldman Sachs International.

By 2005, Draghi's career in public service appeared to be over. But things took an unexpected turn when Antonio Fazio, the governor of the Banca d'Italia, found himself at the centre of a criminal investigation over the planned acquisition of Banca Antonveneta, a domestic bank, by Dutch lender ABN Amro. Fazio had championed a takeover by Banca Popolare Italiana, it was alleged, in exchange for gifts that included a Baume & Mercier watch, a Prada handbag and rare religious manuscripts.[3] Chosen to restore the Banca d'Italia's reputation, Mario Draghi did so in short order.[4] After six years in Rome, during which he delivered harsh truths about public finances to governments of the left and right, he succeeded Jean-Claude Trichet as president of the European Central Bank. Putting an Italian at the helm of the single currency had seemed unthinkable when the Maastricht Treaty was signed, given the country's reputation for inflation and exchange-rate instability, but Draghi once again won over his critics.[5]

The ECB president's London speech was an anodyne affair, in which he defended the euro 'as much, much stronger than people acknowledge' to a sceptical audience of City grandees.[6] That was until he offered 'an alternative message'. 'Within our mandate, the ECB is ready to do whatever it takes to preserve the euro and believe me, it will be enough,' he told his audience.[7] In this one sentence, the European Central Bank president signalled a decisive break from the hesitant policies of his predecessor. The soothing effect on financial markets was almost instantaneous. Rarely had the power of European officials seemed greater in the post-Maastricht period. And yet, EU governments had long since decided to save the euro.

Kerneuropa

Like UK Prime Minister Gordon Brown and French President Nicolas Sarkozy, German Finance Minister Peer Steinbrück initially saw the global financial crisis as an opportunity for the EU, predicting that the United States would 'lose its superpower status in the financial world'.[8] But Steinbrück quickly realised that losing one or more eurozone members was a more realistic possibility than the end of US hegemony. When Hungary, Latvia and Romania, three member states which hadn't adopted the euro, had found themselves facing acute balance of payments problems after the global financial crisis, the EU and IMF provided financial support without a second thought. Under the Maastricht Treaty, eurozone members were prohibited from receiving such assistance and European officials publicly insisted that no exemptions would be allowed. This prohibition was sacrosanct, argued Jürgen Stark, a prominent member of the ECB Executive Board.[9] Steinbrück disagreed. EU treaties 'don't foresee any help for insolvent countries', he acknowledged, 'but in reality the other states would have to rescue those running into difficulty.'[10] Asked whether Germany would countenance the break-up of the euro, he replied 'Could you imagine anyone would be willing to put up with this? We would have to take action.'

Wolfgang Schäuble, Steinbrück's successor as German finance minister, was not so sure. In the 1990s, the then leader of the largest centre-right group in the Bundestag had responded to the idea that Southern European countries might one day join the euro by calling for deeper integration among a hardcore of countries that shared Germany's interests and values. Schäuble's vision of Kerneuropa reflected his longstanding commitment to European integration, as well as to lessons drawn from East Germany's painful absorption into West Germany's economic and monetary union. Although the German economy had recovered its poise by the mid-2000s, after a prolonged period of sluggish growth and rising unemployment, Schäuble seemed sceptical that all EU member states would respect the euro's rules on government borrowing and feared the high price that Germany would have to pay if they couldn't.

Greece had narrowly qualified for the euro in 2001 and thereafter periodically flouted the Maastricht Treaty's fiscal rules, which required member states to keep budget deficits below 3 per cent of GDP. In January 2009, Greece's centre-right finance minister, Yannis Papathanasiou, estimated that the budget deficit for that year would reach 3.7 per cent.[11] Ten months later, Papathanasiou's centre-left successor, Giorgos Papakonstantinou, revealed that the true figure would be 12.7 per cent. This dramatic revision was due not just to the worsening impact of the global financial crisis, the European Commission concluded, but to 'deliberate misreporting' of data on government borrowing.[12] From government estimates of tax revenue, the social security surplus and expenditure on hospitality, the previous government had painted a profoundly misleading picture of Greek public finances.

When PASOK's George Papandreou became prime minister in October 2009, his patrician sense of public service compelled him to level with the Greek people. A centre-left grandson of a liberal prime minister and son of a socialist one, he believed that his country was on an unsustainable path at a perilous time for the international financial system.

After nearly a decade in opposition, Papandreou also had an opportunity to discredit the opposition, while avoiding the familiar cycle of exchange-rate instability and default that accompanied fiscal crises before joining the eurozone. Yields on Greece's triple-digit government debt had remained low during the euro's first decade, yet now they suddenly spiked, making it increasingly costly for the government to issue new debt. Papandreou promised budget cuts and economic reforms, but the country's sovereign debt rating was progressively downgraded as fears of default mounted.

Writing in the *Financial Times* in March 2010, Schäuble offered his thoughts on the future of the euro.[13] Germany had given up the Deutsche Mark on the understanding that the euro would be 'strong and stable', he argued, but the eurozone had 'to integrate further' to deliver on this promise. Acknowledging that the IMF's potential involvement in support for Greece was 'hotly debated', he proposed the creation of a European Monetary Fund which could grant 'emergency liquidity' to member states at risk of default. The catch was the recipients of such support would be subject to a 'cooling-off period' during which they would be excluded from eurozone decision-making. His thoughts were 'in no way directed at the specific measures to stabilise Greece', the German finance minister insisted, but his underlying message said otherwise; it was time for Kerneuropa – a 'core Europe' – and not all member states could count on remaining in the eurozone.

A man of extraordinary fortitude, Schäuble had been confined to a wheelchair in 1990 after being shot at a campaign rally for German unification, but he soon returned to frontline politics. A scandal over party financing cut short his chairmanship of the Christian Democratic Union, his resignation being hastened by Merkel who had offered a damning assessment of the scandal to the *Frankfurter Allgemeine Zeitung*.[14] Returning as a member of Merkel's cabinet, Schäuble offered an ambivalent mixture of support and defiance, coldly defending the chancellor from her detractors, while conveying to all that he knew best. Merkel was all too familiar with such treatment and calculated that her interests were best served by sending a hawk to meetings of EU finance ministers while ensuring that she had the final say over Germany's handling of the euro crisis. Schäuble threatened to resign on more than one occasion, but the chancellor encouraged him to stay, correctly surmising his sense of public service and determination to remain in power.[15]

Schäuble's call for a European Monetary Fund was aimed not only at Papandreou but also at Merkel who had overruled his objections to involving the IMF in any financial support for Greece. The German finance minister had support from his French counterpart, Christine Lagarde, and French President Nicolas Sarkozy, who wanted the EU to lead in this crisis, just as it had done in the early stages of the global financial crisis. Merkel didn't disagree on this point but on the question of how the EU should respond.[16] Without the IMF, it would likely fall to the European Commission to negotiate and enforce the conditions attached to financial support for Greece. The Commission had already failed to forestall Greece's fiscal crisis, even though problems over its public finance statistics had come to light in 2005. The IMF would contribute expertise and funding to any support package, as well as the political detachment that Merkel saw as vital to protect the interests of German taxpayers. In February 2010, eurozone Heads of State or Government sided with Merkel by agreeing to involve the Commission, IMF and ECB in ongoing dialogue with Greece and by agreeing that member states would 'take determined and coordinated action, if needed, to safeguard financial stability in the euro area as a whole'.[17] Welcoming Schäuble's suggestion for how future crises might be handled differently, she told reporters that a European Monetary Fund couldn't be realised without revising the EU treaty.[18] Having led during the turmoil over the European Constitution and Lisbon Treaty, Merkel understood all too well how difficult it was to renegotiate EU treaties, much less win approval for any changes given the risk of referendums in one or more member states. So, rather than risking a ratification crisis on top of an economic one, the chancellor let Schäuble's proposal drift.

For Adam Tooze, an economic historian, Merkel was a pro-market politician determined to force fiscal discipline on Greece and distrustful of the EU's ability to manage the crisis by itself.[19] However accurate this description may be of the German chancellor's economic philosophy, it underestimates her commitment to keeping the eurozone intact despite fierce domestic pressure over providing financial support to a country which was perceived by many German voters to have acted recklessly. For Tooze, Schäuble was the European federalist in this political marriage, and yet the finance minister's vision of European integration posed grave risks to the EU in the name of creating a more perfect (but less inclusive) union.[20] The chancellor may have had fixed views on how to keep Greece in the eurozone, but she never questioned that it would and should remain a member.

As Greece's fiscal situation worsened and German public opinion hardened, the chancellor threw her weight behind financial support for Athens subject to the strictest conditionality. Without Germany, there would have been no EU support for Greece. Without EU support, Papandreou would have had to turn to the IMF, a scenario that Greek voters would almost certainly not have stood for. So, eurozone leaders signed off on Merkel's terms and Papandreou formally requested financial assistance from the EU and IMF. Alexis Tsipras, leader of the Coalition of the Radical Left (SYRIZA), spoke for just thirteen members of parliament, but he captured the mood of many more when he decried the decision as 'a humiliating day for Greece and Europe'.[21] Be that as it may, it was also the day that the Heads of State or Government demonstrated their commitment to saving the single currency.

With a political agreement in place, it now fell to the European Commission, the ECB and the IMF to hammer out the details of an economic adjustment programme with the Greek government in return for €110 billion in loans over three years and to monitor the programme's implementation. The Troika, as this ad hoc arrangement became known, was dismissed by one seasoned scholar of European integration as a form of receivership in which European officials dictated decisions that by rights were the responsibility of democratically elected governments.[22] But such interpretations overstated the power of Commission and ECB officials, and their counterparts from the IMF, whose role was to challenge rather than devise policy commitments made by the Greek government to unlock financial support. Papakonstantinou had already committed to swingeing expenditure cuts in January 2010 in a desperate attempt to reassure financial markets that he had the crisis in hand. EU officials, in particular, pushed him to go further, but the finance minister signed off on the policy commitments and won the backing of the Hellenic Parliament, which preferred to remain in the euro rather than return to the drachma, albeit at considerable economic and social cost.

The Greek government can have laboured under no illusions that these policies would be painful and deeply unpopular. At the beginning of the crisis, economic forecasts predicted a recession in 2009 followed by flat growth in 2010.[23] By May 2010, a deep recession was expected for a further full year and this before the entire effects of the economic adjustment programme had been factored in.[24] Unemployment had been 7.7 per cent of the civilian labour force before the global financial crisis started.[25] It was now expected to reach 13.2 per cent.[26] Greece's largest trade unions responded by announcing a general strike, which closed ports and airports and brought tens of thousands of people onto the streets, calling for an end to austerity and the removal of the IMF. Three days after the loan agreement was announced, rioters firebombed a bank in the city's commercial district, killing three employees through smoke inhalation. One victim, Angeliki Papathanasopoulou, was four months pregnant.[27]

Papandreou pressed ahead with the economic adjustment programme because, to him, it was the least-worst option. However imperfect, the programme offered a chance to win the 'battle of credibility' with financial markets by addressing pathologies in the public sector and tax system that had fuelled years of deficit spending.[28] The cuts would entail suffering and sacrifice, he acknowledged, but the government had sought to minimise the impact on 'the weaker in society'.[29] With a €8.5 billion bond due to mature on 19 May 2010, the time to negotiate an alternative economic adjustment programme and seek parliamentary approval was heavily constrained. The only viable alternative was sovereign default, which the prime minister feared would shred Greece's credibility with citizens and international creditors, disrupt national defence and the provision of vital public services and lead to calls for Greek expulsion from the euro. 'I have done and will always do whatever it takes for the country not to go bankrupt,' the prime minister insisted.[30]

The officials who brokered this deal were publicly supportive of the economic adjustment programme but privately ambivalent. In the IMF, non-European executive directors worried that the Fund had been railroaded by the EU into providing an outsize loan to a government that had failed to demonstrate sustainable debt dynamics.[31] Typically, IMF members are allowed to borrow 435 per cent of their quota over three years. Greece received 3,200 per cent.[32] European officials, meanwhile, came to regret viewing Greece's problems through a fiscal lens rather than focusing on the underlying structural factors which contributed to the country's problems.[33] Even if officials harboured doubts, the decision to act lay with eurozone Heads of State or Government, who gambled that frontloading fiscal cuts would ensure the swiftest possible resolution of Greece's economic problems and maintain the credibility of the single currency.

When national leaders met in Brussels on 7 May 2010, the atmosphere was tense. The sense of euphoria on financial markets following the announcement of the Greek programme had given way to scepticism about its sufficiency and fears that the sovereign debt crisis was spreading to other eurozone members. A case in point was Portugal, which had recovered relatively quickly from the global financial crisis, but still posted persistent budget deficits. The country's economic fundamentals would not have attracted comment during normal times, but now they provoked panic. 'This isn't only a problem for one country. It's several countries. It's Europe. It's global,' ECB President Jean-Claude Trichet told the European Council.[34] 'Come on, come on, stop hesitating!' screamed Nicolas Sarkozy in response, to little avail.[35]

Trichet had been in a bind from the moment Greece's fiscal problems came to light. Financial markets expected the ECB to champion the kind of large-scale government bond purchases initiated by the United States Federal Reserve to drive down the cost of borrowing. But monetary hawks within the ECB's decision-making bodies believed that Trichet had already gone far enough with the Securities Markets Programme, which was used to purchase more than €200 billion in Greek, Irish, Italian, Portuguese and Spanish government bonds between 2010 and 2012. Significant though this sum was, it paled in comparison to the €600 billion in long-term Treasury securities which the United States Federal Reserve committed to buy in November 2010 to help revive its economy after the global financial crisis.

Some voices within the Bank believed that unconventional monetary policies, even if they worked, would reduce the pressure on member state governments to address the problems of fiscal indiscipline and weak financial supervision that caused the euro crisis.[36] Others feared the inflationary consequences of large-scale government bond purchases. ECB Executive Board Member Jürgen Stark and Bundesbank President Axel Weber were the biggest thorns in Trichet's side. The ECB's 'expansionary stance' may have been necessitated by the global financial crisis, but unless they were quickly retracted, inflation could make 'a rapid and powerful comeback', Weber argued in May 2009.[37] The ECB hadn't bought government bonds, Stark told an audience at the University of Tübingen in November 2009, because this would have amounted to 'the monetisation of government debt, a sure road towards inflation over the medium term, with adverse effects on our independence and credibility'.[38]

Because ECB President Trichet either couldn't or wouldn't budge, the Heads of State or Government had little choice but to create a crisis fund of their own. This provided German Finance Minister Wolfgang Schäuble with an opportunity to revive his plans for a European Monetary Fund and, perhaps, his vision of a smaller eurozone built around a hardcore of like-minded member states. But Schäuble, who was struggling with a wound from stomach surgery that had failed to heal, was rushed to hospital, just as EU finance ministers agreed to create not one but two new instruments: a €60 billion fund to be managed by the European Commission, and a €440 billion European financial stability facility to be managed by the finance ministers themselves. Expecting protracted negotiations, financial markets greeted this overwhelming display of financial firepower with a profound sense of relief. But hopes that the worst of the euro crisis was over proved to be premature.

'We All Partied'

On 8 September 2008, as the fallout from Lehman Brothers' collapse engulfed the EU, John Bowe, a director at Anglo Irish Bank, called his colleague, Peter Fitzgerald, to update him on his meeting with the Central Bank of Ireland. 'To cut a long story short we sort of said look, what we need is €7 billion and we're going to give you, what we're going to give you is our loan collateral so we're not giving you ECB, we're actually giving you the loan clause. We gave him a term sheet and we put a pro note facility together and we said that's what we need. And that kind of sobered up everybody pretty quickly, you know,' reported Bowe.[39] 'And is that €7 billion a term?' asked Fitzgerald. 'This is €7 billion bridging,' replied Bowe. 'So . . . so it is bridged until we can pay you back . . . which is never.' How did you 'arrive at the seven?' asked Fitzgerald. 'Just, as Drummer would say, picked it out of my arse,' said Bowe.

Twelve days later, Brian Lenihan Jr, Ireland's finance minister, emerged from all-night talks to announce that the government would provide a blanket guarantee for six banks for two years. Anglo Irish Bank was included on this list.

Another scion of politics, Lenihan was named after his father, a Fianna Fáil minister under Taoiseach Charles Haughey, who had accumulated a vast, unexplained personal fortune as, under his watch, Ireland lurched from economic crisis to economic crisis.[40] But Haughey's commitment to social partnership, tax breaks and the country's nascent financial services sector set in motion Ireland's extraordinary economic revival. When Brian Lenihan Sr needed a liver transplant in 1989, Haughey helped to raise funds for his medical expenses, which the Taoiseach partly used for his own purposes, an official inquiry concluded.[41] Two decades later, as Brian Lenihan Jr presided over the end of Ireland's economic boom, he was diagnosed with pancreatic cancer but carried on as finance minister.

How much pressure the ECB exerted on Ireland over this guarantee was one of the most intensely debated questions surrounding the euro crisis. While the message from Frankfurt – and, more importantly, national capitals – at this time was that member states must stand behind their banking system, the EU didn't force the Irish government's hand. Lenihan and Irish Taoiseach Brian Cowen took the view that allowing Anglo Irish Bank, as the weakest of the country's biggest financial institutions, to go bankrupt would have constituted another Lehman Brothers moment. Since all six banks were solvent, they concluded, a time-limited guarantee was the best way to weather the storm. Far from insisting on this guarantee, the ECB and EU member states were caught off guard by its timing and broad coverage.

One problem with Lenihan's reasoning was that it was premised on an incomplete understanding of the true state of the six protected banks. By joining the euro, Ireland experienced considerably lower interest rates, fuelling a credit boom. But systemic shortcomings in financial supervision, born of a close relationship between politicians, bankers and builders, led to excessive risk-taking by Irish banks and acts of fraud. Under the leadership of David Drumm – or 'Drummer' as his colleagues called him – the size of Anglo Irish Bank's loan book trebled in four years.[42] The bank's share price plummeted after the global financial crisis hit, but Drumm hid the worst of the damage by disguising the true state of the bank's balance sheet.[43] Having nationalised Anglo Irish Bank, the Irish government announced in September 2010 that the costs to the Irish taxpayer from this financial institution alone would be €29.3 billion.

Ireland's government debt before the global financial crisis was just 25 per cent of GDP.[44] By 2010, it was approaching 100 per cent. Like Papandreou and Papakonstantinou before them, Cowen and Lenihan slashed public expenditure in response to the global financial crisis but failed to convince financial markets that things were under control, as bond spreads on Irish debt continued to rise. By November 2010, Irish banks were on life support by means of emergency liquidity assistance from the ECB, but Lenihan still refused to throw in the towel. An EU–IMF loan was inevitable at this point. The Irish finance minister had lost the confidence of financial markets and had no credible alternative despite speculation that Irish Americans might come to the rescue. As the ECB's exposure to Irish banks mounted, Trichet informed Lenihan that emergency liquidity assistance would be cut off unless the Irish finance minister issued a request to EU colleagues for financial support.[45] The ECB also played hardball over whether the Irish government could impose losses on senior bondholders as part of such a package. Having initially opposed the idea, Ireland's central bank and finance ministry had come to see it as a way of reducing the burden of bank bailouts on the Irish state. Fearing that the Irish government's actions might spread to the rest of the eurozone, the ECB vehemently disagreed.[46] The IMF and European Commission eventually sided with the ECB, leaving the Irish government with no choice but to protect senior bondholders if it wanted financial assistance from the EU and IMF. Whether the Troika was overly cautious on this point is moot, but the decision added an estimated €9 billion to Ireland's financing needs and fuelled public resentment in Ireland over the EU and IMF's unwillingness to 'burn the bondholders'.

Seemingly determined to deflect the blame for this national humiliation, Lenihan and cabinet colleagues remained silent, as talks between Irish officials and the Troika played out behind closed doors. In the end, Irish central bank governor Patrick Honohan took matters into his own hands and informed the media that 'a large loan . . . to show Ireland has sufficient firepower to deal with any concerns of the market' was imminent.[47] Three days later, the Irish government formally requested assistance, paving the way for a €85 billion loan financed by the EU, the IMF and selected member states. 'It is the banks and the bank guarantee you gave that has got us into this mess,' a journalist put it to Lenihan. 'Our problems are not just banking problems,' replied the finance minister, who blamed overspending on 'guards, teachers and nurses' despite Ireland's relatively low expenditure on public services. 'Let's be fair about it. We all partied.'[48]

Portugal was next in line, securing €78 billion in loans from the EU and IMF in May 2011. Bond yields on Portuguese debt were approaching double-digits by that point, making the decision all but inevitable even if the economy was in a much stronger position than those of Greece and Ireland. As financial market fears shifted to Spain and Italy, the EU's crisis funds no longer looked so impregnable. In December 2010, member states had agreed to create the European Stability Mechanism, a permanent fund with a lending capacity of €500 billion, bringing the eurozone's combined financial firepower to €1 trillion. But Citigroup economists concluded that the EU would need at least twice this amount if large member states were sucked into the sovereign debt crisis.[49]

Speaking at the Brussels Economic Forum in May 2011, Wolfgang Schäuble argued for fiscal consolidation and measures to boost international competitiveness as the way to convince financial markets, instead of 'throwing other countries' money at the problem'.[50] But it was clear by this point that Greece would need a second round of loans from the EU and IMF. At the beginning of the euro crisis, Schäuble had hinted at Greek expulsion from the euro. Now he told Evangelos Venizelos – Papathanasopoulou's successor as finance minister – to his face to consider a 'timeout' from the eurozone to allow for currency devaluation and debt restructuring.[51]

Merkel, although she had asked Schäuble to remain in post despite his ill health, was having none of this. True, she and Sarkozy encouraged Papandreou to hold an in-out referendum on euro membership in the margins of the G-20 summit in Cannes in November 2011, but this was a defensive tactic designed to counter the Greek prime minister's plan to give voters a say over the terms of a second loan agreement.[52] It worked after a fashion, as Papandreou rescinded his plan for a referendum and resigned the premiership. Lucas Papademos, a former vice-president of the ECB, took charge of a caretaker government, which concluded a second €130 billion loan agreement with the EU and IMF in return for deeper fiscal cuts and a deal on debt restructuring, which halved the value of Greek debt held by private investors. This write-down of Greek debt was a tactical victory for Schäuble, but he had nevertheless been outmanoeuvred by Merkel, who continued to defend Greece's place in the eurozone. 'There is no guarantee that the route we have taken will lead to success and it is possibly not the last time that the Bundestag will have to consider financial assistance for Greece,' a weary Schäuble told German members of parliament.[53]

Merkel and Schäuble disagreed over Grexit, but they both feared a backlash from the Bundesbank and German voters if they bore the costs of creating what was colloquially called a 'big bazooka' to provide even greater financial assistance to ailing eurozone members. At the G-20 in Cannes, French President Nicolas Sarkozy and US President Barack Obama had heaped considerable pressure on Merkel to create a bigger crisis fund, to the point where she burst into tears. 'I am not going to commit suicide,' the chancellor reportedly replied.[54]

Unconventional monetary policies made Merkel wince, but she understood that, in the absence of a big bazooka, the ECB would inevitably have to do more.[55] The chief obstacle to this course of action was that it was Germany's 'turn' to nominate the next ECB president after Trichet, leaving Bundesbank president and noted critic of bond purchases Axel Weber in line for the top job. While German officials talked up Weber's candidacy, Merkel stayed silent as France fielded alternative candidates. By February 2011, Weber had concluded that he lacked sufficient support to become ECB president, recused himself as a candidate and announced his intention not to seek a second term at the Bundesbank.[56] Merkel made little attempt to dissuade Weber and, having taken the highly unusual step of not naming a German candidate for the ECB presidency, threw her support behind Mario Draghi. The Italian was 'very close to our ideas of the stability culture and solid economic policies,' insisted Merkel.[57] But it was arguably the Italian's pragmatism that endeared him to the chancellor, who understood that the ECB's intransigence on large-scale bond purchases couldn't continue if the single currency were to survive.[58]

Trichet was a cautious consensus builder who remained aloof from the Heads of State or Government. Draghi was a schmoozer, who used his time at EU summits to snatch conversations with national leaders and win their trust. He focused most of his energies on Germany, opening back channels with Merkel and Schäuble at which his predecessor, a fierce defender of ECB independence, would have baulked. Draghi also courted Merkel and Schäuble's confidence by insisting on even tighter rules on government borrowing by EU member states as a prerequisite for bolder policies from the ECB.[59]

When Draghi promised to do 'whatever it takes to save the euro', he did so not as a *deus ex machina*, but as a European official who acted with the tacit support of national leaders, who had made clear their determination 'to do whatever is required to ensure the stability of the euro area as a whole', a phrase that had been parsed in the media long before Draghi's speech as 'whatever it takes to save the euro'.[60] In so doing, national leaders didn't publicly instruct the ECB to engage in large-scale bond purchases, which would have contravened the Maastricht Treaty's guarantee on bank independence. But by not voicing a prior objection, they tacitly signalled that they would stand by the bank if it took this momentous step.[61]

Forewarned of Draghi's speech, unlike members of the ECB Governing Council, Merkel and François Hollande, Sarkozy's successor as French president, took the unusual step of issuing a statement after the ECB president's intervention, recognising the responsibility of EU institutions to do everything they could 'to defend the eurozone'.[62] In normal times, such a statement would have fuelled concerns that the Heads of State or Government were seeking to contravene the independence of the ECB. Here it helped to provide Draghi with the political cover he needed to embark on large-scale bond purchases. When Bundesbank President Jens Weidmann predictably warned that Draghi's plan was 'tantamount to financing governments by printing banknotes', Schäuble offered a polite and dutiful rebuke. The ECB had respected its mandate in the past and would continue to do so in the future, the German finance minister insisted.[63]

'You Just Killed the Troika' (2015)

By 2014, the euro crisis appeared, for all intents and purposes, to be over. The EU's €100 billion loan to Spain two years earlier hadn't been, as feared, an *entrada* for a larger rescue package. Rather, it helped Prime Minister José Luis Rodríguez Zapatero to stop the rot in the Spanish banking system without losing market access. Meanwhile, Italy regained the credibility that it had lost under Silvio Berlusconi by appointing Mario Monti, a former European Commissioner, as caretaker prime minister. Ireland's unemployment rate reached 15.5 per cent during its EU and IMF programme, reflecting the heavy toll taken by budget cuts.[64] Irish finance minister Brian Lenihan Jr died seven months after negotiating this programme. Had he lived longer, he would have seen falling unemployment and a banking system that had been stabilised, if not purged, of all its problems, by the time Ireland exited this programme. Portugal also paid a heavy price for its EU and IMF programme, but it too exited on time, regained the confidence of financial markets and resumed economic growth.

The common denominator in all these cases was national leaders' commitment to the single currency and voters' willingness to endure the painful consequences of this choice. The eurozone's newfound resilience was evidenced by financial markets' muted reaction to Cyprus' ill fortunes. In 2009, the United States Navy intercepted a Russian-owned ship bound for Syria with a cargo of ammunition, which was subsequently stored at Cyprus' Evangelos Florakis Naval Base. A fire at the base two years later and a subsequent explosion killed thirteen people and knocked out a nearby electricity station, causing power and water shortages and a deep recession. This crisis added to longstanding problems facing Cypriot banks, which had grown disproportionately big due to offshore deposits, primarily from wealthy Russians, bringing the island's bloated financial system to the brink of collapse after the global financial crisis hit.[65] Although eurozone finance ministers bungled an attempt to impose an emergency levy on Cyprus' wealthiest depositors as a condition for EU loans, financial markets showed little concern that this crisis might reignite problems in the rest of the eurozone, while negotiations over €10 billion in loans from the EU and IMF continued. It was not just the small size of this loan that explained such calm but the reassurance provided by the ECB's bond purchase programme. Not for the first time, however, things were different in Greece.

Elections to the Hellenic Parliament in June 2012 produced an uneasy coalition between New Democracy, the party that had lit the fuse on Greece's sovereign debt crisis, and PASOK, the party that had struggled to contain it. The new government conveyed little confidence that the end of the sovereign debt crisis was in sight, leading to growing support for Syriza's charismatic youthful leader, Alexis Tsipras. A former student activist who had come of age in the anti-globalisation protests of the late 1990s, Tsipras promised a clean break from the country's discredited political elites and a radically different response to the country's economic crisis, which would protect the country's poorest. It was the message that many Greek voters wanted to hear, propelling Syriza to first place in the European Parliament elections in May 2014.

Yields on Greece's long-term debt had spiked even before Tsipras unveiled the Thessaloniki Programme, a manifesto promising a European debt conference to cancel 'the greater part of public debt's nominal values' and at least €4 billion in infrastructure investment.[66] In a deliberate provocation of Germany, the manifesto promised to re-open the question of an interest-free loan that Nazi occupiers forced on the Bank of Greece in 1942. Celebrating Syriza's stunning election victory in January 2015, Greece's new prime minister in waiting, Alexis Tsipras, promised to make the Troika, the ad hoc arrangement which brought the EU, the IMF and the ECB together to negotiate and oversee financial assistance for eurozone members, 'a thing of the past'.[67]

Following the Austrian Freedom Party in 1999, right-wing populists had become a familiar feature of the post-Maastricht period, but this was the first time that left-wing populists had secured a seat at the EU's top table. Donald Tusk, the president of the European Council, offered obligatory congratulations to Tsipras while reminding him that the EU had 'stood by Greece from the first day of the crisis'.[68] The new Greek prime minister saw things differently. By insisting on deeper and deeper cuts to salaries and pensions, he argued, the EU had turned an economic crisis into a humanitarian one.[69] It was time to end austerity, while Syriza restored debt sustainability and undid the 'clientelist and kleptocratic practices of the political and economic elites' that had ruled Greece for so long.

Tsipras understood three political truths. First, other Heads of State or Government would have to acknowledge not just the will of the Greek people, but the outpouring of political frustration that had brought Syriza to power. In this he could count on sympathy, if not support, from European social democrats, who understood that the strict conditions attached to financial assistance were economically ruinous. Second, Northern European countries would not stand for a situation in which Syriza promised to reverse the public sector job cuts, pension cuts and other policies undertaken by Greek governments since 2010 while asking those countries for more financial assistance. Third, the new Greek government had a month left to go before the existing, already extended loan agreement expired, and it was running out of cash fast. Greek banks were already dependent on emergency liquidity assistance from the ECB, which was growing increasingly anxious about this arrangement.

It fell to Yanis Varoufakis, Greece's new finance minister, to find a way forward. A silver-tongued game theorist, he led a peripatetic life as an economics lecturer in Australia, the United Kingdom and the United States and won praise on the left for his biting commentary on the euro crisis, before being elected to the Hellenic Parliament in January 2015. It was not only his patterned shirts and black leather trenchcoat that distinguished Varoufakis from other eurozone finance ministers, but also his willingness to question the fundamental tenets of EU crisis management. His country didn't have a liquidity problem, Varoufakis argued, but a solvency problem that could only be addressed through debt relief and growth-friendly policies rather than further loans and deeper austerity.

Varoufakis presented himself as a pro-European politician, who had dreamt as a child living under the Greek junta that his country would one day join the European Community.[70] And yet, he was sceptical about the single currency's viability and scathing about EU institutions, which he saw as complicit with the IMF in subjecting Greece to an act of fiscal 'waterboarding'.[71] Polemics didn't translate easily into policy, as evident from Varoufakis' attempt to enlist IMF support for debt restructuring while simultaneously threatening to default on loan repayments to the Fund.[72] There was ambiguity too over whether the new Greek finance minister privately saw Grexit as inevitable or even desirable given the steadfast refusal by Heads of State or Government to consider his 'modest proposal' to convert national debt into EU bonds and engage in large-scale infrastructure investment.[73]

Varoufakis' first press conference with Jeroen Dijsselbloem, the Dutch finance minister who chaired meetings of eurozone finance ministers, was visibly tense.[74] 'Taking unilateral steps or ignoring previous arrangements is not the way forward,' Dijsselbloem told members of the media. 'We see no purpose in cooperating with this tripartite committee,' responded Varoufakis. Rising abruptly from his seat, an animated Dijsselbloem whispered 'You just killed the Troika' as he left the podium.[75] 'This is an unearned compliment,' replied the Greek finance minister. Varoufakis' visit to Berlin to meet with Schäuble went no better. 'When are we getting our money back?' a junior minister half-joked as he escorted Varoufakis to meet Schäuble, who refused to shake hands let alone engage with the Greek government's suggestions.[76] 'We agreed to disagree,' Schäuble told the press afterwards. 'We didn't even agree on that,' replied Varoufakis.[77]

As the clock ticked, both sides made their moves. The Greek government was prepared to honour 70 per cent of its predecessor's policy commitments, but it sought time to prepare a more growth-friendly set of reforms, in accordance with its election manifesto.

Eurozone finance ministers agreed to a four-month extension of financial assistance on the understanding that new policies were consistent with programme targets and codified in law. 'As long as the programme isn't successfully completed, there will be no payout,' warned Schäuble, who saw Grexit as increasingly likely.[78] Varoufakis had won time, but he failed to make any headway on debt relief. After private sector debt restructuring in 2012, the bulk of Greek sovereign debt was owed to other sovereigns and the IMF. The IMF was open to debt relief, but it refused, on point of principle, to take any write-downs on the money owed to it. Northern EU members were equally adamant that they would not carry the burden of such restructuring.

However eloquent Varoufakis may have been in his analysis of the eurozone's commitments, other finance ministers didn't trust him. It was not just that they viewed the Greek finance minister as a peacock, who seemed more interested in preening his feathers through magazine spreads than the serious stuff of EU negotiations.[79] It was that they viewed his party's populist manifesto, whether fairly or not, as incompatible with the hard choices required to keep Greece in the eurozone. While he promised economic reforms that the Greek people could own, what Varoufakis ultimately sought was debt relief, either in the form of a debt swap designed to reduce the nominal value of Greek debt or further cancellation. There was also uncertainty over Varoufakis' real end game. Although he resisted Schäuble's calls to make common cause on a possible Greek exit from the euro, the Greek finance minister saw Grexit as preferable to 'capitulation' over a third loan agreement.[80] Varoufakis also floated proposals for the Greek government to pay civil servants' wages in electronic IOUs, an instrument that some economists saw as the reintroduction of a national currency in all but name.[81]

Varoufakis achieved little in the four-month extension he had gained on Greece's loan agreement. Debt relief remained firmly off the political agenda and the additional reforms he promised neither changed Greece's growth prospects nor convinced eurozone partners, who countered with proposals of their own, calling for further higher value-added tax and a redoubling of pension reforms aimed at achieving 'sizeable and sustainable primary budget surpluses'.[82] Dijsselbloem understood that such proposals were anathema to Varoufakis, but he had been in regular contact with Tsipras and hoped that the Greek prime minister would step in and strike a deal. What Dijsselbloem didn't expect was for Tsipras to break off negotiations before putting the EU and IMF's most recent reform proposals to Greek voters in a referendum.[83] In much the strangest act of direct democracy in the post-Maastricht period, voters were asked to approve the latest terms offered by the Troika as set out in two PDF documents, one on economic reforms and the other on debt sustainability analysis. Neither document was even translated into Greek.

Tsipras' referendum announcement was a bold gambit designed to break the deadlock between eurozone finance ministers. It was also a monumental act of self-harm. On 30 June 2015, Greece's second loan agreement expired and the country defaulted on a €1.6 billion repayment to the IMF, the first developed country to do so in the history of the Fund. Since Syriza was elected, Greek banks had been steadily losing deposits, leaving them even more dependent on emergency liquidity assistance. The ECB did not terminate this support after Tsipras walked away from international creditors, but nor was the eurozone monetary authority willing to provide the additional assistance that this diplomatic gambit necessitated. Left to his own devices by Draghi, Tsipras had to close Greek banks, limit ATM withdrawals and impose controls, adding to the sense of national crisis in the run up to the referendum.

That 61 per cent of Greek voters overwhelmingly rejected the terms of the EU and IMF negotiations was no surprise. What was striking, exit polls suggested, was the sizeable majority among all voters for staying in the euro. What separated voters were their beliefs about the consequences of the vote. Around 60 per cent of 'yes' voters believed that a 'no' vote would lead to Grexit, while 90 per cent of 'no' voters expected further talks if they got their way.[84] Varoufakis was overjoyed by the referendum result, counselling Tsipras to introduce electronic IOUs and step up pressure on EU partners for debt restructuring.[85]

But the prime minister was determined to do whatever it took to keep his country in the euro. So he fired Varoufakis and prepared to strike a deal with EU partners.

Greece's new finance minister, Euclid Tsakalotos, was politically to the left of his predecessor but altogether more low-key and pragmatic by inclination. Educated at St Paul's School in London and Oxford University, he spoke Greek with an English accent and English like a character in a Richard Curtis film and immediately put eurozone finance ministers at greater ease. That was everyone except Schäuble, who remained unconvinced by Greece's reform commitments and saw another opportunity to push for Grexit. Determined to secure a third loan agreement, Tsakalotos offered concession after concession, but, at Schäuble's insistence, finance ministers proposed to the Heads of State or Government that Greece be offered a 'timeout' from the eurozone in return for debt restructuring.[86] Dijsselbloem was dismayed but he lacked the authority to resist. Draghi's final attempts to reason with the German finance minister over Greek debt sustainability provoked an angry rebuke. 'I'm not stupid,' replied Schäuble.[87] The German finance minister may simply have been playing bad cop; however, his writings and public interventions on European integration since Maastricht said otherwise. Letting Greece join the euro had been an expensive mistake for Germany and the EU, he implied, and it was better to bear the costs of putting this decision right rather than pay in perpetuity. Merkel, not for the first time, disagreed.

With no deal in sight in the small hours of 13 July 2015, Merkel and Tsipras prepared to leave the conference room. Had they done so, Schäuble would almost certainly have got his way, ending the sense of irrevocability surrounding the single currency and encouraging financial markets to ask which member states might be next to follow Greece into a timeout. Present in the discussions was European Council President Donald Tusk, who firmly told Merkel and Tsipras, 'Sorry, but there is no way you're leaving this room until you agree.'[88] It was not so much an order as a political mantra about how the EU managed crisis after crisis in the post-Maastricht period.

After fourteen hours of talks, the Heads of State or Government announced an €86 billion loan agreement between Greece and the EU. All references to Schäuble's timeout had been removed from the summit conclusion. In exchange, Tsipras agreed to a raft of reform measures, ranging from further cuts to pensions to the liberalisation of milk production and bakeries. He also agreed, with deep reluctance, to a new privatisation fund overseen by EU institutions and authorised to sell up to €50 billion in state assets to repay loans to European creditors. The July 2015 deal left room for 'additional measures . . . aim[ed] at ensuring that [Greece's] gross financing needs remain at a sustainable level' while ruling out debt restructuring.[89]

Varoufakis was devastated by this turn of events, as were the twenty-five members of Syriza's far left, who broke away to form Popular Unity and campaign openly for Grexit. Voters were more forgiving. Forced to call a general election after losing his majority, Tsipras lost only a handful of seats but won a fresh mandate from voters. In contrast, Popular Unity failed to win a single seat. Thereafter, the Greek government delivered on most of its policy commitments with a minimum of political controversy in return for a modicum of debt relief, which gave the country longer to repay rather than less. Although a fifth of the active labour force remained out of work in 2017, unemployment continued to fall as a sustained economic recovery took hold for the first time in a decade.[90] A year later, Greece exited its loan agreement on schedule, giving it access to financial markets once again.

The economic costs of the euro crisis were devastating, especially for Greece, which saw its GDP shrink by 25 per cent, leaving more than a third of the country's citizens in poverty or at risk thereof.[91] Had Merkel and other EU leaders moved more quickly to contain this crisis and allowed for a more gradual fiscal consolidation and greater emphasis on economic growth as a condition for financial assistance, economic hardship on this scale could have been avoided. And yet, the single currency had survived, not simply because of the ECB's actions but, above all, because national leaders demanded it.

The European Left (2008–21)

The global financial and euro crises vitalised right-wing populists at the expense of all European mainstream parties but especially those on the centre left. Alternative for Germany was launched in 2013, by two journalists, Alexander Gauland and Konrad Adam, and an economist, Bernd Lucke, who opposed financial support for eurozone members. It quickly morphed into an anti-EU and anti-immigration party which jarred with its founders' politics to varying degrees but resonated with voters. The arc of the Alternative for Germany's rise intersected the arc of the Social Democratic Party's (SDP) fall, the latter having struggled to find a creditable successor to Gerhard Schröder, who retired from politics in November 2005 after failing to secure a third term as German chancellor. Between 2004 and 2019, the SDP changed leader on average every 349 days. The party's sole route to power during this period lay in periodic grand coalitions with the centre right; such power-sharing proved unpopular with SDP voters, who turned in increasing numbers to right-wing populists. In the United Kingdom, Gordon Brown's leadership in the early stages of the global financial crisis failed to exonerate him of charges that his pro-globalisation policies caused the crisis in the first place, propelling David Cameron's Conservative Party to power. In Italy, Matteo Renzi presented himself as a Tuscan Tony Blair, but the Florentine lacked the former UK prime minister's political instincts. Whereas Blair won three general elections, Renzi quickly lost his way over a foolhardy referendum on reforming the Italian Senate, which voters used to register their discontent at the Italian government's unpopular labour market reforms. Renzi's resignation failed to save the Democratic Party, which lost more than half of its seats in the 2018 election. In Greece, the collapse in support for George Papandreou's PASOK following the euro crisis was so comprehensive that Pasokification became a term to describe European social democracy's extraordinary fall from favour during this period.[92]

Wouter Bos, leader of the Dutch Labour Party, understood how bleak things looked for the left, even before the euro crisis hit. Bos had become Labour leader, after Ad Melkert, Wim Kok's anointed successor, took the party from first to fourth place in the tumultuous election of 2002. Bos quickly reconnected with voters by challenging the government's response to the country's sluggish economic recovery and led Labour back to government as junior coalition partners with Christian Democratic Appeal. A similar move had put the Labour Party on a path to power in the 1990s; now it had the opposite effect.

As finance minister when the global financial crisis hit, Bos faced tough choices over the rescue of Fortis Bank, falling house prices and a recession far deeper than anticipated. Although he won praise for his handling of the crisis, his party haemorrhaged support to Geert Wilders' right-wing populist Party for Freedom. The lesson for the left from this period, Bos told his Amsterdam audience in January 2010, lay not in a return to 'old beliefs in state intervention' but a more realistic reappraisal of what markets could and couldn't do. The lesson of Bokito, a 180-kilo male western gorilla who escaped his enclosure in Rotterdam Zoo in May 2007 and ran amok, Bos suggested, was that 'a very deep and wide ditch provides better security than a good animal trainer'. What sounded like an invocation to rediscover the role of the state in European social democracy turned out to be a valediction. A month after his Amsterdam lecture, Bos retired from politics. While his colleagues promised a 'return to the left', Labour's finance minister Jeroen Dijsselbloem became a poster child for austerity because of his role as Eurogroup chair, to the evident displeasure of voters who deserted the party in droves in spite of falling unemployment and a return to growth. In 2017, the Labour Party lost twenty-nine of its thirty-eight seats, its worst-ever performance.

François Hollande's defeat of Nicolas Sarkozy in France's presidential election in May 2012 raised hopes for the left and then quickly dashed them. A disciple of former Commission President Jacques Delors and a political rival to his daughter, Martine Aubry, Hollande tacked to the left to win the Socialist Party's nomination before tapping into French voters' frustration with President Nicolas Sarkozy. Having promised an economic policy that would put growth ahead of austerity, Hollande then pushed through €20 billion in tax increases and €10 billion in expenditure cuts in his first year, forcing unemployment yet higher in the name of reducing the budget deficit. The new president's popularity plummeted thereafter, leaving him with the lowest presidential approval rating in the history of the Fifth Republic in October 2013.[93] By December 2016, France's unemployment rate finally started to fall, but this came too late to save Hollande or his party.

Some social democrats survived by living on their political wits. In Denmark, Helle Thorning-Schmidt's Social Democratic Party lost seats in the 2011 election but formed a minority left-liberal coalition. Lower taxes for Denmark's highest earners were the price to be paid for holding this motley crew together. The Social Democratic Party drifted further to the right under Thorning-Schmidt's successor, Mette Frederiksen, whose successful anti-immigration platform in the 2019 election led one commentator to question whether the left had really won.[94] In Sweden, the Social Democrats lead by Stefan Löfven maintained a grip on power by mimicking the right-wing populist Sweden Democrat Party's restrictive policies on immigration and asylum. In Finland, Sanna Marin showed that a more progressive politics was possible, albeit in a five-party coalition spanning the centre left and centre right. That all five parties were led by women – four of them in their early thirties – helped to push back against the patriarchal right-wing populist True Finns.

Social democrats in Northern Europe looked over their shoulders at the far right. In Southern Europe, they held hands with the radical left. In Portugal, Prime Minister António Costa's Socialist Party built an unlikely alliance with the Left Bloc, the Portuguese Communist Party and the Green Party, three left-wing parties which were energised by the country's anti-austerity mood. Known as *Geringonça* (the contraption), this coalition was more successful than its moniker suggested, with Costa building a consensus around income tax cuts to stimulate economic growth combined with indirect tax increases to keep government borrowing under control. While critics dismissed this policy as 'austerity by stealth', the country's unemployment fell from over 16 per cent to under 6 per cent between 2013 and 2020.[95] This led to talk of a 'Fourth Way', even before Costa won an unexpected, outright majority in February 2022.[96]

In Spain, Socialist Party leader Pedro Sánchez insisted that he would be unable to sleep at night if he were in a coalition with Podemos, an anti-austerity party started in response to the anti-austerity 15-M Movement.[97] However, Sánchez showed few signs of sleep deprivation after he formed a minority coalition with Podemos in January 2020. The government's ideological differences, minority position and dependence on the Basque and Catalan separatists made it difficult to pass a budget much less secure support for its economic policies. That Sánchez was hailed as a 'beacon for socialism in Europe' showed the depths of darkness in which European socialists found themselves in the late 2010s.[98]

Social democrats had once driven EU strategy. Now they settled for occasional tactical wins. Swedish Prime Minister Stefan Löfven and MEP Maria João Rodrigues, architect of the Lisbon Strategy and by now vice-president of the European Socialists and Democrats, helped to nudge Jean-Claude Juncker's plans for Social Europe in a social democratic direction.[99] The 2017 European Pillar of Social Rights was neither as solid nor as legalistic as its name suggested; but by identifying twenty principles underpinning Social Europe and aiming to make all legally enforceable, it revived ambitions for social regulation that had lain dormant since before the days of the Third Way. In contrast, grand social democratic projects such as François Hollande's European Growth Plan received short shrift.

Angela Merkel's retirement in December 2021, after sixteen years in power, robbed the EU of its most experienced crisis manager. It also created a new opportunity for the European left. A mild-mannered former mayor of Hamburg, Olaf Scholz had risen to become the SDP's lead candidate in the 2021 federal elections. The Christian Democratic Union / Christian Socialist Union performed poorly under Merkel's successor, Armin Laschet, leaving Scholz to form a grand coalition with the Greens and liberal Free Democratic Party. Talk of European social democracy's rival was tempered, however, by Scholz's promise to maintain the 'northeast German mentality' that had characterised Merkel's time of office, not least because of the electoral threat from the right-wing populist Alternative for Germany.[100]

PART III
EUROPE IN THE WORLD

9

Global Europe

'Mr Europe'

The EU's disjointed response to the Yugoslav Wars confirmed Commission President Jacques Delors' worst fears over the common foreign and security policy.[1] Faced with the most serious breach of European peace since the Second World War, the Union's foreign ministers had equivocated while 140,000 people lost their lives. In December 1998, as Slobodan Milošević's forces drove ethnic Albanians from their homes in Kosovo, killing tens of thousands, Tony Blair and Jacques Chirac decided that the time had come for the EU to develop 'credible military forces, the means to decide to use them, and a readiness to do so, in order to respond to international crises'.[2] Convinced by the two leaders' arguments, the European Council launched the European Security and Defence Cooperation. In 2003, the EU deployed 300 military personnel on a peacekeeping mission in the former Yugoslav Republic of Macedonia. Nearly forty such missions followed over the next two decades. Most were time-limited and small-scale in their ambition, but national governments' willingness to commit national troops on the ground under a European flag would have been unthinkable in the pre-Maastricht period.

Javier Solana's appointment as the EU's High Representative in October 1999 was another key moment in the Union's emergence as an international actor.[3] His leadership of the Euro-Mediterranean Conference during Spain's presidency of the EU in 1995 showcased his talent for international diplomacy and propelled him to the position of Secretary-General of NATO, an organisation that he had opposed Spain joining a decade and a half earlier.[4] Solana became the public face of NATO's 'humanitarian' airstrikes against Yugoslavia, which protected Kosovo Albanians displaced by Milošević's forces, yet killed an estimated 500 civilians.[5]

EU foreign ministers feared alienating public opinion and the United States if the European Security and Defence Policy evolved too quickly. Consequently, Solana kept a relatively low profile during the EU's first military missions and instead presented himself, and the EU, as an international mediator, as when he helped to broker a deal to end a five-week siege at the Church of the Nativity in Bethlehem in May 2002.[6] When he visited the White House as NATO Secretary-General, Solana was mocked in *The Onion* as 'a guy in a tie' identified by those present as 'some kind of visiting dignitary, businessman, expert, government official or something'.[7] As the EU's foreign policy chief, Solana became a named straight man, as the satirical newspaper poked fun at US foreign policy figures. 'They're sending Solana but not me? I deserve to go so much more than that guy,' exclaimed a United States senator in one such spoof.[8]

Solana's growing stature gave him a prominent place in public debates leading up to the Iraq War, yet he was only as strong as the support he received from member states. In this case member states were hopelessly divided. A Fulbright scholar who earned his PhD in physics at the University of Virginia, Solana was an Atlanticist by temperament, but he distrusted Bush's evangelical tones and 'binary' world view after the 9/11 attacks.[9] Not so UK Prime Minister Tony Blair, whose passion for politics was intertwined with his spiritual awakening at Oxford, and for whom, it seemed, EU cooperation on security and defence came second to the special relationship between the UK and United States.[10] In the hours after al-Qaeda's attack on the United States, Blair promised that the UK would stand 'shoulder to shoulder with our American friends' and he remained true to his word.[11] French President Jacques Chirac and German Chancellor Gerhard Schröder, although they committed troops to the NATO-led,

UN-approved mission in Afghanistan, refused to back Bush's demands for regime change in Iraq. Chirac saw an opportunity to assert French and European autonomy but his concerns ran deeper. Having served in the Algerian War, Chirac was wary of 'imposing a law on people from the outside'.[12] Schröder was protective of the Franco-German relationship and so reluctant to break with Chirac. With federal elections scheduled for September 2002, the chancellor could also ill afford to back a war that a majority of Germans opposed.[13]

Questioned over European opposition to the war in Iraq, Bush's pugnacious defence secretary Donald Rumsfeld replied, 'You're thinking of Europe as Germany and France. I don't. I think that's old Europe.'[14] Rumsfeld's words stung the EU because they contained a dose of truth. Blair was not alone in supporting Bush. Portugal's youthful prime minister José Manuel Barroso was one of seven other European leaders to sign a letter in January 2003, insisting that Saddam Hussein be disarmed.[15] That the leaders of three soon-to-be EU member states – Poland's Leszek Miller, Hungary's Péter Medgyessy and the Czech Republic's Václav Havel – were fellow signatories made this a continental as well as a transatlantic rift. There was little that Solana could do to overcome these differences in the short term, so he began writing a new long-term strategy for the EU's common foreign and security policy.

Endorsed by the European Council in December 2003, on the day before US special forces apprehended Iraq President Saddam Hussein in Tikrit, the European Security Strategy didn't refer to Iraq.[16] Instead, the document presented the EU as a new sort of global actor for a rapidly evolving international system. 'As a union of 25 states with over 450 million people producing a quarter of the world's Gross National Product (GNP), and with a wide range of instruments at its disposal,' the strategy began, 'the European Union is inevitably a global player.' Strengthening the EU's military capabilities was a key priority, it accepted, while stressing that the most pressing international challenges required civilian capabilities. 'In failed states,' for example, 'military instruments may be needed to restore order.' The document didn't mention Rumsfeld's struggle to bring order to Iraq amid a violent insurgency. It didn't need to.

Among the key global threats identified in the European Security Strategy was the proliferation of weapons of mass destruction. Solana was thinking here not of Iraq but Iran, whose leader Mohammad Khatami admitted in February 2003 that his country had been secretly building facilities capable of enriching uranium.[17] This infrastructure was intended to produce civilian nuclear power, Khatami insisted; Rumsfeld, however, feared that Iran's real aim was to develop nuclear weapons. The Secretary of Defence ordered Pentagon officials to prepare plans for airstrikes against Iran, a country that Bush had included in his 'axis of evil' speech alongside Iraq and North Korea.[18] Solana saw an opportunity for the EU to lead on this issue and travelled to Tehran, where he called for 'full cooperation and transparency' with the International Economic Energy Agency while holding out hope for an EU–Iran Trade and Cooperation Agreement and deeper dialogue on human rights.[19]

After his studies in the United States, Solana had become a professor of physics at Complutense University of Madrid. Although his field was solid-state rather than nuclear physics, he had a fine-grained understanding of centrifuges, isotope separation technologies and hard versus light water reactors, and technical issues on which the politics of Iran's nuclear programme turned. The key to Solana's influence, however, lay in the decision by the foreign ministers of France, Germany and the UK, Dominique de Villepin, Joschka Fischer and Jack Straw, to talk directly with Iran.[20] Initially, Solana found himself sidelined by the so-called EU-3, as this ad hoc triad came to be known, but the High Representative soon became its public face.

The decision to go to war in Iraq had unfolded rapidly. Nine months after his axis of evil speech, Bush had given Saddam Hussein an ultimatum to give up Iraq's weapons of mass destruction. Six months later – after UN weapons inspectors had failed to find such weapons or confirm that they had been destroyed – the US-led invasion of Iraq was underway. The Iran nuclear crisis was glacial by comparison, reflecting the EU's willingness to pursue diplomatic solutions, even after Iran failed to abide by the terms of an interim deal to end uranium enrichment brokered with the EU-3 in October 2003. This willingness remained, even after Mahmoud Ahmadinejad won the Iranian presidency. Khatami was a reformer who was determined to reduce the country's high rates of unemployment and desirous of a more constructive relationship with the West. Ahmadinejad was a charismatic conservative whose trademark white polyester jacket signalled that he was a man of the people. He was also an unpredictable firebrand who denied the Holocaust and threatened to wipe Israel 'off the map'.[21] But the EU still sought common ground with Iran, as when the Europeans offered to supply the Iranian government with a light water reactor. Ahmadinejad showed little interest in a deal, but as EU, UN and US sanctions began to bite, he was prepared to talk, if not to suspend uranium enrichment.[22] Ahmadinejad's successor, Hassan Rouhani, a reformer who had led earlier rounds of negotiations with the EU-3, was determined to end these sanctions and prepared to broker a deal.

Although no agreement with Iran was in sight as his decade as High Representative came to an end, Solana took consolation from the fact that he had helped, in his judgment, to 'put Europe into the world'.[23] Baroness Ashton, a member of the UK House of Lords who had served in Gordon Brown's cabinet, picked up where Solana had left off in discussions with Iran. It was Ashton's successor as High Representative, Federica Mogherini, who chaired the final rounds of negotiation between Iran, the EU-3, China, Russia and the United States in Austria in July 2015. The deal had many authors, but it was Mogherini who joined Iranian foreign minister Mohammad Javad Zarif on the dais at Vienna's Palais Coburg hotel to present the Joint Comprehensive Plan of Action to the world's press.

Like Ashton, Mogherini's character and competence were questioned in a way that men appointed to senior political roles seldom were. When the High Representative role was created, it was often referred to in EU circles as 'Mr Europe'.[24] Even after Ashton's term of office, many still struggled to see women representing the EU on the global stage. 'Ms Mogherini has attended the right schools, majored in the right subjects, completed the right internships, been a member of the right Socialist youth groups – yet there is nothing in her résumé that one could point to as a crucible of leadership,' suggested one journalist as the race to replace Ashton intensified.[25] That Mogherini was Italy's foreign minister, albeit for eight months, made little difference. That she was two years older than the Italian prime minister, Matteo Renzi, didn't stop critics from asserting that she was too young to be entrusted with such responsibility. The prevailing view, even after the Heads of State or Government agreed on her appointment, was that Mogherini 'lacked clout'.[26]

Sworn in as High Representative just as talks with Iran were entering a critical phase, Mogherini quickly established her credibility with EU foreign ministers and took the chair as negotiations over the Iranian nuclear programme went into extra time.[27] US Secretary of State John Kerry was, by now, at the table, Barack Obama's presidency having ushered in a more conciliatory approach to Tehran. Despite this shift, Kerry repeatedly threatened to quit the talks.[28] Mogherini and her team kept the parties talking for more than two weeks in Vienna's Palais Coburg and worked through the night to produce a final text that all sides could live with.

Presented to the world's press on 14 July 2015, the Joint Comprehensive Plan of Action was far from perfect.[29] During the thirteen years of stop-start talks that led to this agreement, Iran continued to flout its obligations under the Nuclear Non-Proliferation Treaty and to support terrorist and militia groups across the Middle East. The agreement itself provided for its own expiry after fifteen years and was backed by a political text rather than a treaty. At best, it prevented Iran from obtaining nuclear weapons; at worst, it merely delayed the time it would take to do so, giving the rest of the world longer to react.[30] Nevertheless, Iran gave significant ground by agreeing to keep uranium enrichment to levels consistent with the production of nuclear energy or medical research, to phase out IR-1 centrifuges, a key component of its nuclear programme, and to impose strict limits on the development of new generation centrifuges and its stockpile of enriched uranium. In exchange, the EU, UN and United States agreed to phase out the sanctions specifically related to the nuclear programme, which had weighed heavily on the Iranian economy over the previous decade. Roundly praised for her role in brokering the deal, Mogherini wasted little time in travelling to Tehran to push for its implementation in full.[31]

A European in the White House (2016–20)

On 8 May 2018, US President Donald Trump announced that he was withdrawing his country from the Iran nuclear deal. It was, he told reporters, 'a horrible, one-sided deal that should have never, ever been made. It didn't bring calm, it didn't bring peace, and it never will.'[32] Trump raised legitimate grievances. As it benefited from the lifting of Western sanctions, Iran remained a supporter of Hezbollah, Hamas and Houthis, a principal backer of Bashar al-Assad's regime in Syria and a state sponsor of terrorism in the Middle East and Europe. However, Trump's problems with the deal appeared to be personal as well as political. Determined to denigrate the policies of his predecessor, Barack Obama, the 45th president insisted that 'A constructive deal could easily have been struck at the time, but it wasn't,' while making unsubstantiated claims about Iran's ability to develop nuclear weapons under the terms of the agreements.

While the Heads of State or Government tiptoed around Trump, Mogherini came out swinging. 'The nuclear deal with Iran is the culmination of 12 years of diplomacy,' she announced after a meeting of EU foreign ministers. 'It belongs to the entire international community. It has been working and it is delivering on its goal, which is guaranteeing that Iran doesn't develop nuclear weapons.' 'Do not let anyone dismantle this agreement,' she urged the Iranian people. 'It is one of the biggest achievements diplomacy has ever delivered, and we built this together.'[33] The High Representative went further in the days that followed. 'It seems that screaming, shouting, insulting and bullying, systematically destroying and dismantling everything that is already in place, is the mood of our times,' she told an audience in Florence. 'While the secret of change – and we need change – is to put all energies not in destroying the old, but rather in building the new.'[34]

Mogherini's real audience was the Iranian government. By taking a tough line against the United States, she hoped to reassure Tehran that the EU and its member states remained committed to the Iran Nuclear Deal and capable of delivering the economic benefits it offered to Iran. The EU had been here before when Trump's predecessor George W. Bush declared the Kyoto Protocol dead. Once again, the Union stuck with its prior agreements and rallied international support. China and Russia sided with the EU rather than the Trump Administration, which set out demands for a new nuclear deal that it knew no government in Tehran would ever agree to.[35] The Joint Comprehensive Plan of Action could have easily collapsed during this period, not least following Iranian President Hassan Rouhani's attempt to seek leverage over sanctions by announcing a new round of uranium enrichment.[36] And yet, the EU and Iran kept talking, in the hope that a more durable deal could be found.

Trump was not the first US president to clash with the EU, yet none were as openly hostile. Before entering politics, the entrepreneur turned reality television star had shown little interest in Europe beyond the fairways of Balmedie and Doonbeg. But this changed, in the early 2010s, as Trump used his outsize presence on social media to pour forth on the political issues of the day, including in Europe. 'The euro, put in place to hurt the US is done! - - will have less negative impact than most think,' he tweeted in June 2012.[37] Blunt, brash and, often, baseless, Trump's tweets contrasted with the circumlocution of many mainstream politicians. To his growing band of supporters, he stood for something different, something authentic and someone who heard their frustration with leaders who championed a more progressive society, while failing to protect them from the pain of globalisation.

Trump's antipathy towards the EU was not by chance. His politics were influenced by, and intertwined with, Europe. Commentators were quick to draw comparisons between Trump and Silvio Berlusconi, the Italian billionaire turned populist prime minister. However, Berlusconi's Euroscepticism flourished only after he left office. Trump's closest progenitor was Sir James Goldsmith, the Anglo-French founder of the Referendum Party. The two crossed paths in the late 1980s while considering rival bids for the ailing airline, Pan Am.[38] Trump was a mid-sized property developer, with a line in casinos and hotels, who sought to emulate financial titans like Goldsmith by joining Wall Street's takeover wars in the 1980s.[39] While Trump lacked Goldsmith's acumen for buying and selling corporations, the two were remarkably similar in other respects. Both were charismatic billionaires whose political ambitions were thwarted by their colourful private lives. Both overcame these obstacles by saying the unsayable and presenting themselves as the voice of the people against the political elite. Both preached the gospel of anti-globalisation and turned on the multilateral trading system. Trump's promise to pull out of the WTO could have come word for word from *Le Piège*, Goldsmith's treatise against the General Agreement on Tariffs and Trade.[40]

Europe's right-wing populists were overjoyed with Trump's unexpected election in November 2016. It was, Front National leader Marine Le Pen exclaimed, 'an additional stone in the building of a new world, destined to replace the old one'.[41] Le Pen was photographed in New York's Trump Tower in the weeks after the result, as was UK Independence Party leader, Nigel Farage, who posed with the president-elect before a golden door in the skyscraper's penthouse suite. EU Heads of State or Government also called Trump to offer congratulations, while fretting about what came next. Angela Merkel went furthest in public, offering 'close cooperation' with Trump based on their countries' shared commitment to 'democracy, freedom and respect for the law and the dignity of man'.[42] That the taciturn chancellor felt compelled to list these values said a lot.

In the late 1980s, as his media profile soared, Trump had taken out an advert in the *New York Times*, *Washington Post* and *Boston Globe* in which he had criticised Japan for 'taking advantage of the United States'.[43] The Japanese government, he argued, was free-riding on the United States' defence spending, while allowing an undervalued yen to drive up trade surpluses with the American economy. 'Let's not let our great country be laughed at anymore,' he urged the newspapers' readers. Trump's views on trade and security had changed little in the intervening years; the difference was that they were now projected onto the European Union, which the president named ahead of Russia and China when asked by a reporter in July 2018 who was his biggest foe globally at that moment. 'I respected the leaders of those countries,' Trump insisted of the EU member states. 'In a trade sense, they have really taken advantage of us, and many of those countries are in NATO. And they weren't paying their bills.'[44]

European officials had spent three years negotiating with the Obama Administration over the ill-fated Transatlantic Trade and Investment Partnership, potentially the largest bilateral trade agreement in history. Now they prepared for a border adjustment tax aimed, in particular, at German automobile firms operating in the United States while importing many of their inputs from abroad. While Republican lawmakers quietly shelved plans for such a tax, Trump imposed duties on European steel, prompting retaliatory measures from EU trade ministers. Seeking to avert a transatlantic trade war, European Commission President Jean-Claude Juncker flew to Washington DC, where he kissed Trump on the cheek and convinced him to revive talks on a zero-tariff trade deal.[45] The talks went nowhere, yet Juncker's charm offensive helped to diffuse tensions.

When he arrived in the Oval Office, Juncker gave Trump a photograph of George S. Patton, the US Army general who died in service during the Second World War and lay buried in Juncker's native Luxembourg.[46] Trump was no student of history, but he cited Franklin J. Schaffner's *Patton* (1970) among his favourite films, and drew on the film's opening scene, in which George C. Scott speaks before an enormous American flag, in his campaign rallies. 'Dear Donald, let us remember our common history,' added Juncker as an inscription to the photo, hoping to avoid a trade war and preserve the transatlantic relationship. The Commission President's efforts made little difference to Trump, who continued to berate NATO members that failed to honour their pledges on defence spending while referring to the organisation as 'obsolete'.[47]

Even before Trump took office, Federica Mogherini argued for change. 'As Europeans, we must take greater responsibility for our security,' a new strategy document for EU foreign affairs and security, prepared by the High Representative, declared in June 2016.[48] Thirteen years earlier, Solana's European Security Strategy had spoken in sacred tones about the United States' 'critical role in European integration' and the enduring importance of NATO and the transatlantic relationship. Mogherini, in contrast, insisted that the EU must be able to act autonomously of NATO 'if and when necessary'.[49] Trump's fractious foreign policy built support for Mogherini's plan. 'We Europeans truly have to take our fate into our own hands,' argued Merkel in a campaign rally in Munich in May 2017.[50] Emmanuel Macron put this even more forcefully in November 2019 when he expressed concerns over 'the brain death of NATO'.[51] Such sentiments drove new EU policy commitments, including a new pact between twenty-five EU member states designed to invest in defence projects, such as the development of armoured vehicles or common responses to cyberattacks.

Significant though such initiatives were, the EU had achieved nothing close to genuine autonomy in the field of security and defence by the early 2020s. No matter how frustrated the Heads of State or Government were with NATO, they weren't prepared to forgo the transatlantic alliance, however frail and fractured it looked. The EU still needed the United States' security guarantee for one reason above all. That reason was Russia.

Russia and Ukraine (2001–21)

Two weeks after the 9/11 attacks, Vladimir Putin delivered an address to the Bundestag in Berlin. Addressing his audience in Russian and German, it was a homecoming of sorts for the president, who had been stationed 200 kilometres south, in Dresden, as a KGB officer towards the end of the Cold War. Putin spoke fondly of the cultural and historic ties that bound Germany to Russia, and of his hopes for European integration. European integration was the triumph of 'consensus over and above national egoism', he argued. 'A united and secure Europe' would be 'the harbinger of a united and secure world.'[52] Six years later, when the Russian president returned to Germany to speak at the Munich Security Conference, his warm tones had given way to sarcasm and scorn. Perhaps he had misunderstood a conference delegate who suggested that the EU and NATO rather than the UN could legitimately authorise the use of force, Putin wryly suggested, while warning Europeans that they risked a new arms race.[53]

Putin's transformation from an apparent admirer of the EU to its antagonist had domestic and international origins. A relative unknown when he was picked by Boris Yeltsin to be prime minister, the former head of the Federal Security Service (the successor to the KGB) never convinced as a liberal democrat. When he stumbled politically, as he did over the Kursk submarine disaster after his election as president, his instinct was to turn on the media and political opponents and play the nationalist card. Restoring Russia's status as a great power was central to this right-wing populist project, which left little room for cooperation and consensus-seeking with the EU. Putin's confidence in the West, and by extension the EU, was also badly shaken by 9/11. After al-Qaeda attacked the United States, Putin had offered himself as an ally to George W. Bush, but the Russian president grew increasingly alarmed at the Texan's foreign policy.[54] Bush's decision to withdraw from the 1972 Anti-Ballistic Missile Treaty served as an early warning. The US president's public support for Georgia and Ukraine's ambitions to join NATO spoke to Putin's worst fears.[55]

That Putin treated the EU as an expansionist acolyte of NATO was ironic. The Union had shown little enthusiasm for taking in additional member states after the Big Bang enlargements of 2004 and 2007 and Ukraine's Orange Revolution made little difference in this regard. After declaring independence from the Soviet Union in 1991, the country experienced a costly and delayed transition to market capitalism, made worse by the Russian financial crisis. One of the few policy-makers to emerge with credibility from this period was Viktor Yushchenko, an unassuming governor of the National Bank of Ukraine, who was unexpectedly invited to become prime minister. After stepping down, Yushchenko allied with Yulia Tymoshenko and other opposition leaders and ran for the presidency against Viktor Yanukovych, the preferred choice of the incumbent, Leonid Kuchma. Disfigured by dioxin poisoning during the campaign, Yushchenko won the first round before narrowly losing to Yanukovych in the second, amid widespread reports of election fraud. Hundreds of thousands of protesters camped out in Maidan, Kyiv's Independence Square, until the supreme court ordered that the vote be re-run, leading to victory for Yushchenko. Promising to take Ukraine into the EU, Yushchenko was hailed as a statesman. He received a cool response from EU leaders, who remained reluctant to take in new members after the Big Bang enlargement of the 2000s, not to mention one that was so intimately connected to, and internally divided over, Russia.[56]

Among the Heads of State or Government, only Lech Kaczyński advocated membership for Ukraine. As confrontational towards Moscow as he was towards Brussels, the Polish president nonetheless saw EU and NATO membership for Poland's neighbour as guarantors against Russian aggression.[57] Kaczyński lacked support from other leaders, who were reminded of their energy dependence on Russia when a dispute between Russia's Gazprom and Ukraine's Naftogaz resulted in a temporary drop in gas supplies to EU member states during an unusually cold spell in January 2006.[58]

European Commission President José Manuel Barroso found it difficult to ignore the pro-democracy protests in Ukraine. Accession to the European Communities had helped to reinforce the path to democracy in Barroso's native Portugal and he was determined that the EU should offer hope to Yushchenko and his supporters. 'Our door remains open. The future of Ukraine is in Europe,' the Commission President told Ukraine Prime Minister Yuri Yekhanurov, while building support within the Commission and among the Heads of State or Government for a new trade deal with Ukraine.[59] Negotiations on the EU–Ukraine Association Agreement were slow to get off the ground. By the time they were concluded, Yanukovych had regained the presidency from Yushchenko.

Although he was Putin's preferred candidate, Yanukovych, like Kuchma before him, sought to balance Ukraine's foreign policy between East and West. Geopolitical considerations informed Yanukovych's thinking, as did the fact that Russia and the EU each accounted for around a quarter of Ukraine's exports.[60] The new president's initial response was to press ahead with the EU Association Agreement; but facing public criticism from Putin, he sought new terms with the EU and announced plans to join Russia's proposed Eurasian Customs Union. For Barroso, Yanukovych's attempt to ride both horses was out of the question. Ukraine couldn't be a part of the EU's free trade agreement while forming a customs union with Russia, Belarus and Kazakhstan.[61] In 2004, protesters in Maidan wore orange ribbons. Now, ten years later, they waved European flags and demanded that Yanukovych sign the Association Agreement.

Fearing war, the foreign ministers of France, Germany and Poland brokered a deal between Yanukovych and Ukrainian opposition groups for constitutional reforms and fresh presidential elections. However, before this agreement could be implemented, Yanukovych fled the country in fear of his life. Five days later, pro-Russian forces seized government buildings in Crimea, which had remained home to the Russian navy's Black Sea fleet after Ukraine became an independent country. By the time Ukraine's newly elected president, Petro

Poroshenko, flew to Brussels to sign key elements of the EU Association Agreement, Russia had completed its annexation of Crimea. To Poroshenko, the move marked the 'first most decisive step' towards EU membership.[62] Barroso remained hopeful, yet EU Heads of State or Government had gone about as far as they were willing to go at that point.

Relations between Russia and the EU went from bad to worse over Ukraine. When Malaysian Airlines Flight 17 from Kuala Lumpur to Amsterdam was shot down by pro-Russian separatists over eastern Ukraine in July 2014, Dutch Foreign Minister Frans Timmermans' tearful speech to the United Nations Security Council about the 298 people who lost their lives in the attack and the rebels' reluctance to return their bodies and allow access to the crash site, galvanised the EU, which stepped up sanctions against Putin's inner circle of advisors and oligarchs. Russia responded with sanctions of its own against EU foodstuffs, leading to a substantial loss of trade on both sides.[63] Neither sanctions nor EU member states' repeated attempts to broker peace in Ukraine's Donbas region made a difference to Putin, who allowed the slow-burning Russo-Ukraine war to run while threatening to send hundreds of thousands of Russian troops into eastern Ukraine.

It was not only the EU's neighbours that became embroiled in this new cold war but also its member states. The EU's Baltic members – as former Soviet republics with large Russian minorities – were most vulnerable. When Estonian Prime Minister Andrus Ansip decided to remove Enn Roos' *Bronze Soldier* (1947), a war memorial in Tallinn which originally commemorated the Red Army's liberation of Estonia's capital during the Second World War, he was rebuked by Putin for sowing 'discord and mistrust'.[64] Riots and looting involving more than a thousand ethnic Russians followed, drawing attention to the discrimination they faced under Estonia's citizenship laws and raising fears that Russia might intervene. The day after the statue's removal, Estonian ministries, news organisations and banks were hit by a massive cyberattack, which Ansip claimed originated in Russia.[65] Reports of Russian interference in French, German and Spanish elections and support for right-wing populists added to concerns that Putin, having once looked to the EU with hope, was seeking to destroy it from within.[66]

Despite these threats, the EU treated Moscow with kid gloves, undermining the Union's credibility as a global actor. Successive Italian prime ministers, from Silvio Berlusconi to Giuseppe Conte, led efforts to relax sanctions against the Putin administration. German Chancellor Angela Merkel, like her Italian counterparts, sought continued cooperation with Moscow in the field of energy. South Stream, a proposed gas pipeline from Anapa in Russia to Tarvisio in Italy, was abandoned in December 2014, partly in response to EU sanctions. But work on Nord Stream 2, a pipeline from Russia to Germany under the Baltic Sea was completed six years later. When Putin demanded in December 2021 that NATO troops be withdrawn from the Baltic States and Poland in return for a peaceful settlement with Ukraine, it fell to US President Joe Biden to engage in diplomatic discussions.[67] The EU was merely an onlooker.

Systemic Rival

Expectations ran high when Pascal Lamy, Jacques Delors' loyal lieutenant, returned to Brussels as Trade Commissioner in 1999. Over the previous decade, the EU had, in the words of one Commission official, 'rediscovered multilateralism'.[68] Forming an influential caucus with Canada, Japan and the United States, the EU had steered the Uruguay Round of the General Agreement on Tariff and Trade to a successful conclusion and created the World Trade Organization. The 123 contracting parties to the Marrakesh Agreement agreed to cut tariffs on industrial goods and phase out quotas on textiles while leaving contentious issues such as agriculture and services to future talks.[69] Lamy represented the EU in negotiations over this built-in agenda, which he argued could only be dealt with through an entirely new global trade deal. WTO members agreed and so the Doha Development Round was born.

Lamy had served as *chef de cabinet* for Delors, running the Commission president's private office and pursuing his political agenda with ruthless efficiency. The two men shared a commitment to Social Catholicism.[70] For Delors, this meant buttressing the single market with Social Europe. For Lamy, it meant addressing the social dimension of globalisation. When violent anti-globalisation protesters disrupted the WTO ministerial in Seattle in 1999, Lamy was one of few policy-makers present to call on global leaders to answer the demonstrators' demands for higher social and environmental standards.[71] Doha, with its desire for a more equitable trading system, was tailor-made for Lamy, who was subsequently called from Brussels to Geneva to become the WTO's new director-general. The Exocet, as Lamy was known, used his considerable diplomatic skills to seek movement from industrialised countries on agricultural products and concessions from developing countries on industrial goods, but he missed his target by some distance. 'Members have simply not been able to bridge their differences,' the director-general informed the Geneva press corps in July 2008 after four years of negotiations and five ministerial conferences.[72]

Doha's collapse was a bitter blow not only for Lamy but also for the EU's global ambitions. Having put 'effective multilateralism' at the heart of its foreign policy, the Union learned how ineffective it could be outside its own finely tuned institutional structures. At the height of the Third Way, world leaders had shared a positive vision of global-isation and a willingness to strike a deal. Now they preferred no deal to a domestic backlash against a bad one or the uncertain gains from reducing barriers to investment, trade protection and intellectual property rights. Industrialised countries had also lost influence to developing ones, which, as in the environmental sphere, had the power to make or break a global deal. While holding out hope for the WTO, the EU promised 'faster and more comprehensive trade liber-alisation within the framework of its bilateral relations'.[73] China, it concluded, was 'the biggest single challenge of globalisation'.

By the time the Maastricht Treaty was signed in 1992, relations between the EU and China had returned to normal. Condemning the

Chinese government's response to the Tiananmen Square protests in 1989, EU Heads of State or Government had recognised protesters' democratic demands as legitimate, imposed sanctions and broken off ministerial and high-level contacts. This cold shoulder lasted a little over a year. Bilateral trade with China was blossoming even before Deng Xiaoping's southern tour reignited the country's transition to a market economy. The EU's political dialogue with China, launched in 1994, sought trade and investment opportunities for European businesses and a channel to address concerns over the EU's widening trade deficit with China. It also reflected the EU's belief in its own normative powers, with a new EU–China Human Rights Dialogue offering a diluted version of the Union's approach to economic and political reform in Central and Eastern Europe. For China, this dialogue was preferable to political isolation; periodic lectures on fundamental rights and the rule of law were a small price to pay for closer economic and political ties with the West, at a time when the Clinton Administration continued to shun Beijing.

By 2020, China and the EU had become one another's most important trading partners. While the EU–China Human Rights Dialogue continued to meet, it offered little more than a salve for European consciences. 'Getting China right' originally meant diffusing disputes over Chinese bra imports, and an undervalued renminbi.[74] Now it meant navigating China's increasingly tangible presence within the European economy. A case in point was the Greek port of Piraeus, in which Cosco, the state-backed Chinese shipping company, acquired a stake in 2008.[75] Within a decade, Cosco had become the port's majority shareholder, as Greek authorities sought to pay down their public debt by privatising state assets and stimulating investment and job creation.

Dubbed 'the head of the dragon' by Chinese premier Xi Jinping, Piraeus port formed a central part of the Belt and Road Initiative, a series of infrastructure projects from East Asia to Europe designed to foster closer economic and political ties with Beijing.[76] The deal enjoyed public support in Greece, at first, although frustration grew over Cosco's failure to deliver on investment pledges and commitments on safe working conditions in the port. The death of a dock worker, Dimitri Dagkli, after he was hit by a container crane, prompted a twenty-four-hour strike by port workers, amid signs that Greek authorities were having second thoughts about China.[77] By this point, human rights groups had already sounded the alarm over Greek diplomats' decision to block EU criticism of China in the UN's Human Rights Council.[78] It was better to take this issue up in the EU–China Human Rights Dialogue, the diplomats unconvincingly insisted.

Piraeus was no isolated case. By 2018, Chinese companies had acquired stakes in the ports of Antwerp, Bilbao, Dunkirk, Le Havre, Marsaxlokk, Nantes, Rotterdam, Valencia and Zeebrugge.[79] Four years later, Cosco acquired a 24.9 per cent stake in a terminal in the German port of Hamburg. The deal had caused significant tensions in the German cabinet over national security, and words of warning from the country's president about 'one-sided dependencies' towards China.[80] However, Hamburg's Mayor Peter Tschentscher was adamant that the city could not afford to lose Chinese ships to other European ports if the investment was blocked.[81] After intense public debate, Chancellor Olaf Scholz, himself a former mayor of Hamburg, brokered a face-saving compromise, which prevented Cosco from acquiring the blocking minority that the business had originally sought, and which Scholz had originally supported, ahead of his official visit to Beijing to meet President Xi Jinping.[82] The visit went smoothly, yet it did little to help Scholz's strained relationship with French President Emmanuel Macron over the EU's policy towards China.

Such controversies were not limited to maritime ports.[83] In November 2021, Cainiao Network, the logistics arm of Chinese tech firm Alibaba, opened its largest-ever e-commerce hub at Liege Airport.[84] At the signing ceremony for this deal three years earlier, Belgian Prime Minister Charles Michel praised Wallonia's attractiveness as an investment location. But Belgian MPs soon raised questions about national security.[85] The purchase of Frankfurt Hahn Airport by Shanghai Yiqian Trading Company in 2016 provoked a similar reaction.[86]

The Heads of State or Government's response to such developments was conflicted. In March 2020, Emmanuel Macron, joined by the leaders of Belgium, Greece, Ireland, Italy, Luxembourg, Portugal, Slovenia and Spain, wrote to Michel, by then the president of the European Council, to insist that 'no strategic assets fall prey of hostile takeovers'.[87] By this point, member states had already agreed on new measures for screening foreign direct investment on grounds of national security.[88] And yet, nine months later, Michel and Macron joined a call with Xi Jinping to reach an agreement in principle on an ambitious new EU–China investment agreement.[89]

Trying, but failing, to reconcile such contradictions, the European Commission produced a strategy paper in March 2019 describing China as 'a cooperation partner', 'a negotiating partner' and a 'systemic rival'. When Chinese foreign minister Wang Yi questioned this characterisation, the EU's High Representative, Federica Mogherini, suggested that the Commission's paper had been for internal debate. Determined to take a tougher line, Mogherini's successor, Josep Borrell, decried China's harsh treatment of the Uyghurs, a mostly Muslim ethnic minority, and announced targeted sanctions against four Chinese officials.[90] When China responded with sanctions of its own against MEPs, national parliamentarians and EU academics, the European Parliament announced that it would not approve the EU–China investment agreement.[91] Behind the scenes, EU member state governments scrambled to save a deal that had taken seven years to negotiate.[92]

The European Union and Africa (2000–20)

The tension between self-image and self-interest was a recurring theme in the EU's common foreign and security policy. The first EU–Africa Summit in Cairo in April 2000 heralded a new global partnership between Africa and Europe 'on the basis of shared values of strengthening representative and participatory democracy, respect for human rights and fundamental freedoms, the rule of law, good governance, pluralism, international peace and security, political stability and confidence among nations'.[93] The EU's commitment to such values rang hollow due to its historical amnesia over European imperial rule in Africa and because its normative agenda was riven with contemporary contradictions. Together the EU and its member states provided more development aid to Africa each year than any other donor. But the conditions attached to this aid came at a high price, as in the Cotonou Agreement's attempt to link aid to the opening up of previously protected economic sectors. Although Burundi, Nigeria and Tanzania slowed the ratification of economic partnership agreements, the EU's common agricultural policy continued to weigh on African farmers, even after the phasing out of export subsidies for European agricultural products.[94]

The Cairo Summit also rested uneasily with the EU's patchy commitment to human rights in Africa. Just six years earlier, the Union had looked on as the assassination of Rwandan President Juvénal Habyarimana led Hutu extremists to kill up to 800,000 Tutsis in one hundred days. EU Heads of State or Government expressed their 'horror' at this genocide, yet they made no attempt to intervene either diplomatically or militarily, despite the billions the EU had spent on aid for Rwanda in recognition of the country's special relationship with Europe.[95] The only Western country to answer the United Nations' call for humanitarian intervention was France, which had provided economic and military support to Habyarimana as part of its dense web of cultural, business and political links with Francophone countries after decolonisation. The nearly 2,500 French troops deployed under Opération Turquoise helped to create a safe zone of sorts in south-west Rwanda, but France stood accused of being too close to its former Hutu allies.

Led by Paul Kagame, a Tutsi refugee who grew up in Uganda, the Rwandan Patriotic Front ended the genocide and formed a new government in Kigali, which brought political stability to Rwanda and set in motion a remarkable economic recovery. Kagame, who won the Rwandan presidency in 2000, was soon feted as an African visionary who used Western aid to emulate Singapore's model of efficient public services and market capitalism. And yet, Rwanda's long period of uninterrupted growth couldn't disguise Kagame's disdain for political opponents and his controversial military operations in neighbouring Congo. In 2012, the United Nations accused Rwanda of supporting Congolese rebels who had committed war crimes, leading the EU and several member states to cut aid flows to Rwanda. Fearing China's growing influence in Africa, the EU soon reversed this decision, consolidating Kagame's grip on power.[96]

In Rwanda, France did what the EU was not prepared to do. Over time, the EU was accused of privileging French interests in Africa. A case in point was EUFOR Tchad/RCA, an EU military mission which deployed 3,700 military personnel from 14 EU member states to Chad and the Central African Republic in March 2008. France had a longstanding military presence in its two former colonies, but President Nicolas Sarkozy sought urgent help to deal with more than half a million people displaced by the Chadian civil war and ethnic cleansing in Sudan's Darfur region.[97] When Chad's president, Idriss Déby, a close ally of Sarkozy, objected to United Nations involvement in his country, EU foreign ministers agreed to dispatch 3,700 military personnel from 23 EU member states to protect displaced people and facilitate humanitarian aid. Only Germany and the UK refused to commit troops, leaving the mission in the incongruous position of relying on Russian helicopters to complete its tasks.

For fifteen months, EUFOR Tchad/RCA carried out nearly 2,500 patrols and 500 air missions, helping to improve security in an area the size of France.[98] It largely achieved its modest goals, with the one serious mistake occurring when a vehicle carrying two team members unintentionally crossed the border into Sudan and drew fire from local forces. The first soldier to die in the line of duty for the EU, French Sergeant Gilles Polin, was given full military honours at the Citadel of Bayonne, his coffin draped in the tricolour, as French President Nicolas Sarkozy and EU High Representative Javier Solana looked on.

The EU's experience in Chad and the Central African Republic spoke to European preconceptions of Africa as a failing continent.

Ethiopia's extraordinary economic performance in the 2000s and 2010s shattered this image. Fuelled by a public investment boom, the country's real GDP growth rate averaged 10.1 per cent between 2004 and 2020.[99] During this period, GDP per capita increased nearly three-fold and average life expectancy increased from 54 to 65.[100] The policy choices made by Prime Minister Meles Zenawi and other Ethiopian policy-makers drove this economic success story. But the EU and its member states played a part by providing nearly €800 million in overseas development assistance to Ethiopia each year.[101] Ghana, another beneficiary of EU aid, showed that economic development need not come at the expense of political reform. By 2022, the West African country ranked higher than Hungary for political rights and civil liberties, according to Freedom House.[102] To Assita Kanko, a Belgian MEP born in Burkina Faso, the impact of European aid on ordinary Africans remained open to question. 'Every time European leaders came to Africa and announced huge cheques under the press spotlights,' she recalled of her childhood in Ouagadougou, 'families watched the news and wondered where the money would go.'[103]

Hailed as one of Africa's strongest economic performers in the 2000s, Mali was caught in a cycle of violence in the 2010s driven by separatist forces, who sought to build a breakaway state in the north of the country, and mutinous military groups, who deposed the country's democratically elected president, Amadou Toumani Touré, in a coup. Like the rest of the Sahel, Mali also provided sanctuary for Jihadi groups, such as al-Qaeda in the Islamic Maghreb, a loose network of terrorist cells which grew out of the Algerian civil war and soon spread to neighbouring countries. Determined to protect France's interests in its former colony, François Hollande sent fighter jets and ground troops to Mali in January 2013 to retake Gao, Kidal and Timbuktu from al-Qaeda in the Islamic Maghreb. Although the operation was a tactical success, France was soon drawn into a more ambitious and open-ended counter-terrorism operation in Mali, Chad and Niger.

Adamant that Europe shoulder some of this burden, Hollande had already convinced other Heads of State or Government to back an

EU mission in Mali, albeit one limited to training and advising the Malian military in the fight against Jihadi groups.[104] Twenty-two EU member states joined this mission over the next decade, including the United Kingdom and Germany, which did so with little enthusiasm and with the knowledge that it would have damaged their standing in the EU to turn their back on a counter-terrorism operation. Two military coups in August 2020 and May 2021, left Mali with an unelected government which, as France wavered over its presence in the country, turned to Russian mercenaries. With one eye on his re-election bid, perhaps, Hollande's successor, Emmanuel Macron, pulled French troops from the country's own mission and the EU's in February 2022.[105] Without France, the EU's mission in Mali lacked credibility, speaking to concerns that the common foreign and security policy privileged one member state's regional interests in African above all others. Having wrestled with whether to stay in Mali to limit the spread of Jihadi groups or cut ties with a country that seemed to be spiralling out of control, EU foreign ministers decided in April 2022 to end the mission.[106]

China showed few such compunctions about its role as a security actor in Africa. In 2013, the People's Liberation Army joined MINUSMA, the UN mission in Mali. This was the first time that China had committed combat troops to UN peacekeeping, but not the last. By December 2021, China had more than 1,700 troops stationed in Abyei, Mali, Congo and South Sudan.[107] It also had a permanent military base in Djibouti, which was home to up to 2,000 naval personnel.[108]

EU member states' unease about committing troops to military operations in Africa left foreign ministers reliant on more tenuous ways of pursuing regional interests. When Jihadi militants forced French energy firm TotalEnergies SE to suspend work on its US$20 billion liquified natural gas project in Mozambique's Cabo Delgado province in April 2021, EU foreign ministers agreed on a small-scale training mission led by Portuguese special forces.[109] But the EU also relied on Rwanda to send a much larger force to drive Jihadi forces out of Cabo Delgado. For Rwandan President Paul Kagame, the mission helped to counter past criticism of his interventionist foreign policy. For the EU, it seemed more cost-effective to pay Kagame for a mission so squarely aimed at French economic interests rather than the 800,000 Mozambicans displaced by Jihadi violence.[110]

At the European Union–African Union Summit in Brussels in February 2022, the EU pledged €150 billion in investment for Africa by the end of the decade.[111] Significant though this commitment was, the summit's talk of 'human rights for all, gender equality and women's empowerment in all spheres of life, respect for democratic principles, good governance and the rule of law, actions to preserve the climate, environment and biodiversity, sustainable and inclusive economic growth, the fight against inequalities, support for children's rights, and the inclusion of women, young people and the most disadvantaged' seemed even less credible than similar promises in Cairo twenty-two years earlier.[112]

Despite the common foreign and security policy's shortcomings, the EU achieved a role on the world stage that few thought possible when the Maastricht Treaty was signed in February 1992. The Heads of State or Government did so not by ceding control over questions of war and peace to European officials but by championing their collective interests, where possible, in an unsettled and increasingly multipolar international system. Where member states' interests overlapped, the EU shaped world events in ways that none of its constituent countries could have done alone. Where member states significantly diverged, the union found itself buffeted by global forces. And yet, Maastricht's vision of the European Union as a global actor survived, as national leaders regrouped around international challenges where they could make a collective difference. One such challenge, by some measures the greatest of the post-Maastricht period, was climate change.

10

Ecological Europe

Support and Solidarity from Brussels

In October 1992, Petra Kelly was found murdered in her home in Bonn. Her partner, Gert Bastian, lay dead nearby, having, the police concluded, shot Kelly and then shot himself.[1] Europe's best-known environmentalist, Kelly had co-founded the Greens (Die Grünen) twelve years earlier and lent her name and formidable intellect to a variety of causes. She started her professional career in Brussels as a trainee in the European Commission before becoming an official in the Economic and Social Committee, a consultative body of the then European Community. Kelly's prior interest in politics stemmed from her time as a student in Washington DC, where she met anti-nuclear activists such as Ralph Nadar and volunteered for Senator Robert F. Kennedy's presidential campaign. She had a strong aversion to nuclear energy, believing that her sister's early death had been hastened by her exposure to a nuclear plant near their home in Virginia.[2] So when West Germany responded to the 1973 oil shock by announcing plans to build eight new nuclear power stations, Kelly felt compelled to act. Speaking to 10,000 demonstrators at Wyhl – the location of one such plant – she offered support and solidarity from Brussels.[3]

The prevailing view among environmentalists at this time – and for a decade or more to come – was one of Euroscepticism.[4] In the UK, for instance, Teddy Goldsmith's Ecology Party viewed the single market as demonstrating 'the worst failings of an over-centralised, growth-orientated bureaucracy'.[5] Its successor, the Green Party, campaigned to take the UK out of the European Communities in the 1989 European Parliament election and won 2 million votes for its principled opposition to European integration. However, from the moment Kelly spoke at Wyhl, she saw the potential for a pan-European anti-nuclear movement and asked not only what the European Community could do to protect the environment but also whether environmentalism was the issue that the Community had been waiting for. From Carnsore Point in Ireland to Creys-Malville in France, Wyhl inspired a new wave of anti-nuclear protests, which Kelly believed could unite Europeans.[6] Her political instincts were shrewd, and her timing remarkable. Three months before the first European Parliament election in June 1979, a partial meltdown at the Three Mile Island Nuclear Station in Pennsylvania heightened public concerns over nuclear power across the world. The Greens won no seats in this contest, yet they secured nearly 900,000 votes and established environmentalism as a rising force in West Germany and across the European Community.

Kelly's commitment to European integration was by no means unconditional. A year before her death, as negotiations over the Maastricht Treaty entered a crucial phase, she gave a wide-ranging speech at Oregon State University in which she warned that Europe was seeking to build 'a second military-economic superpower'.[7] What was needed, she argued, was 'an ecological and demilitarized Europe, a pacifist and feminized Europe that is in solidarity with the Third World and that rethinks and redesigns its economic and industrial policies'. Kelly had lost her seat in the Bundestag by this point, paying the price for the Greens' opposition to German unification. The party had close ties to East Germany and opposed what they saw as Helmut Kohl's determination to impose Western capitalism on the old German Democratic Republic. Kelly saw the embryonic EU's policy towards Central and Eastern Europe in similar terms, criticising member states for putting economic transition before the ecological transformation that was urgently required in Eastern Europe.

Seeking, as she did throughout her career, to fuse environmentalism with European solidarity, Kelly proposed a suite of EU environmental policies in her speech, including 'new ecological taxation systems, new eco-taxes, new tax systems in both East and West Europe, and strong regulations on chemicals, and prohibitions on carcinogenic substances'.

Kelly feared what direction the EU would take, but she was more worried about the future of the Greens. Environmentalism was, to her mind, a transnational social movement dedicated to anti-militarism, ecology and non-violence. The Greens existed to achieve these aims, not to win political office. It was and should remain, Kelly insisted, an anti-party. At the time of her death, Kelly had lost this struggle over the soul of her party to colleagues such as Joschka Fischer, a student radical turned ecologist, turned Minister for the Environment in Hesse, who sought high office even if it meant compromising on foundational principles. Fischer succeeded in what he set out to do, becoming vice-chancellor and foreign minister of Germany in 1998 in the country's first Red–Green coalition at the federal level. In government, the Greens introduced more favourable tariffs for renewable energy producers and reached a deal to phase out nuclear power by 2022. They also supported NATO enlargement and the deployment of German troops in Kosovo. Kelly would have brooked no such compromises over foreign policy in the name of environmental legislation, as non-violence for her went hand in hand with protecting the planet.

Although the Greens lost their political innocence as she feared, Petra Kelly's vision of European integration was partly realised before she was killed by her partner, Gert Bastian. A former major general in the West German army turned anti-nuclear campaigner, he believed, perhaps, that his past dealings with the East German secret police were about to be exposed. Whatever the reasons for Bastian's heinous act, Kelly's vision was realised in the growing salience of environmental issues among the people of Europe; by 2019, 94 per cent of EU citizens described protecting the environment as important to them, while 83 per cent saw EU legislation as necessary for this purpose.[8] It

1. Danes vote 'yes' to the Maastricht Treaty at the second time of asking in May 1993. Impassioned debates in both referendum campaigns foreshadowed how hotly contested the politics of European integration would be in the post-Maastricht period.

2. Jacques Delors warns MEPs in February 1993 that the 'very idea of a united Europe could be in peril'. The European Commission President had deep misgivings about Maastricht and feared a resurgence of nationalism in the new European Union.

3. Sir James Goldsmith campaigns for a public vote on whether the UK should remain in the EU in January 1997. The Anglo-French billionaire's Referendum Party won no seats in the UK general election four months later, but his warnings that elites were 'seeking to destroy the identity of every European nation' inspired a new generation of right-wing populists.

4. European Commissioner for Culture Viviane Reding attends the Cannes Film Festival in May 2001. The EU's MEDIA programme contributed to the growth of cross-border film and TV productions. These European works didn't serve a federalist agenda, as some had feared, but they were critically acclaimed and widely watched by EU citizens.

5. Václav Havel meets European Commission President Jacques Delors in March 1991. The Czech dissident turned Head of State initially called for a new Confederation for Europe, but he and other Central and Eastern European leaders quickly made joining the EU a priority.

6. Prime Minister Leszek Miller and Foreign Minister Włodzimierz Cimoszewicz sign Poland's Treaty of Accession in April 2003. EU leaders cooled on the idea of further enlargements after they welcomed twelve new member states in the 2000s. The Union's stop-start accession negotiations with Turkey were one consequence of this hesitancy.

7. Dutch 'no' voters celebrate the defeat of the European Constitution in June 2005. The Maastricht Treaty's 'leftovers' could have been quickly settled, but they triggered a decade of treaty revisions which aggravated rather than alleviated the problems of legitimacy facing the enlarged EU.

8. Michael O'Leary campaigns for a 'yes' vote in Ireland's second referendum on the Lisbon Treaty in October 2009. The Ryanair CEO said he had 'nearly died of boredom' reading the treaty, which salvaged most of the European Constitution. And yet, he proved a powerful advocate for the Union despite earlier criticisms of European officials for acting like they were in 'fucking North Korea'.

9. Wim Kok, Social Democratic prime minister of the Netherlands, welcomes the UK's new Labour prime minister, Tony Blair, to Amsterdam in June 1997. The Third Way helped left-wing parties to regain power in the 1990s, but this influential political philosophy asked little of the EU. The global financial crisis that began in 2007 returned Social Democrats to the political wilderness in many member states.

10. Soldiers on patrol outside the European Commission's Berlaymont headquarters in February 2015. The EU stepped up cross-border cooperation on justice and home affairs in response to 9/11 and terrorist attacks in Belgium, France and Spain, but it faced criticisms from civil liberty groups for eroding Europeans' right to privacy.

11. A young refugee goes about her daily life in the Mória camp on the Greek island of Lesvos in June 2015. Reports that the EU had lost control of its borders during this period were overstated, but this narrative, and the harsh policies it produced, showed how much right-wing populism had been mainstreamed in Europe.

12. EU High Representative Federica Mogherini and Iranian Foreign Minister Mohammad Javad Zarif present the Iran nuclear deal to the world's press in July 2015. When US President Donald Trump withdrew his country's support two years later, Mogherini scrambled to save an agreement that the EU had spent more than a decade negotiating.

13. Gisela Stuart, Boris Johnson and Michael Gove hold a sombre press conference after the UK's referendum vote to leave the EU in June 2016. Johnson had agonised over which side to support before lending his star power to Leave. Having promised 'intense and intensifying European cooperation', the former Brussels journalist backed a hard Brexit and realised his ambition to be prime minister.

14. Hungarian Prime Minister Viktor Orbán is questioned by MEPs in January 2017 over his commitment to democracy and the rule of law. The Commission and European Parliament struggled to uphold the EU's fundamental values without stronger backing from the Heads of State or Government, who remained reluctant to confront one of their own.

15. Greta Thunberg, founder of the School Strike for Climate, addresses the European Parliament's Environment Committee in April 2019. The EU helped to forge a High Ambition Coalition within the United Nations Framework Convention on Climate Change, but it s efforts didn't go far enough for the Swedish activist, who warned MEPs that 'our house is on fire'.

16. The Party for Freedom's Geert Wilders, the Northern League's Matteo Salvini and National Rally's Marine Le Pen share a platform before the 2019 European Parliament elections. The EU proved a soft target for right-wing populists, who capitalised on the Union's handling of global crises and public disquiet over European integration and globalisation.

17. Ursula von der Leyen (centre) discusses the EU's response to the Covid-19 pandemic with Mark Rutte, Angela Merkel, Giuseppe Conte, Charles Michel and Emmanuel Macron in July 2020. The European Commission President helped to overcome the Union's early disjointed response to coronavirus, but she took her political cue from national leaders.

18. President of Ukraine Volodymyr Zelenskyy addresses an extraordinary session of the European Parliament by video link in March 2022. The EU had misread the risks from a resurgent Russia, despite warnings from Central and Eastern European leaders, but the Union moved rapidly to provide military aid to Zelenskyy and temporary protection to Ukrainian refugees. Whether the war-torn country would ever join the EU remained unclear, even after it was declared a candidate for membership.

19. António Costa, Emmanuel Macron, Roberta Metsola and Ursula von der Leyen participate in the closing ceremony of the Conference on the Future of Europe in May 2022. 'If we as citizens have been capable of working together and reaching a consensus you can and must do the same,' Jorge Pazos, a delegate from the Canary Islands, told the leaders.

20. Athens after May Day protests in 2013. The EU neither became a superstate after Maastricht nor withered in the face of nationalism. The Heads of State or Government stood together in times of global turmoil, even if they did not always live up to the ideals of unity, solidarity and harmony embodied by the circle of stars on the European flag.

was realised in the growing strength of the Greens/European Free Alliance, which won 67 seats and nearly 20 million votes in the 2019 European Parliament elections. It was also realised in the Heads of State or Government's willingness to put environment policy at the heart of the European project. European environmental policy began at the Paris Summit in 1972 and gathered strength in the Single European Act, yet it found form in the Maastricht Treaty, which included 'respecting the environment' among the EU's over-arching aims.[9]

World Leader Pro Tempore

By the late 1980s, the European Community had a reputation as an environmental laggard, reflecting divisions between its member states. Helmut Kohl wanted concerted action at Community level but not at the expense of West German industry.[10] Margaret Thatcher, who had worked as a research scientist before dedicating herself to politics, identified global warming as a growing concern in a speech to the Royal Geographical Society in 1988, but the UK prime minister was more interested in cutting back 'endless regulation' in the European Community than championing new laws to protect the environment.[11] François Mitterrand declared his love of nature but he demonstrated little practical interest in French environmental policy.[12] Consequently, expectations were low when European Commission President Jacques Delors appointed Carlo Ripa di Meana as Commissioner for the Environment in 1989, yet the Italian brought the same energy to this portfolio as he had done to cultural policy in Delors' first term.

Eager to make his mark, Ripa di Meana put forward a flurry of proposals designed to raise environmental standards at home and the EU's standing abroad. He backed the creation of the European Environmental Agency to offer independent scientific advice and took legal action against the UK over the quality of drinking water and environmentally contentious impact assessments on road-building projects in Oxleas Woods and Twyford Down, earning plaudits from protesters and a nickname, 'the Grim Ripa', in the British press.[13] Ripa di Meana also sought to increase the Community's influence in international environmental conferences, especially those organised by the United Nations, which remained reluctant to give the European Commission a seat at the top table. Praised for his role in negotiations on the Basel Convention on hazardous waste, Ripa di Meana pushed for the right to attend and speak on behalf of the European Community at the UN Earth Summit in Rio de Janeiro in 1992.

Rio built on two decades of stop-start discussions within the UN among industrialised and developing countries. It was the first Earth Summit since the UN Intergovernmental Panel on Climate Change published its inaugural assessment report. Reflecting the state of scientific consensus on this subject, this study concluded that human activities were substantially increasing the atmospheric concentration of greenhouse gases and predicted, under its business-as-usual scenario, that the global mean temperature would rise by 3 degrees Celsius above pre-industrial levels by the end of the twenty-first century. The 1987 Montreal Protocol raised expectations about environmental diplomacy, as did George H.W. Bush's promise to be America's 'environmental president'.[14] Bush made good on this pledge by securing sweeping amendments to the Clean Air Act, but he soon abandoned his environmentalism after incurring the wrath of industry groups and his own Republican Party. The United States, he made clear in advance of the summit, would not accept binding limits on greenhouse gases. Dismayed but still determined to act, Ripa di Meana presented the European Community as the world's global environmental leader pro tempore. He had already convinced European environment ministers to adopt a target for stabilising greenhouse gas emissions at 1990 levels and proposed an ambitious new carbon tax, the first of its kind among industrial economies. In presenting his proposals for this tax, Ripa di Meana called on Japan and the United States to follow the European Community's lead. The Commissioner's more immediate problem was that he lacked support from some EU member states and fell foul of the rest when he sought to dilute his proposal. Having repeatedly threatened to boycott the Earth Summit without an agreement in principle on a carbon tax, Ripa di Meana sent his director-general to Rio instead. 'I have decided not to go to a conference where it seems everything or virtually everything has been arranged,' he told reporters, calling for an environment policy 'based on binding obligations and precise undertakings, not on words'.[15]

'What shall we do without Carlo?' asked the British environmentalist David Nicholson-Lord after Ripa di Meana announced his resignation.[16] Although Jacques Delors mooted the idea of repatriating powers over environmental policy to member states after the fallout over Rio, Ripa di Meana won this argument in absentia. The 1992 Earth Summit may have failed to deliver binding commitments on the reduction of greenhouse gases, yet it created a framework for future negotiations which the EU proved determined to lead. The European Commission played an important role in these negotiations, not because it found a way to work around uncooperative member states, but because a new generation of national leaders who took environmental issues and the electoral threat from green parties more seriously won office and looked to the Union to do more. A key actor in this respect was Germany's youthful environment minister Angela Merkel, who took the chair when the parties to the United Nations Framework Convention on Climate Change met in Berlin in April 1995 to take stock of progress since the Rio Earth Summit. With a PhD in quantum chemistry, Merkel easily grasped the science of climate change; however, it was her talent for summitry which came to the fore in Berlin, as she skilfully built consensus between the 160 countries present about the need for binding commitments to reduce greenhouse gas emissions. The EU not only participated as a full member in these talks, but also bolstered Merkel's efforts for an ambitious deal by proposing that industrialised countries reduce greenhouse gas emissions by 15 per cent of 1990 levels.[17] The United States, in contrast, argued that emissions should be stabilised and insisted that developing countries be part of any deal, perhaps because it knew that poorer countries would baulk at the economic costs of doing so.

In May 1996, the EU became the first international organisation to insist that global temperature rises be limited to 2 degrees Celsius above pre-industrial levels. Hitherto, economists and atmospheric scientists had used this target as a crude proxy for the point at which global warming would do extreme and irrevocable harm to the planet. After this aim was endorsed by Merkel and other EU environment ministers, it became the benchmark against which global environmental diplomacy would be judged and an indelible marker of Europe's influence on this policy domain. Crucial too was the EU's willingness to lead by example by accepting deep cuts to greenhouse gas emissions.

Before the Conference of Parties in Kyoto in 1997, the EU announced that it was prepared to cut greenhouse gas emissions by 15 per cent from their 1990 level by 2010.[18] That member states reached an agreement on this goal despite their initial differences was a testament to their capacity for deliberation and consensus-seeking. Germany, the Netherlands and Denmark were most ambitious. All three had high environmental standards and feared for their international economic competitiveness unless their trading partners took climate change more seriously. They were supported by two of the EU's newest member states, Finland and Sweden, which had been in the vanguard of international action on climate change since the 1960s. Belgium, France, Italy, Luxembourg and the UK were more hesitant, fearing that their failure to raise environmental standards earlier would impose excessive burdens now. The EU's poorest member states, Greece, Ireland, Portugal and Spain, opposed measures that could harm their economic development. It fell to the Netherlands – a country that was uniquely sensitive to rising sea levels – to find a way forward. Using her country's presidency of the EU, Margreeth de Boer, the Dutch environment minister, drew member states out on how far they were willing to go and convinced many to go further.[19]

By demonstrating that sovereign states with different interests and domestic politics could forge a common response to climate change, the EU made a major contribution to Kyoto.[20] The United States, having initially sought only to stabilise greenhouse gases by 2010, agreed to cuts of 7 per cent, compared to 6 per cent in Japan and 8 per cent in the EU. That the EU couldn't speak with one voice was a recurring criticism from US policy-makers, but it was the Union and its member states that swiftly ratified the Kyoto Protocol, while the United States spoke in tongues. President Bill Clinton signed the agreement and then refused to submit it to Congress without 'meaningful participation by key developing countries'.[21] His successor, George W. Bush, shared none of his father's environmental instincts and made clear his 'unwillingness to embrace a flawed treaty'.[22] The Kyoto Protocol was 'dead', National Security Advisor Condoleezza Rice told European ambassadors in March 2001.[23] The EU carried on, convincing Vladimir Putin to secure the treaty's ratification in exchange for supporting Russia's accession to the WTO, and pressing ahead with the EU Emissions Trading Scheme, a pioneering attempt to reduce greenhouse gases through a cap and trade system.[24]

Thus emboldened, the EU set its sight on a successor to the Kyoto Protocol. The convergence in views among national leaders was striking. Tony Blair was a late convert to environmentalism but, as he approached the end of his time in Downing Street, he compared climate change to fascism and proposed legislation designed to cut UK emissions by 60 per cent by 2050.[25] A faint smell of fossil fuel had always followed Gerhard Schröder, in spite of his commitment to Kyoto, but his successor as German chancellor, Angela Merkel, cut a far more credible figure after her successful stint as environment minister.[26] She also found an ally in French President Nicolas Sarkozy, who had struggled to win support at home for his ambitious environmental pledges and so revived the idea of an EU carbon tax.[27] Although such pledges were partly performative, they reflected a growing political consensus about the EU's role in combatting climate change. Try as some Eurosceptic parties did to poison the well of environmental politics, 62 per cent of Europeans counted climate change among the most serious problems facing the Union.[28] Even a Martian could see, UK opposition leader David Cameron told an audience in Brussels, that the EU should be focusing on 'the environmental challenge of climate change'.[29] Three decades after Petra Kelly spoke at Wyhl, the environment had become, as scholars Louise Van Schaik and Simon Schunz put it, the EU's 'saviour issue'.[30]

The accession of Austria, Finland and Sweden in 1995 raised expectations about EU environmental policy. The Big Bang enlargement of the 2000s lowered it. The EU's newest member states were mostly poorer than Greece, Ireland, Portugal and Spain had been when they joined the European Community and far more dependent in some cases on fossil fuels. Around 97 per cent of electricity generated in Poland, for instance, came from burning coal and lignite.[31] And yet, the EU's aspirations of global leadership on climate change were largely undimmed, as preparations for a post-Kyoto agreement intensified. In March 2007, the Heads of State or Government made 'a firm independent commitment' to reduce greenhouse gas emissions by 20 per cent by 2020 relative to 1990 levels.[32] They also endorsed cuts of 30 per cent if industrialised economies and a sufficient number of developing countries signed up to a sufficiently ambitious deal.

Countering past criticisms that the EU's negotiating positions lacked credibility, EU environment ministers and the European Parliament agreed to binding legislation which committed the Union as a whole to 20 per cent cuts in greenhouse gases, a 20 per cent share of renewables in energy consumption and 20 per cent greater energy efficiency by 2020.[33] 'Any package with a title of matching 20 numbers has got to be primarily political,' argued one economist, but it was no less bold an exercise in environmental diplomacy for this.[34] The potential for political deadlock within the EU was significant. Poland's prime minister Donald Tusk, for one, faced significant domestic opposition from his country's powerful coal industry and over the potential for substantially higher consumer electricity prices. However, rather than veto the climate change package, he made common cause with the leaders of other Central and Eastern European member states and put their collective concerns to Nicolas Sarkozy, who was determined to conclude France's six-month presidency of the EU with a deal. EU leaders finally agreed to stick with the 20-20-20 targets, while offering leeway to the EU's newest member states.[35] While these and other concessions were criticised for diluting the deal, it still went far beyond anything considered by the EU's international partners.

Billed by EU Environment Commissioner Stavros Dimas as the 'world's last chance', the Conference of Parties in Copenhagen in December 2009 brought 120 Heads of State or Government, 10,500 delegates and 13,500 observers to the Danish capital to hammer out a post-Kyoto agreement.[36] The prevailing mood was one of 'cautious optimism' – not least because of the EU's pre-commitments – making the summit's anticlimactic conclusion all the greater.[37] In his inaugural address on the steps of the United States Capitol, President Barack Obama promised to respond to 'the threat of climate change, knowing that the failure to do so would betray our children and future generations'.[38] In the halls of Copenhagen's Bella Centre, he told EU leaders that their plans for binding emissions targets were unworkable and left for a meeting with the leaders of Brazil, China, India and South Africa to strike a deal based on general principles, ill-defined national commitments and some new money for developing countries. To Obama's credit, he read the room correctly and judged that a non-binding accord was preferable to non-agreement. To the EU's dismay, its delegates weren't even in the room as the US president made this calculation.

In the days following the summit, German Environment Minister Norbert Röttgen and his British counterpart Ed Miliband pinned the blame on China for blocking a deal that many developed countries and most developing ones wanted.[39] But the EU drew heavy flak for its 'herbivorous' approach to negotiations.[40] 'The EU frankly doesn't have the political clout to determine the outcome at Copenhagen,' concluded Peter Haas, a professor of environmental politics.[41] EU scholars were also scathing. After 'saving the Kyoto protocol', concluded Karin Bäckstrand and Ole Elgström, the EU 'came to Copenhagen with a strong normative agenda, unrealistic expectations, a miscalculation of the geopolitical context and without offering additional unilateral concessions'.[42] The EU's failure to convince developing countries and lingering doubts over the commitment of all member states to the 20-20-20 targets were 'inconvenient truths', suggested researchers Charles F. Parker and Christer Karlsson.[43]

No stranger to such reproaches, the EU invested its energies after Copenhagen not in internal recriminations but in recalibrating its environmental diplomacy. Previously, the EU had offered significant cuts to emissions upfront in the hope that the United States and other major players would follow. The EU's pledge in October 2014 to cut greenhouse gas emissions by at least 40 per cent by 2030 was consistent with this approach; however, the Union broke from past practice with its attempt to build a broad-based alliance in support of an ambitious global deal.[44] A breakthrough came at the Conference of Parties in Durban in November 2011, when the EU jointly agreed with Australia, Norway and Switzerland to extend their commitment to the soon-to-expire Kyoto Protocol until 2020. In return, all parties agreed to seek a new global agreement with 'legal force' to take effect in 2020. The EU also found unlikely allies in small, low-lying island nations.[45] These countries lacked economic weight and political power, but their vulnerability to rising tides embodied the existential challenges of climate change. European Environment Commissioner Miguel Arias Cañete's visit to the Pacific Islands Leaders Forum in Papua New Guinea was part of this new diplomatic strategy, as was the EU's practical support to Samoa, the Solomon Islands and Vanuatu in submitting their emission reduction plans and other climate actions to the UN.[46] The EU also provided support to Marshall Islands Foreign Minister Tony de Brum, a uniquely talented politician who could make the case for a global deal in a way that few Europeans could match.

Cañete was comfortable in smoke-filled rooms; his visits to Morocco, Brazil and Ecuador helped to build support for the EU's approach to climate change, but as a patrician politician with family ties to Spanish oil companies, he lacked moral authority. When

Jean-Claude Juncker nominated Cañete to the environment port-folio, environmental campaigners called him 'Señor Petrolhead' and cried foul.[47] As a boy, de Brum lived through 105 nuclear tests by the United States in and around the Marshall Islands, informing his efforts, as an adult, to hold the world's nine nuclear powers to account in the International Court of Justice, and his commitment to environmental politics more generally. Critics questioned whether the EU was using the Marshall Islands as 'moral cover', but such criticisms downplayed de Brum's success at winning the EU and others over to his argument that global temperature rises must be limited to 1.5 per cent to avoid an environmental catastrophe.[48]

At the Conference of Parties in Paris in December 2015, the extent of the EU's diplomatic efforts since Copenhagen became apparent. With three days to go, Cañete and de Brum held a joint press conference to announce that more than 90 countries had pledged their support for a binding global agreement and rigorous procedures for tracking and reviewing states' emissions commitments.[49] De Brum, as head of this High Ambition Coalition, sat at the centre of the dais, flanked by German Environment Minister Barbara Hendricks, her counterparts from Colombia, Gambia and Mexico, and Giza Gaspar-Martins, the Angolan chief negotiator of the Least Developed Countries group. Todd Stern, the United States Special Envoy for Climate Change, was conspicuous by his presence, reflecting Barack Obama's disappointment at the deal he brokered in Copenhagen and his determination to do better before leaving office. 'It is a kind of performance. It makes no difference,' responded Chinese Vice Foreign Minister Liu Jianmin when asked about the EU's diplomatic efforts.[50] And yet, the High Ambition Coalition gained members and momentum and upped the pressure on China to engage more constructively than it had done in Copenhagen. At the closing plenary, Cañete and de Brum led coalition members into the auditorium at Paris le Bourget. Pausing for the press before entering the room, the Commissioner looked around and asked, 'Where's the American?'. 'Welcome, Todd. Let's go,' cried Cañete, as Stern slowly made his way to the front row.[51]

The Paris Agreement offered a complex and heavily caveated commitment by the parties to the United Nations Framework Convention on Climate Change to limit global temperature rises to 'well below' 2 degrees Celsius, while seeking efforts to lower this limit to 1.5 degrees Celsius.[52] This agreement would not have been possible without China and the United States. By committing the United States to reduce emissions by between 26 and 28 per cent below their 2005 level by 2025 and China to reach peak emissions by 2035, the joint announcement on climate change by Barack Obama and Chinese President Xi Jinping in 2014 was a major step towards the final agreement.[53] However, Obama and Xi walked a path that had been partially forged by two decades of EU environmental diplomacy. This effort didn't begin and end in Brussels, but by showing how heterogenous states could find common ground on climate change and building an even bigger coalition of developed and developing countries, the EU made a decisive contribution to the final deal.

Energiewende

On 23 July 2002, two Brussels security guards lowered and folded the blue-black flag of the European Coal and Steel Community at a discrete ceremony in front of the Breydel building, and handed it to Enrico Gibellieri, President of the Consultative Committee, who passed it to Commission President Romano Prodi.[54] The history of European integration is a chronicle of deaths prematurely foretold, but on this occasion, one of the three Communities on which it was founded was formally dissolved. This moment had been envisaged in the Treaty of Paris (1951), which provided for its own expiry after a half-century, by which point the European Coal and Steel Community had long faded from view. While it inspired the European Economic Community and the European Atomic Energy Community in 1957 and the EU in 1992, the founding Community failed to establish a genuine common market for coal and steel. Member states preferred to nurture national coal and steel industries, even if this resulted in over-supply and under-competitiveness, and this practice continued until coal consumption declined and steel imports from developing countries became more cost-effective. The few remaining functions carried out by the European Coal and Steel Community could be more easily done by the European Economic Community, the Commission concluded in 1991. Euratom, having no expiry date, remained, but it was 'of little consequence for most Member States, apart from France', concluded EU scholar Pamela Barnes.[55] The Community's fortieth birthday in 1997 went largely unnoticed, amid public celebrations and criticisms of its better-known twin.

Energy was central to the EU's origins, yet it seemed to be of declining relevance to its future by the 1990s. The EU's environmental concerns and ambitions reversed this trend, as member states embraced renewable energy with varying degrees of enthusiasm. Germany set the pace, providing generous subsidies to hydro, wind and solar energy producers and biofuel firms. This *Energiewende* (energy transformation) was underway before the Fukushima nuclear accident, but it was utterly changed by it. On the afternoon of 11 March 2011, an earthquake registering 9.1 megawatts – one of the largest on record – struck off the coast of northeast Japan, causing a 14-metre tsunami. These twin catastrophes set in motion a Level 7 meltdown at the Fukushima Daiichi Nuclear Power Plant, in response to which 150,000 people were evacuated from their homes. More than 14,000 kilometres away, in Germany, this accident revived memories of Chernobyl and an anti-nuclear movement still active since the days of Petra Kelly. Following mass demonstrations and a surprise election victory for the Greens in her party's stronghold, Baden-Württemberg, Angela Merkel faced intense pressure to act. Hitherto, the chancellor had resisted the Social Democrats and the Greens' pledge to phase out nuclear power. Now she announced that her government would take all nuclear plants offline by 2022. Merkel had already committed at this point to making renewables the largest component of Germany's energy mix by 2050 while using nuclear power as a 'bridging technology'.[56] This bridge was now hastily dismantled.

In less than a decade after Fukushima, Germany went from having no turbines in the North and Baltic Seas to being the world's second-biggest producer of offshore wind power.[57] A rapid growth in photovoltaics, especially in southern Germany, increased solar energy capacity by 30,000 megawatts between 2010 and 2016. Thanks to such investments, the share of renewables in the country's primary energy consumption rose from 4.2 per cent in 2000 to 15.0 per cent in 2019.[58] That nearly three-quarters of Germany's energy mix still came from fossil fuels by the end of this period was partly due to the gap left by nuclear energy, but it also reflected the German government's continuing reliance on coal and gas.[59] West Germany had started to phase out domestic coal production in the 1950s as imported coal and oil provided more competitive sources of energy.[60] However, it was not until 2020 that the Bundestag passed a law to phase out coal-fired power stations over eighteen years; the opening of the brand new Datteln 4 power plant that year illustrated just how long this lead time was.[61] Like her predecessors, Merkel remained steadfast in her commitment to natural gas, both as a standalone energy source and a new 'bridge' to renewables.[62] This choice was a pragmatic one, but it exacted a heavy toll on the environment and Europe's energy security.

By 1993, Germany was importing around 40 per cent of its natural gas from Russia and it grew no less dependent in the three decades that followed.[63] The member states that joined the Union in the 1990s and 2000s were more dependent still. Estonia, Latvia and Lithuania remained on the Russian power grid and secured 100 per cent of natural gas imports from the privatised remnants of the Soviet gas ministry, Gazprom. The Commission sounded a silent alarm over this situation in 2000, promoting cooperation with Russia in a Green Paper on energy security while inviting EU member states to consider whether they should do more to stockpile gas reserves. EU energy ministers showed little desire to cooperate in this sensitive domain and instead did what they could on a country-by-country basis to protect their energy security. Six years later, amid tensions between

Moscow and Kyiv's new pro-Western government, Gazprom cut supplies to Ukraine, causing supplies to Austria, Germany, France, Hungary and Poland to drop by up to a third. When tensions between Russia and Ukraine flared up again in 2009, sixteen EU member states saw their gas imports stop entirely.

The Lisbon Treaty gave the EU a new role in promoting energy security and solidarity, but both goals remained elusive. In 2011, BASF, E.ON and Gazprom completed the first phase of Nordsteam, allowing gas to flow from Vyborg in Russia to Lubmin in Germany under the Baltic Sea. While this route allowed Germany to bypass Ukraine, it also circumvented existing pipelines to and through EU members in the Baltics and Central and Eastern Europe. As prime minister of one of the states affected, Poland's Donald Tusk was especially concerned. His call for an energy union in which the EU would negotiate gas contracts on behalf of member states was publicly presented as a way to 'confront Russia's monopolistic position'.[64] However, it betrayed fears of oligopsony in which some EU member states had more buying power than others. In 2015, by then president of the European Council, Tusk convinced the Heads of State or Government to sign up for an energy union, but it bore little resemblance to his original proposal.[65] Member states agreed instead to reduce their energy dependence while notifying each other of bilateral negotiations on gas contracts.

'Spoiled Irresponsible Children'

In August 2018, Greta Thunberg, a 15-year-old Swedish girl, skipped class to sit outside the Riksdag with a sign that read 'school strike for climate'. Cross-posting a picture of herself on social media, she added a caption: 'We children don't usually do what you grown-ups tell us to do. We do as you do. And since you don't give a shit about my future. I don't give a shit either.' A week later, Thunberg was joined by classmates, teachers and parents. Her daily protests continued until the Swedish general election and thereafter she returned to parliament every Friday. Three months later, 17,000 students in 24 countries joined a Fridays for Future protest to call for action on climate change. In September 2019, an estimated 4 million people in 153 countries took to the streets in support of this movement on the same day.[66]

Thunberg's original protest was aimed at the Swedish government, which she saw as falling short of its commitments to the Paris Agreement. But her arguments added up to a more fundamental critique of the contradictions inherent in European environmental politics. In 2017, Sweden had passed legislation promising to achieve net-zero carbon emissions by 2045, putting it in the global vanguard of climate action. Thunberg's central thesis was that this was not enough to achieve the Paris Agreement's headline goal of keeping the global rise in temperature well below 2 degrees Celsius; instead countries such as the UK and Sweden needed to reduce emissions by at least 15 per cent per year to achieve this goal.[67] In 2018, as the country experienced devastating wildfires and its warmest summer on record, Sweden's emissions had risen by 0.5 per cent. Why, Thunberg asked, were people not treating this as an emergency? 'They keep saying that climate change is an existential threat and the most important of all,' she noted, 'and yet they just carry on as before.'[68]

For two decades, the EU had championed itself as a global environmental leader. Thunberg arrived in Brussels in February 2019 to puncture this claim. Speaking at Petra Kelly's alma mater, the Economic and Social Committee, surrounded by other Swedish schoolchildren, Thunberg dismissed claims by Miguel Arias Cañete and others that a 45 per cent cut in greenhouse gas emissions by 2030 – as compared with the 40 per cent pledged by the EU in advance of the Paris Summit – was within reach.[69] 'Some people say that is good or that is ambitious,' Thunberg said, 'but this new target is still not enough to keep global warming below 1.5 degrees Celsius . . . You can't just sit around waiting for hope to come, you're acting like spoiled irresponsible children.'[70]

Thunberg visited Strasbourg in April 2019 to tell MEPs that Europe's house was on fire. She visibly fought back tears as she told the hemicycle – packed with parliamentarians and their staffers – that 200 species were becoming extinct every day. Was it right to let a 16-year-old shoulder this burden, much less one with Asperger's syndrome? Were politicians exploiting Thunberg's growing renown to burnish their public profiles? Whatever the answers to these questions, there could be no doubting Thunberg's talents as a political and scientific communicator. Her speeches mixed emotional and moral appeals with cutting-edge scientific research. A British rock band, The 1975, even put a selection of the Swede's public remarks to music.

On social media, Thunberg responded to detractors with determination, humour and self-deprecation. When Vladimir Putin described her as 'a kind but poorly informed teenager', she included this phrase in her Twitter bio. When Brazil's president, Jair Bolsonaro, called her a *pirralha* (a brat), she did the same.[71] Environmental activism gave her life meaning, Thunberg argued, and her Asperger's syndrome informed her politics by understanding climate change 'in black or white terms' while others failed to see through the grey.[72]

Thunberg might have helped to recast environmental politics in Europe and beyond, yet she didn't act alone.[73] The Paris Agreement raised expectations about what states could do and drew attention to the 1.5 degrees Celsius target, for which Tony de Brum and others had long argued. US President Donald Trump's decision to withdraw the United States from the Paris Agreement played well with his supporters but it emboldened those who sought to defend the commitments made by the Conference of Parties in December 2015 and to go beyond them. Thunberg was not the only environmental activist who made a difference. In Belgium, Anuna De Wever rose to public prominence as an 18-year-old organiser of the Fridays for Future protests, forcing the resignation of a Flemish minister who falsely claimed that it was a political 'set up'.[74] In Portugal, 10-year-old Mariana Agostinho joined five other young environmental activists in taking all EU member states to the European Court of Human Rights for failing to meet their obligation on climate rights. Significantly, the litigants claimed that climate change had directly interfered with their right to life, their right to respect for family and private life and their right to non-discrimination, citing the heatwaves and forest fires experienced by Portugal as a result of climate change among their supporting evidence.[75] Nor was such passion wasted on the young. In the UK, 91-year-old John Lymes was arrested outside the Cabinet Office in October 2019 for participating in a display of civil disobedience by Extinction Rebellion.[76]

Growing public concern for the environment, driven in part by such activism, put pressure on European politicians to act. When Ursula von der Leyen appeared before the European Parliament in July 2019, as president-elect of the European Commission, she had little choice but to display her green credentials. She was more dependent than her predecessors on the votes of the Greens/European Free Alliance because of this party's strong showing in European Parliament elections three months earlier and her lukewarm support from socialist MEPs. Unimpressed by the president-elect's promise to be 'more ambitious' on climate change, the Greens/European Free Alliance announced their intention to vote against von der Leyen, who sought to save her candidacy by promising a green deal for Europe in her first 100 days in office.[77] Although this pledge was not sufficient to win around the Greens/European Free Alliance, in the end she secured sufficient support from other parties and kept climate change at the centre of her presidency.

Von der Leyen's European Green Deal was sweeping in its vision and blurred around the edges.[78] At its centre was a bold pledge to make the EU climate-neutral by 2050, meaning that it would produce no net emissions of greenhouse gases by mid-century. This goal would be codified in a proposed European Climate Law to reduce net greenhouse gas emissions by at least 55 per cent by 2030 compared to 1990 levels. Less clear was where the proposed €1 trillion in investment to help achieve these ambitious goals would come from and precisely how the EU could or would decouple economic growth from resource use, although a host of new strategies on topics ranging from biodiversity to an environmentally friendly food system were promised to square these aims. Instead of flinching at the European Green Deal, national leaders were broadly supportive, in keeping with their growing ambitions for European environmental policy since Maastricht. Only Poland's president Andrzej Duda refused to endorse the goal of making the EU climate-neutral by 2050, but this move was less about ideological differences than maintaining his leverage in negotiations over European funding to help coal-dependent regions move away from fossil fuels.[79] In December 2020, the Heads of State or Government gave their political backing to a new net emissions target designed to cut greenhouse gas emissions by 55 per cent by 2030 compared to 1990.[80] Thunberg remained unimpressed, describing these targets as 'surrender'[81] and called on environmental protesters to shine a light on how 'those who are seen as leaders are so unbelievably far from doing what is enough'.[82] Had she lived, Petra Kelly would surely have shared such scepticism.

11

Borders

Schengen (1995–2021)

On 25 March 1995, passengers arriving at Brussels Zaventem airport from Barcelona, Madrid and Malaga had to show their passports to border guards.[1] The following day, this decades-old requirement was dropped. Belgium, Luxembourg and the Netherlands had already eliminated border controls within their Benelux Union in 1970. When France and Germany announced their intention to do likewise in 1985, following protests by truck drivers over long delays at the Franco-German border, Benelux ministers proposed a joint endeavour.[2] Meeting on a riverboat moored in Schengen – a Luxembourg village hitherto known for its dry white wines, if at all – ministers from the five countries agreed to the 'gradual abolition of checks at their common borders'.[3]

It took five years of negotiations before the states agreed on a way to do this and a further five before this approach was implemented. By this point, Greece, Italy, Spain and Portugal had joined the so-called Schengen area, leaving Ireland and the UK as the only holdouts among EU member states. Although Prime Minister John Major had promised to put the UK at the heart of Europe, he was implacably opposed to any initiative which might be seen to weaken British control over British borders.[4] Successive Irish governments also chose to remain outside Schengen, determined both to preserve the country's common travel area with the UK and a soft border with Northern Ireland.[5]

230

The removal of border checks didn't materialise overnight. Drivers passing through Schengen to nearby Metz or Saarbrücken still faced checks, as governments tested a new information system to share data on persons and property in the interests of national security. Aside from occasional glitches, the Schengen Information System worked, but France's new Europe minister harboured serious concerns. Once known as the 'boy wonder' of Alpine politics, Michel Barnier had been elected to France's National Assembly aged 27 by the voters of Savoie, a mountainous region on the Franco-Italian border.[6] He had risen to national prominence as co-president of the 1992 Winter Olympics in Albertville, after which he joined the cabinet of Édouard Balladur as environment minister. There, Barnier cultivated a reputation as a plainspoken negotiator, who convinced the Ukrainian government to close the three remaining nuclear reactors at Chernobyl.[7] His message on Schengen was characteristically blunt. 'It is clear, particularly with regard to soft drugs, that the practices of certain member states, combined with the relaxation of border controls, was creating drug tourism,' Barnier told parliamentarians in 1995.[8] Without action to address this issue, he concluded, removing border controls was inconceivable.

The certain member state in question was the Netherlands, which had allowed cannabis to be sold and consumed in licenced coffee shops since the 1970s, as part of efforts to manage the risks associated with drug use. Jacques Chirac had scored points on the presidential campaign trail by publicly criticising the Dutch approach, even though his call for an EU-wide ban on the sale of all narcotics stood next to no chance of success. Dutch policy was built on a national consensus, which viewed drugs through a public health lens rather than a criminal justice one and sought to break the link between soft and hard drug usage. But Chirac showed no interest as French president in learning from this approach, preferring to pose as the law-and-order candidate at home and on the European stage.

Chirac's primary concern was that Schengen, an agreement inherited from his socialist predecessor, left him vulnerable to Jean-Marie

Le Pen's far-right populist Front National. Members of this right-wing populist party had protested on the Franco-Italian border on the day before the Schengen Implementing Convention entered into force. When the Armed Islamic Group of Algeria killed 8 and injured 157 in a series of improvised explosions across France in the summer of 1995, Le Pen saw an opportunity to capitalise further on anti-migrant sentiment.[9] Determined to protect Chirac's right flank, Barnier told the National Assembly that it was no longer possible to talk about free movement without taking into account the terrorist attacks that had happened in his country.[10]

For a while, it looked like Schengen might collapse, but this early storm blew over. Chirac mended fences with his Dutch counterpart, Wim Kok, who agreed to a series of non-binding EU declarations on drugs which allowed the French president to claim influence while making little practical difference to national policies.[11] France, meanwhile, quietly agreed to the removal of routine land border checks with Schengen partners, while continuing to stop travellers on an ad hoc basis. Occasional checks were permitted under Schengen within twenty kilometres of common borders where police feared threats to public safety. But national police forces' apparent use of racial profiling in such cases suggests that checks were motivated by prejudice as much as security concerns and that borders were more open for some Europeans than others.[12]

Denmark joined Schengen in 2001 because it was determined to preserve its pre-existing passport union with Finland and Sweden. And yet, the Danish government continued to absent itself from EU justice and home affairs under opt-outs secured in advance of the country's second referendum on the Maastricht Treaty. The political contradictions behind this position became apparent when the Amsterdam Treaty absorbed Schengen, turning this intergovernmental area of decision-making into a fully fledged EU policy. It was also manifest in Denmark's periodic decisions to introduce temporary border controls with other EU member states. The Schengen Agreement allowed for such controls but they had traditionally been used to manage crowds at international gatherings, be it Pope Benedict's tour of Malta or the Hells Angels' visit to Iceland.[13] The Danish government's decision to introduce border checks with Germany and Sweden in May 2011 without prior notice seemed to be driven instead by right-wing populists, who fanned public concern over cross-border crime from Central and Eastern Europe and demanded a government response.[14]

Such political machinations weren't limited to Denmark. Had he won re-election in May 2012, French President Nicolas Sarkozy would have found it difficult to wriggle out of a campaign promise to suspend his country's membership of Schengen pending reform to the EU's policies on immigration and asylum.[15] Michel Barnier offered a variation on this pledge in his short-lived run for the French presidency in 2021, when he promised to suspend all immigration to France for between three to five years while he renegotiated Schengen.[16] Although it provoked widespread criticism, Barnier's willingness to make this pledge showed the extent to which right-wing populist positions had become mainstreamed in European politics in the post-Maastricht period.

Of the thirteen countries that became EU members after 2000, nine joined the Schengen area, as they were obliged to do under the terms of accession. Slovenia's border dispute with Croatia delayed the latter's acceptance, as did EU concerns over irregular migration from Bosnia-Herzegovina. But Croatia's conservative prime minister Andrej Plenković used his good offices with the European People's Party, and reputation as a pro-EU reformer, to secure a positive decision in December 2021.[17] Cyprus, like Ireland, feared that removing border checks with EU members would complicate the search for peace on its island. After hopes of unification faded, Cypriot President Nicos Anastasiades finally applied to join Schengen in 2019.[18] Still, the Commission refused to take a quick decision on Cypriot accession, in part, because of the administrative challenges presented by the Green Line dividing the island.

In 1995, Dutch Prime Minister Wim Kok had found himself caught between Jacques Chirac and Jean-Marie Le Pen in debates over Schengen. Fifteen years later, it was Kok's successor as Dutch prime minister, Mark Rutte, who seemed to be running scared of right-wing populists. Taking a page from Chirac's playbooks, Rutte announced that he would veto Bulgaria and Romania's participation in Schengen because of what he saw as the failure of these member states to tackle corruption and organised crime.[19] Romanian President Traian Băsescu pushed back against Rutte, whom he saw as pandering to Geert Wilders, a right-wing populist who had demonised Bulgarian and Romanian workers in the Netherlands.[20] But Basescu's criticisms went unanswered.[21]

Freedom of Movement

Maastricht's signatories were strongly committed to free movement within the Union even if they shied away from removing checks on common borders. One of the treaty's key innovations was to grant EU citizenship to the roughly 350 million people living in the Union when Maastricht entered into force.[22] To some, this decision constituted another encroachment on national sovereignty, although EU citizenship was derived exclusively from national citizenship.[23] To others, the treaty drew another artificial dividing line between those born in the EU and immigrants, leading to further social stratification within the Union.[24]

EU citizens were given the right to vote and stand in municipal elections in any member state, and the right to move and reside freely within the territory of any EU country. Maastricht also reiterated the freedom of workers to seek and accept employment in another member state without discrimination based on grounds of nationality, twenty-five years after the Council of Ministers had enshrined this principle in legislation, if not always in practice.[25] When asked, EU citizens valued freedom of movement. In a Eurobarometer conducted in the spring of 1997, respondents aged between 15 and 24 years put the ability to go wherever they wanted at the top of the list when asked what Europe meant to them.[26] Among the population at large, the freedom to travel, study and work was consistently recognised as one of the most tangible benefits of European integration.[27]

Despite such public support, the number of EU citizens who exercised their right to free movement remained low.[28] So much so that in 1997 the European Commission invited Simone Veil, former president of the European Parliament and French Minister of Social Affairs, to prepare a report on how more Europeans could be encouraged to take advantage of their right to live and work in other countries.[29] That less than 1.5 per cent of EU nationals were resident in another member state, the Veil Report concluded, was due to a host of invisible barriers, ranging from difficulties accessing employment services to inadequate language training and unequal tax treatment. This view of EU citizens as home birds was also informed by the experience of past enlargements. When Portugal and Spain joined the European Communities in 1986, fears over mass migration from these comparatively poor countries to the rest of the EU proved unfounded. In fact, as political scientist Sebastian Royo notes, the number of Spanish and Portuguese residents in other member states in the decade after enlargement fell by more than 200,000.[30] Far from driving people abroad, the Iberian enlargement gave them the economic confidence to return home.

Twelve out of the fifteen EU member states introduced temporary restrictions on free movement in response to the Big Bang enlargement of May 2004. The governments of Ireland, Sweden and the UK had economic and political reasons for doing otherwise. All three were experiencing rates of economic growth above the EU average at the time, and all three had below-average unemployment rates.[31] Central and Eastern Europe's well-educated, low-paid workers offered a quick fix for the resulting labour shortages. The UK and Sweden were also led by Third Way prime ministers who saw free movement as a fact of life and anti-immigration rhetoric from right-wing populists as something to be tackled head-on. Speaking to the Confederation of British Industry in April 2004, UK Prime Minister Tony Blair acknowledged that immigration was a live issue, while defending his decision to open his country's labour market to nationals of the new member states.[32] There were already 100,000 people from Eastern Europe studying or working in the UK, which had half a million job vacancies, he told his audience. The choice was to 'use the opportunities of accession' or 'hold our economy back and in all likelihood see a significant increase in illegal working'. Swedish Prime Minister Göran Persson was less sure. Whereas Blair sought to face down his critics, Persson flip-flopped over the risks of 'welfare tourism'.[33] However, as head of a minority government, the prime minister lacked the votes to introduce temporary restrictions on free movement.[34]

Ireland's Taoiseach Bertie Ahern was a political chameleon, who had led a centre-right party for a decade, before declaring himself to be a committed socialist. He was steadfast in his allegiance to Irish business, which was in dire need of workers, as economic growth rebounded after the slowdown of the early 2000s. In the 1950s, and again in the 1980s, Irish people moved abroad in their tens of thousands in search of work, but this situation was reversed in the 1990s, as a long economic boom and falling unemployment created labour shortages in sectors such as agriculture, catering and construction. Between 2001 and 2004, Irish authorities issued more than 30,000 permits per year to nationals from outside the European Economic Area.[35] These numbers fell sharply after enlargement, which offered employers a deep and permanent pool of young, well-educated workers without the need for costly and time-consuming paperwork. There was little to be gained economically or politically from a transition period. Attempts by Anthony Coughlan and other 'no' campaigners to mobilise Irish public opinion against EU migration during Ireland's second referendum on the Nice Treaty had backfired, giving Ahern political licence over his handling of enlargement.[36]

For all their enthusiasm about free movement, Blair, Persson and Ahern assumed that immigration flows after the 2004 enlargement would be modest. These assumptions turned out to be badly wrong. One study commissioned by the UK Home Office on the eve of the Big Bang enlargement anticipated net migration flows of between

5,000 to 13,000 per year to the UK from the ten new member states up to 2010.[37] The forecast was heavily qualified because of the absence of robust data, but even so, it proved woefully inaccurate. Between 2004 and 2010, long-term net migration from Central and Eastern European member states to the UK increased by 353,000.[38] In the EU as a whole, nearly 3 million people moved between the EU's new and old member states between 2003 and 2008.

That so many new EU citizens chose to exercise their right to free movement shouldn't have been so surprising. Aside from Cyprus, Malta and Slovenia, the new member states had income levels below Portugal, the poorest country in the EU-15. The average standard of living in Bulgaria, Latvia, Lithuania, Poland and Romania was less than half the EU average.[39] Those who voted for EU membership in accession referendums typically believed in the economic gains from European integration.[40] And yet, few expected to reap such benefits overnight. In 2004, a minority of new member state nationals expected their circumstances to improve within twelve months.[41] Given the Heads of State or Government's determination to limit the cost of enlargement, EU financial support for new member states through the structural and cohesion funds would be a slow drip rather than a deluge.[42]

Previous waves of EU–UK migration had been piecemeal and focused disproportionately on London and surrounding regions, but those who arrived after 2004 were more likely to locate in the West Midlands and North West of England.[43] A case in point was Greater Manchester, which soon had more Polish inhabitants than many midsize Polish towns.[44] Blair's decision to avoid temporary restrictions on free movement was a significant pull factor, although not the only one. The UK economy's long boom and flexible labour market also played a role, as did the prevalence of English-language learning in Polish secondary schools and the presence of friends, family and recent immigrant networks.

Public opposition in the UK towards immigrants and immigration had steadily fallen in the two decades before the Big Bang enlargement, but this trend was reversed thereafter.[45] Right-wing tabloids played a part in this shift. In 2009, the Federation of Poles in Great Britain contacted the Press Complaints Commission over a series of articles in the *Daily Mail* which used expressions such as 'feckless', 'chancers', 'race riots', 'swamp the NHS', 'fears for schools', 'cut-price treatment', 'push British graduates to back of the jobs queue' and 'killers, drug smugglers and rapists' in stories concerning Polish people living in the UK.[46] The newspaper denied being 'anti-Polish', while agreeing to amend or remove certain articles.[47]

UK Independence Party leader Nigel Farage also drew repeated links between EU immigration and crime. When asked whether he would be concerned about having a group of Romanian men as neighbours, he replied 'if you lived in London, I think you would be'.[48] 'Let me be clear that UKIP is not a racist party,' wrote Farage in an open letter following the furore over his remarks, while reporting, inaccurately, that 92 per cent of all ATM crime committed in London was by Romanians.[49] In a survey conducted in May 1992, less than 5 per cent of respondents identified immigration as the most important issue facing Britain.[50] By May 2016, this figure had reached 38 per cent, ranking above every other issue.[51]

In 2002, nationals from the twelve member states that would join the EU later that decade accounted for 0.5 per cent of Ireland's population.[52] By 2008, this figure had risen to 4.5 per cent.[53] The biggest share of new arrivals came from Poland, the largest of the new member states, followed by Lithuania, one of the smallest. Although the latter had become one of the fastest-growing economies in Central and Eastern Europe, unemployment remained stubbornly high after the Russian financial crisis of the late 1990s. More than 1 per cent of Lithuania's entire population moved to Ireland in the space of two years. Central and Eastern European migrants to Ireland experienced acts of discrimination and outright racism but nothing like the tabloid backlash witnessed in the UK at this time.[54] On the contrary, Dublin's *Evening Herald* boosted its circulation by publishing *Polski Herald*, a weekly Polish-language supplement.[55]

The economic gains to Ireland and the UK from the EU's Big Bang enlargement were considerable. The new member state nationals who arrived after 2004 had higher skill levels and higher rates of economic activity on average than their Irish and British counterparts. They came to work, not draw welfare, adding an estimated 1.0 per cent to the UK's growth potential, and up to 3.0 per cent to Ireland's.[56] The benefits for the new member states were less clear cut. Although emigration provided a safety valve for Central and Eastern European countries which entered the EU with very high unemployment, population outflows led to a permanent loss in output potential in Lithuania, among other new member states.[57]

Economic data painted only part of the picture. They didn't capture the sense of dislocation and detachment experienced by those who left their homes in search of work. Or how Hungarian schools, Lithuanian mass and Latvian festivals became a feature of Irish and British life. Sporting events convey the scale and pace of change. When the Polish men's football team arrived in Dublin in May 1991 for a UEFA European Championship qualifier, they passed through Dublin Airport without fanfare. When their successors returned fourteen years later, they were greeted with bread and salt, Polish symbols of homecoming.[58] Red flares filled Lansdowne Road before kick-off, giving the match the look and feel of a local derby. Within a few short years, Olaf Boruc, Hugo Gwiazdowski and Patryck Swieczka Andrzejczak lined out for the Republic of Ireland's youth team, all three born in Ireland to Polish parents. When Emma Raducanu, whose Romanian father brought her to live in the UK in 2004, won the US Open Tennis Championships in 2021, Nigel Farage tweeted his congratulations and called her a 'global megastar'.[59] 'He won't be able to afford to live next door,' responded Gary Lineker, a former England football captain.[60]

The societal impact of EU enlargement is portrayed in two films, John Carney's *Once* (2007) and Piotr Domalewski's *I Never Cry* (2021). Filmed on handheld cameras on a shoestring, Oscar-winning *Once* tells the story of an unnamed Czech immigrant to Ireland, who works as a cleaner and sells magazines and flowers on Dublin's Grafton Street. There she meets a busker, who works in his father's Hoover repair shop. The woman returns the next day with her broken vacuum cleaner, which she wheels through the city, as she and the busker discuss their shared passion for music. They play together and fall in love, but the woman stays true to her Czech husband, who remains reluctant to join her and the couple's daughter in Ireland. What happens between the woman and the busker goes largely unspoken. They connect, cultural theorist Marita Ryan argues, through music, which provides a 'creative space' and site of 'friendship and understanding'.[61]

Carney acknowledges the difficult living conditions endured by many new member state migrants, yet *Once* provides only glimpses of their precarious working conditions and what happened to the loved ones they left behind.[62] *I Never Cry* tells the story of Ola Hudzik, a Polish teenager who travels to Dublin to bring home the remains of her father, Christoph, whom she barely knew. Although Christoph was killed by a falling shipping container, his family are not entitled to compensation, Ola learns, because he worked a second shift under another colleague's name in breach of the 'European Union standard'. 'It turns out everyone was doing it,' his Irish foreman admits.

Domalewski describes a world in which Europe is integrated economically but not socially. Christoph lives his life with other EU migrants, whom he depends on for companionship, accommodation and employment while sending money to his daughter, disabled son and wife in Olsztyn. 'What was he like?' Ola asks. 'Like everybody else, they're not really here. It is very hard to get to know someone when they are somewhere else.' Despite this dark portrait of EU enlargement, *I Never Cry* holds out hope of sorts. Seeing Ola's distress, a group of Irish teenagers invite her to a pub, where they drink Guinness with vodka chasers until sunrise. A bacchanalian evening, it is also a shared experience between young Europeans.

The Global Refugee Crisis (2015)

The idea of a borderless EU was always a myth. As well as their contingent commitment to free movement within the Union, member states manage and protect the EU's external border with the rest of the world. In 1990, the Schengen states introduced a common visa system for third-country nationals entering their shared territory. In the same year, the twelve member states of the then European Community signed the Dublin Convention, which sought to prevent individuals from claiming asylum in more than one country. One member state would be responsible for assessing an individual's claim for asylum. The criteria for deciding such responsibility were complex. However, an individual entering the EU irregularly – with the aid of people smugglers, for example – would generally be transferred back to the first member state in which they set foot to have their asylum claim assessed. Maastricht provided for cooperation on immigration and asylum policy but steered clear of such specificities. While the EU as a whole faced rising asylum claims due to events in Eastern Europe and the former Yugoslavia, the Heads of State or Government were divided on how to respond. Helmut Kohl favoured a centralised response.[63] As head of an affluent member state bordering Central and Eastern Europe, Germany feared that it would receive a disproportionate share of migrants. The UK shared such concerns, with Prime Minister John Major facing pressure from within his own Conservative Party to take a tougher line on asylum policy.

Between 1992 and 1996, the annual rate of asylum claims to the EU fell from 672,385 to 227,805.[64] This trend was soon reversed, as Slobodan Milošević's forces displaced hundreds of thousands of ethnic Albanians in Kosovo. In the Amsterdam, Nice and Lisbon Treaties, member states agreed on what they had been unable to do at Maastricht, by creating a fully fledged EU immigration and asylum policy and new rules for processing asylum claims. By the mid-2000s, all EU members except Bulgaria, Cyprus, Croatia, Ireland, Romania and the UK were part of Schengen and all except Denmark had signed up to the Dublin Convention, which was now part of EU law. Eurodac, a database which fingerprinted all asylum seekers and irregular migrants entering the Union, was also operational.

An early warning over the fraught politics of EU asylum policy occurred in December 1997 when, on the day after Christmas, a ship carrying hundreds of Kurdish refugees from Turkey and Iraq docked at Badolato on Italy's Ionian coast. When a similar incident occurred six months earlier, Italian authorities quickly deported the individuals, but two things had changed in the interim. First, Schengen and Dublin had become fully operational in Italy, meaning that the country's authorities were now under an obligation to assess asylum claims. Second, encouraged by the Catholic Church, Italian public opinion shifted towards supporting Kurdish refugees, who had been caught between Saddam Hussein's forces in Iraq and the ongoing Turkish-Kurdish conflict. Gerardo Mannello, the mayor of Badolato, captured this mood of solidarity when he provided housing for twenty Kurdish families and temporary accommodation for the rest.[65] Our 'doors must be wide open', declared Italian President Oscar Luigi Scalfaro in his New Year's address.[66]

Italy won worldwide praise for its actions, but the German government was alarmed by what it saw. Many Kurdish refugees were determined to reach family and friends in Northern Europe and Italy's lax approach to asylum claims and returns provided these individuals with ample opportunity to continue their onward journeys. This was contrary to the spirit of Dublin, which put the onus on Italian authorities to assess the asylum claims of those arriving in their country through irregular means. But those who admonished Italy for its porous borders, such as German interior minister Manfred Kanther, showed little appreciation of just how difficult it was to patrol 7,500 kilometres of coastline.[67] EU member states neither supported Italy in this invidious task nor seriously considered relocating asylum seekers from Italy to other EU member states. The EU's response to Kurdish refugees, who lived under threat of torture and death in detention in Turkey, was no less disingenuous. Only a handful of EU member states agreed to resettle Kurdish refugees directly from Iraq and Turkey, while others, including Germany, returned Kurds to Turkey throughout the 1990s. Those who paid smugglers US$3,000 to cross the Mediterranean on a rusty boat did so because they had no alternative.[68]

This early test showed that EU asylum policy was a fair-weather affair. When international conflicts abated and asylum applications fell, these agreements helped the EU to manage its borders reasonably well. When the weather turned, as it did in Afghanistan in 2001, Iraq in 2003 and Chad in 2005, and asylum applications spiked, the EU struggled to cope. For the individuals caught up in these conflicts, seeking refuge in the EU was, however treacherous, preferable to remaining in the region or holding out hope for resettlement. For southern member states, this meant arrivals that were difficult to manage, not simply because of their scale, but because many of those arriving were determined to reach family and friends elsewhere. For the northern member states, the influx of people whose asylum claims should have been processed elsewhere was not only contrary to EU asylum policy; it was also a boon for far-right populists, who thrived on media narratives about nation states being engulfed by migrants irrespective of the numbers involved. These contradictions put intense strain on Schengen and Dublin, although these agreements proved more resilient than they looked.

The Heads of State or Government, as they so often did when faced with global emergencies, forged a collective response to the refugee crises. While they failed to address the economic deprivation and political instability that drove people from their countries, national leaders were successful at disrupting irregular migration flows in the short term, at least. A case in point occurred in Spain in October 2005, as up to 500 people per day climbed over a razor-wire fence between Morocco and Spain's North African enclave Ceuta in a desperate attempt to enter the EU.[69] Frontex, the EU's new border agency, watched on, but it was soon drawn into events after a heavy-handed response from Spanish and Moroccan police created new business for people smugglers operating on the West African coast. In 2006, an estimated 31,000 people attempted to reach Spain's Canary Islands by rickety fishing boats from Senegal.[70] Around 6,000 individuals died or were reported missing. Frontex initially sent experts to help process asylum claims and manage returns, before contributing to joint sea and air patrols off the coast of Senegal. By intercepting and turning back boats, these patrols helped to disrupt this route.[71] However, in so doing, the EU effectively redirected irregular migration flows to Lampedusa, an Italian island near Libya, which received a record 31,252 arrivals in 2008.[72] A deal between the EU and Muammar Gaddafi saw Libya tighten border controls in exchange for €60 million in aid, but the challenges facing EU asylum policy were only just beginning, as the Arab Spring swept Gaddafi from power and triggered unrest in North Africa and the Middle East.

The world faced an acute refugee crisis in 2015, as the number of people seeking international protection from persecution and conflict under the United Nations High Commissioner for Refugees (UNHCR) mandate reached 16.1 million, the highest level since the end of the Cold War.[73] This was a global crisis in both its origins and impact. More than half of all refugees in 2015 came from Syria, then in its fourth year of a bloody civil war, Afghanistan, a country still reeling from the US-led invasion fourteen years earlier, and Somalia, which had faced perpetual bloodshed since President Siad Barre's dictatorial regime collapsed in 1991.[74] The majority of these refugees went to Ethiopia, Iran, Jordan, Lebanon, Pakistan and Turkey, where they remained in makeshift accommodation, or sought resettlement to Europe, North America and Australia.

In 2015, a record 1.3 million people claimed asylum in the EU.[75] Most came from Afghanistan, Iraq and Syria. The rest came from other parts of the Middle East, Africa and Central and Eastern Europe, alongside 18,000 people who were brought by smugglers and traffickers from Bangladesh. While the Libya–Italy route remained a key one, 840,000 people arrived in Greece by dingies and makeshift boats from Turkey's Aegean coast.[76] It was not simply the sudden increase in the number of people arriving into the EU that made this global refugee crisis so challenging for the Union.[77] It was the fact that arrivals were concentrated in a small number of entry points in Southern and Central Eastern Europe, leaving border officials in these locations overwhelmed and those who arrived seeking either to remain in cramped conditions or continue their perilous journey to other parts of the Union. Nowhere was this clearer than in Lesvos, a Greek island with a population of 85,000, which received 500,000 arrivals in 2015.[78] Mória, and other refugee centres on the island, had neither food, accommodation nor sanitary facilities for such numbers, leaving families sleeping in tents and under trees surrounded by rubbish while they awaited transfer to Athens.[79] Once there, most began the journey on foot through to Western Europe via the former Yugoslav Republic of Macedonia, Serbia, Hungary and Austria.

Germany was by far the most popular destination for those entering the EU. In 2015, it received 442,000 asylum claims in 2015, giving the right-wing populist Alternative for Germany a new cause to rail against alongside Chancellor Angela Merkel's handling of the euro crisis.[80] When she visited a makeshift reception centre for refugees in Dresden in August 2015, Merkel was heckled and booed by Alternative for Germany members. 'There can be no tolerance for people who question the dignity of other people,' she told assembled journalists.[81] 'We have managed so many things – we will also manage this situation,' she added.[82] In truth, Merkel had limited options. The Dublin Convention was under severe strain by this point. Greece and Italy simply couldn't process asylum claims on the scale required and given the determination of those arriving in these member states to go elsewhere. Even if she had chosen to do so, Merkel couldn't have easily relocated hundreds of thousands of people because they should have claimed asylum elsewhere. Although her words were, in this sense, a reflection of political reality, Merkel could have bowed to right-wing populists, as UK Prime Minister David Cameron did, when he referred to refugees arriving in Europe in 2015 as a 'swarm'.[83] Instead, Merkel set Dublin to one side and accepted that Syrians could claim asylum in Germany even though they had entered the EU through other member states. One month later, as the numbers arriving in Germany continued to rise, Merkel introduced temporary border controls with Austria. Hungary, Malta, Slovenia and Sweden soon introduced similar arrangements.[84]

As the EU grappled with the global refugee crisis, Syrians fled for their lives. A barber by profession, Abdullah had moved from Damascus to the border town of Kobani in northern Syria in July 2011 as violent protests gripped the capital.[85] Struggling to make ends meet, he commuted to Damascus for work. On his return journey one day, he was captured by a group of rebels, who pulled his teeth out on account of his Kurdish heritage. Shortly afterwards, Abdullah moved to Turkey, where he was joined by his wife, Rehanna, and sons after the Islamic State laid siege to Kobani. He had no desire to live in Europe; he planned to join his sister in Canada, but since he and his family lacked passports, they needed authorisation from the Office of the United Nations High Commissioner for Refugees, which was inundated with requests. Running short of money and options, Abdullah asked his sister for money to pay smugglers to take him and his family from Turkey's southwestern coast to the Greek island of Kos. Twice abandoning crossings, the family tried a third time on an inflatable boat meant for eight people but carrying sixteen. Shortly after leaving the port of Bodrum, the boat capsized, leaving Abdullah, his wife and sons clinging to the deflating vessel for nearly three hours. Rehanna couldn't swim and eventually succumbed. Her son Ghalib, aged 6, was found dead in a Turkish cove the next morning. One hundred metres away, his 3-year-old brother, Alan Kurdi, lay prone and lifeless on the shore, where he was photographed by Nilüfer Demir, who had got up early to capture images of departing refugees. As Abdullah prepared to bury his family, Demir's image of Alan appeared in newspapers and television screens around the world. The public outcry was instantaneous, putting sudden pressure on politicians in Europe and beyond to act.

After seeing Demir's photograph, a dismayed François Hollande called Angela Merkel, who agreed on the need for 'a permanent and obligatory mechanism' to relocate refugees between EU member states.[86] Other EU Heads of State or Government took convincing, especially Hungarian Prime Minister Viktor Orbán, who faced growing electoral competition at home from Jobbik, a far-right party, which had called for all migrants to be stopped at the border to protect 'poor Hungary'.[87] Not to be outdone, Orbán ordered a four-metre-high razor-wire fence to be built on the border with Croatia and Serbia and warned of threats to 'Europe's Christian culture'.[88] Under proposals presented by Commission President Jean-Claude Juncker in September 2015, Hungary would have taken in around 1,000 asylum seekers from Italy and Greece in return for 54,000 asylum seekers being relocated from Hungary to other member states. Jobbik still objected to any EU-wide response to the crisis and so Orbán insisted that Hungary would take no part in the scheme. When EU interior ministers agreed to relocate 120,000 asylum seekers from Italy and Greece, Orbán challenged the decision before the European Court of Justice.[89] There was next to no chance that the Court would rule in the Hungarian government's favour. The appeal was for domestic consumption, as was Orbán's decision to call a referendum on whether the EU should be allowed to resettle non-Hungarians without the consent of the country's parliament. The result was a foregone conclusion after most opposition parties boycotted the referendum, although the 98 per cent 'no' vote was invalidated when turnout failed to reach the required threshold.

The EU's difficulties in handling the crisis ran deeper than Hungary. Juncker's plan to distribute asylum seekers according to a 'key' determined by the population, wealth and unemployment rate of the receiving country was a technocratic solution to an intensely political problem. The real key was public opinion. In a poll published in 2018, 77 per cent of EU respondents supported taking in refugees fleeing persecution and war, compared to 66 per cent in the United States.[90] But eight of the ten EU members surveyed two years earlier believed that refugees increased the threat of terrorism in their country.[91] By 2017, only 28,000 people had been relocated under the Union's scheme.[92]

As with earlier crises, European politicians talked about addressing the root causes of irregular migration, while focusing their energies on tightening border controls. On the day after Alan Kurdi's death, François Hollande also phoned Recep Tayyip Erdoğan to discuss how to stem the flow of people across the Eastern Mediterranean.[93] In 2015, nearly 2 million people had sought refuge in Turkey, leaving the country more concerned about its own humanitarian crisis than policing EU borders. The Union responded by pledging €3 billion to support humanitarian assistance and public services for Turkey's refugees, but what Erdoğan wanted most of all was to revive his country's stop-start talks on membership.[94] The EU reluctantly agreed, in response to which Erdoğan offered to return all irregular migrants crossing from Turkey to the Greek islands. For every Syrian returned to Turkey, the Union agreed to resettle one person.

The impact of this deal was almost instantaneous, with arrivals in Greece falling by more than 400 per cent in 2016.[95] As of 2021, nearly 4 million Syrians remained under 'temporary protection' in Turkey.[96] The deal worked up to a point. Illegal crossings on the Aegean Sea fell by 95 per cent between 2015 and 2017, reducing the pressure on European asylum policy.[97] But this came as scant consolation for the half a million people still waiting to have their asylum claims processed. By this point, 20,000 men, women and children were still stranded in the Mória Refugee Camp, where the conditions endured by these would-be EU citizens remained in clear violation of the Union's fundamental values.[98]

During this period, the European Union was haunted by the claim that it had lost control of its borders. This suggestion was inaccurate, however much it embellished right-wing populist narratives about a continent engulfed by immigration and Islam.[99] Much like the Union itself, the agreements of Schengen and Dublin were repeatedly written off, but both endured, even as the number of refugees worldwide soared.[100] Although temporary border restrictions became more common, Schengen still fostered free movement between countries to a degree unimaginable in most parts of the world. The Dublin Convention remained dysfunctional, but its practice of requesting that member states take charge of, or take back, asylum claimants for which these countries had legal responsibility resumed. Although Greece accepted only a fraction of such requests made by other member states in 2019, Italy accepted a majority.[101]

Faced with a global crisis, EU member states had stood together once again, helping to return a semblance of normality to the Union's asylum policy after the momentous events of 2015. And yet, the harsh border policies pursued by some countries – from Italian Deputy Prime Minister Matteo Salvini's attempts to deny entry to migrants saved from the Mediterranean, to the Greek coast guards' alleged push back of boats in the Aegean – showed how normalised right-wing populist policies towards irregular migrants had become since Maastricht.[102] Such policies won votes but they endangered lives and did little to address the reasons why so many people risked so much to reach the EU.

At an emergency meeting with African Heads of State or Government in Valetta in November 2015, EU leaders agreed to create a new €4.5 billion Emergency Trust Fund for Africa to address the 'root causes' of irregular migration into Europe.[103] The instrument was soon criticised for pressuring countries such as Ethiopia, the Gambia, Morocco and Niger into accepting agreements on the return and readmission of migrants rather than investing in economic development.[104] Such short-termism proved counterproductive, as ever. On a single day in May 2021, 1,500 children walked or swam around the razor-wire fence between Morocco and Spanish Ceuta. Some came with small backpacks; most arrived with nothing.[105]

12

Terror

Molenbeekphobia

On 22 March 2016, a 27-year-old European man, Khalid El Bakraoui, detonated a bomb on an underground train beneath the EU Quarter in Brussels, killing himself and twenty other people.[1] One hour earlier, his older brother, Ibrahim, and an accomplice had set off two nail bombs in Zaventem airport, killing themselves and twelve people. As the Rue de la Loi filled with emergency services and armed soldiers, EU institutions issued an alert telling all staff to remain at home or in their offices. The 1992 Maastricht Treaty had formalised EU efforts to combat terrorism, building on two decades of informal cooperation between member state authorities. EU counter-terrorism policy developed sporadically in the quarter-century that followed, especially in response to large terrorist attacks in Europe and beyond, but the EU had never before had to deal with an atrocity on this scale planned and executed in the Union's de facto capital.

Those who could, walked away from Maelbeek station. Those who couldn't, received medical attention from emergency services, local doctors and a handful of Commission first-aiders, who had trained for workplace emergencies and now found themselves in a war-like zone. Several EU buildings were evacuated, and one turned into a temporary field hospital, but staff mostly remained in their offices, watching unfolding events on television screens or from their windows, as they made panicked calls to loved ones. The city's schools were either on Easter break or winding down for the holidays, leaving officials' children dotted around the city doing different activities. One group of children, en route to a museum, narrowly missed the metro explosion, while several officials, and their families, were in Zaventem airport as nail bombs destroyed the departure hall.

Right-wing populists had stoked fears of European nation states being under siege from the moment the Maastricht Treaty was signed. Proponents of this political ideology sought to portray themselves as the authentic voice of the people in troubled times. Eurocrats and immigrants were integral to this narrative, which presented European officials as unelected (mostly foreign) bureaucrats intent on over-riding national democracy in the name of European federalism, and immigrants as a drain on welfare states and a threat to Christendom. The Brussels bombings allowed right-wing populists to connect these claims by portraying the EU as a victim of the forces it had unleashed. 'Free movement,' declared UK Independence Party leader Nigel Farage on the day after the attack, 'is a lovely idea when everything is going swimmingly, but it has become the means by which weapons, terrorists and criminal gangs can move around Europe completely uninterrupted.'[2]

Right-wing populist discourse, whether intentionally or not, filtered into the mainstream media.[3] Much of this coverage focused on Molenbeek, a Brussels commune with a large Muslim population, which had links to the bombings, as well as earlier terrorist incidents, including the murder of four people at the Jewish Museum of Belgium in May 2014, the shooting dead of twelve people at French satirical magazine, *Charlie Hebdo*, in January 2015 and the November 2015 Paris terror attacks. In the last of these incidents, one of the most shocking acts of terrorism witnessed in post-war Europe, suicide bombers blew themselves up outside the Stade de France, as François Hollande watched France play Germany inside before gunmen fired indiscriminately on al fresco diners across the city and into the crowd at an Eagles of Death Metal concert in the Bataclan. In total, 131 people were killed in five separate locations across the city, and more than 400 were injured.[4] As false claims spread on social media that

Molenbeek was Europe's first 100 per cent Muslim city – it was a place in which people of all faiths and none lived – traces of these narratives seeped even into the left-leaning press.[5] For the *Guardian*, Molenbeek was fast becoming 'Europe's jihadi central'.[6] For the *New York Times*, it had become 'The Islamic State of Molenbeek'.[7]

Terrorist connections with Molenbeek were all too real, yet claims that the EU capital was overrun by foreign extremists were grossly inaccurate. Four of the five Brussels bombers were born in the EU and the other had moved there as a young child. Khalid and Ibrahim El Bakraoui were born in Laeken, the Brussels suburb in which the Heads of State or Government had announced the Convention on the Future of Europe. The brothers had fallen into a life of crime and most likely been radicalised in prison.[8] After his release, Ibrahim breached the terms of his parole by travelling to Turkey, where he made contact with Salafi-jihadists on the Syrian border, before being deported to the Netherlands, from where he returned home. Although Belgium was described as a hotbed for 'returnees', they numbered around 125 people among the country's estimated 800,000 Muslims.[9] The terror attacks were perpetrated by relatively small cells operating on limited financial resources.

While it suited commentators such as US presidential candidate Donald Trump to describe Brussels as a 'hellhole' intent on Sharia law, it was anything but.[10] Molenbeek had a heavy police presence, even before Belgian Prime Minister Charles Michel announced a city-wide lockdown to capture Salah Abdeslam, a Belgian-born perpetrator of the Paris terror attacks. The authorities finally apprehended Abdeslam four days before the Brussels bombings and, in doing so, may have led the bombers to strike when they did. In his will, Ibrahim El Bakraoui described his fear of ending up 'in a cell' with Abdeslam. Having considered an attack on Charles Michel or further operations in France, El Bakraoui and his colleagues suddenly switched focus to Brussels' transport system.[11]

In 2013, Belgium's unemployment rate was 8.5 per cent.[12] Not so in Molenbeek, where an estimated 30.5 per cent of the civilian labour force was out of work, two-thirds of them for a year or more.[13] The unemployment rate for young people was over 40 per cent, with the proportion of such job-seekers lacking an upper-secondary qualification well above the regional average. These conditions were familiar to many ethnic minorities in the EU, with people of Turkish, Moroccan and Antillean descent in the Netherlands, for instance, facing double the national unemployment rate.[14] Molenbeek's mixture of joblessness and crime was familiar to many European suburbs, including Malmö's Rosengard, where Osama Krayem was born. The high-tech hub that developed next to the Øresund Bridge meant little to Krayem, who grew estranged from his moderate family before being radicalised online and joining the Islamic State in Syria.[15] Posing as a Syrian refugee, Krayem returned to Belgium, where he joined Khalid El Bakraoui on the Brussels metro attack, which the former fled after failing to detonate his explosive vest, only to be arrested by police after giving away his location on Facebook.[16]

The victims of the Brussels bombings came from all parts of Europe, as well as China, India, Peru and the United States of America. Included among their number was Patricia Rizzo, whose grandparents had moved from Italy to Belgium in the early years of the European Community.[17] After studying in Brussels, Rizzo held a variety of jobs in EU agencies before joining the European Research Council, a funding body dedicated to the spread of scientific ideas across Europe. Rizzo's family travelled from one Brussels hospital to another after she was reported missing, but she had been killed on the Metro on her way to work.

Europol

Although European law enforcement authorities had cooperated through Interpol, an international body, since 1923, the Maastricht Treaty's establishment of a European Police Agency was significant. Interpol was a police-led initiative, which helped national officers to communicate with each other and issue alerts over fugitives and missing persons. Europol was created by the Heads of State or Government, who instructed police forces to work together to combat drug trafficking, organised crime and terrorism. Launched in 1999, Europol didn't have independent investigative powers, but it was given the authority to provide intelligence analysis and other forms of operational support to cross-border police operations. No area of policy-making is more sensitive than national security and so the willingness of EU member states to work together in this domain, however tentatively at first, was a major step for the Union.

European counter-terrorism policy had its origins in the Trevi Group, an informal network of ministers and officials which formed in response to the murder of eleven Israeli athletes and coaches and one police officer by members of a Palestinian militant organisation at the Olympic Games in Munich in 1972, as well as the rise of far-left terrorist groups such as the Red Army Factions in West Germany and the Red Brigades in Italy. Left-wing violence was greatly diminished by the 1990s, but ethnoreligious conflict continued, as evidenced by the 1998 Omagh Bombing, in which dissident Irish Republicans killed twenty-eight in a street crowded with back-to-school shoppers. It wasn't until the Armed Islamic Group of Algeria detonated a series of improvised explosive devices across France in 1995, however, that terrorism made it to the top of the European agenda. 'Terrorism constitutes a threat to democracy, to the free exercise of human rights and to economic and social development, from which no Member State of the European Union can be regarded as exempt,' EU interior ministers declared at a meeting in La Gomera after these attacks.[18] Henceforth, increasing the exchange of operational information about terrorist groups would be a priority.

Sharing information on counter-terrorism didn't come naturally to national police forces, who feared jeopardising any leads if they shared intelligence too widely. At first, Europol analysts manually collated what data they could on terrorist groups and financing and shared their findings with relevant authorities. Then, in 1999, EU justice ministers agreed that Europol should take charge of a new

European information system that national police forces would feed into and draw on. It took time to build this system and longer still to engender trust in it, with national police forces remaining under no legal obligation to share what they knew with European partners.

The terrorist attack that injected the greatest urgency into Europol's work occurred not in Europe but in New York, Pennsylvania and Virginia on 9/11, when al-Qaeda operatives hijacked and crashed four passenger planes and killed 2,977 victims. Watching the attacks on New York's Twin Towers from Brighton, where he was due to address the Trade Union Congress, Tony Blair set aside the speech he had come to give and declared 'mass terrorism' to be 'the new evil in our world today'.[19] In an emergency summit held ten days later, EU Heads of State or Government declared 'the fight against terrorism . . . a priority objective of the European Union'.[20] An expression of solidarity with a close ally at a time of national tragedy, it was also an admission: the 9/11 attacks had been partly planned in Hamburg, where Egyptian ringleader, Mohammed Atta, was known to German police.[21]

Faced with a global challenge, EU member states, as they so often did in the post-Maastricht period, stood together. One beneficiary of this stance was Europol, which was given new powers to ask national police forces to investigate specific cases, a dedicated Counter Terrorism Task Force, as well as the authority to share information with the Federal Bureau of Investigation. Despite such commitments, national tendencies died hard. When al-Qaeda in Iraq detonated high explosive bombs on two commuter trains in Madrid in March 2004, killing 193 people and injuring more than 2,000, Spanish police refused to tell their EU counterparts what types of explosive had been used.[22] French Interior Minister Nicolas Sarkozy lambasted Europol after the Madrid bombings, accusing the agency of assigning too few staff to its Counter Terrorism Task Force.[23] But Europol officials briefed back that its efforts had been seriously hampered by national authorities' reluctance to share live operational data.[24] Although member state governments reiterated their commitment to share such information, national security services remained as wary of each other as ever.[25]

Terrorist groups undoubtedly exploited gaps in European counter-terrorism policy. That the Paris attacks had been planned by a cell operating in Belgium was no coincidence. Salah Abdeslam and his associates found a laxer security environment in Belgium because of the country's fragmented federalism and exploited gaps in intelligence sharing. Stopped at the Franco-Belgian border hours after the Paris attacks, Abdeslam's car was waived through after a yet-to-be-updated police database failed to sound the alarm. He remained at large in Belgium until police traced him through fingerprints found at a Brussels property rented under a false name by Khalid El Bakraoui.[26] After they apprehended Abdeslam, security services raced to find El Bakraoui, but their efforts came too late to prevent the Brussels bombings.[27]

A Welshman in Washington DC

In James McTeigue's *Ninja Assassin* (2009), Naomie Harris plays a Europol agent investigating an international crime syndicate's role in political assassinations. She moves freely around Berlin, interviewing witnesses and wielding her firearm against masked swordsmen. Her British boss, played by Ben Miles, deploys heavily armed special forces, apprehends suspects at will and maintains high-tech safehouses around the German capital. Rob Wainwright bore a striking resemblance to Ben Miles, but the similarities ended there. Born in the Welsh Valleys, Wainwright served as an intelligence analyst for MI5, the UK Security Service, before becoming director of Europol, the first non-police officer to hold the role. Early on in his tenure, he travelled to Washington DC where he met with Robert Mueller, the director of the Federal Bureau of Investigation (FBI), to request support.[28] Four years earlier, the FBI had sent a handful of liaison officers to The Hague, but Wainwright sought a greater US presence to both increase Europol's intelligence capabilities and boost its credibility with national governments. The United States remained the most important intelligence interlocutor for most EU member states, especially after 9/11, and so seeing Americans invest in Europol encouraged member states to follow suit. In 2009, Europol had around 600 full-time and seconded staff. By 2018, it had double that.

Europol enjoyed significant operational successes under Wainwright's leadership. In 2014, the agency coordinated the arrest of 1,027 individuals involved in human trafficking, illegal migration and trade in firearms.[29] Thousands of law enforcement officers from all EU member states and international partners such as Australia, Colombia and the United States took part in the raids, which were directed from The Hague and carried out over eight days. Thirty children were saved from trafficking as a result of the operation. Three years later, Wainwright took to the podium at the United States Department of Justice to announce that Europol, the FBI, the US Drug Enforcement Agency and the Dutch police had shut down AlphaBay and Hansa, two of Europe's largest dark markets for illegal trade in drugs and firearms.[30] At the beginning of his tenure, Wainwright had struggled to be heard across the Atlantic.[31] Now the Welshman was feted in Washington DC.[32]

Despite these achievements, Europol still found it difficult to gather and process information on European terrorist groups. As was so often the case in the post-Maastricht period, European officials lacked the authority and resources to do their job without strong political support from the member states. Although they were known to European intelligence services, the Brussels bombers had hidden in plain sight, in part, because national authorities failed either to share or use information effectively. Ibrahim El Bakraoui, for instance, had been identified as a potential terrorist by Turkish authorities and extradited to the Netherlands but, as his name didn't appear on any terrorist list, he was not detained.[33] Although Dutch authorities passed on concerns to their Belgian counterparts, the latter were slow to act. In the days leading up to the Brussels attacks, it was the FBI that shared information with the Dutch about El Bakraoui being wanted in

Belgium.[34] Europol's new European Counter Terrorism Centre, which carried on the work of the post-9/11 Counter Terrorism Task Force, was caught flatfooted. That Belgium no longer stationed a liaison officer in The Hague at this point didn't help.[35]

Meeting two days after the Brussels attacks, EU justice ministers agreed to create a new European Counter Terrorism Centre at Europol and to deal, as a matter of urgency, with sizeable data gaps in its European information system. In 2014, the system had identified around 3,000 foreign terrorist fighters.[36] By the beginning of 2016, Europol had identified 18,000 such individuals and associates by drawing data from a much wider range of agencies. The EU body also stepped up its support for counter-terrorism operations, as in its coordinating role in disrupting the Amaq news agency and other parts of the Islamic State propaganda machine in 2018, and its support for a Spanish police investigation of an Islamic State cell in Barcelona and Madrid, which stopped a planned terrorist attack in 2021.[37]

Despite such efforts, Jihadi attacks in Europe continued, as when Mohamed Lahouaiej-Bouhlel, a Tunisian-born resident of Nice, drove a cargo truck into a Bastille Day crowd on the Promenade des Anglais in July 2016, killing eighty-six people, and the Berlin Christmas Market attack in December of the same year, when Anis Amri, a failed asylum seeker from Tunisia, drove a truck through a festive crowd near the city's Bahnhof Zoo, killing eighteen. Neither Amri nor Lahouaiej-Bouhlel was part of a terrorist cell; rather they were radicalised through comparatively brief interactions with radical preachers, underlining the scale of the challenges facing European security services.[38]

Right-wing terror attacks in the EU also rose in the post-Maastricht period.[39] In the UK, one person was killed and nine injured in June 2017 when a far-right supporter drove a van into a group leaving the Finsbury Park Mosque. The perpetrator, Darren Osborne, was a long-term unemployed man with no great interest in right-wing politics until he was radicalised over a matter of weeks by material he accessed online.[40] In Germany, Tobias Rathjen wrote a series of online racist manifestos before opening fire in February 2020 on two hookah lounges in Hanau, killing nine people and injuring five.[41] The Heads of State or Government decried such attacks and offered condolences, but for once showed little interest in formulating a collective European response.

The European Arrest Warrant

António Vitorino understood that Europe would never be the same after 9/11. A brilliant legal thinker, he had become a member of the Portuguese assembly aged 23, a judge in the country's constitutional court aged 33 and, following a spell as deputy prime minister and defence minister, European Commissioner for Justice and Home Affairs, three months shy of his forty-third birthday. Vitorino quickly established himself as one of Brussels' most talented officials. He helped to write the EU Charter of Fundamental Rights and championed efforts to create a European area of freedom, security and justice. Progress towards the second of these goals was piecemeal, with member states keen to cooperate on issues such as organised crime, drug trafficking and counter-terrorism but reluctant to cede sovereignty in such a sensitive domain.

One issue that Vitorino took a particular interest in was the difficulty of extraditing suspected criminals between EU member states. A case in point was Rachid Ramda, an Algerian man granted asylum in the UK wanted in connection with the Armed Islamic Group of Algeria's bomb attacks on France in 1995. Against the wishes of the UK government, the British courts refused to hand Ramda over to French authorities, citing concerns over their handling of the case, leaving the suspect languishing in London's Belmarsh prison for four years without standing trial. EU member states had signed two conventions in the mid-1990s which sought to speed up extradition, but they were slow to ratify agreements, which in Vitorino's view didn't go far enough. European officials could do little in this sensitive policy domain without the express approval of member states so Vitorino instructed his officials to prepare proposals for a European Arrest Warrant, which he made public six days after 9/11.[42] Determined to act together, national leaders put Vitorino's proposal at the top of the EU's new plan to combat terrorism after the al-Qaeda attack on the United States.[43]

Influential though Vitorino was, he didn't convince member states to do what they would not otherwise have done. Most Heads of State or Government supported the proposal, albeit reluctantly in some cases, as a way to show decisive action against terrorism after 9/11.[44] Silvio Berlusconi was the only real hold-out, perhaps, as the political scientist Christian Kaunert conjectures, because the Italian prime minister feared extradition one day given how frequently he faced prosecution.[45] Such was the momentum behind the Commission proposals that Berlusconi eventually relented, allowing the European Arrest Warrant to become law in June 2002.

The warrant proved its worth on 29 July 2005 when the Carabinieri raided an address in Rome and apprehended a naturalised British citizen, Osman Hussain, who eight days earlier had tried, but failed, to detonate a hydrogen peroxide bomb on an underground train in London's Shepherd's Bush tube station.[46] One of four unsuccessful attacks on the UK capital that day, the 21 July attack came a fortnight after four suicide bombers had killed 52 people and injured 784 on London's transport network. That Hussain had left London by Eurostar and passed through France and Italy revealed serious short-comings in European intelligence sharing. That he was arrested in a matter of days and returned to the UK in a matter of weeks showed, however, that the days of terrorists seeking safe haven in other member states were drawing to a close. However, this didn't stop some members of the British Conservative Party from rebelling against the European Arrest Warrant long after it had become law.

Under the Lisbon Treaty, the European Court of Justice was given oversight of cooperation among member states in the area of criminal justice for the first time. Fearing a Eurosceptic rebellion in the

House of Commons, UK Prime Minister Gordon Brown hit upon a formula that would allow the UK to opt out of all justice and home affairs policies adopted before the Lisbon Treaty before deciding whether to opt back in.[47] When Brown's successor, David Cameron, announced in 2013 that the British government would opt out of 135 areas of cooperation and opt into 35, this looked like a win for Eurosceptics in the ruling Conservative Party. But Jacob Rees-Mogg, mannered son of anti-Maastricht campaigner, William, saw an opportunity to make life difficult for the prime minister. In 1993, William Rees-Mogg had joined forces with Sir James Goldsmith over a High Court challenge against the Maastricht Treaty. Twenty-one years later, Jacob Rees-Mogg backed efforts by Stuart Wheeler, treasurer of the UK Independence Party, to seek a judicial review of the British government's decision to opt back into the European Arrest Warrant.[48] The second challenge failed, just as the first had done; however, the affair brought attention to the first-term MP for North East Somerset, who had hitherto lacked his father's public profile. It also stoked media fears that foreign police officers and EU judges were trampling British citizens' rights.[49]

Privacy

The European Arrest Warrant was, for António Vitorino, just one front in the EU's fight against terrorism. As a former defence minister, he placed particular emphasis on intelligence sharing, both among EU member states and between the EU and its international allies. In May 2004, Vitorino travelled to Washington DC to meet with Tom Ridge, the United States Secretary for Homeland Security.[50] There, they put the final touches to a new EU–US agreement on passenger name records. After 9/11, US security services sought access to the data that commercial airlines had long kept on their passengers' contact details, travel plans, credit card information and dietary preferences. Civil liberties groups pushed back against the sharing of such information on domestic flights, but the Department of Homeland Security insisted that international carriers operating US-bound flights comply or risk losing their landing rights.

Frits Bolkestein, the single market Commissioner, was keen to strike a deal.[51] European carriers had been hard hit by the slump in air travel after 9/11 and they could ill afford to lose access to the lucrative market for transatlantic flights. European interior ministers were equally keen, identifying a common EU approach to passenger name records as a top priority for combatting terrorism after the 2004 Madrid bombings.[52] Johanna Boogerd-Quaak, a Dutch MEP, was unconvinced. The Commission, she concluded in a report for the European Parliament's Committee on Civil Liberties, Justice and Home Affairs, had acted without legal basis and due regard for the EU Data Protection Directive, which established strict conditions on the transfer of data between EU member states and between the Union and third countries and respect for EU citizens' fundamental right to privacy, as enshrined in the European Convention on Human Rights. Passenger name records had been collected by airlines for commercial purposes, the MEP warned, but they were now being repurposed in the name of public security and without rules determining how such data would be used and stored.[53] The European Parliament agreed with Boogerd-Quaak and voted by a margin of 276 to 260 to take the Commission to the European Court of Justice. The Court annulled the EU–US Passenger Name Record Agreement on procedural grounds, although its judgment left room for the Union to draft a new agreement with the Bush Administration.[54]

Two months after she presented her report to the Committee on Civil Liberties, Justice and Home Affairs, Boogerd-Quaak came a distant second in the European Parliament elections, to her former parliamentary aide, Sophie in 't Veld, who became the sole representative of her party, Democrats 66, in Strasbourg. But in 't Veld took the baton from her former boss and became the European Parliament's most prominent civil rights campaigner. She enjoyed a high profile, yet was powerless to prevent the EU and United States signing an amended Passenger Name Record Agreement. Undeterred, in 't Veld used her limited speaking time in the European Parliament to deliver one blistering speech after another on the risks to privacy and data protection. 'We may not have powers, but we are not stupid,' she told Franco Frattini, Vitorino's successor as EU Justice Commissioner, when he came to Parliament to discuss the EU's new agreement on passenger name records (PNR) with the United States.[55] 'We need evidence that the use of PNR data actually leads to greater security.' A relative unknown in the Netherlands when she arrived in Strasbourg, in 't Veld quickly became one of Europe's best-known MEPs.

Called to give evidence to the UK House of Lords European Union Committee in April 2008, a rare privilege for an MEP, let alone one from another member state, in 't Veld explained the wider significance of this seemingly technocratic issue. PNR was not just about air travel or transportation more generally, she warned.[56] It had implications for the information that public authorities could collect: 'telecommunications data ... postal data, medical data, bank data, credit card data, there are smart cameras, smart microphones, satellite surveillance, you name it ... Frankly, I am getting the feeling that citizens are increasingly under surveillance and the right to hold the executive to account is being eroded rapidly.'

It was around this time that in 't Veld, a sought-after speaker in the United States among civil liberties groups, suspected that she was being targeted by the Department of Homeland Security. Each time she boarded a plane to cross the Atlantic, she noticed that her boarding pass was stamped with four S's, singling her out for additional questions and checks under the so-called Secondary Security Screening Selection process.[57] Determined to know why this was happening, in 't Veld submitted a freedom of information request to US authorities, who released twenty-eight pages of information. Convinced they and other US agencies had more, in 't Veld filed suit in the US District Court for the District of Columbia, which ruled in favour of the Department of Homeland Security but drew further attention to the cause of data protection and privacy in the age of terror and counter-terrorism.

When the Lisbon Treaty entered into force in December 2009, the European Parliament gained powers that it had previously lacked concerning EU deals with third countries. In 't Veld moved quickly to recommend that MEPs withhold consent for the new EU–US passenger name record agreement, which hadn't yet been ratified by all member states.[58] The Commission, she insisted, should return to the negotiating table with its American counterparts and agree on a more coherent set of principles with regard to the sharing of data in this sensitive domain. When the Commission came back to the European Parliament in 2012, with what it argued was 'robust privacy safeguards for passengers', in 't Veld remained unconvinced.[59] The European Parliament refused to back her on this occasion, giving its consent to the deal after a decade of wrangling. It was, the Dutch MEP concluded, a 'heavy blow to citizen freedoms'.[60]

In 't Veld might have lost the vote, but her views about creeping threats to privacy in the EU were vindicated when, in 2011, the Commission proposed that passenger name records be shared on flights to and within the EU.[61] The Dutch MEP initially stopped the Commission in its tracks, convincing colleagues on the European Parliament's Committee on Civil Liberties, Justice and Home Affairs to reject the proposal as incompatible with EU fundamental rights.[62] However, the European Parliament faced intense pressure from the Heads of State or Government following the *Charlie Hebdo* shooting in Paris in January 2015. That the shooters carried out the attacks in their country of birth and residence made no difference. In a statement adopted a month after the attack, national leaders put public pressure on the European Parliament, which finally voted in favour of the European Passenger Name Records Directive one month after the Brussels bombings. In 't Veld voted against.[63] 'It remains to be seen,' she concluded, 'whether we will get the security that everyone is talking about.'

On 23 May 2021, Ryanair Flight 4978 between Athens and Vilnius was forced to land in Minsk after being informed by Belarusian authorities that a bomb was on board. When the aircraft landed, local security services detained Roman Protasevich, a young journalist who had opposed the draconian policies of Belarus' authoritarian president Alexander Lukashenko, and his girlfriend, Sofia Sapega, a 23-year-old law student who had no track record of political involvement. It was, Ryanair CEO Michael O'Leary announced, 'a state-sponsored hijacking'.[64] Paraded before cameras on the days that followed, Protasevich and Sapega admitted their guilt, but they gave every indication that they were doing so under duress.[65] How Belarusians came to know that Protasevich and Sapega were on board was unclear. While suspicion centred on three individuals who failed to reboard the aircraft in Minsk, human rights activists continued to question the role that passenger name records might have played in the incident.[66]

For all of its shortcomings, the EU's counter-terrorism efforts saved lives and showed member states' determination to act together, in even the most sensitive areas of policy-making. And yet, the actions taken by the EU and its member states weighed heavily on the Union's legitimacy. To pro-European liberals, the EU's determination to gather and share intelligence with each other and with the United States violated the fundamental rights to which the EU and its member states had pledged themselves. To Eurosceptics, initiatives such as the European Arrest Warrant provided further proof, if it was needed, of the EU's onward march into areas of national sovereignty.

The Heads of State or Government's preoccupation with Jihadi terrorism, though unavoidable, was also a boon for right-wing populist parties and those who marched to their drumbeat against Muslim Europeans. The European Fundamental Rights Agency reported 'increased hostility' towards Islamic communities in the EU in the wake of 9/11 and a similar trend was observed after incidents such as the Paris attacks in November 2015.[67] One study of local crime figures in Manchester found a persistent spike in anti-Muslim hate crimes in the weeks following Jihadi terrorist attacks.[68] Significantly such attacks peaked after media coverage, which the authors of the study adjudged to be more inflammatory than news about other terrorist attacks.

The Brussels bombings of 22 March 2016 were remembered by survivors and witnesses, as well as those who lost loved ones, in makeshift and permanent memorials. For nearly two months, the city's residents left flowers, flags, candles and other memorabilia at the Bourse, a popular meeting point located in one of the city's busiest thoroughfares. It was, Ana Milošević, an expert of European memorials, observes, a spontaneous attempt by citizens to come to terms with the causes and consequences of the horrific attacks.[69] A permanent memorial was unveiled in the EU Quarter on the first anniversary of the attacks. Jean-Henri Compere's *Wounded But Still Standing in Front of the Inconceivable* (2017) begins as a series of pockmarked horizontal steel planes before a smooth section slopes upwards to the sky. In Molenbeek, meanwhile, Mustapha Zoufri's eternal flame encased in a steel-latticed cuboid, *The Flame of Hope* (2016), had been conceived as a tribute to Belgium's Moroccan immigrants before the artist rededicated it as a symbol of solidarity which bound the city together.[70]

PART IV
'DO NOT BE LATE'

13

Brexit

The Anti-Federalist League

In May 2010, Nigel Farage climbed into a passenger seat of a light aircraft in Hinton-in-the-Hedges. The MEP had spent the morning flying over Buckingham, the constituency in which he was standing for election, towing a 'Vote for your country – Vote Ukip' banner. After take-off, the banner became wrapped around the tailplane, causing the aircraft to nosedive into a field. Fortunate to survive, Farage walked away from the wreckage, bloodied and with a bruised lung, and lit a cigarette.[1] The right-wing populist UK Independence Party secured no seats in that day's general election or any other in the three decades after its establishment in 1993, with the sole exception of Clapton in 2015. But on 23 June 2016 Farage won the political prize that he had coveted for three decades when 17 million voters went to the polls and ticked the box for the United Kingdom to leave the European Union.

Three prime ministers played a pivotal role in events leading to and from this historic juncture: David Cameron, Theresa May and Boris Johnson. None would have chosen of their own volition for the UK to leave the EU in the way that it did. Instead, short-term decisions taken by all three prime ministers to appease Eurosceptics in their own party, who in turn feared Nigel Farage's electoral threat, had consequences that spiralled out of control. Although they had hoped for a different result, EU Heads of State or Government quickly lost confidence in British political leaders and moved to safeguard the Union's interests. Protecting Ireland was important; preventing other right-wing populists from mimicking Brexit was more important still.

A commodities trader by profession, Farage quit the Conservatives over John Major's support for the Maastricht Treaty. He was an ideal candidate for Sir James Goldsmith's Referendum Party, but by the time it was founded, Farage had already joined Alan Sked's Anti-Federalist League. Sked was a professor of international history at the London School of Economics who had grown disillusioned with the EU after a career spent teaching European studies. Under his leadership, the League was a pressure group in the tradition of Victorian anti-corn law campaigns rather than a modern political party, but Farage and others demanded a rethink. The renamed UK Independence Party was launched in 1993 and, despite its promise to be a 'non-racist party with no prejudices against foreigners or lawful minorities of any kind', embraced right-wing populism.[2] Dismayed by the party's new direction, Sked left three years later.[3]

Although it attracted new members, the UK Independence Party remained in the shadows of the Referendum Party, lacking Goldsmith's charisma and money. A one-man political show, the Referendum Party fell apart when Goldsmith died; however, the UK Independence Party still struggled to find a leader who could connect with voters. They seemed to have found their man in Robert Kilroy-Silk, a Labour MP turned daytime television presenter who had left his job at the BBC following a furore over a newspaper column in which he had questioned Muslim people's contribution to society.[4] But Kilroy-Silk seemed preoccupied with his own political brand and soon left to form his own short-lived party. This left Nigel Farage, by now an MEP for South East England, with top billing.

Britons' awareness of the European Parliament increased as the legislature acquired a bigger role in EU decision-making, even though many MEPs remained unknown to the public. Not so Farage, who used his limited speaking time in the European Parliament to powerful effect, piquing the interest of the national media. Initially, Farage sought to expose instances of financial impropriety and maladministration.[5] But he found a larger audience with ad hominin attacks on EU political figures, as when he told European Council President Herman Van Rompuy that he had 'the charisma of a damp rag and the appearance of a low-grade bank clerk'.[6] Such interventions were juvenile and also tailor-made for social media. He soon became a mainstay on BBC's *Question Time*, where his plainspoken, provocative answers contrasted with the management-speak of Third Way politicians. A tabloid darling, he was frequently photographed holding a pint of real ale, although he reportedly preferred wine.[7]

Under the UK's first-past-the-post electoral system, the UK Independence Party couldn't mount a credible challenge against incumbents in general elections, but the party still exerted significant indirect influence on the Conservatives and Labour. Having declared himself 'sick of constant British vetoes' in Brussels, Conservative leader Michael Howard responded to UKIP's strong polling numbers by promising a referendum on the European Constitution.[8] It was a 'tidying up exercise', UK Prime Minister Tony Blair insisted of the European Constitution at first, before bowing to pressure to give the British people a say.[9] Blair's decision to cancel this referendum after 'no' votes in France and the Netherlands denied Farage an opportunity to defeat the treaty, while helping to build his profile and power base. When the prime minister came to Strasbourg in December 2005 to mark the end of the UK's six-month presidency, Farage called him a 'cheese-eating surrender monkey' for concessions made to Jacques Chirac in negotiations over the UK's budget rebate.[10] 'You sit with our country's flag, but you do not represent our country's interests,' replied Blair. 'This is the year 2005, not 1945. We're not fighting each other anymore. These are our partners, our colleagues and our future lies in Europe.' The prime minister won this exchange, but it did Farage's reputation no harm. Nine months later, the MEP was elected UK Independence Party leader.

Banging On About Europe (1992–2012)

Michael Howard's successor as Conservative leader, David Cameron, was a moderniser who believed that his party could only regain power by occupying the centre ground of British politics. His problem was that he could only test this proposition by winning and maintaining the trust of his party's increasingly populist right wing, for whom principled opposition to the EU had become a shibboleth since Margaret Thatcher's fall from power. Cameron professed himself a Eurosceptic since no aspiring leader of his party could credibly do otherwise by the mid-2000s, but he was neither strongly for nor against European integration. As a special advisor to Norman Lamont in 1992, Cameron had watched the Chancellor of the Exchequer defend in vain sterling's place in the exchange rate mechanism. The experience filled the future prime minister with an apparent distrust of European *grand projets*, especially the euro. Unlike Lamont, however, he remained committed to UK membership of the EU.

Cameron's real passion was for domestic policy. After his election to Parliament, he joined the Home Affairs Committee and championed a more liberal approach to drug policy to the consternation of his colleagues. As a dark horse candidate for the Conservative Party leadership five years later, he won media plaudits for his 'new compact' to deal with 'drug dependency, family breakdown, persistent unemployment, [and] poor public space', leaving older rivals such as David Davis for dust.[11] As opposition leader, Cameron promised to protect the National Health Service and spoke movingly of the doctors and nurses who had cared for his son, who would die aged 6 due to complications from cerebral palsy and epilepsy.[12]

Inheriting an economy still reeling from the global financial crisis, Cameron divided his time as prime minister between cutting the UK's double-digit budget deficit and championing the Big Society, a Third Way-inspired programme which sought to empower charities, NGOs and other civil society groups to promote more inclusive local communities. These projects were incongruous, in as much as cuts to public services in the name of fiscal responsibility imposed disproportionate pain on the poorest in society. However, the more glaring inconsistency at the heart of Cameron's centrist premiership is that he remained beholden to his party's right-wingers, who refused their leaders' entreaties to stop 'banging on about Europe' rather than 'the things that most people care about'.[13]

In his campaign to become party leader, Cameron had promised to pull the Conservatives out of the European People's Party over the latter's statutory, yet largely symbolic, pledge to 'federal integration in Europe'.[14] This gambit helped Cameron to beat his Eurosceptic rival, David Davis, who had refused to tie his hands through such a promise, while emboldening those Conservatives who sought confrontation with the EU. Soon Cameron bowed to pressure to promise a referendum on the Lisbon Treaty if it hadn't been ratified before the next general election.[15] Although the treaty had entered into force by the time the Conservatives formed a coalition government with the Liberal Democrats in May 2010, Cameron promised his party that he would not let matters rest.[16]

Other Heads of State or Government prepared for the worst when Cameron made his debut at the European Council, but they encountered a pragmatist in search of a quiet life rather than a staunch Eurosceptic. A month earlier, while the Conservatives and Liberal Democrats hammered out their coalition agreement, Labour's caretaker chancellor, Alistair Darling, had agreed to the creation of the European financial stabilisation mechanism, an EU fund to manage the euro crisis. Cameron had every right to cry foul; Darling had consistently ruled out such support prior to the election.[17] Instead, the new prime minister made clear that he wanted a 'successful euro' and would support measures to reinforce the single currency providing they entailed no transfer of powers from Whitehall to Brussels.[18] 'Whether they require treaty changes or not, our position will be the same,' he told fellow Heads of State or Government. 'We will back measures that help sort out the eurozone.' Having feared a new era of confrontation with the United Kingdom, national leaders breathed a sigh of relief. None more so than Angela Merkel, who travelled to the UK prime minister's official country residence, Chequers, to discuss Cameron's plans for closer cooperation on all manner of global challenges.

That Cameron acclimatised to the European Council so easily shouldn't have been so surprising. His call as opposition leader for the EU to focus on the three Gs of globalisation, global warming and global poverty was simply a reformulation of the Third Way thinking that had dominated EU discourse since the 1990s.[19] So too was his attempt to limit transfers of powers to Brussels, lest it fuel a Eurosceptic backlash. The key difference was that other Heads of State or Government, including his predecessors as UK prime minister, had contained this political pressure, by and large, whereas Cameron quickly succumbed to it. As first Ireland and then Portugal were drawn into the euro crisis, Conservative backbenchers began to ask questions. It was time for the prime minister, they argued, to extract concessions in return for British acquiescence. Some senior Tories suggested an opt-out from EU labour laws, in effect restoring the deal that John Major had secured at Maastricht.[20] Others sought to restrict the entitlement of 'benefit tourists' coming from the Union.[21] The concessions themselves were less important than the confrontation. Europe's difficulty was the UK's opportunity.

When Angela Merkel and Nicolas Sarkozy suggested in February 2011 that EU member states sign a Competitiveness Pact, Cameron was initially tempted to join.[22] The German chancellor and French president had no great desire to grant further powers to the EU; their aim instead was to reassure domestic audiences and financial markets that the Union had learned the lessons of past policy mistakes. Cameron could have played along, using EU-wide commitments, to reinforce his own efforts to get government borrowing under control. Instead, he allowed his advisors and party members to exaggerate the pact's significance and frame it as a threat to UK interests. Having won plaudits for his pragmatic performance at the European Council, Cameron now left the room when the pact was discussed.

Like the Competitiveness Pact, the Fiscal Compact was an attempt to reset credibility after the euro crisis by codifying EU member states' commitment to fiscal discipline and closer economic policy coordination. There was never any question of the UK taking part, but this didn't stop backbenchers from piling pressure on David Cameron to seek strategic advantage. In October 2011, eighty-one Conservative members of parliament backed a rebel motion for a referendum on EU membership. The motion was never going to pass, yet its backers made clear their expectation that Cameron 'deliver' in negotiations over the Fiscal Compact or face further rebellions.[23]

As late-night talks over the Fiscal Compact entered their end game in December 2011, the prime minister made his move. He would only support the agreement, Cameron informed the other Heads of State or Government, if the UK were given guarantees regarding EU involvement in financial supervision and the future of the single market. Merkel and Sarkozy had no intention of giving Cameron a veto over such sensitive policy issues so they pressed ahead with prepared plans for an intergovernmental treaty among a subset of EU member states. This might even have been the Franco-German leaders' plan all along. Sarkozy had long argued for European economic government among eurozone members and seemed to have finally won Merkel around to this proposal as the euro crisis exposed the need for fundamental reforms to the single currency's design. In any case, Cameron returned home to cheers from his Eurosceptic backbenchers for finally standing up to EU partners.

Signed by twenty-six Heads of State or Government in March 2012, the Fiscal Compact made little difference to the workings of the EU. Sarkozy's talk of economic government had always been over-blown. The French president had no intention of allowing EU institutions to direct French economic policy. Nor had Merkel, who used the Fiscal Compact to assuage economic conservatives in her own party before giving her tacit support to large-scale bond purchases by the ECB. Cameron's clumsy attempt to exert leverage over this issue eviscerated his image as a European pragmatist. At home, it confirmed the prime minister's political malleability and emboldened those who sought a referendum on UK membership of the Union.

The clearest winner from this period was Nigel Farage, who was buoyed by the Conservative leader's refusal to commit to an in-out referendum. In the 2010 general election, the UK Independence Party had secured just 3 per cent of all votes. By the end of 2012, it was polling above 12 per cent and its leader talked openly of an electoral pact with the Conservatives. '[W]e're a different party with a different manifesto,' Farage told reporters at the UK Independence Party conference in Birmingham, 'but if we were offered a deal that made it easier to push open a door marked "independence for the United Kingdom" of course we'd consider it.'[24] This deal was unconscionable for Cameron, who despite his willingness to court Eurosceptics to win the leadership of his party, had dismissed the UK Independence Party as 'fruitcakes, loonies and closet racists'.[25] Talk of a leadership challenge against Cameron emerged even before Farage's party secured 22 per cent of the vote in a by-election in Rotherham in December 2012.[26]

An Island Story (2013)

David Cameron was not a leader who appeared prone to excessive introspection. A direct descendent of King William IV and a grandson and great-grandson of MPs, he replied when asked why he wanted to be prime minister: 'Because I think I'd be rather good at it.'[27] Over Christmas 2012, Cameron reflected on his political predicament and decided to give a major public speech in which he would promise a referendum on the UK's continued membership of the EU if and only if his party won the next general election. Had Cameron faced down Eurosceptics in the Conservative Party, as John Major had done over the Maastricht Treaty, he might have avoided a public vote or delayed one until the EU had weathered the euro crisis. But the risks to Cameron's leadership from Eurosceptic rivals, and to his own party in the 2014 European Parliament election and the 2015 UK general election, informed his decision to do otherwise. That British voters might opt to leave the EU was a risk that he understood all too well, Cameron later insisted.[28] However, the prime minister almost certainly underestimated his own powers as a political salesman and the strength of feeling against the EU in some parts of British society after three decades in which politicians and the tabloid press had railed against creeping control by Eurocrats.

Initially, Cameron planned to announce his referendum pledge in Berlin. However, the timing clashed with the fiftieth anniversary of the Élysée Treaty and drew polite discouragement from Merkel. Cameron then settled on the Netherlands, a country that wore its own doubts about European integration on its sleeve, but he was detained at home over a hostage crisis in Algeria, in which six Britons and thirty-one other foreign workers had been killed. So the speech was moved to Bloomberg's new European headquarters on the site of a Roman road in the City of London, where the prime minister announced that he would hold a referendum on whether the United Kingdom should remain in the EU if the Conservatives won the next general election.

As a boy, Cameron had been captivated by Henrietta Elizabeth Marshall's *An Island Story*, a chauvinistic history of his country told through genteel English monarchs, greedy French and belligerent Germans.[29] Now, as prime minister, he told his Bloomberg audience that the UK's 'island story' shaped its 'argumentative', 'forthright', 'passionate' and 'pragmatic' approach to Europe, which set it apart from other member states.[30] 'We can no more change this British sensibility than we can drain the English Channel,' he insisted. 'And because of this sensibility, we come to the European Union with a frame of mind that is more practical than emotional.' These words showed Cameron to be a British exceptionalist, who was either unable or unwilling to acknowledge what he saw at EU summits: that all leaders were shaped by their national stories, protective of their sovereignty and determined to defend their countries' interests. The Bloomberg speech also confirmed that Cameron was no Eurosceptic but someone who saw the EU as having helped to heal the 'wounds of history'. Recalling a visit to Berlin after the Wall came down, he spoke of his youthful excitement at 'a great continent ... coming together' and his enduring belief that the UK's national interest was better served by being a member of the EU.

The prime minister won praise for his 'genuinely pro-EU contribution', but the primary purpose of his speech was to convey his deep frustration with the course of European integration.[31] His concerns were three-fold. First, the euro crisis was, he argued, threatening the interests of non-eurozone members. Plans for fiscal union and banking union, he warned, would compromise the UK's access to the single market. Second, the EU was falling behind in, what he called, 'the global race of nations'. The fragmented single market and penchant for regulation and bureaucracy were, in his view, to blame for Europe's declining competitiveness and share of world output. Finally, the EU was plagued by 'public disillusionment' and a sense that the Union was 'done to people rather than acting on their behalf'. Although these problems permeated the EU as a whole, Cameron told his audience, they were acutely felt in the United Kingdom. The British people, he warned, had become resentful of interference, angry over 'legal judgments made in Europe' and disenfranchised by 'referendums promised – but not delivered'. 'Democratic consent for the EU in Britain is now wafer thin', the prime minister concluded. The time had come to hold a referendum on whether to stay in the Union.

Given the urgency of these problems, why did the prime minister not call a referendum there and then? As always, his thinking was informed by the euro, the project that repelled him but to which he was invariably drawn. It made little sense to ask the British people to vote on membership, he insisted, until they knew what sort of EU would emerge from the euro crisis. When the euro crisis drove the next round of change to the EU treaties, he pledged to seek a new settlement to safeguard British interests and address the economic and political problems he had outlined. If this treaty amendment was not forthcoming, he would seek a new settlement alone.

There were other reasons for Cameron's delay. Three polls conducted in the days before the Bloomberg speech gave the Leave side a sizeable lead over Remain.[32] Seeking a new settlement, as Harold Wilson had done in 1975 before holding a referendum on membership of the European Community, relieved Cameron of the pressure to defend the status quo. It also bought time to find a new and improved relationship with the EU and for the UK's pro-European campaigners and pressure groups to find their voice. Above all, delaying the referendum offered a chance to reverse the Conservative's political fortunes. By promising to hold the referendum if his party won the 2015 general election, Cameron laid a trap for Labour leader Ed Miliband, who had already seen off calls from within in his own party for a referendum, and UK Independence Party leader Nigel Farage, who stood for little else. The device snapped shut more forcefully than expected, helping the Conservatives to win a parliamentary majority for the first time in two decades and trapping the prime minister in the process.

Other Heads of State or Government were prepared to play along with the newly returned UK prime minister, although not at any cost. Cameron's suggestion that the UK negotiate new terms as part of a wider package of treaty reforms to save the single currency was greeted with stony silence.[33] The worst of the euro crisis was over by mid-2015 and even if it hadn't been, linking the future of the single currency to a hard-to-win UK referendum made little sense. Having tried and failed to use the euro crisis to gain leverage in negotiations over the Fiscal Compact, Cameron tried and failed again. He had no choice now but to seek a bespoke solution to the problems that had bedevilled the UK's relationship with the EU.

Touring EU capitals to make the case for his new settlement, Cameron remained vague about what kind of deal he sought. This frustrated Heads of State or Government, who nonetheless understood that the Conservative leader was in a bind. While the British public might be convinced by concessions, a vocal minority in his party sought a rupture from, rather than reconciliation with, the EU.

When Cameron finally played his hand in a letter to European Council President Donald Tusk in November 2015, he asked for changes that were limited in scope and largely symbolic.[34] On the euro, for example, the prime minister sought reassurances that non-eurozone members wouldn't be obliged to join the proposed European banking union even though the EU was in no position to demand otherwise. On competitiveness, Cameron's call for a clear long-term commitment to boost EU competitiveness and productivity looked like the Lisbon Strategy reheated. On sovereignty, his call for a British opt-out from 'ever closer union' took issue with a preambulatory clause in the treaty, which was occasionally referenced by EU judges but made no discernible difference to UK membership of the Union.[35] Cameron's biggest ask was on immigration, where he sought an 'emergency brake' to limit the rights of EU workers to seek benefits and social housing for four years.

It was, Donald Tusk insisted, 'a significant and far-reaching agenda', which some national leaders found 'difficult'.[36] In truth, only Polish Prime Minister Beata Szydlo expressed significant reservations and, even then, signalled her willingness to reach an agreement.[37] Workers from Central and Eastern Europe seemed to be the target of Cameron's emergency brake, yet the vast majority of those who moved to the UK after the EU's 2004 enlargement came to work rather than sign on. In 2016, more than a million Poles were living in the UK, but the Department of Work and Pensions recorded less than 6,000 Polish people as receiving working-age benefits. Predictions of an Anglo-French spat over the new settlement didn't materialise. In the end, the French government was content to secure minor revisions to the agreement to ensure that it didn't unduly favour the City of London.[38]

Agreement on the new settlement had ostensibly been reached by the beginning of 2016, yet Cameron still needed to show that he had pushed things to the brink and extracted every possible concession from EU partners. Late-night talks in Brussels duly followed but they were largely for show. Steeling herself for this spectacle, Angela Merkel left the Justus Lipsius Building to visit Maison Antoine, one of the best-known *friteries* in the EU Quarter.[39] As she ate double-fried chips with sauce andalouse from a paper cornet, the German chancellor glanced over her shoulder at the UK's ITN news before continuing her snack. Hours later, Cameron emerged from the European Council to announce that he had secured 'special status' for the United Kingdom in the EU and that the final compromise on in-work benefits and other aspects of the deal were 'enough' for him to back Remain in the referendum.[40] 'This is a truly pathetic deal,' argued Nigel Farage, who had resumed the leadership of his party after four days in the political wilderness; 'Let's leave the EU, control our borders, run our own country and stop handing £55 million every day to Brussels.'[41]

Breaking Point (2016)

Boris Johnson, the *Daily Telegraph*'s Brussels correspondent turned mayor of London, made his name as a purveyor of Euromyths about straight bananas, one-size-fits-all condoms and teabag recycling, but he was, at heart, a European.[42] The son of a former Commission official, Johnson had attended the European School in Brussels and generally supported the UK's membership of the Union during his eight years running the Greater London Authority. In late 2012, as David Cameron wrestled with whether to call an EU referendum, Johnson declared such a vote to be 'unnecessary'.[43] In the months immediately after Cameron's referendum pledge, Johnson remained publicly undecided about how to vote, arguing in his *Daily Telegraph* column that 'the question of EU membership is no longer of key importance to the destiny of this country'.[44] A rational person, he accepted, had good reasons to vote for Remain.

On the day after Cameron unveiled his new settlement, Johnson wrote drafts of his weekly column in support of EU membership and against it. His real agony was political rather than intellectual. Although he had been talked about as a future Conservative leader, Johnson remained a figure of fun prone to political fabrication. He had been sacked as a *Times* trainee for making up a quote from his historian godfather.[45] He suffered the same fate when, as the Conservative's shadow spokesperson for the arts, he lied about his private life to Conservative leader Michael Howard.[46] As mayor of London, he got stuck on a Thameside zip wire, a Union Jack in each hand, after reportedly lying to the operators about his true weight.[47] Re-entering parliament in 2015, as his second term as mayor drew to a close, Johnson was one of the most recognisable figures in British politics. His quick wit, unkempt appearance and faint Churchillian stoop made him stand out from contemporary politicians; however, he lacked a broad power base in the Conservative Party and seemed unlikely to challenge those, like Home Secretary Theresa May, who had occupied great offices of state under Cameron. Joining the Vote Leave campaign, while May reluctantly supported Remain, instantly endeared Johnson to Eurosceptic hardliners in the Conservative Party. By overcoming his own ambivalence towards the EU, Johnson had shaken off his image as a political dilettante and become David Cameron's heir apparent.

Johnson brought star power to Vote Leave, while Dominic Cummings provided discipline and a determination to win. Referendums were a way of life in some EU member states, but they were exceptional in the United Kingdom's parliamentary system. Tony Blair's constitutional reforms opened the door to local referendums, including a 2004 vote on the establishment of an elected assembly in the north-east of England. Cummings advised the insurgent 'North East Says No' campaign to victory, warning voters that the assembly would cost £1 million and arguing that this money would be better spent on health care.[48] Cummings repurposed this argument for the EU referendum, telling voters that leaving the European Union would mean an extra £350 million per week for the National Health Service. The figure was inaccurate, but it proved no less effective for this, linking EU withdrawal, as it did, to a treasured national institution.

Cummings' other masterstroke was to keep UK Independence Party leader Nigel Farage at arm's length from the official Leave campaign. Farage had done more than any other British politician to secure the referendum, but he remained a divisive figure who risked discouraging voters who wanted to register their disapproval with the EU and Cameron without being seen to endorse a right-wing populist, Cummings calculated. Johnson, in contrast, was the acceptable face of Brexit because of – not in spite of – his misgivings about leaving the EU. Even so, Johnson remained an unpredictable figure, as when he told reporters in an early Leave press conference that a 'no' vote would serve as a pretext for seeking a better deal and a second referendum.[49]

Britain Stronger in Europe, the official campaign for Remain, lacked all conviction. Stuart Rose, former chairman of Marks and Spencer, was a reluctant leader, as well as a politically inexperienced one. This inexperience was supposed to have been an advantage; public trust in business was 46 per cent in the UK in 2016 compared to 36 per cent for trust in government.[50] It turned into a millstone. Among wealthier, university-educated, politically engaged individuals with a declared interest in politics, 60 per cent tended to trust business. Among low-income groups, the same figure fell to 35 per cent.[51] The second of these groups swung much more strongly to Leave but were now invited by a businessman with little or no national profile to change their mind. Appearing before the Treasury Select Committee in the early weeks of the campaign, Rose accepted the premise of his questioner that British wages would go up if free movement were to end following Brexit. His public appearances were kept to a minimum thereafter and he later expressed regret that he had been corralled into leading the campaign. That the question about wages had been posed by a pro-EU Labour MP, Wes Streeting, revealed a wider truth about how divided the Remain campaign was over the referendum and how costly these divisions proved to be.[52]

David Cameron, the man who had called the referendum, proved to be an ineffectual campaigner. In 2013, the prime minister had promised to put his 'heart and soul' into a campaign for continued membership, but he spent three years either sidestepping the EU as a subject of political debate or keeping up the pretence that he might campaign for Leave if other Heads of State or Government didn't give him what he wanted.[53] As these talks drew to a close, the prime minister's communication director, Craig Oliver, rode a funicular at Davos and found himself 'wondering – should that PR have started properly in 2013, when the referendum pledge was made?'[54] Such hindsight came too late for the prime minister, who had 121 days between the announcement of the new settlement and referendum day to reverse a political lifetime of public ambivalence about Europe. Although he campaigned with his characteristic energy and confidence, he came up short. Speaking in the Great Court of the British Museum, the prime minister summoned up two thousand years of history and warned of future conflict unless Europeans stood together. '"Brexit" could trigger World War Three, warns David Cameron', said the sceptical headline on the next day's *Daily Mirror*, to the delight of those campaigning to quit the EU.[55]

Whereas Vote Leave drew on Cummings' experience of 'North East Says No', the Remain campaign relied on Better Together, the anti-independence side in Scotland's 2014 referendum on whether to become a sovereign state. Under Chancellor George Osborne's leadership, the Treasury had skewered the Scottish government's post-independence policy pledges, suggesting that its promises on childcare, corporation tax and air passenger duty alone would cost Scottish taxpayers £1.6 billion.[56] Adding to the Scottish government's own goal over whether it could keep sterling, adopt its own currency or be obliged to join the euro under the terms of accession to the EU, those who argued to preserve the United Kingdom as a political union won the economic arguments hands down. Borrowing from this playbook, Osborne instructed the Treasury to weigh the benefits of remaining in the EU against various forms of Brexit. Its headline message was that Brexit would cost the country between £20 billion and £45 billion in tax receipts and the average household £4,300 per year.[57] While arguments of this kind cut through in Scotland, they proved blunt in the UK as a whole. One reason was that Vote Leave remained deliberately vague about what kind of Brexit it sought, whereas the Scottish government chose to set out detailed plans for how it would govern after independence. This made it easier for Vote Leave to question the credibility of the Treasury's analysis and to dismiss the whole exercise, as Boris Johnson succinctly put it, as 'Project Fear'.[58]

A second lesson drawn from Scotland's independence referendum was that cross-party platforms were effective but costly. Two days before polls opened, Labour leader Ed Miliband and the Liberal Democrats' Nick Clegg signed a guarantee with David Cameron to transfer extensive new powers to the Scottish parliament in the event of a vote to remain in the UK. This gamble helped to prevent Scottish independence, yet it tarnished Labour and the Liberal Democrats, who were all but eradicated north of the border in the 2015 general election. During the EU referendum campaign, Tim Farron, Clegg's successor, consented to a brief photo opportunity with David Cameron at Oval Cricket Ground, while Labour leader Jeremy Corbyn refused to attend. A left-wing radical who had staged a stunning upset in the race to succeed Ed Miliband, Corbyn had made the leadership ballot thanks, in part, to the insistence of MPs, including the newly elected Jo Cox, who didn't share his politics but believed that their party should listen to a wider range of voices.[59] Corbyn had campaigned for the UK to leave the European Community in 1975 and opposed every treaty revision since, including Maastricht, which he dismissed at the time as creating a 'bankers' Europe'.[60] However, he led a largely pro-European Parliamentary Labour Party, which insisted that he speak up for Remain. He did so without energy or enthusiasm, avoided campaign events and even took a short holiday in the run up to the vote. 'On a scale of one to ten, where one is couldn't care less and ten is jumping on the couch like Tom Cruise on *Oprah*, how passionate are you about staying in the EU?' a comedian asked Corbyn on Channel 4's *The Last Leg*. 'Seven, seven and a half,' responded the deadpan Labour leader.[61]

Former Prime Minister Tony Blair had no such difficulties supporting Remain. But Remain was wary about aligning itself too closely with a politician whose political reputation in the UK had been ruined by his decision to go to war in Iraq. Undeterred, Blair joined John Major in Derry-Londonderry, where the two ex-prime ministers walked side by side along the Peace Bridge, a symbol of reconciliation between the city's Catholic and Protestant communities part-funded by the EU. Speaking at an event at Ulster University, the two politicians warned in no uncertain terms that leaving the EU could threaten the Northern Ireland peace process and lead to a hard border on the island of Ireland. Leavers rejected such warnings out of hand. There was 'no reason' to believe that free travel between Ireland and Northern Ireland would be affected by leaving the EU, UK Secretary of State for Northern Ireland Theresa Villiers argued, to a chorus of criticism from previous occupants of this political office.[62] And yet, the future of Northern Ireland barely registered as an issue in the nationwide debate, which was dominated by discussions over English identity and the expected economic gains from leaving the EU.

The one Labour politician who really cut through in the campaign was Gisela Stuart, whose animus towards the EU had only intensified since her unhappy experience as one of the two UK parliamentarians in the Convention on the Future of Europe. Six months after the Convention came to an end, Stuart had criticised the text it helped to produce – the European Constitution – while arguing for a reformed EU with the UK at its centre.[63] Thirteen years later, having drifted even further to the right to save her seat in the historically Conservative stronghold of Edgbaston, she became chair of Vote Leave. Stuart was not well known nationally, but her support helped soften the campaign's image as a caucus of Conservative Eurosceptics. That Stuart was born in West Germany had once been a political liability; it now proved a political asset. Voting for Leave didn't mean being a 'little Englander', Stuart told journalists; it meant realising that the UK didn't need the EU to escape 'narrow nationalism' in the way that her country of birth did.[64]

As in EU referendums in other member states, the UK found limited room for a genuine pan-European debate. An exception to the

Heads of State or Government's policy of non-interference was Irish Taoiseach Enda Kenny, who made several appearances in the UK to drum up support for Remain. That 330,000 Irish people living in the UK could, unlike most other EU citizens, vote in the referendum provided a pretext for doing so. Kenny's chief concern, born of his bitter experience of Ireland's referendums on the Nice and Lisbon Treaties, was that British politicians had underestimated the challenge posed by right-wing populists who were willing to peddle Euromyths and half-truths. Kenny also feared the economic and political fallout from Brexit for both the Northern Ireland peace process and Irish trade with the UK, which economists predicted could fall by as much as a fifth if the UK left the EU.[65] There were concerns too that Brexit could lead to border controls between Ireland and Northern Ireland and otherwise destabilise the peace process. Cameron seemed comfortable with Kenny and the two planned a joint appearance at an event for the Irish community in Manchester before Downing Street had second thoughts. The problem was not with the Taoiseach but Cameron, who his advisers worried was playing badly in the north of England. The day after this event had been scheduled, Jo Cox was murdered on a street in Birstall, West Yorkshire, by a far-right supporter who shot and stabbed the pro-Remain MP and shouted 'Britain First. Britain will always be first.'[66]

In an age of political obfuscation, Cox told it like it was. Aghast at Corbyn's failure to connect with traditional Labour voters and at his lack of engagement in the referendum campaign, she wrote an op-ed expressing regret for nominating him. It was time for Corbyn and those around him, the MP argued, to 'come out of their bunker, stop blaming everybody else, and show the discipline and determination to drive our message home.'[67] Cox was a progressive politician who had cut her political teeth as an assistant to a Labour MEP in the European Parliament before working for Oxfam. Although she was critical of EU trade policy for its impact on developing countries, she believed that the EU could and should be a force for good in the world and that British leadership in Brussels was central to this ambition. Cox received a torrent of abuse on social media for her stance against Corbyn, yet she encouraged him to use his 'unique voice' in the campaign or face consequences if Labour voters failed to turn out for Remain. Had Cox lived, she had the determination and political skillset to become Labour leader. Instead, she died at the hands of a man who, asked to identify himself in court, replied, 'My name is death to traitors, freedom for Britain.'[68]

Two hours before Cox's murder, Nigel Farage unveiled a poster showing hundreds of young men standing in a tightly packed line seemingly waiting to enter the UK. Captioned 'Breaking Point', the poster urged voters to 'break free' and 'take back control'. In fact, the image showed Syrian and Afghan refugees crossing the Croatia–Slovenia border at the height of the global refugee crisis in 2015. In taking this photograph for Getty Images, Jeff Mitchell had sought to show the struggles faced by these individuals as they crossed Europe on foot and by train in search of international protection.[69] Most sought a new life, not in the United Kingdom, which promised to resettle 20,000 Syrian refugees, but in Germany, which welcomed more than one million arrivals in 2015. However, such context was stripped from Farage's poster, which cropped a child and a white adult man from Mitchell's photograph, fuelling right-wing populist narratives about the UK being engulfed by economic migrants intent on exploiting the EU's commitment to free movement of people. This is 'not our campaign' and 'not my politics', insisted Boris Johnson when asked about the image. A vote to leave the EU would, he insisted, 'neutralise anti-immigrant feeling generally'.[70] Johnson was, he insisted, 'passionately pro-immigration and pro-immigrants' despite his own track record of racially insensitive remarks and false alarms about Turkey's imminent accession to the EU during the referendum campaign.

Suspended for five days following Cox's death, campaigning resumed in time for BBC's Great Debate in Wembley Arena to go ahead. Scottish Conservative leader Ruth Davidson, Labour's London Mayor Sadiq Khan and Frances O'Grady, general secretary of the Trades Union Congress, spoke for Remain. Boris Johnson, Gisela

Stuart and Andrea Leadsom, a Conservative MP, spoke for Leave. 'The European Union was a noble dream in the last century. But today it has failed. It has turned into a nightmare,' Stuart told the audience, while reminding Labour voters of Rose's claims about the EU's impact on British wages.[71] Out-debated by Davidson, who insisted that Vote Leave had 'lied about the costs of Europe', 'lied about Turkey' and 'lied about the European Army', Johnson shifted uneasily at the podium throughout the evening and had few memorable lines. That was until his closing remarks when he looked straight into the television cameras and borrowed a line from Nigel Farage's Brexit battle bus: 'If we vote leave and take back control, I believe that this Thursday can be our country's Independence Day' – to thunderous applause from the assembled audience.

At 10 p.m. on 23 June 2016, YouGov called the referendum result for Remain. The vote was unlikely to go his way, Nigel Farage conceded, while insisting the UK Independence Party 'will only continue to grow stronger in the future'.[72] Ninety minutes later, Sue Stanhope, Regional Counting Officer for the North East, announced that Sunderland had voted Leave by a large margin, as the winning supporters cheered and punched the air. One by one, local counts in the North West, South West and South East of England went the same way, as did results in East Wales and Antrim and Down in Northern Ireland. By the time the BBC's David Dimbleby announced the result, Farage had retracted his concession speech. 'Let June 23 go down in our history as our independence day,' he declared, while grinning and holding his arms aloft.[73] The mood at Boris Johnson's hastily arranged press conference at Vote Leave headquarters couldn't have been more different. Bowing his head and folding his hands before speaking, as if in silent prayer, he insisted that 'nothing will change over the short term'.[74]

David Cameron had insisted throughout the campaign that he would stay as prime minister if the result didn't go his way. However, having called the vote and lost, he concluded otherwise. 'I held nothing back, I was absolutely clear about my belief that Britain is stronger, safer and better off inside the European Union and I made clear the referendum was about this and this alone – not the future of any single politician, including myself,' he announced from a podium outside 10 Downing Street.[75] Although he marked his own scorecard leniently, Cameron's resignation revealed an essential truth. For all his frustrations with Brussels bureaucracy, both real and exaggerated, the prime minister believed in the EU as a project that could protect and promote the UK's national interest in an era of globalisation. Having failed to convince voters of what he privately thought but had so rarely conveyed publicly before the referendum campaign, his tenure was over. He had gambled and lost.

Seven days later, Boris Johnson's supporters gathered in St Ermin's Hotel in Westminster for the official launch of his leadership campaign. To their astonishment, he announced that having consulted with party members, he would not be standing for the leadership of his party. Hours earlier, his campaign manager and fellow Leaver, Michael Gove, had questioned the former mayor's fitness for high office and launched his own bid to be Conservative leader. Gove stood next to no chance of winning, not least because of the manner in which he had elbowed his political friend and ally to one side. Theresa May was now the only credible contender to lead the party and was duly appointed prime minister when her last remaining challenger, Andrea Leadsom, resigned after questioning whether the Home Secretary had a 'tangible stake' in the future as a woman without children.[76]

'Brexit Means Brexit' (2016–19)

Theresa May was a political survivor with a strong sense of public service. Under New Labour, Home Secretaries resigned or were replaced every two years, on average, amid the stresses and scandals which apparently came with the job. May retained this role throughout David Cameron's six years as prime minister. She stood up to the powerful police trade union, championed efforts to end modern slavery and made a concerted effort to reduce net migration to the UK from the hundreds to the tens of thousands. The last of these goals was not of May's choosing; it emerged from an extemporised commitment made by David Cameron in a live television interview.[77] However, she took it no less seriously and made tough immigration and asylum policies her political mission at the Home Office. Her draconian measures made little difference to the number of asylum claims, which waxed and waned with world events, but they endeared her to her party's right-wing and helped to keep the UK Independence Party at bay. Now, as prime minister, May inherited yet another ill-thought-through initiative from Cameron and she proved no less determined to deliver. 'Brexit means Brexit,' she insisted.[78]

May had campaigned for Remain, which appealed to the Conservatives' shellshocked pro-EU wing. But she had done so half-heartedly, which gave her a degree of credibility with her Eurosceptic colleagues. But May was no Eurosceptic. In her one set-piece speech during the referendum campaign, she had warned in no uncertain terms about the economic costs of being shut out of the single market and cast doubt on whether the UK could negotiate more favourable trade deals outside the EU's customs union. Once she entered Downing Street, May reversed her position and made leaving the EU her overriding focus.

'Brexit means Brexit' was not quite as tautological as it sounded. The history of the EU was littered with examples of re-run referendums – over Maastricht, Nice and Lisbon – and a public petition for a second vote on UK membership gathered 2.5 million signatures in twenty-four hours. European Council President Donald Tusk left open the door to this possibility, with his expression of personal regret and insistence that 'there's no way of predicting all the political consequences of this event, especially for the UK'.[79] May was adamant that this would not happen. 'There will be no attempts to remain inside the EU, no attempts to rejoin it by the back door, and no second referendum.'[80] The people had spoken loud and clear and it was politicians' responsibility to deliver change and make a success of it. Those who suggested otherwise 'didn't get it'.

One problem with 'Brexit means Brexit' is that it gave May no specific mandate on how to approach withdrawal negotiations and what the future relationship between the EU and UK should be. Her decision to appoint Boris Johnson as foreign secretary was not so much an act of magnanimity as an attempt to bind the Leave campaign's most prominent member to her approach. And yet, as always, Johnson got off lightly. David Davis, a Eurosceptic former Europe minister and Cameron's one-time rival was given responsibility, as the UK's new Secretary of State for Exiting the EU, for leading talks with Brussels. Cocksure, Davis promised a slew of trade deals within two years and predicted that the UK would soon be outperforming the EU.[81]

In November 2016, Davis travelled to Brussels to meet with Michel Barnier, the Commission's chief Brexit negotiator. Two decades earlier, the two men had served on the Westendorp Group, which had helped to prepare the Amsterdam Treaty. Now they met to negotiate a withdrawal agreement and a treaty governing the future relationship between the UK and the EU. Temperamentally, the two men couldn't have been more different. Davis was a libertarian, who already seemed troubled enough with the British state's interference in citizens' lives to countenance a new layer of supranational governance. He was also a showman who was fond of grand political gestures, as when he resigned his seat as MP in 2008 over the government's counter-terrorism legislation and sought to make the by-election into a referendum on civil liberties. Barnier was a Gaullist, who saw the EU as a way to reinforce the nation state, not to dismantle it. An introvert, he stood tall, said little but exuded the confidence of a former two-term Commissioner and French foreign minister. National leaders appointed their own EU spokespeople, sparking fears of a turf battle, yet Barnier quickly won their trust.

The EU's immediate priority in Brexit negotiations was to ensure that the UK honoured its financial obligations to the Union, respected the rights of EU citizens living in the UK and took no action that could lead to a hard border on the island of Ireland. Enda Kenny, the

Irish Taoiseach, played a central role in setting the third of these priorities by ensuring that all members of the Twenty-Seven – as the remaining member states now styled themselves – understood the high stakes for Ireland from Brexit and the EU's responsibilities to the Northern Ireland peace process.[82]

The EU's willingness to stand by Ireland to this degree served a strategic purpose, as the political scientist Brigid Laffan argues.[83] To the UK, it sent a clear signal that EU member states would stand together in the face of Brexit, putting its remaining member states' collective interests over those of a departing one. This helped the EU to maximise its leverage in negotiations and to prevent London from playing EU member states off against one another. Standing by Ireland also provided a tangible example of how the Union could help to protect its member states in a moment of economic and geopolitical turmoil. Here the EU sought to counter politicians such as Marine Le Pen in France and Geert Wilders in the Netherlands, who treated Brexit as a victory for their disruptive brand of right-wing populism. By offering the UK a future relationship that was visibly inferior to EU membership, the Heads of State or Government were determined to show EU citizens how costly leaving the Union would be.

What the UK sought from Brexit negotiations was more difficult to pin down. Three days after the referendum, Boris Johnson outlined his vision of a soft Brexit in which the UK would extricate itself from EU law and the jurisdiction of the European Court of Justice while retaining access to the EU single market and continuing to cooperate in areas such as the environment, foreign policy, defence and counter-terrorism.[84] At the time, Johnson spoke for many Leavers, who acknowledged the closeness of the referendum result and the UK's continuing economic and political interdependence with EU member states. But the idea of leaving the EU single market and customs union suddenly gained ground among Leavers for a variety of reasons.

The sudden switch in support from a soft to a hard vision of Brexit was not confined to Conservatives. The scholar Richard Tuck spoke for many Lexiteers – left-wing advocates of Brexit – when he recalled how his willingness to compromise after the referendum was soon overtaken by suspicion of those who sought to remain in the EU. 'All compromise proposals', he soon concluded, 'leave open a route quite quickly back into the EU in some fashion.'[85] Conservatives had another reason to fear a soft Brexit because it left their right flank exposed to Nigel Farage, who was on the lookout for a new political position as his time as an MEP drew to a close. A prominent supporter of Donald Trump, Farage responded enthusiastically when the president-elect declared that he would make a 'great' UK ambassador to the United States.[86] Fortunately for May, the UK had always sent career diplomats to Washington DC, allowing her to sidestep Trump's unsolicited suggestion.

While Barnier shuttled between national capitals, seeking to understand member states' concerns, especially those of the Irish government, Davis seemed disinterested in the fine details of negotiations and made little effort to build consensus within his own party. Barnier paid particular attention to Ireland's land border with Northern Ireland, which he was already familiar with from his time as European Commissioner for Regional Policy. Appearing before a House of Commons Select Committee in July 2016, Davis referred to the border as an internal one, raising questions about whether he even understood that Ireland was a sovereign state.[87] When he finally visited the border two years later, he did so without telling the press or Northern Irish politicians, for the sole purpose, it would seem, of having his photograph taken.

The less that Davis and other Leavers did to advance Brexit negotiations, the more it fell to May to find a way forward. The prime minister's speech at Lancaster House was an opportunity to level with voters, Parliament and her party about what sort of Brexit she believed to be in the national interest and on offer from the EU.[88] Instead, she came out for a hard Brexit, insisting that the UK would leave the customs union and the single market and that, if it came to it, 'no deal for Britain is better than a bad deal for Britain'. Entirely at odds with May's warnings about Brexit during the referendum campaign, the speech sought to keep Leavers in check and to appeal to right-wing Eurosceptic newspapers. 'Give us what we want, or you'll get crushed', offered *The Times* by way of summary, while the *Daily Mail* heaped patronising praise on 'The Steel of the New Iron Lady'.[89] Farage seemed happiest of all. 'Real progress', he tweeted. 'I can hardly believe that the PM is now using the phrases and words that I've been mocked for using for years.'[90]

To EU Heads of State or Government, who increasingly despaired of the UK, May's speech seemed entirely for domestic consumption. So it proved when the prime minister formally notified the European Council of the UK's decision to withdraw from the EU under Article 50 of the Treaty on European Union and then called a snap general election. From that moment, the British government had two years to conclude a withdrawal agreement, unless EU leaders unanimously agreed to an extension. This timetable would have been tight even if the prime minister had secured a cross-party consensus over how to respond to the referendum result, as Denmark had done in 1992 when voters rejected the Maastricht Treaty. But May would have struggled to replicate this approach even if she hadn't found the idea of doing a deal with Jeremy Corbyn's Labour Party unconscionable.[91]

May's arguments for Remain during the referendum campaign revealed a concern for the economic costs to the UK of erecting trade barriers with the EU, as well as discomfort with the free movement of workers within the union.[92] On that basis, the prime minister's personal preference was probably for a comparatively soft form of Brexit in which goods, services and capital, although not workers, could flow relatively freely between the EU and the UK. But it was next to impossible to win domestic support for this outcome while May remained beholden to hardline Eurosceptics in her own party. Rallying voters and the tabloid press around the national flag through her Lancaster House speech and her decision to trigger Article 50 provided May with a chance to increase her parliamentary majority and so decouple herself from those in her party who sought the hardest form of Brexit.

Like Cameron before her, May stepped up to the craps table and rolled snake eyes. Thanks to Labour's stronger than expected performance under Jeremy Corbyn in the 2017 General Election, the Conservatives lost their slim majority and returned as a minority government propped up by the Democratic Unionist Party. May was now beholden both to Eurosceptics in her own party and Northern Irish MPs who had campaigned for Brexit but now worried that it might advance the political cause they feared most: a united Ireland. It was a catastrophic political error from the prime minister, who compounded her problems by pressing ahead with her plans for a softer Brexit, setting her on a collision course with her backbenchers and Farage.

By February 2018, Michel Barnier's patience was wearing thin. Two months earlier, the negotiating teams published a statement of progress on their talks thus far. The so-called Joint Report indicated that the UK was ready to meet the EU's requests on financial obligations and citizens' rights and that the two shared a commitment to avoid a hard border on the island of Ireland. What the Joint Report didn't say, and what Theresa May wouldn't say, is how the UK would fulfil its stated ambition to leave the EU single market and customs union, while fulfilling its pledge to avoid a hard border on the island of Ireland. So, with the blessing of EU member states, the Commission published a draft withdrawal agreement, which indicated that Northern Ireland would align itself to the EU's customs union and some single market rules, thus avoiding the need for checks between Ireland and Northern Ireland. Great Britain, meanwhile, would leave the EU single market and customs union, giving the UK control of its own trade policy. The catch was that goods being shipped from Great Britain to Northern Ireland would require customs checks to ensure that the UK didn't have a backdoor into the EU's single market.

The leader of the Northern Irish Democratic Unionist Party, Arlene Foster, was incensed by the Commission's draft, which she saw as threatening Northern Ireland's place in the UK.[93] Although she had campaigned for Brexit, Foster had no desire to see a return to political violence in her homeland. As a child, she had been forced to move after her home was targeted by Republican paramilitaries over her father's role as a Royal Ulster Constabulary reservist. Equally, Foster couldn't, as a committed unionist, countenance the creation of an economic border between Northern Ireland and Great Britain to avoid one between Ireland and Northern Ireland. This was about economics as well as politics. Northern Ireland was much more integrated with the British economy than Ireland, leaving Northern Irish businesses exposed to time-consuming and costly checks on goods from their most important customers and suppliers. Having reassured Foster that the UK would remain united after Brexit, May had little choice but to side with the Democratic Unionist Party; now she came under pressure from the EU to present alternatives.[94] Before the prime minister could do so, however, she needed to square cabinet colleagues.

In July 2018, cabinet members arriving at Chequers had their mobile phones confiscated before being handed a one hundred-page document, which represented May's best attempt to deliver Brexit. Under the Chequers Plan, the UK as a whole sought to align itself with the EU's customs union and some provisions of the single market, allowing frictionless trade between the two. Despite her sabre-rattling over a 'no deal', May had proposed an economic relationship which sought to keep the UK as close as possible to the EU, subject to Leavers' demands to leave the EU single market and customs union proper. One by one, her cabinet's most prominent Leavers signed up to the deal. One by one, they had second thoughts and tendered their resignations. Davis was first to go, declaring 'the return of control to parliament more illusory than real'.[95] Next came Johnson. 'The trouble is that I have practised the words over the weekend and find that they stick in the throat,' Johnson wrote. 'Since I cannot in all conscience champion these proposals, I have sadly concluded that I must go.'[96]

May's premiership was on borrowed time. She occupied a minority position in a minority government and could count on little or no support from Labour, which was as divided over Brexit as her own party. Jeremy Corbyn had survived a leadership challenge after the referendum and clung to power by exceeding low expectations in the 2017 general election. Facing fierce pressure from his party's pro-EU wing to back a second referendum, he resisted doing so due to his ambivalence towards European integration and because he feared that Leave-voting Labour supporters would desert the party in droves if he did. So instead, Corbyn obfuscated over his preferred form of Brexit and slow-walked discussions over a referendum. Nor could May rely on the moral support that EU leaders typically offered each other in times of political crisis. At the European Council in Salzburg, Emmanuel Macron informed her that the Chequers Plan was 'a good and a brave step' but 'not acceptable' without clarity on how frictionless trade would work in practice.[97]

Faced with this dispiriting situation, May did what she always did and pressed on. In November 2018, EU and UK negotiators announced that they had reached an agreement on a withdrawal agreement. This text provided much the same guarantees on financial obligations and citizens' rights as the Joint Report. The key addition was the Northern Ireland backstop, under which the UK would remain part of the EU's customs territory until an alternative solution could be found to avoid a hard border on the island of Ireland. It was, May told the House of Commons, 'the best deal that could be negotiated'.[98] Her critics began to circle. To Arlene Foster, the fact that Northern Ireland alone would remain aligned to EU single market rules under the backstop was unacceptable.[99] For Boris Johnson, remaining in the EU customs territory left the UK with a form of 'colony status'.[100] Three times, MPs voted for May's deal and three times they rejected it. Before the final vote, May announced her intention to resign. 'I believe it was right to persevere, even when the odds against success seemed high,' she announced on the steps of Downing Street, her voice cracking as she thanked voters for 'the opportunity to serve the country I love'.[101]

Getting Brexit Done (2019)

In December 2019, UK Prime Minister Boris Johnson drove a JCB emblazoned with the slogan 'Get Brexit Done' through a wall of white bricks marked 'Gridlock' to thunderous applause from Conservative Party activists.[102] It was an inspired election slogan, which channelled British voters' frustration after three years of soul searching over how to deliver the result of David Cameron's referendum. Nigel Farage's Brexit Party, formed in response to Theresa May's deal, had received 5 million votes in the 2019 European Parliament election, but he lost supporters in droves once Johnson became prime minister, talked up the prospect of 'no deal' and, egged on by Downing Street's new chief strategist, Dominic Cummings, prorogued parliament for five weeks when MPs insisted that he seek an agreement.[103] The Brexit Party's offer of an electoral pact went unanswered by Johnson. By now, the prime minister appeared to have stolen every stitch of Farage's political clothing.

Johnson's prorogation of parliament, which was overturned by the UK Supreme Court as unlawful, was all part of his right-wing populist show. Only he, he insisted, could deliver the true will of the people against Remainers intent on blocking Brexit. When the prime minister flew to the European Council in October 2019 to sign a revised withdrawal agreement, there was a collective sigh of relief across the UK. After months of warnings over high tariffs, supply chain problems and medicine shortages, any deal was better than no deal. The Heads of State or Government seemed to share this sentiment, offering smiles and backslaps to their departing colleague, as he attended his first and last European Council as the leader of an EU member state.[104]

Hailed by British tabloids as a skilled negotiator, Johnson's deal was virtually identical to the one sketched by the Commission in its draft withdrawal agreement a year earlier. Theresa May's backstop was gone, replaced with a protocol, which aligned Northern Ireland, but not Great Britain, to the EU's customs union and certain single market rules. A hard border between Ireland and Northern Ireland had been avoided at the expense of customs checks on goods being shipped from Great Britain to Northern Ireland. No Conservative government 'could or should' agree to a border in the Irish Sea, Johnson had told the Democratic Unionist Party conference, eleven months before he did exactly that.[105]

The EU, although it gave ground by accepting that British officials could perform these customs checks, largely achieved what it had sought from Brexit negotiations. Beyond immediate concerns over financial obligations, citizens' rights and Northern Ireland, the EU had put its integrity ahead of its future relationship with the UK. The Political Declaration, which accompanied the withdrawal agreement, envisaged further negotiations on a 'comprehensive and balanced' UK–EU free trade area while signalling that this deal would yield nothing like the benefits of Union membership.[106] However much some EU leaders regretted Brexit, the messy manner of the UK's departure was not entirely unwelcome. Within a year of the UK referendum, Marine Le Pen had abandoned her pledge to take France out of the EU.[107] In the Netherlands, Geert Wilders experienced a similar change of heart.

Returning to London, Johnson presented his 'great deal' to Parliament, heralding his country's right to determine its own future, while rekindling its past as an 'open, generous, global, outward-looking and free-trading' nation.[108] Five days later, he called a general election. By now, the Labour Party had committed to hold a second referendum and to campaign for Remain. However, the window of opportunity for such a vote had long since closed. Yet again, Jeremy Corbyn faced low expectations but this time he underperformed, helping the Conservative Party to its best general election result since Margaret Thatcher's second term.

With a majority of eighty seats, Boris Johnson encountered none of the problems that Theresa May had done in securing parliamentary approval for his deal. How much the new prime minister truly believed in the agreement he had struck with the EU was never entirely clear. He had wagered his political career on a referendum that he probably expected to lose and then won the premiership only by championing a form of Brexit far harder than the one he had called for after the referendum. Whether Johnson fully understood the political wager he had placed or came to believe his own boosterism was difficult to discern, but it mattered little to British parliamentarians who approved the Brexit Bill with ease, allowing the EU–UK withdrawal agreement to take effect. On 1 February 2020, an official unhooked the Union Jack from its halyard in the atrium of the Europa Building in Brussels and walked away with the British flag draped unceremoniously over her arm, while street-sweepers in London cleaned College Green after the previous night's festivities.[109]

A New Stage

The Trade and Cooperation Agreement signed by the UK and EU in December 2020 secured the sovereignty that the British government had desired over its economic policy. By leaving the single market and customs union, the United Kingdom was now free to seek bilateral trade deals with countries of its choosing and to respond to global opportunities and crises without its EU partners. The price paid for such sovereignty was a bare-bones deal with the Union, which ensured tariff-free trade, but only for goods originating in the UK and EU. British businesses paid nearly £10 billion in EU tariffs in the first three-quarters of 2021 alone, either because their products were partially made in other parts of the world or because they were unable to provide the necessary paperwork to EU customs officials.[110] The agreement facilitated trade in some services, such as telecommunications, while curtailing access for financial services, costing the City of London £2.3 trillion in the value of derivatives trade in one month alone.[111] UK farmers no longer received subsidies from the European Union's common agricultural policy, although EU trawlers retained residual rights to fish in UK waters.[112] British citizens would need a visa waiver to visit EU member states and, in most cases, a permit to work there. Once a mainstay of European music festivals,

British bands could no longer count on performing at Rock Werchter, Roskilde and Sziget. United Kingdom university students could no longer spend a year abroad under the EU's Erasmus Programme, while British school trips to continental Europe plummeted because of the cost and inconvenience. The UK continued to share passenger name records and criminal records, but it was no longer a member of Europol or a participant in the European Arrest Warrant. The UK also took no part in the Common Security and Defence Policy or any aspect of the EU's Common Foreign and Security Policy.

Despite Brexit, the EU remained a potent issue in British politics. One reason is that this situation suited Boris Johnson. Having made his name as a Brussels-bashing journalist and won high office by backing Leave, the prime minister remained no less dependent on the EU as a political foil after UK withdrawal. From initially denying the EU's ambassador to the UK full diplomatic credentials to sending two navy frigates to Jersey over a row about post-Brexit fishing licences, Johnson missed no opportunity to rally British tabloids around the Union Jack and against the circle of stars. Euroscepticism had always been a displacement activity for the Conservative Party – over the end of the Cold War, over Thatcher's downfall, over New Labour – and so it remained while the search for Brexit's dividend continued. Hailed as a 'new dawn' by Johnson, the free trade agreement signed by the United Kingdom and Australia in June 2021 was expected to yield benefits for the UK in the region of 0.02 per cent of GDP.[113] The overall cost of leaving the EU on UK growth potential, meanwhile, was forecast at 4 per cent.[114]

In a poll conducted by Queens University Belfast in October 2021, 53 per cent of Northern Irish respondents agreed that the protocol was an appropriate response to Brexit, compared to only 46 per cent four months earlier.[115] In the same survey, 62 per cent agreed that the arrangement could benefit Northern Ireland. And yet, the Northern Ireland Protocol remained deeply unpopular with unionist politicians, who felt betrayed by Johnson's handling of Brexit and concerned that Northern Ireland's booming trade with Ireland in the early months of Brexit was weakening the former's ties to Great Britain. In March 2021, loyalists rioted on the streets of Derry-Londonderry for four consecutive nights throwing petrol bombs at police officers in protest against the protocol. Similar disturbances occurred in West Belfast in November 2021.

To John Gillingham, a historian of European integration writing two years after the referendum, British politics seemed remarkably stable.[116] But the long-term risks to the integrity of the United Kingdom from Brexit were real. In a poll published in August 2021, two-thirds of Northern Irish respondents believed that a referendum on Irish unity should be held because of Brexit even if most said they would vote to stay in the UK.[117] Another referendum on Scottish independence also seemed more likely after Brexit, if not any more winnable. That Scottish voters had been urged to vote against independence in 2014 to protect Scotland's membership of the EU and then been subject to Brexit despite their majority vote for Remain crystallised the case against being governed by London. But the prospect of border controls at Berwick-upon-Tweed if Scotland left the UK and joined the EU greatly complicated the economic case against independence. Although a pact between the Scottish Nationalist Party and Scottish Greens in August 2021 produced a clear pro-independence majority in Holyrood, Johnson refused to accept calls for a second independence referendum.

That Northern Ireland and Scotland might one day rejoin the EU seemed possible. That the United Kingdom might do so seemed remote in the extreme. And yet, one of the ironies of the 2016 referendum was how it spurred pro-EU sentiments among some sections of British society. In London's St Pancras station, Tracy Emin's light sculpture welcomed Eurostar passengers with 'I want my time with you' written in pink neon writing.[118] In Dover, on the side of a derelict building, a Banksy mural showed a workman chipping away at a star on the European flag.[119] The anonymous artist planned to replace it with an image of a crumpled flag on the day the UK left the Union, but the mural was mysteriously whitewashed. 'Never mind,' Bansky replied. 'I guess a big white flag says it just as well.'[120] These artists not only expressed their thoughts on Brexit. They also reflected shifts in public opinion towards the EU after the referendum. In a poll conducted by Savanta in December 2022, 51 per cent of respondents said that they would vote for the UK to rejoin the EU.[121] This figure rose to 67 per cent for those aged between 18 and 34.[122]

Try as Boris Johnson did to dampen such pro-EU sentiment through cultural initiatives such as UNBOXED – an event dedicated to British creativity known colloquially as the Festival of Brexit – it was only a matter of time before global events threw the UK and EU together. In November 2021, twenty-seven asylum seekers died in the English Channel after setting sail from Normandy for the Kent coast on an inflatable dinghy. A record 21,000 people made this perilous journey in 2021, as the Taliban's return to power in Afghanistan, continued instability in Syria and other world events impinged on Europe.[123] The UK prime minister's Twitter spat with French President Emmanuel Macron caught the headlines in the days following the tragedy.[124] But talks between EU and UK officials on a returns agreement continued behind the scenes. The UK's relationship with the EU wasn't over. It was merely entering a new stage.

14

Next Generation EU

'Mortal Danger' (2020)

There have been few more moving renditions of Beethoven's Ninth Symphony than the online version posted by nineteen self-isolating members of the Rotterdam Philharmonic Orchestra on 20 March 2020.[1] This performance of the European anthem resonated all the more by going viral on the same day that the Heads of State or Government met via video link to discuss the Covid-19 pandemic. Whereas the musicians enraptured those who heard them, the European Council's stuttering response enraged those who wanted coordinated action. In a rare public intervention, Jacques Delors, the 94-year-old former president of the European Commission, warned that a 'lack of European solidarity' had put the EU in 'mortal danger'.[2]

One month earlier, Mattia Maestri, a 38-year-old manager from Codogno in Italy's Lombardy region, was hospitalised with low oxygen levels. A keen runner, Maestri had struggled with a fever, persistent cough and shortness of breath for the previous ten days. Alarmed by a CT scan of their young and physically fit patient's lungs, the doctors broke protocols and tested for a new respiratory virus that had emerged in the Chinese city of Wuhan weeks earlier.[3] Maestri tested positive, becoming Europe's 'patient zero'.[4] By the time he was discharged from Codogno hospital several weeks later, his father had died, and Covid-19 was spreading rapidly across the continent.

Europe had faced health emergencies in the post-Maastricht period, including HIV, of which there were more than 700,000 diagnoses in the EU and European Economic Area by 2019.[5] However, the EU's response to earlier epidemics and pandemics was largely limited to modest funding for research and development and information exchange between health officials and ministers. The Maastricht Treaty made little difference in this regard. Although it introduced health protection as an aim of EU cooperation, health policy remained a matter for member states. The ferocious backlash from British politicians and tabloids against the European Commission's 1996 ban on British beef exports during the Bovine Spongiform Encephalopathy (BSE) crisis merely reinforced this point. Although the British government had admitted by then that the neurodegenerative disease could pass to humans, Prime Minister John Major still threatened to bring EU decision-making to a standstill over the export ban.[6]

When H1N1 – more commonly known as swine flu – reached Europe from North America in April 2009, EU health ministers declared the virus to be a 'potential global threat' and promised coordinated measures by the Commission, member states and the EU's newly created European Centre for Disease Prevention and Control (ECDC).[7] But when the pandemic turned out to be less severe than anticipated, the European Parliament criticised some member states' response as 'disproportionate' and unduly influenced by the World Health Organization and pharmaceutical companies.[8] While France and the United Kingdom invested in very costly vaccination programmes, the report noted, Poland didn't and yet faced much the same death rate as these member states.

On 9 January 2020, the ECDC reported a small number of pneumonia cases 'of unknown aetiology' at a market in the Chinese city of Wuhan. But, based on the limited information provided by Chinese authorities, the EU agency judged the risk that the virus would enter the Union and spread widely to be 'low to very low'.[9] Heavily caveated to begin with, this risk assessment was quickly revised. By 2 March, the ECDC was reporting more than 2,000 Covid-19 cases in the EU and neighbouring countries and 38 deaths.[10] The probability of new clusters of the kind witnessed in Lombardy was now 'moderate to high'. The European Fine Art Fair went ahead in Maastricht a week later, but other large-scale cultural and sporting events across the continent were soon cancelled. By the end of the month, more than 600,000 coronavirus cases had been reported in the European Union, European Economic Area and UK, and 51,059 people had died.[11] Schools, universities and workplaces moved online across the EU, as one member state after another went into lockdown.[12]

At the beginning of March, Ryanair CEO Michael O'Leary had called for an end to the 'lunacy on social media' over the coronavirus.[13] 'Let's not have irrational panic measures,' he urged. By the end of the month, European airlines were flying empty passenger planes between EU airports, just to reserve their landing slots. By the end of the following financial year, Ryanair had gone from a €1 billion profit to a €1 billion loss.[14] The airline industry was one of several sectors decimated by the sudden halt to face-to-face contact, including cultural and creative industries and the hospitality sector.[15] On the eve of the pandemic, the Commission had expected the EU economy to grow by 1.5 per cent in 2020, the seventh year of growth since the euro crisis.[16] By the summer of 2020, the Commission was expecting the economy to contract by a record 8.3 per cent.[17]

It was not just the speed with which Covid-19 spread or the pandemic's sudden, devastating impact on economic growth that alarmed EU watchers; it was also member states' willingness to suspend European policy commitments in the name of crisis management. The temporary reintroduction of border controls was a familiar feature of the Schengen Agreement, but never before had so many member states introduced checks on land, sea and air borders at once. Soon, the Heads of State or Government had agreed to restrict non-essential travel into the Schengen area, with some going further by unilaterally restricting or suspending the right of individuals to seek asylum in the EU.[18] Pleas to evacuate Mória went unheeded even after a fire broke out in the virus-ravaged refugee camp, killing a young girl.[19] When Hungary's National Assembly declared a state of emergency, which allowed Prime Minister Viktor Orbán to rule by decree for an unspecified duration, European democracy itself seemed to be in peril.

Personal protective equipment for health care workers was at a premium in the early weeks of the pandemic. So too was EU member states' willingness to work together. In France, President Emmanuel Macron made no apology for requisitioning 6 million surgical masks from Mölnlycke, a Swedish medical company based in Lyon, before they could be exported to Belgium, Italy, the Netherlands, Portugal and Spain.[20] Nor did German Chancellor Angela Merkel for her government's decision to ban the export of masks, gloves and protective suits to other EU member states.[21] 'When Europe needed to prove that this is not only a "fair weather Union",' lamented European Commission President Ursula von der Leyen, 'too many initially refused to share their umbrella.'[22]

Three video summits by the European Council in three weeks produced few concrete policy commitments. Although they declared their commitment to 'smooth border management' within the EU, national leaders didn't say how the Schengen Agreement would be salvaged. While they acknowledged the gravity of the Covid-19 pandemic, they remained non-committal on what the EU could or should do beyond the 'extensive action' already taken by member states to protect their economies. Unless a 'unified, powerful and effective response' could be achieved, warned Spanish Prime Minister Pedro Sánchez, populist forces would be unleashed once again, 'putting at risk the entire European project'.[23]

'Mr Nobody'

Giuseppe Conte was a surprise choice to serve as Italian prime minister when the Five Star Movement's Luigi Di Maio and the Northern League's Matteo Salvini formed a new populist government.[24] A specialist in private law, Conte had risen largely without trace to become a professor at the University of Florence and a member of various low-profile public bodies before he struck up a friendship with Di Maio and advised the insurgent left-wing party on justice and home affairs policy. Italy had previously had technocratic prime ministers, but they tended to be well-known public figures such as Romano Prodi. Nicknamed 'Mr Nobody', Conte had a low profile, even inside academic circles, and nearly scuppered his chances of becoming prime minister when accused of embellishing his visiting positions at various universities.[25] When he finally took the oath of office, Conte seemed to be no more than a frontman for politicians too controversial to lead in their own right.

Presenting himself to Italians as 'the people's lawyer', Conte stood by as Di Maio and Salvini toyed with the idea of settling government debt through mini-treasury bills, a scheme that cast doubt on the country's legal obligations to investors and membership of the eurozone.[26] When Salvini initially refused in July 2018 to let 450 migrants who had been rescued from the Mediterranean disembark in an Italian port, the prime minister turned to other EU member states for help rather than taking the Northern League's leader to task.[27] Conte did speak out when Salvini proposed a register of Roma, as a possible prelude to deporting non-Italian members of this ethnic minority, but the prime minister remained in post.[28] And then, just as Salvini prepared to trigger fresh elections to capitalise on his rising poll numbers, Conte resigned, publicly denouncing his former colleague as a dangerous opportunist. Applauded for his bravery, his earlier support for the Northern League now seemingly overlooked, Conte was invited by the Italian president to form a new government, which he unexpectedly did by brokering an agreement between the Five Star Movement and more moderate parties of the centre and centre left. Denied a general election, Salvini returned to the opposition benches to brood, leaving Conte not only in power but in charge.

When Covid-19 hit, Conte rose to the challenge. As UK Prime Minister Boris Johnson boasted of shaking hands 'with everybody' and allowed packed sporting events to go ahead, the Italian prime minister locked down towns, regions and eventually the entire country in quick succession.[29] Channelling Johnson's hero, Winston Churchill, Conte described the unfolding pandemic as 'Italy's darkest hour', but promised to use the full resources of the state to contain the outbreak.[30] Conte's words connected with Italians, who stayed at home to protect one another, and moved work, schooling and social lives online where possible. Other European countries followed Italy's lead, including the UK, where Johnson had initially sought to protect businesses, mindful perhaps of the economic costs of Brexit. Ten days after the UK finally entered a nationwide lockdown, the prime minister was battling to breathe in an intensive care ward in London's St Thomas' hospital.

Conte's immediate worry was how to support Italian hospitals, which found themselves suddenly overwhelmed with Covid-19 patients. In Bergamo, the army was called in to construct a field hospital. Soon, they were helping to transport bodies to other parts of the country, such was the demand for undertakers. But anxiety over the economic impact of the pandemic, both in terms of health care expenditure and the costs to businesses of losing workers and customers, soon intensified. In March 2020, Conte announced a plan to borrow an extra €25 billion to cope with the pandemic.[31] By early April, this figure had doubled. Italy's debt to GDP ratio was close to 140 per cent before the pandemic hit, leaving financial markets concerned about additional borrowing.[32] As risk premia on Italian debt rose, it seemed only a matter of time before the government would need external financial assistance. Two years after Greece had exited its third loan agreement, the single currency's problems seemed to be starting all over again.

A key difference this time, as the scholar Luuk van Middelaar notes in his chronical of the pandemic, was not just that EU policy-makers had recent experience of crisis management but the speed with which they put this learning into practice.[33] European Central Bank President Mario Draghi's promise in 2012 to do whatever it takes to save the euro had come after years of wrangling over the merits of large-scale bond purchases. A little over a month after Europe's first recorded fatality from Covid-19, Draghi's successor,

Christine Lagarde, unveiled a €750 billion pandemic emergency purchase programme.[34] The European Stability Mechanism had been created after many months of negotiation between member states over how to handle the euro crisis. Within the first few weeks of the pandemic, eurozone finance ministers put the European Stability Mechanism on standby to help with the 'healthcare, cure and prevention' costs of the crisis.[35] But these measures didn't go far enough for Conte, who bristled at the strict conditionality and stigma attached to European Stability Mechanism loans. The prime minister was mindful too of Salvini's earlier attempts to whip up popular opposition to this crisis fund, which the Northern League leader had warned would bring 'ruin for millions of Italians and the end of our national sovereignty'.[36] Were Italy now forced to seek funding from the same body, leaving the country under the surveillance of international creditors, Salvini would have a field day. It was time for EU member states to show genuine solidarity, Conte told his fellow Heads of State or Government, or the populists would win.

Throughout the euro crisis, German Chancellor Angela Merkel resisted policy solutions that would be seen to pass the economic problems of other eurozone members onto the German taxpayer. She remained steadfast in this view, telling Conte and Spanish Prime Minister Pedro Sánchez that their plans for coronabonds – debt instruments issued collectively by member states – would never win the approval of the Bundestag.[37] Inevitably such a scheme would be portrayed as the frugal North subsidising the profligate South. But the chancellor understood that she couldn't force the Italian prime minister to use a policy instrument that he was politically opposed to and that the single currency would be at risk until an alternative course of action could be found. With an approval rating above 80 per cent in the early months of the pandemic, Merkel had political capital to spend.[38] The right-wing populist Alternative for Germany, in contrast, lost political momentum after trying but failing to blame foreigners for the virus, which by now was becoming a German, European and global emergency.

During the euro crisis, Merkel had to contend with French President Nicolas Sarkozy's frenetic diplomacy, followed by his successor François Hollande's domestic woes. Now the Élysée Palace was occupied by a politician who had presented himself to the French people as a progressive pro-EU alternative to Marine Le Pen's reactionary nationalism and won. Macron was determined to leave his mark on the EU and, having fallen short in his efforts to create a meaningful eurozone budget capable of adjusting to macroeconomic shocks, he seized his chance when Covid-19 struck to propose something altogether more ambitious. In phone call after phone call to Berlin during the early months of the pandemic, he sought common ground with Merkel, who worried that the pandemic could devastate the EU and, perhaps, also her legacy.[39] The chancellor was willing to do a deal but on her terms.

In May 2020, Macron and Merkel presented a joint plan for a €500 billion EU recovery fund to support European regions and sectors hardest hit by the crisis. European taxpayers would underwrite the fund, not pay for it upfront. Instead, the Commission would borrow on behalf of the EU and repay this loan in due course using the Union's 'own resources'. Hitherto, the EU budget was small and resolutely balanced. Under this plan, the EU would borrow on the scale of a large state to help restart the European economy.

Had von der Leyen headed up this audacious proposal, her ideas would likely have been dismissed. Instead, she waited until Macron and Merkel had tabled their idea and then moved at lightning speed to make it happen. Like Delors in his prime, she studied the political weather and was ready to move when the wind from national capitals changed. Appearing at the European Parliament in May 2010, the Commission President outlined plans for Next Generation EU, under which the Commission would borrow €750 billion on behalf of the EU to finance grants and loans to member states. Previous generations had grappled with the reconstruction and reuniting of Europe, she argued, and it now fell to the current cohort to chart a common course out of a global pandemic.

Inevitably, it was up to the Heads of State or Government to make or break this proposal. Predictably, Dutch Prime Minister Mark Rutte pushed back, fearing that a settlement which looked overly generous towards Southern Europe would play into the hands of right-wing populist Geert Wilders and his younger Eurosceptic rival Thierry Baudet in the following year's general election. Prior to the summit, Dutch Finance Minister Wopke Hoekstra had been rebuked for asking why some member states had left themselves so vulnerable to economic surprises such as Covid-19. A veteran of the euro crisis, who had taken tough and unpopular decisions to restore his country's public finances, Portuguese Prime Minister António Costa dismissed Hoekstra's remarks as repugnant to everything the EU stood for, leaving the Dutch finance minister politically isolated.[40] Fearing a similar fate, Rutte switched his attention from Southern to Central and Eastern Europe. EU recovery funds must not be disbursed, the Dutch prime minister insisted, to member states that failed to respect EU values on democracy and the rule of law.[41] This put Polish Prime Minister Mateusz Morawiecki and Hungarian Prime Minister Viktor Orbán on the defensive and threatened to derail any deal.

It took four days and nights – the second-longest EU summit since Nice in December 2000 – before European Council President Charles Michel announced that a deal had been reached on Next Generation EU. As usual in such cases, everyone got something. Macron got his recovery fund. Merkel made sure it was temporary. Rutte secured a veto over the disbursement of grants and loans and Morawiecki and Orbán ensured that references to democracy and the rule of law in the final agreement were suitably vague. The real winner was Conte, who secured the display of European solidarity that he had sought. It was a historic moment for the EU, he concluded, and one that made him feel proud to be Italian.[42]

In June 2021, Ursula von der Leyen signed off on Italy's plan to spend nearly €200 billion in EU grants on loans in schemes including ultrafast broadband for 8.5 million homes and businesses, green trains and high-speed railway connections.[43] By this point, Matteo Renzi had withdrawn his new centrist party, Italia Viva, from government, following a row with Conte over how to spend the Next Generation EU funds. Having survived a vote of confidence in the Italian Parliament, Conte ran out of political good fortune when he was unable to form a new government. Failing to find a caretaker prime minister from the ranks of the Five Star Movement, Italian President Sergio Mattarella turned to the one person he thought could steer the country through a national crisis: Mario Draghi. The former ECB president had never before held elected office nor publicly expressed a desire to do so. But he accepted Mattarella's invitation and, with unexpected support from Matteo Salvini, Matteo Renzi and Silvio Berlusconi, formed a government of unity. The move was a testament to Italian politics' resilience in the post-Maastricht period, as well as its most troubling pathologies.[44]

When the pandemic hit, former IMF chief economist Olivier Blanchard warned of a second euro crisis if investors baulked at Italy's rapidly rising debt ratio, triggering a self-fulfilling sovereign debt crisis.[45] That this scenario didn't come to pass was due to the Italian government's determination to privilege economic growth over fiscal stability. Short-term work schemes and emergency loans and guarantees for businesses limited the economic damage from lockdowns, the lifting of which led to a remarkable rebound in economic activity.[46] Having contracted by 8.9 per cent in 2020, the Italian economy grew by 6.5 per cent in 2021, its strongest performance since the country's post-war boom came to an end.[47] By itself, the Italian government's expansionary fiscal policy had the potential to trigger a sovereign debt crisis, especially after the country's primary balance (a key measure of fiscal sustainability) turned negative in 2020. But Next Generation EU helped to reduce Italian bond yields even before the first funds reached Rome by signalling that the Union stood behind its member states and the single currency. So too did the ECB's bond purchase programme, which reached nearly €2 trillion by December 2020.

Italy was no isolated case. The European Union as a whole expanded by 5.3 per cent in 2021, its fastest growth rate since the single currency began.[48] Unemployment – long the Achilles heel of the European economy – reached a post-Maastricht low of 6.7 per cent in 2022. And yet, the EU's rapid recovery from the pandemic shock brought a new set of economic challenges. Chief among them was inflation, driven by supply chain problems and rising energy prices caused by the global economy's hard reset. Frequently criticised for its deflationary bias, the eurozone recorded an annual inflation rate of close to 9 per cent in June 2022.[49] The ECB insisted that it would meet its 2 per cent target in the medium term as it raised interest rates for the first time in a decade, but a painful process of economic adjustment lay ahead.

Vaccine

A licenced physician with a master's degree in public health and a PhD in medical research, von der Leyen brought a unique skill set to the EU's handling of Covid-19. The first Commission President to live in the Commission's Brussels headquarters, she and her team worked late nights to walk back member states' uncoordinated approach to the pandemic. First, she convinced national leaders to rescind bans on exporting personal protective equipment to other EU member states in exchange for a Union-wide export ban to the rest of the world.[50] Then she introduced a 'green lane' scheme to keep internal border checks on freight vehicles to less than fifteen minutes.[51] Most member states complied, ending the long waits faced by truck drivers in the early weeks of the pandemic. For a moment, the single market and the spirit of European solidarity had seemed in peril. By mid-2020, intra-EU trade in goods had largely returned to normal.[52]

In its lessons learned on the EU's response to H1N1, the European Parliament had called for joint procurement in future pandemics to avoid the uncoordinated and costly outlays by national governments witnessed in response to swine flu. Member states duly agreed that the Commission could purchase 'medical countermeasures' on their behalf when faced with serious threats to cross-border health.[53] Von der Leyen's initial attempt to use these powers to purchase joint stocks of personal protective equipment failed, but the Commission soon signed contracts with medical manufacturers to supply masks, gloves, face shields and ventilators. Although this equipment didn't materialise quickly, the contracts helped the Commission turn the page on the EU's crisis response and build its credibility as a crisis coordinator. In June 2020, von der Leyen announced that the Commission would enter into negotiations with individual vaccine producers to develop and purchase Covid-19 vaccines on behalf of the EU.[54]

When Mattia Maestri had presented symptoms at Codogno hospital, the Commission had already launched a €10 million call for urgent research into the coronavirus, including on a vaccine. In the months that followed, the European Investment Bank provided €175 million in financing to CureVac and BioNTech, two German pharmaceutical companies which began vaccine development within a matter of weeks after the virus' genetic sequence was made public.[55] Having invested in such research, the Commission feared that others might reap the rewards when reports emerged that US President Donald Trump sought exclusive rights to CureVac's highly promising mRNA vaccine.[56] The Commission also worried about vaccine nationalism closer to home when France, Germany, Italy and the Netherlands signed an advance deal for up to 400 million doses of the Oxford–AstraZeneca Covid-19 vaccine. But these countries soon agreed to von der Leyen's joint purchase plan after a furious backlash from smaller EU member states, which understandably feared that they would miss out.[57]

Never before had EU officials held so many European lives in their hands. Never before had the European Commission entered such high-stakes negotiations with big businesses at the centre of world events. Sandra Gallina, one of the Commission's most experienced trade negotiators, led EU talks with Johnson & Johnson, Sanofi, CureVac, Moderna and BioNTech, which by now had partnered with US company, Pfizer.

By December 2020, Gallina had secured advance purchase agreements for 860 million doses of vaccines that had passed stage three clinical trials and received conditional authorisation from the European Medicines Agency. CureVac had failed to live up to its promise, despite significant EU investment, but the Pfizer–BioNTech Covid-19 vaccine, another beneficiary of European funding, passed with flying colours. On 27 December 2020, Claudia Alivernini, a nurse at the Lazzaro Spallanzani Hospital in Rome, became the first Italian citizen to be vaccinated against Covid-19. It was, she told reporters, 'an act of love and responsibility towards the community'.[58] 'Now let's see when you die' came the response from one anti-vax campaigner on social media. The populist backlash against the EU's pandemic response had begun.

Antivax

Alternative for Germany was not the only right-wing populist party caught cold by Covid-19. In the Netherlands, Geert Wilders and Thierry Baudet initially blamed Prime Minister Mark Rutte for his slow response to the pandemic and called for a strict nationwide lockdown.[59] When Rutte relented, the two populist leaders found it difficult not to support government policy in the short term. In Italy, Matteo Salvini insisted, at first, that he didn't have a mask and wouldn't wear one.[60] But days later he donned a face covering in the colours of the Italian flag and urged his compatriots to do the same.

By November 2020, nearly 9 million people in the EU had a recorded case of Covid-19 and more than 265,000 people had died.[61] The lifting of lockdown measures six months earlier had been greeted with widespread relief. But, with vaccines still in clinical trials, the opening up of schools and workplaces led to a new wave of infections and fatalities. Further lockdowns were unavoidable yet unpopular. In a Eurobarometer survey conducted in the summer of 2020, 62 per cent expressed satisfaction with measures taken by national governments to fight the coronavirus.[62] By winter, this figure had fallen to 43 per cent. Over the same period, the percentage of people who found it difficult to cope with measures to fight the pandemic, especially confinement, increased from 32 to 40 per cent. While a clear majority of respondents agreed that a vaccine was the only way to end the pandemic – and that the EU was playing a key role in ensuring access to vaccines – a similar percentage expressed uncertainty over the long-term side-effects of being inoculated.

Sensing a political opportunity, Thierry Baudet appeared before the Dutch parliament with a bullhorn to protest against further lock-down measures and reportedly told party members that the Hungarian financier-philanthropist George Soros had created Covid-19 to take away people's freedom.[63] Dismissed as a crank, and temporarily stripped of his party's leadership, Baudet's about-face endeared him to a small, vocal group of Dutch citizens who took to the streets to demonstrate against the government's handling of the crisis. When these protests turned violent after Prime Minister Mark Rutte imposed a night-time curfew, Baudet joined Geert Wilders in condemning the rioters. However, Baudet then stole a march on his populist rival by coming out strongly against vaccines which, he claimed without corroborating evidence, had severe side-effects.[64] Dismissed in the early months of the pandemic, Baudet's Forum for Democracy won six additional seats in the March 2021 election, while Wilders' Freedom Party lost three. Covid-19 cases spiked in the Netherlands later that year, including in Rotterdam Zoo, where Bokito the gorilla, who had lived an unadventurous life since his dramatic escape in May 2007, caught the virus but soon recovered.[65]

Not all right-wing populists were prepared to play politics with the pandemic to this degree. In the 2010s, Salvini had mimicked the Five Star Movement's sceptical stance towards childhood vaccines and the legal mandating thereof, even as parents' growing alarm over such political messages contributed to measles outbreaks across the country. However, he lacked the courage of his convictions when faced with a pandemic that had killed more than 100,000 Italians by the end of 2020. In July 2021, Salvini received his first dose of the vaccine and then joined protests against Prime Minister Mario Draghi's decision to deny access to bars, restaurants and gyms for those who hadn't been vaccinated.[66] That Salvini still supported Draghi's caretaker government reinforced the sense of opportunism surrounding such opposition. But with popular demonstrations against the Covid-pass gaining momentum – and the Northern League's right-wing populist rival, Brothers of Italy, riding high in the polls – Salvini didn't dare do otherwise.

Alternative for Germany responded to its disappointing performance in the 2021 federal election by doubling down on its opposition to masks and vaccines. When Bernd Grimmer, a party member who served in the regional parliament of Baden-Württemberg, died from the virus in December 2021, Alternative for Germany leaders defended their unvaccinated colleagues' choice.[67] Grimmer knew the risks, they insisted: 'Freedom was more important to him.' Behind this tragedy lay the story of how a politician who had served alongside Petra Kelly in the early days of the Greens had drifted to the right and embraced a policy that preserved his sense of freedom but cost him his life. Meanwhile, in France, Sir James Goldsmith's erstwhile political ally, Philippe de Villiers, blamed 'Big Pharma, Big Data, Big Finance, the Bill Gates Foundation and the Davos Forum' for the pandemic, while Éric Zemmour, a polemical journalist turned populist politician, sought to outflank Marine Le Pen, by declaring fears over Covid to be overstated and opposing vaccine boosters for those aged under 65.[68]

Despite such pandemic politics, France, Germany and Italy boasted vaccination rates about the EU average of 71.7 per cent of the population by February 2022.[69] Not so Romania and Bulgaria, which had rates of 41.9 per cent and 29.2 per cent respectively. Both countries paid a price for their underfunded health care systems and haphazard vaccine rollout. But they were the victims too of political leaders who failed to push back against systematic disinformation about the coronavirus vaccine from social media influencers, such as Ventsislav Angelov, who filmed himself attacking a GP who had performed vaccinations.[70] By this point, more than 34,000 Bulgarians had died from the coronavirus. In Romania, Diana Iovanovici Şoşoacă, a charismatic senator prone to political stunts, achieved nationwide attention by distributing false information outside vaccination centres and calling on young people to 'party hard' rather than risk death.[71] By October 2021, the country was losing 500 people per day to the virus.[72]

The EU was relatively unscathed politically from this phase of the pandemic. Few questioned whether the European Commission should have been allowed to borrow €750 billion to fund grants and loans for EU member states or to keep such funding flowing as economic growth surged, and with it inflationary pressures. Nor did the EU's plans for a carbon border adjustment tax and plastic tax to repay such borrowing generate much public attention. Such scrutiny would surely come later, alongside hard bargaining and deliberation over whether to make the EU's extraordinary response to Covid-19 permanent.

The most perilous moment for the EU came in January 2021 when AstraZeneca announced that it would deliver 30 million vaccines in the first quarter rather than the 80 million doses promised.[73] The United Kingdom suffered no such shortfall and, indeed, continued to receive doses of AstraZeneca produced at a factory in the Netherlands until the EU imposed export controls.[74] Fearing a public backlash against the EU if unvaccinated Europeans died as a result of this delay, Commission President Ursula von der Leyen decided to trigger a safeguard clause in the Northern Ireland Protocol – the agreement between the EU and UK to avoid a hard border on the island of Ireland after Brexit – to prevent EU-made vaccines from being exported to the UK via Ireland. The safeguard was designed to deal with serious economic, societal or environmental difficulties, but von der Leyen failed to appreciate the sensitivities surrounding border checks of any sort on the island of Ireland and to consult relevant stakeholders.

What followed was a fast-paced masterclass in what happens when European officials get ahead of member states on matters of national sovereignty. Two hours after reports emerged of von der Leyen's decision, Irish Foreign Minister Simon Coveney announced that he was in contact with the European Commission over its announcement, which had been widely condemned in Ireland and, in a rare show of unity, by Northern Ireland's nationalist and unionist leaders.[75] Just over three hours later, the Commission announced that it would not trigger the safeguard clause after all.

Although this furore didn't help the EU's already strained relations with the British government, which had condemned the Commission's initial decision but continuously threatened to suspend the Northern Ireland Protocol in the months that followed, EU member states moved on.[76] The Commission clawed back credibility by reaching a legal settlement with AstraZeneca, which ensured that the remaining doses would be delivered, and signing new contracts with other vaccine providers.

Member states' vaccination programmes soon scaled up and by July 2021, the EU had pulled ahead of the United States in terms of the percentage of people receiving a second dose.[77] Five EU member states, meanwhile, were ahead of the UK by this point. The most serious vaccine shortfalls occurred in Africa, where just 15 per cent of the continent's adult population had been fully vaccinated by March 2022. Although the EU was the world's biggest vaccine exporter, it supplied ten times more doses to the rest of Europe than to Africa.[78]

As the pandemic wore on, anti-lockdown protests occurred across Europe, as well as other parts of the world. National governments bore the brunt of these demonstrations, but the EU didn't escape entirely. In March 2021, Tom Meert, an IT manager from Leuven without prior political experience, formed Europeans United, a pressure group dedicated to open and democratic debate about pandemic restrictions.[79] Joining forces with Worldwide Demonstration, an international anti-lockdown group accused of pedalling conspiracy theories and extreme political views, Europeans United coordinated a series of open-air protests in Parc du Cinquantenaire in Brussels'

EU Quarter.[80] Calling on the EU to sanction member states for breaching fundamental values, the group's rallies grew steadily larger. They also grew more violent. On 23 January 2022, a crowd of 50,000 protesters spilled out of the park into Rond-point Schuman and fought running battles with police in front of the Berlaymont. The European External Action Service, headquarters of the EU's diplomatic corps, bore the brunt of the violence as masked individuals used sticks, stones and poles to smash in the building's windows. Distancing himself from rioters, Meerts told his supporters, 'They are the old world, we are the new.'[81]

15

Ukraine

'Going Nowhere Fast'

At 4.00 a.m. local time on 24 February 2022, Russian troops entered Ukraine for the second time in a decade. Shortly afterwards, Russian television broadcast an address in which President Vladimir Putin announced a 'special military operation' to achieve 'the demilitarisation and denazification' of Ukraine.[1] 'We are not going to impose anything on anyone by force,' Putin insisted. But the explosions that rocked Kyiv, Kharkiv, Odesa and Mariupol that morning showed this promise to be no more credible than the Russian president's claim that Ukraine was run by NATO-backed 'extreme nationalists and neo-Nazis'.[2] The extreme nationalist, in this case, was Putin, who in a speech three days earlier had claimed Ukraine as part of Russia's 'history, culture, and spiritual space' and denied its right to statehood.[3] Russian intelligence probably expected Ukraine's government to fall within a matter of hours or days; if so, it badly miscalculated, as did many Western analysts.

Volodymyr Zelenskyy played the Ukrainian president on television before doing so in real life. *Servant of the People* (2015–19) tells the story of Vasily Petrovich Goloborodko, an everyman history teacher whose diatribe against Ukraine's corrupt political elite goes viral, leading to his unlikely election as president. A homage to Frank Capra's *Mr Smith Goes to Washington* (1939) and the sentimental works it inspired, *Servant of the People* turned Zelenskyy into a household figure and encouraged his bid for the presidency, which he won by a landslide in April 2019. Like his on-screen alter ego, Zelenskyy surprised his detractors. To some, the new president was no more than a political satirist or a puppet of the oligarchs who supported his election bid. But Zelenskyy showed himself to be a serious-minded politician who tried to limit the political power of oligarchs and their control of the media, even if he fell well short in his promise to end political corruption. In foreign policy, the president struggled from the outset. His pledge to bring peace to Donbas came to little. By the beginning of 2022, more than 14,000 people had been killed and more than one million people displaced in a slow-burning war between Ukrainian forces and Russian-backed separatists.[4] To the Trump Administration, Zelenskyy seemed like a soft touch.[5] European Union leaders remained frustrated with the sluggish pace of political reform under Zelenskyy's presidency and unmoved by his calls for Ukraine to be considered for membership.[6]

When Russia invaded in February 2022, Zelenskyy could have tried to cut a deal with Putin or fled to safety with his family. Instead, he announced a general military mobilisation, prevented all men aged 18 to 60 from leaving the country and called up civilians with prior military experience. Members of the Rada, Ukraine's parliament, were given assault rifles, and bridges in and out of the country's major cities were blown up to slow the Russian army's advance. Possessed of far superior strength and capabilities, Russian forces had invaded from three fronts: the north, with logistical support from Belarus, Crimea and eastern Ukraine. Their primary aim, it seemed, was to encircle and then quickly capture Ukraine's capital. But Russian forces, although their missiles reduced homes, suburbs and whole towns to rubble, encountered stiff resistance across the country, as well as unforeseen difficulties in maintaining supply chains. The Ukrainian government's estimates that nearly 20,000 Russian troops were killed in the first month of the invasion may well have been exaggerated, yet even the Kremlin admitted to 'significant losses'.[7]

Zelenskyy proved to be a skilful wartime leader, who recorded televised addresses and selfie videos not only to rally his fellow citizens but to reach out to Russian citizens who risked their safety by demonstrating against Putin. Above all, the Ukrainian president sought international sympathy for his country, putting pressure on world leaders to provide humanitarian and military aid. Whereas Putin's long and rambling public addresses convinced few who didn't already support him, Zelenskyy used his training as an actor and comedian to build support in Europe, the United States and beyond. Swapping his smart suits for khaki fatigues, he presented himself to the world as a defiant resistance leader for the digital age. An early video recorded on the night after the invasion in which Zelenskyy and a group of political leaders appeared on the streets of Kyiv and announced their determination to defend their country quickly gained more than a million views on YouTube.[8] Little known outside his country before the invasion, Zelenskyy was soon heralded as an 'internet star'. Having pulled *Servant of the People* from its US catalogue in 2021, Netflix reversed its decision. 'You asked and it's back!' gushed the streaming service three weeks after the invasion.[9]

By the end of March 2022, the war seemed to be, in the words of UN Secretary-General António Guterres, 'going nowhere fast'.[10] Five rounds of peace negotiations, held in Belarus and then Turkey, made little headway. By the end of the year, nearly 18,000 civilians had been killed in Ukraine as a result of the invasion, including 429 children.[11] Most lost their lives in indiscriminate airstrikes, rocket attacks or shelling. Although Russian authorities denied mass killings in Bucha, satellite images corroborated testimony that hundreds of innocent civilians had been tied up, shot and dumped in the streets of this Kyiv neighbourhood. In the coastal city of Mariupol, hundreds were trapped in the rubble of the Regional Drama Theatre, which had been transformed into a makeshift air-raid shelter. The word 'children' had been sketched in large letters on the asphalt surrounding this building in the days before this attack.[12] Russian authorities denied claims of genocide, although it was difficult to do otherwise while sticking to Putin's script about this being a 'special military operation' which bore civilians no harm.

Sanctions

The European Union had seen no shortage of foreign policy crises in the post-Maastricht period, but none on this scale since the Yugoslav Wars. Then national leaders had vacillated despite their commitment to a common foreign and security policy. Now they moved together with astonishing speed to hold Russia to account for its breach of the European security order. Immediately before the invasion, the EU extended restricted measures to the 351 members of the Russian Duma who had called on Vladimir Putin to recognise Donetsk and Luhansk's declaration of independence from Ukraine.[13] On the day after, Putin and his foreign minister, Sergey Lavrov, were among those added to this list.[14] In the weeks that followed, three further rounds of sanctions targeted Russian oligarchs, including Roman Abramovich, owner of London's Chelsea Football Club.[15] The EU also closed its airspace to Russian planes and prohibited Russia's central bank from accessing reserves held in the EU.

These actions and those implemented by the EU's international partners had a devastating impact on the Russian economy. The rouble quickly lost 60 per cent of its value against the euro, leading the Central Bank of Russia to double its main interest rate overnight. Although the currency recovered much of its value in the weeks that followed, the rouble was no longer freely convertible.[16] Meanwhile, Russian consumers faced a sudden jump in prices and a shortage of essential products and the Moscow Stock Exchange shut for nearly a month. When the Russian government sought to repay dollar-denominated debt in roubles, being unable to raise the necessary foreign currency, it was declared in a state of selective default by Standard and Poor's.[17]

Despite the stringency of these sanctions, the EU baulked at the one measure that had the greatest potential to end the war: banning imports of Russian oil and natural gas. When the Heads of State or Government had discussed the growing importance of energy security at the Hampton Court Summit in October 2005, the EU was importing 124 billion cubic metres of gas each year from Russia.[18] By 2020, this figure had risen to 155 billion. Germany, despite its embrace of renewables, still relied on natural gas for about a quarter of its energy consumption and on Russia for half of its natural gas imports. Under intense public and diplomatic pressure, German Chancellor Olaf Scholz did what his predecessor, Angela Merkel, had refused to do, by suspending Nord Stream 2, the controversial gas pipeline running from Russia to Germany under the Baltic Sea which had long been opposed by Poland and the EU's Baltic member states.[19] But Scholz ruled out a ban on Russian gas imports for fear of pushing the German economy into recession. As the war drove gas prices higher, the EU's daily energy bill to Russia went from around €200 million per day to around €800 million.[20]

As a former Soviet republic which later joined NATO, Lithuania remained especially vulnerable to Russia's revanchism. It was also the most foresighted in seeking energy security. When it joined the EU in 2004, the Baltic republic imported 100 per cent of its natural gas from Russia, leaving it increasingly concerned over its energy security as Putin's foreign policy turned more threatening. In 2014, one year after Russia and Belarus conducted the largest war game in Europe since the end of the Cold War on Lithuania's border, Lithuanian President Dalia Grybauskaitė formally opened a floating liquefied natural gas terminal in the Port of Klaipėda. Using this facility to store gas shipped from Hammerfest in Norway, Lithuania halved its import dependence on Russia within five years. Six weeks after Russia invaded Ukraine, Grybauskaitė's successor, Gitanas Nausėda, announced a complete ban on Russian gas imports. 'Years ago my country made decisions that today allow us with no pain to break energy ties with the aggressor,' the Lithuanian president declared on Twitter. 'If we can do it, the rest of Europe can do it too!'[21]

Despite Nausėda's pleas, there was little that most EU member states could do in the very short term. Underground gas storage was running at around a quarter of full capacity in early 2022, leaving the Union with barely enough gas to make it to the summer.[22] As a whole, there were only twenty-six liquefied natural gas terminals in the Union by this point. Germany had none, signing its first contract to build one only after Russia invaded Ukraine. Further contracts quickly followed, although they came with a long lead time and covered only a fraction of Germany's energy needs. In July 2022, EU member states agreed to reduce gas demand by 15 per cent, but it was not entirely clear how this voluntary commitment would be met.[23] As rising fuel and food prices linked to the war added to acute inflationary pressures in the eurozone, it remained uncertain how long the EU's resolve towards Russia would last.

Putin soon ratcheted up the pressure by demanding that 'unfriendly countries' settle their gas bills in roubles rather than euro or dollars. When Bulgaria, Denmark, Finland, Poland and the Netherlands refused, Russia cut off gas deliveries, leaving these and other EU member states scrambling to sign contracts with alternative suppliers. The United States and Qatar provided valuable lifelines, with the result that Russia's share of total EU gas imports fell to 13 per cent in October 2022 compared to 39 per cent twelve months earlier.[24] This diversification, coupled with a concerted effort by EU businesses and consumers to reduce their energy usage and an unusually warm European winter, helped to avoid widespread gas shortages. But concerns over energy supplies remained, especially as liquefied natural gas storage was depleted once again. The EU's efforts to wean itself off Russian gas also brought new dependencies. When a corruption scandal involving a group of MEPs and officials from Mauritania, Morocco and Qatar came to light in December 2022, a Qatari diplomat warned of consequences for his country's cooperation with the EU in the field of energy security.[25]

'Told You So' Moment

A political survivor, Josep Borrell was appointed Spain's foreign minister by Pedro Sánchez in 2018, twenty-five years after he had served in Felipe González's last government. The second of these roles almost came to an abrupt end when Borrell was sanctioned for insider trading over the sale of shares of an energy firm whose board he served on.[26] But the Catalan retained the support of Sánchez, who championed him for a top European job. Aged 72 when he became the EU's High Representative for Foreign Affairs and Security Policy, Borrell found Federica Mogherini a hard act to follow. The Italian had patiently gained the trust of EU foreign ministers. Borrell shot from the hip and too often missed.

When the High Representative visited Moscow in February 2021, he sought to show that the EU could do Realpolitik.[27] The Union and Russia had fundamental differences, Borrell accepted in a press conference with Russian foreign minister Sergey Lavrov, while arguing that the two could work together to promote shared interests such as preserving Iran's nuclear deal. And yet, having struck a pragmatic tone, Borrell criticised Russia for the recent arrest of poisoned opposition leader Alexei Navalny and its heavy-handed treatment of pro-democracy protesters who sought the politician's release. Put on the defensive, Lavrov accused German military doctors of fabricating Navalny's toxicology reports and equated Russian protesters with those who stormed the United States Capitol earlier that month. As a blank-faced Borrell looked on, the Russian foreign minister accused the EU of being an 'unreliable partner' and brought proceedings to a close. Immediately after the press conference, Russia expelled three European diplomats for attending pro-democracy protests, without first informing the High Representative, who faced calls for his resignation when he returned to Brussels.[28]

Borrell kept his job but found himself sidelined by member states, who preferred to deal with Putin directly as Russia amassed troops on Ukraine's border. Emmanuel Macron took the lead, using France's six-month presidency of the EU as a pretext for visiting Moscow in early February 2022. However, the president received a frosty reception from Putin and came away with little for his diplomatic efforts. Olaf Scholz fared no better when he visited Russia soon afterwards. Powerless to prevent war, the Heads of State or Government turned to the EU once the conflict was underway to shore up the European security order. Borrell returned to centre stage once again to announce that the EU would provide €450 million worth of weapons and other lethal military equipment via the European Peace Facility to help Ukraine defend its territory. Although the EU had financed nearly forty military and civilian missions by this point, including two advisory missions in Ukraine, it had never before provided weapons to a country under attack. In the months leading up to the war, Borrell had floated the idea of an EU training mission, of the kind undertaken in Mali, but now Belgium provided machine guns, Germany anti-tank weapons and missiles, and Latvia drones, among other contributions. By July 2022, this commitment had been scaled up to €1.5 billion.

The United States sent twice as much military aid to Ukraine in the first six months of the war, fuelling familiar criticisms that the EU was not pulling its weight geopolitically. The Union also faced questions over whether it was meeting Zelenskyy's increasingly urgent requests as Russian forces tightened their grip on Donbas. Germany bore the brunt of this criticism, until the Bundestag finally approved the delivery of heavy weapons in April 2022 despite vocal opposition from the right-wing populist party Alternative for Germany, and several high-profile artists and intellectuals on the left.[29]

European commitments of this sort would have been unthinkable before Maastricht, as would the speed with which national leaders forged consensus over Europe's fractured security architecture. Emmanuel Macron had argued for 'a common strategic culture' in European security and defence policy from the very outset of his presidency, but he had failed to win over Angela Merkel, who remained uneasy about committing German troops and taxpayers in this highly sensitive domain.[30] Although he presented himself as the continuity chancellor, Olaf Scholz tore up Merkel's approach in the days after the invasion of Ukraine by announcing a new €100 billion fund to modernise Germany's military and meet its pledge to NATO to spend 2 per cent of the country's sizeable GDP on defence expenditure. Polish

Prime Minister Mateusz Morawiecki also spurred the EU into action. Dispensing with his usual right-wing populist rhetoric, Morawiecki argued for European unity, seeing an opportunity, perhaps, to win other national leaders around to his party's hostile stance towards Russia, while distracting the EU from his government's controversial judicial reforms. It was, as the journalist Judy Dempsey put it, the Polish leader's 'told you so' moment.[31] Hungarian Prime Minister Viktor Orbán had no such antipathy towards Russia, yet was content to recuse his country from supplying weapons to Ukraine, rather than prevent EU partners from doing so.

Having presented this remarkable package to the world's press, Borrell then fluffed his lines by telling MEPs that the EU would provide 'fighting jets' to Ukrainian forces.[32] Dmytro Kuleba, Ukraine's foreign minister, had requested such support and received positive noises from some European governments. But the politics and practicalities of such support were far from settled.[33] One problem was that Ukrainian pilots were trained only to fly Soviet-era aircraft of the kind still used by Central and Eastern European member states. While Bulgaria, Poland and Slovakia were keen to help, they feared weakening their defences if they sent MiG-29 and Su-25 fighters to Ukraine. Just as important was the concern that Russia might view such support as an act of war. The Russian defence ministry had already warned Romania against hosting Ukrainian jets; although this claim was uncorroborated, it put the EU on notice about the high stakes surrounding its actions.[34]

At this point, the Polish government had already mooted the possibility that it could send Russian-era fighter jets to Ukraine via a United States airbase in Germany.[35] But the Pentagon quickly dismissed this convoluted and potentially combustible idea, as did NATO which ruled out any such support for Ukraine. It was another embarrassing incident for Borrell, who, walking back his earlier claim, now insisted that the EU was 'mainly supporting the Ukrainian army with basic ammunition'.[36] 'Borrell's attempt to demonstrate Europe's strength,' as the political scientist Stefan Auer put it, 'ended up as a very public display of its relative weakness.'[37]

As was so often the case in the post-Maastricht period, power flowed from national governments, who cooperated when it was in their interests to do so. EU officials who understood this point could make a decisive contribution to such cooperation. Those who didn't frequently found themselves whistling in the wind. Later that month, Borrell prematurely announced an additional €500 million in EU military support for Ukraine before the Heads of State or Government had signed off on this sum. 'No, no, no,' responded Dutch Prime Minister Mark Rutte, 'it has not been decided together.'[38]

To win approval for the Maastricht Treaty in a second referendum, Danish political parties had secured an opt-out from EU security and defence cooperation, which remained resolutely in place in the three decades that followed. That 67 per cent of Danish voters backed the abolition of this opt-out in a referendum held in June 2022 showed the war's sudden impact on European integration. So too did EU member states' endorsement of Josep Borrell's revised 'strategic compass'.[39] Despite its elliptical name, this plan included several concrete policy commitments, including the establishment of a 5,000-strong EU rapid deployment capacity geared towards a range of crises and the conduct of regular live EU military exercises. Historic though these decisions were, the war seemed to have an even greater short-term impact on NATO.

In March 2022, Zelenskyy renounced his ambitions to join NATO in the hopes of reaching a peaceful settlement with Russia. Although Ukraine applied to join the alliance six months later, after five rounds of peace talks had fizzled out, the war made it even less likely that NATO members would accept this application. As Ukraine's chances of joining NATO receded, other European countries revisited their reasons for remaining outside. In neutral Ireland, public support for NATO membership increased from 34 per cent in January 2022 to 48 per cent three months later.[40] Although it seemed unlikely that the country would renounce its neutrality any time soon, the sight of Russian naval exercises 200 miles from the Cork coast earlier in the year had started a national conversation. Things moved quicker in

Finland and Sweden, which prepared to join NATO in the summer of 2022, despite warnings from former Russian President Dmitry Medvedev that the Kremlin could deploy nuclear weapons in the Baltics in response to such a move.[41] Whether a reinvigorated transatlantic alliance left room for the EU to deepen cooperation in the sphere of security and defence remained to be seen.

'We Are Helping Refugees'

Five million Ukrainians, most of them women and children, fled their country in the first eight weeks of the war.[42] More than half arrived in Poland, which set the tone for the rest of the EU by greeting the first wave of refugees with welcome signs and tears. Local authorities in border towns such as Medyka, Korczowa and Przemyśl created makeshift reception centres in sports halls, warehouses and shopping malls as people arrived in their tens of thousands per day. Volunteers from all over the country and Europe came to help, offering food, first aid and transport. Clowns and musicians came to entertain the exhausted children and thousands of Poles opened their homes to refugees for months.[43]

Critics were quick to accuse Poland of double standards, and not only because of the hostility and discrimination shown towards people of colour fleeing Ukraine.[44] Months earlier, the country had been confronted with a humanitarian crisis after Belarus cut sections of its barbed-wire border with Poland and actively encouraged irregular migrants to enter the EU. Although this crisis was caused by Belarus in retaliation for EU sanctions over the forced diversion of Ryanair Flight 4978, Polish security forces drew international condemnation for using teargas to push back refugees, who were mostly young men from Iraq, Syria and Yemen.[45] The solidarity shown by Poles towards their Ukrainian neighbours was particular rather than universal, rooted in Slavic identity and shared memories of Communism, but it was no less genuine for this. In an opinion poll conducted in March 2022, 90 per cent of Polish respondents agreed that Ukrainians fleeing the war should be accepted into Poland.[46] Hungary, Romania and Slovakia, the three other EU member states which bordered Ukraine, responded with a similar generosity of spirit.

Elsewhere in the EU, public opinion also swung strongly behind Ukraine. In Rotterdam, the Erasmus Bridge was lit in blue and yellow, as was the Öresund Bridge linking Copenhagen and Malmö and numerous other landmarks across the EU, from the Brandenburg Gate to the Eiffel Tower. Too often in the post-Maastricht period, European politicians took a harsh line towards immigrants and refugees to score points in the media and keep right-wing populists at bay. Now EU leaders raced to keep up with public sentiment by making it as easy as possible for Ukrainians to find a safe haven from the war.

Under the EU–Ukraine Association Agreement, Ukrainians could enter the Union for ninety days. On 4 March 2022, member states agreed to activate the Temporary Protection Directive, giving Ukrainians who entered the EU immediate protection for up to two years, including access to accommodation, health care, education and other essential social services. This was another momentous step for member states to have taken. Adopted after the Yugoslav Wars, the directive offered a circuit breaker of sorts for the EU's asylum system when confronted with a mass influx of displaced people. Although it had faced such circumstances before – most noticeably during the global refugee crisis in 2015 – this was the first occasion that the Commission had proposed its use. That the Heads of State or Government agreed, Hungary's Viktor Orbán included, illustrated member states' determination to act together and their fears of a public outcry if they didn't.

European transport operators played their part during this period by offering free passage across the EU. In the weeks following the invasion, Ukrainian families carrying what possessions they could, and in some cases pets, became a familiar sight on European trains. In the Berlin Hauptbahnhof and numerous other European train stations, those arriving were greeted by volunteers in facemasks and high-vis jackets, who advised on how to make contact with those who had offered sofa beds and spare rooms.[47] European airlines, although their businesses had been badly hit by the closure of Ukrainian and Russian airspace to flights originating in or bound for the EU, helped to ship humanitarian cargo. Refuting claims that Ryanair had hiked prices on some routes due to surging demand from Ukrainian refugees, Michael O'Leary promised that his would be the first airline to return once Ukraine had 'seen off the Russians'.[48]

The war put the EU's right-wing populists in a bind. For years, these challenger parties looked to Russia for moral and financial sustenance, which they received in abundance. Senior members of the Alternative for Germany and Austrian Freedom Party all forged links with the Kremlin, as did the Northern League's leader, Matteo Salvini, who praised Vladimir Putin as 'the best statesmen currently on earth'.[49] Responding to the sudden shift in public opinion, Salvini visited the Polish city of Przemyśl to express his support for Ukrainian refugees. In a joint press conference, the town's mayor, Wojciech Bakun, thanked Italian NGOs for their help before inviting Salvini to come to the Ukrainian border 'to see what your friend Putin has done'. 'We are helping refugees,' insisted a stunned Salvini, before rushing to his car.[50]

'Do Not Be Late'

When the European Council met in Brussels in March 2022, two additional Heads of State joined the proceedings. The first was Joe Biden, who became the first sitting United States president to attend the EU's most senior decision-making body in person. The president looked at home as he entered 'the egg in the cage', the Europa Building's main conference room, where he shook hands with old friends and new. There was room enough for Biden at the summit's circular table, which had after all been built for twenty-eight. The second guest was Volodymyr Zelenskyy, who joined by video link from his wartime headquarters to thank the EU for what it had done, but above all to impress on its leaders how much more Ukraine needed if it was to survive as a sovereign state.

In the preceding weeks, Zelenskyy had addressed legislatures around the world, from Japan's House of Representatives to a joint session of the United States Congress, in each case tailoring his plea for help to the historical experience of his audience. In his remarks to the European Council, Zelenskyy evoked the memory of Borys Romanchenko, a 96-year-old Holocaust survivor who lost his life when the Russian military bombed his home in Kharkiv.[51] Europe had united around Ukraine, he told the Heads of State or Government, acknowledging the powerful impact that sanctions and the cancelling of Nord Stream 2 were having on Russia. But the Ukrainian president also spoke plainly to each of his fellow leaders, suggesting that such measures had been 'a little late' and offering a report card in the style of the schoolteacher he once played on television.

> Lithuania stands for us. Latvia stands for us. Estonia stands for us. Poland stands for us. France – Emmanuel, I really believe that you will stand for us. Slovenia stands for us. Slovakia stands for us. The Czech Republic stands for us. Romania knows what dignity is, so it will stand for us at the crucial moment. Bulgaria stands for us. Greece, I believe, stands with us. Germany . . . A little later. Portugal – well, almost . . . Croatia stands for us. Sweden – yellow and blue should always stand together. Finland – I know you are with us. The Netherlands stands for the rational, so we'll find common ground. Malta – I believe we will succeed. Denmark – I believe we will succeed. Luxembourg – we understand each other. Cyprus – I really believe you are with us. Italy – thank you for your support! Spain – we'll find common ground. Belgium – we will find arguments. Austria, together with Ukrainians, it is an opportunity for you. I'm sure of it. Ireland – well, almost.

Hungary was the one member state that drew the Ukrainian president's opprobrium. 'Listen, Viktor, do you know what's going on in

Mariupol?' he asked the country's right-wing populist prime minister. 'You have to decide for yourself who you are with.' One week later, when Viktor Orbán won a fourth consecutive term, he made fun of Zelenskyy's criticism and called for deeper ties between Russia and Hungary. However, the Ukrainian president's remarks seemed more pertinent than ever.

One of Zelenskyy's principal aims in attending the European Council was to open the door to accession talks. Like NATO, the EU had long been ambivalent over whether to grant Ukraine membership of its club. When protesters waved the circle of stars in Kyiv's Maidan Square in 2014, the Heads of State or Government defended Ukrainians' 'right to choose their own future' while avoiding all talk of EU enlargement.[52] Given the outpouring of public sympathy for Ukraine after Russia invaded in February 2022, it became increasingly difficult for EU leaders to hold this line. Three decades earlier, the EU had promised membership to a subset of Central and Eastern European countries to encourage stability and reform after the Cold War. Now national leaders faced pressure to do the same for Ukraine, a country fighting not only for change but its very existence.

On 28 February 2022, Zelenskyy signed a formal request to join the EU. Applications quickly followed from Georgia and Moldova, two countries which had pursued pro-Western foreign policies over the previous decade and now feared being drawn into a protracted regional conflict. Ukraine sought to join the EU with immediate effect but there was no chance of this happening. It would most likely take Ukraine years to achieve the stable political institutions and market economy status required under the EU's Copenhagen Criteria and a decade or more to negotiate terms of accession. A more probable scenario was that Ukraine would suffer the same fate as Turkey, which saw membership negotiations proceed in fits and starts with little prospect that they would ever be concluded. Emmanuel Macron, for one, gave few grounds for optimism when he warned against opening talks with a country that was at war while acknowledging that it would be unfair to say that Ukraine could never join. The

European Political Community – a Macron-inspired summit of forty-four European countries – seemed partly designed to deflect talk of EU enlargement, just as Jacques Delors' idea of concentric circles had been thirty years earlier.

Volodymyr Zelenskyy could have laboured under no illusions that his country would join the EU anytime soon or perhaps even at all. However, the Ukrainian president hadn't time to play the EU's long diplomatic game. So he talked about membership as if it were already happening and applied as much moral pressure as he could muster. 'And now you and I are preparing Ukraine's membership in the European Union,' Zelenskyy told the European Council. 'Finally. Here I ask you – do not be late. Please.'[53] In June 2022, the European Council unanimously approved Ukraine and Moldova as candidate countries and left the door ajar for Georgia. 'Ukraine's future is within the EU,' declared Zelenskyy, but the Heads of State or Government refused to be drawn on when, or even whether, the EU would ultimately take in new members.[54]

16

'To the People of Europe'

The Debate (2022)

Launching U2's European tour in August 2018 with an opinion piece in the *Frankfurter Allgemeine Zeitung*, Bono announced that the band would be waving a 'big, bright, blue EU flag' at their concerts.[1] His audience might be annoyed or bored by this act, the singer accepted, but it was offered as a provocative and radical gesture. His warning about 'grievance', 'violence' and 'nationalism' had little changed in the quarter-century since he took to European stages before a disintegrating circle of stars, yet his views on the EU had evolved. 'Europe, which for a long time triggered a yawn today sparks a kitchen-table screaming match,' Bono concluded. 'Europe is the theatre of powerful, emotional, clashing forces that will shape our future.'

Four years later, in April 2022, a fierce debate over the future of Europe was raging in France, where a passionately pro-European incumbent faced a right-wing populist challenger who promised to halt the march to a 'European federal superstate'.[2] When the MEP Jean-Marie Le Pen reached the same stage of this contest in 2002, with a pledge to renounce the Maastricht Treaty, the result sent shock waves across Europe.[3] Two decades later, Marine Le Pen, who distanced herself from her father's Holocaust denial but inherited his Euroscepticism, surprised nobody by making it to the second round against Emmanuel Macron for the second successive election.[4] True, the candidate had faced stiff competition from Éric Zemmour, a firebrand right-winger who promised to deport all immigrants who failed to find work after six months and to take only one hundred asylum seekers per year, and Jean-Luc Mélenchon, a veteran left-winger who promised to end the free movement of capital and restore France's fiscal sovereignty.[5] But she held her nerve as Zemmour flamed out and Mélenchon fell short. Softening her image over the previous five years, Le Pen appeared to many voters and the media as a more moderate figure. However, most EU watchers looked on with alarm as a politician who promised to replace the Union with a European Alliance of Nations received 8 million votes.[6]

That Emmanuel Macron had won the French presidency in 2017 aged 39, having never held elected office, was another marker of Europe's political turbulence in the post-Maastricht period. Two years earlier he had resigned as France's economy minister under a socialist government – his first job in frontline politics – to lead a progressive movement which morphed into a centrist political party. To its critics, La République En Marche! was a populist vanity project, which traded on Macron's youth and charisma and substituted serious debate for empty promises about changing politics.[7] Such criticisms weren't without foundation. Macron was a political celebrity who attracted huge crowds to his raucous rallies, where he offered himself as an alternative to mainstream politicians. In this respect, his project was not dissimilar to Marine Le Pen's, being suffused with anti-elitism. But the former minister took policy ideas seriously, enlisting his supporters to gather 100,000 testimonies from members of the public about what worked and didn't in modern France and what mattered most to them. This was not mere marketing but a novel attempt to crowdsource new policy ideas for Macron's manifesto.[8]

La République En Marche! sounded the death knell for the French Socialist Party, which had been on a downward trajectory since the days of François Mitterrand and Jacques Delors before hitting new lows under François Hollande. Had Hollande ruled out running for a second presidential term earlier, he might have made room for Macron, but the latter had already surmised from the state of the left in other European countries that the Socialist Party's fortunes were unlikely to recover. Besides, Macron always had an uneasy relationship with the party, whose left-wing reviled his pro-market views and prior experience as an investment banker. Despite – and perhaps because of – these tensions, Macron was a late archetype of the Third Way.

At the crux of Third Way thinking – which helped European social democratic parties return from the political wilderness in the 1990s – was the belief that classic tax and spend policies targeted at traditional left-wing voters couldn't win elections anymore. Such policies no longer worked, it argued, and this political constituency had disintegrated. To gain power, Third Way politicians believed, globalisation must be accepted and harnessed as a force for good. Macron was no socialist, by his own admission; nevertheless, former Commission President Jacques Delors' insistence that the founder of La République En Marche! was anything but social democratic seemed like sour grapes.[9] Macron, for better or worse, had much in common with Third Way politicians such as Gerhard Schröder, Wim Kok, Poul Nyrup Rasmussen and, most of all, Tony Blair. He shared their determination to reduce unemployment through labour market policies, which made it easier to hire and fire workers and incentivised unemployed people to look for work. He was also drawn towards the knowledge economy, calling for France to become a 'start-up nation' and to lead the next generation of innovation in areas such as artificial intelligence and green technology. Above all, he mirrored the Third Way's belief that globalisation should be defended from those who sought to reintroduce national borders.[10]

Despite his affinity with the Third Way, Macron departed from this doctrine in important respects. As UK prime minister, Blair had waxed lyrical about European integration, while championing light-touch cooperation with EU partners. This hesitancy was partly intellectual; the Third Way was essentially a theory centred on national politics. But it was also instrumental, being born of a desire by social democrats to protect themselves from right-wing populists, who whipped up Eurosceptic sentiment. The Lisbon Strategy, the Third Way's signature policy for the EU, promised a great deal yet asked little of the Union. Macron could have proposed a similar policy programme or matched his opponents' referendum pledge, as Blair did on the European Constitution. Instead, he called for the EU to defend the interests of France and other member states against China, Russia and the United States, as well as Google, Apple and Facebook. Rather than siphoning off Le Pen's supporters, Macron sought to build an alternative coalition among those who were repelled by her right-wing populism. French presidential candidates had wrapped themselves in the European flag before but never as tightly as Macron, who took to the stage at his victory rally in May 2017 to Beethoven's Ninth.

Macron's turbulent first term betrayed his political naivety and insufficient regard for the effects of his policies. His decision to raise fuel levies while cutting taxes for wealthy individuals and big business produced a ferocious backlash from the *gilets jaunes*, a movement named after the high-vis jackets protesters wore during months of public demonstrations. But the president's ratings partially recovered during the Covid-19 pandemic, even if his early image as a political empath was replaced by a reputation for aloofness and arrogance. The EU's response to the coronavirus pandemic also helped Macron to overcome his initial struggles on the European stage, which saw him shelve manifesto commitments to establish a eurozone parliament and settle for a eurozone budget instrument, which at €17 billion was too small to make a difference in macroeconomic terms. Next Generation EU, which authorised the European Commission to borrow up to €750 billion to provide grants and loans to member states, was a major win for Macron's vision of providing tangible support to EU citizens in times of global crisis.

When Russia invaded Ukraine in February 2022, things looked bleak for Marine Le Pen, who hurriedly pulped over a million campaign leaflets showing her standing next to Vladimir Putin.[11] Macron had taken a risk in travelling to Moscow before the invasion and talking to the Russian president by phone afterwards. But the French president's longstanding calls for European sovereignty allowed him to project leadership, as the Union scrambled to reduce its dependence on Russian gas and oil and deepen European cooperation on security and defence. Le Pen was damaged by her past support for Russia, but this did not stop her using rising energy prices as a result of the war to hammer home criticisms of Macron for failing to protect households' purchasing power. Jean-Marie Le Pen's chances of beating Jacques Chirac in the second round of the 2002 presidential election were virtually non-existent. The third-place candidate in the first round, Lionel Jospin, had only been narrowly beaten and his supporters rallied around Chirac who pleaded with voters to 'defend human rights' and France's 'place in Europe and the world'.[12] Two decades later, the third-place candidate Jean-Luc Mélenchon issued a similar plea, but to many of his supporters voting for Emmanuel Macron over Marine Le Pen seemed like a choice between 'la peste et le choléra'.[13]

In 2017, Marine Le Pen had paid a high price for her lacklustre performance against Macron before a primetime audience of more than 16 million viewers. Five years later, it was Macron who looked nervous, resting his chin on his clenched fists in an overbearing manner. Le Pen was smiling and energetic throughout. Having shorn her manifesto of its most controversial elements, she made a forceful case on domestic policy, criticising the president's failure to address inflationary pressures and for his unpopular plan to raise the retirement age. Aside from her promise to ban the wearing of hijabs in public, she kept past comments about French minorities hidden from view. Macron challenged her on the facts, and on her party's reliance on loans from Russian banks, yet Le Pen largely held her own.

It was on the subject of Europe that the debate truly came to life. 'You still want to withdraw from the euro, but you haven't really said it,' said Macron to Le Pen, whose eyes visibly widened as the president accused her of concealing her true intentions towards the EU.[14] Under his leadership, he insisted, the EU had stood together during the pandemic and was now working together on Ukraine. 'There is no European sovereignty because there is no European people,' responded Le Pen, who criticised the president for displaying the European flag under the Arc de Triomphe during the country's six-month presidency of the Union. She didn't wish to leave the EU, she insisted, but she did want the European Commission 'to show respect for sovereign nations'. 'How come France can never defend its own interests?' Le Pen asked, recalling her experiences as an MEP. 'Maybe you didn't go to parliament often enough,' replied Macron, who insisted that he had worked 'day after day after day' to win other leaders over to his policy proposals. In the end, Macron was comfortably re-elected as Head of State, albeit with 58.6 per cent of the second-round vote compared to 66.1 per cent five years earlier. Le Pen conceded quickly and graciously, her eyes firmly on the future.

Five months later, in a general election held after Mario Draghi's caretaker coalition collapsed, Giorgia Meloni's right-wing populist Brothers of Italy emerged as Italy's largest political party. In 1992, Meloni had joined the youth wing of the neo-fascist Italian Social Movement and spoken openly of her admiration for Benito Mussolini.[15] Now, as presumptive prime minister, she entered talks with Matteo Salvini's Northern League and Silvio Berlusconi's Forza Italia about forming a new government. The speed with which many media commentators rushed to allay fears over the election result showed how routine right-wing populism had become in Europe since the Maastricht Treaty.[16] Meloni had toned down her past criticism of the EU, commentators insisted.[17] Besides, the war in Ukraine, the cost of living crisis and the fear of losing access to Next Generation EU funding gave her little choice but to avoid confrontation in Brussels.[18] That Meloni had promised a naval blockade of the Mediterranean to end irregular migration and warned against the 'ethnic replacement of Europe's citizens' both assertions were downplayed in such analysis.[19] Not for the first time, the desire to maintain EU cooperation took precedence over the Union's fundamental values. 'I'm happy with the environment I found myself in,' declared Italy's right-wing populist prime minister on her first official visit to Brussels in November 2022.[20]

Back to the Future (2018–22)

As French voters went to the polls in April 2022, a different sort of debate over the future of Europe was playing out across the EU. The Conference on the Future of Europe had been formally opened at the European Parliament building in Strasbourg in May 2021, where Emmanuel Macron, António Costa, the Portuguese prime minister, and David Sassoli and Ursula von der Leyen, the presidents of the European Parliament and European Commission respectively, sat wearing face masks on a circular stage before a giant video wall of self-isolating Europeans.[21] The occasion had the look and feel of a pandemic-era television show, even before the opening credits cut between major moments of EU history, from the introduction of the euro to the global refugee crisis to scenes of everyday European life, from homeschooling to a concert by Strasbourg electro-swing band Lyre Le Temps. Macron spoke first, hailing the conference as an unprecedented opportunity 'to listen to the entire continent about what kind of future they want'. Sassoli came next, urging citizens to help EU leaders understand 'the spirit of the times'. Costa invited Europeans to come forward with their 'priorities' and their 'dreams'. For von der Leyen, the conference was about discovering 'a shared vision of what we want our Union to be'.

The real driving force behind the Conference on the Future of Europe was Emmanuel Macron. Faced with Marine Le Pen's manifesto commitment in 2017 to hold a referendum on EU membership, the French president could so easily have matched this pledge for the sake of political expediency. Had he succumbed to this temptation – as UK Prime Minister David Cameron had done when faced with similar calls from the UK Independence Party and members of his own Conservative Party – Frexit may well have followed Brexit. To lose one member state was unfortunate. To lose two could have been fatal for the EU. Keenly aware of these stakes, Macron called instead for the people to be given a voice on the future of Europe through citizens' conventions. Having beaten his opponent with a promise to change the European Union, Macron came under pressure to deliver as soon as he set foot in the Élysée Palace.

EU leaders must break the 'taboo' on major treaty changes, argued Macron in the early weeks of his presidency only to receive a luke-warm response from Angela Merkel.[22] The future French president was still finding his way as a recent graduate when Merkel became German chancellor in November 2005, finding herself in the eye of a storm over referendum votes against the European Constitution in France and the Netherlands. The chancellor eventually brokered a solution in the form of the Lisbon Treaty, but the experience drained Merkel's enthusiasm for treaty revisions as a means to settle grand debates about the future of Europe. To Merkel, Macron risked desta-bilising the EU after a decade of global crises by triggering hard-to-win referendums and disruptive legal challenges. To Macron, Merkel's reticence left the EU vulnerable to future global turmoil and the politicisation thereof by right-wing populists.

Merkel was unmoved, but Macron continued to make his case. The EU must, the French president told an audience at the Pnyx in Athens, reclaim the concept of sovereignty from 'those who pretend that looking inwards is a defence'.[23] It was time, he argued, to forge a new European sovereignty capable of protecting Europe from 'great global shifts'. From climate change and counter-terrorism to diplo-macy and digital policy, this new vision of sovereignty meant allowing Europe to choose its place in the world. Macron said little in this speech that other national leaders hadn't said before. However, none had articulated the EU's role as a bulwark against globalisation quite so clearly or staked so much political capital on building it. A new treaty shouldn't be decided 'sneakily behind closed doors in Paris, Brussels or Berlin', Macron ventured. Instead, the EU should hold 'democratic conventions' with citizens 'to discuss the Europe they want to see'.

Writing an open letter to the 'people of Europe' in March 2019, the French president presented Brexit as a cautionary tale in which popu-list politicians wilfully lied to voters about 'access to the EU market' and 'the risks to peace in Ireland of restoring the border'.[24] But the implicit subject of this article was Marine Le Pen, who had rebranded her party and sought a pan-European populist alliance with Matteo Salvini in that year's European Parliament elections. 'Retreating into nationalism offers nothing, it is rejection without an alternative,' argued Macron, who called instead for the EU to protect Europeans from 'major shocks of the modern world' through policies such as a European minimum wage, European support for 'strategic industries' and a combination of 'stringent' border controls with solidarity towards asylum seekers. To work through these and other issues, he reiterated his call for a conference on Europe, involving citizens and civil society representatives, to consider the possibility of treaty change.

European Parliament President David Sassoli endorsed Macron's call for a Conference on the Future of Europe, not because he shared the French president's vision of European sovereignty, but because he saw an opportunity to reassert MEPs' influence after Ursula von der Leyen's controversial appointment as Commission President. Under Lisbon, the Heads of State or Government promised to take the results of European Parliament elections into account before nominating a new Commission President. Stealing a march on this process, European political parties put forward Spitzenkandidaten (lead candidates) before European voters went to the polls in May 2014, turning the contest into an embryonic European general election. After the European People's Party received the most votes in this contest, national leaders reluctantly accepted the party's nominee, Jean-Claude Juncker, as Commission President. When the European Parliament elections produced a similar result five years later, they rejected the centre right's candidate Manfred Weber. A Bavarian MEP who had led the European People's Party group in the European Parliament for five years, Weber was well connected. But he had tarnished his reputation by standing by Hungarian Prime Minister Viktor Orbán and lacked high-level experience in German politics. In nominating German Defence Minister Ursula von der Leyen instead, the Heads of State or Government sought a more qualified candidate to lead the Commission and to reassert their control over choosing the EU's top official.

Responding to this powerplay, David Sassoli called in July 2019 for a 'conference on EU democracy' to revisit the Spitzenkandidat process and the democratic functioning of the Union more generally.[25] Uncertain if she had the majority support among MEPs that she required to be confirmed as Commission President, von der Leyen endorsed Sassoli's proposal. Concerned that they and other national leaders might lose control over this reform process, Macron and Merkel finally acted in tandem. In November 2019, the French and German governments proposed a Conference on the Future of Europe involving EU institutions and citizens to identify reform ideas. Papering over Franco-German differences, this document alluded to the possibility of treaty change after such reflections, without making a firm commitment. There was no such equivocation in the proposal over who would ultimately decide on such reforms. The conference would present its 'final document' to the European Council 'for debate and implementation'.[26]

That the Conference on the Future of Europe's opening ceremony went ahead in May 2021 was due to a series of last-minute concessions. Compromise, as was so often the case, came at the expense of complexity. The new body would be led not by a single figure as Macron and Merkel had wanted but by the presidents of the Commission, Parliament and Council. Despite its clunky institutional design, the Conference on the Future of Europe broke new ground by including 108 EU citizens in its plenary body.[27] These individuals would be drawn from four European citizens' panels, which would begin the process of reflection on Europe's future, giving the people a seat at the table in discussions over the Union's future to a degree never seen before.[28]

EU commentators followed the drafting of the European Constitution between 2002 and 2004 with a sense of excitement. Not so the Conference on the Future of Europe. This 'will not be the place where the future of the EU will be decided', argued Thu Nguyen, a researcher at Jacques Delors' think tank, Notre Europe.[29] The conference, she argued, was ill-timed, too short and constrained by its cumbersome institutional structures. The process 'has been painstakingly designed to go nowhere', agreed one journalist.[30] A Eurobarometer conducted in autumn 2021 found that 33 per cent of respondents had heard about the conference.[31] Of these, 23 per cent didn't really know what it was about. Eighteen months after it launched, the conference had fewer than 4,000 Twitter followers.

Despite its shortcomings, the Conference on the Future of Europe was an innovative attempt to bridge the divide between the EU and its people, which drew on the experience of citizens' assemblies and mini-publics in Ireland and France, among other EU member states, where such fora had helped to find common ground on issues ranging from electoral reform to abortion.[32] Hitherto, EU voters passed judgement on treaty revisions in national elections or referendums after they had been signed by the Heads of State or Government. Now, the EU asked 800 randomly selected citizens to debate what changes they would like to see before governments had decided on whether to embark on treaty reform. The participants were contacted by a market research company, which selected a representative sample taking into account the age, gender, socioeconomic status, education levels and geographic background of participants while ensuring that one-third were aged between 16 and 25 years. Those who accepted attended weekend meetings held first in Strasbourg, then online and finally in Florence, Dublin, Natolin and Maastricht. Meetings were moderated by experts and facilitators, with simultaneous interpreters ensuring that citizens could speak in their own languages.

Images of EU citizens sitting in the European Parliament's hemicycle engaged in principled debate went unnoticed by most Europeans, in contrast to video footage of violent protesters storming the United States Capitol months earlier. One Maltese woman told fellow delegates that it had taken fifteen hours to get to Strasbourg; unable to find her onward connection from Frankfurt, she had spent

all night in a bus station. Maybe, she offered as an opening suggestion, all airport signs in Europe could be in English.[33] The citizens'
panels that followed were freewheeling and unfocused, at times, but
participants remained positive about their experience, despite the
technical challenges and time commitment involved and uncertainty
about whether their recommendations would be taken seriously. For
some, the conference was a chance to talk about political causes that
mattered to them. For others, it was an exciting opportunity to learn
more about politics and see the European Union up close.

Not for the first time, citizens took the Union's policy-makers by
surprise. Among the 178 recommendations produced by the four
European citizens' panels were calls for investment in new bike lanes,
kindergartens and playgrounds, free first-aid courses and EU support
for palliative care and assisted dying.[34] That an estimated 12 per cent
of recommendations required the transfer of new competences to
the EU may have reflected a degree of misunderstanding about
how the Union worked.[35] Indeed, a recurring theme among the
panels was the need for the EU to educate its citizens about European
institutions, policies and processes as well as combatting disinformation and fake news. At the same time, the citizens' panels looked to
the EU to take on new tasks in sensitive domains such as education,
health care and social policy and seemed open to the treaty changes
this entailed.

The citizens who took part in this exercise showed a limited appetite for the institutional reforms championed by David Sassoli before
his untimely death from pneumonia in January 2022. Indeed, they
favoured democratic checks and balances that went beyond the
European Parliament, including EU-wide referendums on 'excep-
tionally important matters' and the creation of a new permanent
body of EU citizen representatives.[36] They also called for the revival
of plans for a European Constitution, nearly two decades after the
European Convention failed.

The final report of the Conference on the Future of Europe whit-
tled the citizens' panels' suggestions to 49 proposals. However, what

remained offered a reasonable sample of the ideas produced through twelve months of intensive discussion across Europe. Most of the recommendations could be realised under the EU's existing legal structures, but this didn't prevent Macron and MEPs from claiming a mandate for treaty revision. The conference was at risk of becoming a Rorschach test in which European elites saw their preferred approach to reforming the Union. And yet, the EU citizens present at the closing ceremony saw things differently. Encircling the dais, they spoke passionately about their experience of the panels and hopes for the future of Europe. Jorge Pazos, a delegate from the Canary Islands, conveyed this mood of civic authority by describing how the European Parliament's hemicycle had become his second home. 'If we as citizens have been capable of working together and reaching a consensus,' he told Macron and the other leaders present, 'you can and must do the same.'[37]

Hopes and Fears Revisited

The ministers who signed the Maastricht Treaty on 7 February 1992 had high hopes. Built on the edifices of the older European Community, the European Union marked a 'new stage in the process of European integration' which would help to end 'the division of the European continent', the treaty's preamble declared.[38] Maastricht also triggered strong but strikingly different warnings from European Commission President Jacques Delors and Anglo-French businessman Sir James Goldsmith. Delors didn't oppose the Maastricht Treaty; nor could he hide his disappointment about the 'sterile ambiguity of many articles' or fears that cooperation between member states had 'weakened'.[39] For Goldsmith, who had hitherto supported European integration, Maastricht sought 'to destroy the identity of every European nation'.[40] Looking back after three decades, neither man's fears were justified. The European Union was driven not by faceless technocrats in the three decades after Maastricht, this book has argued, but, above all, by the Heads of State or Government of its member states who looked to the Union to manage a succession of global crises from the end of the Cold War to Covid-19. The EU weathered these crises, yet national leaders' naïve understanding of globalisation allowed new opportunities for right-wing populists to stir up discontent over European integration, while challenging the principles of democracy, rule of law and minority rights. The history of the EU since Maastricht is one of endurance as well as an account of how the ideals of unity, solidarity and harmony embodied by the circle of stars on its flag were partially eroded.

Although he was prone to pessimistic pronouncements about European integration, Delors was right about some of Maastricht's specific defects. During negotiations over economic and monetary union, one of the treaty's signature projects, the then Commission President anticipated two key problems.[41] The first was that the EU would struggle to enforce limits on government borrowing once the euro was created. The second was that member states would find it difficult to adjust to major economic shocks without a common budget instrument. The Greek government's failure to disclose the true scale of its budget deficit before the 2007–8 global financial crisis was one catalyst for the sovereign debt difficulties which came close to tearing the eurozone asunder in the decade that followed. EU member states' decision to suspend such rules when the Covid-19 pandemic hit and create a temporary budgetary instrument, Next Generation EU, helped avoid a second euro crisis. It was also a vindication for the former Commission President.

While he proved prescient about the euro, Delors' more fundamental concerns about national leaders' dedication to the European project were misplaced. When he warned MEPs in 1993 that member states' commitment to European integration was fading, the Frenchman failed to predict how invested the Heads of State or Government would remain in the Union in the three decades that followed.[42] Faced with a string of international crises, national leaders' instinct to work together to advance their collective interests grew steadily sharper. Such cooperation did not always come quickly, as evidenced by the delays over financial assistance for Greece during the euro crisis. Nor was it cost-less, as illustrated by the harsh conditions attached to such support. But EU member states' determination to forge a common response to international challenges in the three decades after Maastricht went well beyond the norm in a period marked by diminished expectations about inter-state cooperation. Older international organisations, such as the United Nations, and newer ones, such as the Group of Seven and Group of Twenty, came nowhere close to matching such efforts. Regional organisations from Mercosur in Latin America to the Association of Southeast Asian Nations lagged even further behind.

The sixteen countries that joined the EU between 1995 and 2013 underlined not only the Union's power of attraction but also the Heads of State or Government's commitment to European integra-tion. National leaders embraced the EU's Big Bang enlargement for its economic opportunities and the political stability it promised at a time of geopolitical upheaval in Europe. So successful was EU enlarge-ment in both respects that the Union struggled to foster economic and political reforms in neighbouring countries without the offer of membership. The EU's doubts over enlargement after the Big Bang did little to help the cause of democratic reform in Turkey and left Ukraine vulnerable to Russia's increasingly belligerent foreign policy under Vladimir Putin.

Russia's invasion of Ukraine in February 2022 showed that Delors had been right to worry about the pan-European security architec-ture after the Cold War. But his fears about the recrudescence of nationalism and a breakdown of European cooperation were over-stated. In the first six months of the war, the EU provided €2.5 billion in arms to Ukrainian forces and sanctuary to more than 5 million citizens fleeing the conflict. Although it remained to be seen whether the Heads of State or Government's decision to recognise Ukraine as a candidate country would really lead to membership, the Union stood ready to play a major role in the country's reconstruction.

The UK's referendum vote to leave the EU in 2016 was a bitter blow for the Union, but Brexit didn't occur because a Head of State or

Government turned on the EU. It happened, above all, because three UK prime ministers gambled and lost. David Cameron proved unable to salvage his country's place in the EU (and his political career) by negotiating a 'new settlement' with the Union and putting the results to an in-out referendum. Theresa May was a Remainer who sought a comparatively soft form of Brexit but found this goal beyond her reach when she called a snap general election and lost her parliamentary majority. Boris Johnson became the kind of reckless nationalist that Delors warned of in 1993. And yet, this child of a European official and former Brussels hack most likely backed Leave in the expectation that he would lose. Having unexpectedly won, Johnson ended up championing a far harder form of Brexit than he had called for in the aftermath of the referendum because it helped him to become prime minister. While the UK's political classes tied themselves in knots over Brexit, EU Heads of State or Government protected their collective interests over Northern Ireland and the Single Market, while right-wing populists across Europe quietly cancelled their plans for immediate in-out referendums.

Jacques Delors was by no means the only public figure who doubted whether the EU would survive. Serious news outlets made a concerted attempt to explain EU summits, meetings and decisions to their readers and viewers. But too many journalists, broadcasters and editors relied on lazy tropes about the EU being on the verge of collapse. Some historians shared this taste for the macabre, most noticeably John Gillingham, who published the EU's 'obituary' in February 2016, four months before British voters went to the polls.[43] Although he doubled down on this prediction after Brexit, Gillingham's warnings about the EU being engulfed by mass migration and economic depression didn't age well.[44]

The problem with such doomsaying, as the EU historian and political theorist Luuk van Middelaar argues, is that it 'underestimates the invisible glue that holds the club together'.[45] But the trouble with van Middelaar's glue is that it proved better at bonding small groups of politicians than the populace at large. In a Eurobarometer conducted at the beginning of 2022, the Union conjured up a positive image for only 44 per cent of people.[46] From the moment the Maastricht Treaty was signed, the EU fell consistently short in its efforts to bring the Union closer to citizens, who voted in increasing numbers for right-wing populists presenting themselves as defenders of the people against sinister elites intent on building a European superstate. The Heads of State or Government's handling of the euro and global refugee crises was a boon for right-wing populists, who portrayed the EU as dominating national democracy while remaining subservient to global forces. Although the EU endured, it did so by storing up reservoirs of distrust and ill will that its opponents wasted no opportunity to release.

National leaders' initial response to right-wing populism after Maastricht was to defend and codify the Union's commitment to fundamental values such as democracy, human rights and the rule of law. But they struggled to enforce these values and stood silently as politicians who openly flouted such norms gained power and set the political agenda. Leaders' willingness to tolerate Viktor Orbán – as he went from liberal protégé to proponent of illiberal democracy – was the most egregious example, albeit not the only one. From the Northern League's demonisation of asylum seekers and minorities in Italy to the Law and Justice party's assault on judicial independence in Poland, EU leaders looked the other way. The EU's values were further undermined through its human rights dialogue with China, which took on an increasingly performative character as economic ties between the two sides strengthened, and by the Union's half-hearted efforts to bring economic prosperity and political stability to West Africa among other regions.

Sir James Goldsmith can be seen, in retrospect, as a forebear of the anti-globalist movement. Behind the apocalyptic language of *Le Piège* and its English translation, *The Trap*, the businessman understood that the sacralisation of free trade would benefit businesses and consumers far more than workers and so generate significant societal strains. EU Heads of State or Government would have done well to heed such warnings at the earliest opportunity, but they remained wedded for too long to Third Way thinking and showed too little solidarity with Europeans affected by falling wages and other downsides to unfettered globalisation. Next Generation EU, which provided €750 billion to EU member states in grants and loans to aid their economic recovery from the Covid-19 pandemic, showed that a more caring EU was possible, although it remained to be seen whether such solidarity would persist once the exigencies of this public health emergency had passed.

Goldsmith was a polemicist who offered no clear-cut alternatives beyond patriarchal appeals for poorer countries to settle for a happy life and a slower pace of development.[47] And yet, the business tycoon's real insight was political rather than economic. He understood quicker than most contemporaries that the Maastricht Treaty had created a soft target that political outsiders could use to rail against elites, immigrants and other external threats. *The Trap* was not so much an economic treatise as a populist playbook from which politicians from Declan Ganley to Marine Le Pen drew inspiration, whether consciously or not. Donald Trump was an honorary member of this club given his strong backing of Brexit and insistence that the EU was a 'foe' despite the United States' strong support for European integration since the late 1940s.[48]

Goldsmith's warnings that Maastricht marked the beginning of a European superstate were always hyperbolic. The Treaty did touch upon two highly sensitive areas of policy in addition to economic and monetary union: foreign and security policy and justice and home affairs. But cooperation in these fields proceeded cautiously and flowed through rather than around national governments. The sight of High Representative Federica Mogherini and Iranian foreign minister Mohammad Javad Zarif presenting the Iran Nuclear Deal to the world's press in July 2015 confirmed the EU's above-title billing on the international stage. However, Mogherini had been flanked in the preceding negotiations by the foreign ministers of France, Germany and the United Kingdom and without the EU3's explicit support would have found it difficult to bring such talks to a conclusion. The thought of Europol investigating cross-border crimes and assisting in counter-terrorism operations would also have had Goldsmith reaching for George Orwell's *Nineteen Eighty-Four* once again.[49] But this EU agency remained heavily dependent on national police forces and security services to do its job.

The borderless Europe that right-wing populists stoked fears over after Maastricht was more imagined than real. Although budget airlines such as Ryanair and cross-border television shows such as *Bron|Broen* (*The Bridge*) helped to unite Europeans in new ways, the Union remain fragmented in important respects. The Single Market Programme was completed on schedule on 31 December 1992, but technological change created new opportunities for cross-border trade which the EU hadn't legislated for. A case in point is telecommunications, which witnessed greater competition within member states, especially as mobile phones came to market, but no genuinely pan-European providers. Although the Commission hailed the abolition of roaming charges as a European success story, it was one premised on the persistence of nationally segmented markets. The same was true of digital services more generally, where geo-blocking in television, film and music streaming remained pervasive despite European officials' best efforts. Millions more people exercised their right to free movement after the EU's Big Bang enlargement, yet labour mobility remained relatively low.

The Schengen area's efforts to remove border checks between European countries and establish common policies on immigration and asylum also showed that the EU was more bordered than borderless. Most Union citizens could move between member states with an ease that would have been hard to imagine before Maastricht, although Europeans of colour were still much more likely to be stopped by police close to internal borders on grounds of public safety. Temporary border checks were always allowed under Schengen, but they became increasingly common in the 2010s for reasons that seemed partly influenced by the anti-immigration rhetoric of right-wing populists. A driver going from Gela in Sicily to Palojoensuu in Finland along the E35 in 2022 had no guarantee of an uninterrupted journey.

The EU's borders remained more visible still for those who made the perilous journey to Greece from Syria and other conflict zones only to be returned to Turkey under the terms of the EU's controversial deal with President Recep Tayyip Erdoğan. Kurdish refugees arriving on Italy's Ionian coast in December 1997 had been welcomed by political leaders. Twelve years later, irregular migrants on the *Open Arms* rescue ship were denied entry to Italian ports at the behest of the country's right-wing populist deputy prime minister, Matteo Salvini, a decision decried by many Italians and for which he later stood trial.[50] The securitisation of European borders and the dehumanisation of asylum seekers was by no means confined to the Italian government, as razor-wire fences on Hungary's border with Croatia and Serbia and the use of water cannon by Polish authorities on the Belarussian border attested. The speed with which the EU offered temporary protection to the millions of people fleeing Ukraine after Russia invaded in February 2022 showed how contingent such policies were on shifting media coverage and public opinion.

As an MEP, Sir James Goldsmith saw first-hand how much power the Heads of State or Government exercised over the EU, but it served his Eurosceptic agenda to exaggerate the influence of Eurocrats. This political tactic would be copied by numerous right-wing populists in the post-Maastricht period, from Nigel Farage's description of Commission President José Manuel Barroso as 'planning world domination' to Geert Wilders' conspiratorial claim that the European Commission was plotting to 'replace' Europe's population.[51] This 'thin-centred' ideology worked by portraying right-wing populists as the true representatives of the people against a sinister elite. European officials were an easy mark since they were small in number and invisible to most Europeans' day-to-day lives. The Commission's staff numbers had grown from 15,000 on the eve of Maastricht to 31,000 by 2022; however, this left the main administrative body of the EU, a

Union of half a billion people, with the same number of officials as Luxembourg, a country with a population of less than one million.[52]

The EU remained both familiar and foreign. In a survey conducted in the summer of 2022, a record 64 per cent claimed an understanding of how the Union worked.[53] But citizens' knowledge of political personalities still generally stopped at national borders. UK Justice Secretary Michael Gove's invitation to Britons in June 2016 to name the five presidents that ran Europe correctly assumed that most couldn't.[54] Even those who could name Jeroen Dijsselbloem, Mario Draghi, Jean-Claude Juncker, Donald Tusk and Martin Schulz – heads of the Eurogroup, the European Central Bank, the Commission, the European Council and the European Parliament respectively – were unlikely to know much about who these individuals were and what they stood for. Besides, these leaders didn't run Europe. Gove did, along with the ministers who sat alongside him in the EU's Council of Ministers and their political superiors who made up the European Council. The EU after Maastricht was not a skirmish between disembodied states and supranational institutions, but an arena in which vivid faces engaged in an intense debate over Europe's past, present and future.

That the EU was driven by Heads of State or Government, who in turn answered to national electorates, provided an elegant rebuke to claims that the Union suffered from a democratic deficit.[55] And yet, national leaders found it increasingly difficult to confer legitimacy on the EU in this manner as their own authority was increasingly questioned. In a Eurobarometer published in early 2022, just 35 per cent of respondents said that they tended to trust national governments. Trust in national parliaments was not much higher, which is one reason why the pressure built to hold referendums on EU treaty revisions. When the Treaty of Rome was signed in March 1957, none of the founding members seriously considered giving voters a direct say on whether to create the European Community. After Maastricht, making major treaty revisions without triggering a hard-to-win referendum in one or more member states became virtually inconceivable.

Without Commissioners such as Carlo Ripa di Meana, Karel Van Miert and Viviane Reding and their staff, the consensus that prevailed among EU member states would not have been turned into policies and laws with practical consequences and the potential to effect change. And yet European officials seldom steered European integration in a direction that member states didn't want to go. Where they did, as in Commission President Jean-Claude Juncker's refugee resettlement plan, national leaders quickly reasserted their authority and changed course.

Few European officials made a bigger impact after Maastricht than Ursula von der Leyen, who in her first three years as Commission President unveiled an ambitious package of environmental policies, the European Green Deal, and coordinated the EU's impressive response to the Covid-19 pandemic. Von der Leyen didn't devise such policies from scratch; had she done so they would likely have sunk without trace. Instead, she scanned the political horizon, saw how far member states were prepared to go and presented policy proposals at high speed. She made mistakes, most noticeably in considering a ban on vaccine exports from Ireland to Northern Ireland without due regard for the peace process. But the fact that few fully acknowledged her accomplishments, which made her the most successful Commission President since Delors, provided a glimpse into the gendered politics of leadership in Europe.

No global challenge was greater in the post-Maastricht period than climate change.[56] The European Union showed genuine leadership on this issue through its concerted efforts to reduce greenhouse gas emissions at home and to secure binding commitments from other parties to the United Nations Framework Convention on Climate Change. Despite EU leadership, average global temperatures went from close to their pre-industrial average in 1992 to between 1.1 and 1.2 degrees Celsius higher three decades later.[57] Temperatures ran even higher in Europe, as mild winters followed summers scarred by wildfires and flash floods.

On 19 July 2022, newspapers reported a surface temperature of 39.5 degrees in Maastricht, one of the highest recorded in the Netherlands since records began.[58] The sun was also shining that day on the Western Uplands, on the Moyne Park estate in Abbeyknockmoy, on the silent streets of Cambuslang and, farther eastward, on the Øresund Bridge. It was shining on the Mediterranean, on the Palais des Congrès Acropolis in Nice, on the ashes of Mória and on the Bodrum shoreline. It was shining on the Great European plain, on Place Jo Cox in Brussels, on the river Moselle in Luxembourg and on the Central European University in Vienna. It was shining on Wenceslas Square in Prague, on the Polish city of Przemyśl and on the old town of Uzhhorod, where actors from the Mariupol Drama Theatre gathered to perform.[59]

The Main Ensemble

European Officials

Catherine Ashton (Baroness)	High Representative of the Union for Foreign Affairs and Security Policy (2009–14)
Michel Barnier	European Commissioner (1999–2004, 2010–14), Member of the Convention on the Future of Europe (2002–3), EU Brexit negotiator (2016–21)
José Manuel Barroso	President of the European Commission (2004–14)
Frits Bolkestein	European Commissioner for Internal Market (1999–2004)
Josep Borrell	EU High Representative for Foreign Affairs and Security Policy (2019–)
Miguel Arias Cañete	European Commissioner for Climate Action (2014–19)
Édith Cresson	European Commissioner for Research, Science and Innovation (1995–99)
Jacques Delors	President of the European Commission (1985–95)
Jeroen Dijsselbloem	President of the Eurogroup (2013–18)
Mario Draghi	President of the European Central Bank (2011–19)
Jean-Claude Juncker	President of the European Commission (2014–19)

THE MAIN ENSEMBLE

Pascal Lamy	European Commissioner for Trade (1999–2004)
Charles Michel	President of the European Council (2019–)
Federica Mogherini	High Representative of the Union for Foreign Affairs and Security Policy (2014–19)
Romano Prodi	President of the European Commission (1999–2004)
Viviane Reding	European Commissioner for Education and Culture (1999–2004), European Commissioner for Information Society and Media (2004–10), European Commissioner for Justice, Fundamental Rights and Citizenship (2010–14)
Carlo Ripa di Meana	European Commissioner for Culture (1985–89), European Commissioner for the Environment (1989–92)
Jacques Santer	President of the European Commission (1995–99)
Javier Solana	High Representative for the Common Foreign and Security Policy (1999–2009)
Jürgen Stark	European Central Bank Executive Board Member (2006–11)
Frans Timmermans	First Vice-President of the European Commission (2014–19), Executive Vice President of the European Commission for the European Green Deal (2019–)
Jean-Claude Trichet	President of the European Central Bank (2003–11)
Donald Tusk	President of the European Council (2014–19)

Karel Van Miert	European Commissioner for Transport and Consumer Protection (1983–89), European Commissioner for Competition (1993–99)
Günter Verheugen	European Commissioner for Enlargement (1999–2004), European Commissioner for Enterprise and Industry (2004–10)
António Vitorino	European Commissioner for Justice and Home Affairs (1999–2004), Member of the Convention on the Future of Europe (2002–3)
Ursula von der Leyen	President of the European Commission (2019–)
Rob Wainwright	Director of Europol (2009–18)
Margot Wallström	European Commissioner for the Environment (1999–2004), First Vice-President of the European Commission and European Commissioner for Institutional Relations and Communication Strategy (2004–10)

Heads of State or Government

Valdas Adamkus	President of Lithuania (1998–2003, 2004–9)
Bertie Ahern	Irish Taoiseach (1997–2008)
Andrus Ansip	Prime Minister of Estonia (2005–14)
José María Aznar	Prime Minister of Spain (1996–2004)
José Manuel Barroso	Prime Minister of Portugal (2002–4)
Traian Băsescu	President of Romania (2004–14)
Silvio Berlusconi	Prime Minister of Italy (1994–95, 2001–6, 2008–11)
Tony Blair	Prime Minister of the United Kingdom (1997–2007)

Gordon Brown	Prime Minister of the United Kingdom (2007–10)
Jerzy Buzek	Prime Minister of Poland (1997–2001)
David Cameron	Prime Minister of the United Kingdom (2010–16)
Jacques Chirac	President of France (1995–2007)
Emil Constantinescu	President of Romania (1996–2000)
Giuseppe Conte	Prime Minister of Italy (2018–21)
António Costa	Prime Minister of Portugal (2015–)
Mario Draghi	Prime Minister of Italy (2021–22)
Andrzej Duda	President of Poland (2015–)
Mikuláš Dzurinda	Prime Minister of Slovakia (1998–2006)
Recep Tayyip Erdoğan	Prime Minister of Turkey (2003–14), President of Turkey (2014–)
Mette Frederiksen	Prime Minister of Denmark (2019–)
Felipe González	Prime Minister of Spain (1982–96)
Dalia Grybauskaitė	President of Lithuania (2009–19)
António Guterres	Prime Minister of Portugal (1995–2002)
Ferenc Gyurcsány	Prime Minister of Hungary (2004–9)
Václav Havel	President of Czechoslovakia (1989–92), President of the Czech Republic (1993–2003)
François Hollande	President of France (2012–17)
Boris Johnson	Prime Minister of the United Kingdom (2019–22)
Jean-Claude Juncker	Prime Minister of Luxembourg (1995–2013)
Jarosław Kaczyński	Prime Minister of Poland (2006–7)
Lech Kaczyński	President of Poland (2005–10)
Enda Kenny	Irish Taoiseach (2011–17)
Helmut Kohl	Chancellor of (West) Germany (1982–98)
Wim Kok	Prime Minister of the Netherlands (1994–2002)

Ewa Kopacz	Prime Minister of Poland (2014–15)
Ivan Kostov	Prime Minister of Bulgaria (1997–2001)
Sebastian Kurz	Chancellor of Austria (2017–19, 2020–21)
Stefan Löfven	Prime Minister of Sweden (2014–21)
Emmanuel Macron	President of France (2017–)
John Major	Prime Minister of the United Kingdom (1990–97)
Sanna Marin	Prime Minister of Finland (2019–23)
Theresa May	Prime Minister of the United Kingdom (2016–19)
Vladimír Mečiar	Prime Minister of Slovak Republic (1993–94, 1994–98)
Giorgia Meloni	Prime Minister of Italy (2022–)
Angela Merkel	Chancellor of Germany (2005–21)
Stjepan Mesić	President of Croatia (2000–10)
Charles Michel	Prime Minister of Belgium (2014–19)
Leszek Miller	Prime Minister of Poland (2001–4)
François Mitterrand	President of France (1981–95)
Mateusz Morawiecki	Prime Minister of Poland (2017–)
Gitanas Nausėda	President of Lithuania (2019–)
Viktor Orbán	Prime Minister of Hungary (1998–2002, 2010–)
Turgut Özal	President of Turkey (1989–93)
George Papandreou	Prime Minister of Greece (2009–11)
Göran Persson	Prime Minister of Sweden (1996–2006)
Romano Prodi	Prime Minister of Italy (1996–98, 2006–8)
Anders Fogh Rasmussen	Prime Minister of Denmark (2001–9)
Poul Nyrup Rasmussen	Prime Minister of Denmark (1993–2001)
Matteo Renzi	Prime Minister of Italy (2014–16)
Pedro Sánchez	Prime Minister of Spain (2018–)

Jacques Santer	Prime Minister of Luxembourg (1984–95)
Nicolas Sarkozy	President of France (2007–12)
Simeon Saxe-Coburg-Gotha	Prime Minister of Bulgaria (2001–5)
Poul Schlüter	Prime Minister of Denmark (1982–93)
Olaf Scholz	Chancellor of Germany (2021–)
Gerhard Schröder	Chancellor of Germany (1998–2005)
Wolfgang Schüssel	Chancellor of Austria (2000–7)
José Sócrates	Prime Minister of Portugal (2005–11)
Laimdota Straujuma	Prime Minister of Latvia (2014–16)
Beata Szydło	Prime Minister of Poland (2015–17)
Margaret Thatcher	Prime Minister of the United Kingdom (1979–90)
Helle Thorning-Schmidt	Prime Minister of Denmark (2011–15)
Alexis Tsipras	Prime Minister of Greece (2015–19)
Donald Tusk	Prime Minister of Poland (2007–14)
Lech Wałęsa	President of Poland (1990–95)
José Luis Rodríguez Zapatero	Prime Minister of Spain (2004–11)
Volodymyr Zelenskyy	President of Ukraine (2019–)

Right-wing Populists

Konrad Adam	Co-Founder, Alternative for Germany (2013)
Justin Barrett	No to Nice Campaign, Ireland (2001–2)
Thierry Baudet	Founder, Forum for Democracy, the Netherlands (2016)
Silvio Berlusconi	Founder, Forza Italia (1994, 2013)
Nigel Farage	Leader, UK Independence Party (2006–9, 2010–16) and Brexit Party (2019–21)
Pim Fortuyn	Founder, Pim Fortuyn List (2002), the Netherlands

Declan Ganley	Founder, Libertas (2008), Ireland
Alexander Gauland	Co-Founder, Alternative for Germany (2013)
James Goldsmith	Founder, Referendum Party, United Kingdom (1994); Founder, Movement for France (1994)
Jörg Haider	Chair, Austrian Freedom (1986–2000)
Boris Johnson	Vote Leave Campaign (2016)
Jarosław Kaczyński	Co-Founder, Law and Justice, Poland (2001)
Lech Kaczyński	Co-Founder, Law and Justice, Poland (2001)
Jean-Marie Le Pen	Founder, Front National, France (1972)
Marine Le Pen	President, Front National (2011–18) and Rassemblement National, France (2018–22)
Bernd Lucke	Co-Founder, Alternative for Germany (2013)
Giorgia Meloni	Co-Founder, Brothers of Italy (2012)
Mateusz Morawiecki	Law and Justice, Poland
Viktor Orbán	Co-Founder, Fidesz, Hungary (1988)
Matteo Salvini	Federal Secretary, Northern League, Italy (2013–)
Heinz-Christian Strache	Chair, Austrian Freedom Party (2005–19)
Beata Szydło	Law and Justice, Poland
Geert Wilders	Founder, Party for Freedom, the Netherlands (2006)

Animals

Bokito	A gorilla in Rotterdam Zoo (1996–2023)

Timeline

23 July 1952	European Coal and Steel Community established
1 January 1958	European Economic Community and European Atomic Energy Community established
1 January 1973	Denmark, Ireland and the United Kingdom join the European Community
1 January 1981	Greece joins the European Community
7 January 1985	Jacques Delors becomes President of the European Commission
14 June 1985	Schengen Agreement signed
1 January 1986	Portugal and Spain join the European Community
1 July 1987	Single European Act enters into force and Single Market Programme begins
6 February 1989	Polish Roundtable Talks begin
16 June 1989	Viktor Orbán's speech at the reburial of Imre Nagy
9 November 1989	Fall of the Berlin Wall
19 June 1990	Schengen Convention signed
2 August 1990	Gulf War begins
17 August 1990	Yugoslav Wars begin
26 December 1991	Soviet Union dissolved
7 February 1992	Maastricht Treaty signed
2 June 1992	Danish voters reject the Maastricht Treaty

16 September 1992	United Kingdom leaves the exchange rate mechanism
1 October 1992	Petra Kelly murdered
31 December 1992	Single Market Programme completed
18 May 1993	Danish voters approve the Maastricht Treaty
22 June 1993	Heads agree that associated countries of Central and Eastern Europe will become EU members
1 November 1993	Maastricht Treaty enters into force. The EU is established
7 April 1994	Rwanda genocide begins
1 January 1995	Austria, Finland and Sweden become members of the EU
25 January 1995	Jacques Santer becomes President of the European Commission
26 March 1995	Schengen Agreement and Schengen Convention enter into force
2 October 1997	Amsterdam Treaty signed
28 February 1998	Kosovo War begins
25 March 1998	First EU–China Summit
1 January 1999	Euro launched
15 March 1999	Santer Commission resigns
1 May 1999	Amsterdam Treaty enters into force
1 July 1999	Europol becomes fully operational
16 September 1999	Romano Prodi becomes President of the European Commission
12 December 1999	Turkey becomes a candidate for EU membership
4 February 2000	Austrian Freedom Party enters government
24 March 2000	Lisbon Strategy launched
26 February 2001	Nice Treaty signed
11 September 2001	Al-Qaeda attacks on New York, Pennsylvania and Virginia

TIMELINE

7 October 2001	US-led invasion of Afghanistan begins
28 February 2002	Convention on the Future of Europe meets for the first time
21 April 2002	Jean-Marie Le Pen makes it to the second round of the French presidential election
6 May 2002	Pim Fortuyn murdered
31 May 2002	EU ratifies the Kyoto Protocol
1 February 2003	Nice Treaty enters into force
20 March 2003	Iraq War begins
31 March 2003	EU launches first military mission in former Yugoslav Republic of Macedonia
13 January 2004	European Commission proposes the EU Services Directive
11 March 2004	Madrid train bombings
1 May 2004	Cyprus, Czech Republic, Estonia, Hungary, Latvia, Malta, Lithuania, Poland, Slovakia and Slovenia join the EU
29 October 2004	European Constitution signed
22 November 2004	José Manuel Barroso becomes President of the European Commission
29 May 2005	French voters reject the European Constitution
1 June 2005	Dutch voters reject the European Constitution
3 October 2005	EU begins accession negotiations with Turkey
17 December 2005	The former Yugoslav Republic of Macedonia becomes a candidate for EU membership
1 January 2007	Bulgaria and Romania join the EU
13 December 2007	Lisbon Treaty signed
12 June 2008	Irish voters reject the Lisbon Treaty
15 September 2008	Lehman Brothers files for bankruptcy
26 November 2008	European Economic Recovery Plan agreed
2 October 2009	Irish voters approve the Lisbon Treaty
1 December 2009	Lisbon Treaty enters into force

2 May 2010	Greece receives €110 billion in financial assistance from the EU and IMF
17 December 2010	Montenegro becomes a candidate country for EU membership
1 March 2012	Serbia becomes a candidate country for EU membership
26 July 2012	European Central Bank President Mario Draghi promises to do 'whatever it takes to save the euro'
23 January 2013	David Cameron promises to hold a referendum on the UK's membership of the EU
1 July 2013	Croatia joins the EU
18 March 2014	Russia annexes Crimea
21 March 2014	EU–Ukraine Association Agreement signed
27 June 2014	Albania becomes a candidate country for EU membership
26 July 2014	Viktor Orbán's 'illiberal state' speech in Băile Tuşnad
1 November 2014	Jean-Claude Juncker becomes President of the European Commission
7 January 2015	*Charlie Hebdo* shooting
5 July 2015	Greek voters reject terms of EU–IMF financial assistance
14 July 2015	Iran Nuclear Deal (Joint Comprehensive Plan of Action) agreed
2 September 2015	Alan Kurdi, a 2-year-old Syrian boy, drowns in the Mediterranean Sea near Bodrum, Turkey
22 September 2015	EU establishes migrant relocation and resettlement scheme
13/14 November 2015	Paris attacks
18 March 2016	EU–Turkey deal signed
22 March 2016	Brussels bombings
16 June 2016	Jo Cox, Member of UK Parliament, murdered

TIMELINE

23 June 2016	UK voters opt to leave the EU
5 October 2016	EU ratifies the Paris Agreement
29 March 2017	Theresa May triggers Article 50
11 April 2017	Marine Le Pen makes it to the second round of the French presidential election
8 May 2018	Donald Trump withdraws the United States from the Iran Nuclear Deal
1 June 2018	The Northern League and Five Star Movement form coalition government in Italy
1 December 2019	Ursula von der Leyen becomes President of the European Commission
24 January 2020	European Centre for Disease Prevention and Control warns of novel coronavirus
31 January 2020	UK withdraws from the EU
14 December 2020	EU creates €750 billion Next Generation EU fund
21 December 2020	European Medicines Agency approves first Covid-19 vaccine
30 December 2020	UK and EU sign Trade and Cooperation Agreement
15 April 2021	European Covid-19 deaths pass one million
7 May 2021	Conference on the Future of Europe opening ceremony
24 February 2022	Russia invades Ukraine
28 February 2022	EU provides lethal military equipment to Ukraine
4 March 2022	EU invokes Temporary Protection Directive for people fleeing war in Ukraine
10 April 2022	Marine Le Pen makes it to the second round of the French presidential election
23 June 2022	Ukraine and Moldova become candidates for EU membership
22 October 2022	Giorgia Meloni becomes Prime Minister of Italy

Acknowledgements

In 1992, as a teenager growing up in Dublin, I was too young to have a vote in Ireland's referendum on the Maastricht Treaty and unsure, in any case, of what it really meant. I was cognisant, however, that something called European integration was happening around me. TV ads urged businesses and consumers to prepare for the soon-to-be-completed single market. Nightly news showed Irish politicians arriving for meetings in Washington DC, their limousines flying European flags on their front wings. MTV Europe helped me to understand that my generation crossed borders, as did a high-minded band formed in the school next to mine by my cousins' neighbour.

Over the next three decades, the EU would come to fascinate and frustrate me. As an undergraduate at Trinity College, Dublin, I raged against the Union's apparent indifference to workers, while enjoying cheap flights to European countries. As a postgraduate at the College of Europe in Bruges, the EU became a subject of late night discussions over strong Belgian beers with classmates from all over Europe. Similar conversations marked my time at the London School of Economics, where I wrote a PhD on the euro, as it took its first uncertain steps. As an economist at the European Commission, I marvelled at how officials and politicians could work so seamlessly together on complex policy problems, while the Union struggled to connect with citizens. As a professor at Birkbeck College and, later, Loughborough University, I watched the idea of leaving the European Union go from the margins of political debate to a daily, divisive reality and learned from my extraordinary students.

ACKNOWLEDGEMENTS

This book bears many stamps from this European journey, on which I was guided by some remarkable teachers, mentors and colleagues. I am especially grateful to Kenneth Armstrong, Samantha Ashenden, Iain Begg, Simon Bulmer, Michele Chang, Alex Colás, Olivier Costa, Servaas Deroose, Kenneth Dyson, Jason Edwards, Bob Hancké, David Howarth, Erik Jones, Wolfram Kaiser, Joost Kuhlmann, Brigid Laffan, Hartmut Lehmann, Joni Lovenduski, Deborah Mabbett, Ivo Maes, Imelda Maher, Uwe Puetter, Claudio Radaelli, Pat Reilly, Ben Rosamond, James Savage, Waltraud Schelkle, Colin Scott, Amy Verdun, Helen Wallace and Ben Worthy. Conversations with Stijn Billiet, Marcus Birch, John Brennan, Richard Crowe, Mark Du Bois, Tobias Eichner, Alma Erenstein, Giles Goodall, Peter Griffith, Benoît Keane, Edwin Lerew, Benedicta Marzinotto, Iacopo Mugnai, Andreas Nägele, Cormac O'Daly, Marco Simoni, Lukas Spielberger, Sotiria Theodoropoulou and Nick Vincent over many years also helped me to see the Union from different vantage points.

This is my seventh book but the first aimed at a general readership. It wouldn't have happened without Chris Bray, a talented writer who was generous with his time and advice, and Michael Alcock, who ably represented me as my agent and believed in the book from the beginning. Jo Godfrey and her colleagues at Yale University Press gave me the time and encouragement I needed to cross the finish line. Sinclair MacKay kindly read my book proposal and helped me to think of the title. I am grateful to the European policy-makers and practitioners, who spoke to me under conditions of anonymity, and Pandelis Nastos at the European University Institute, who helped me to navigate the Historical Archives of the European Union.

Many gifted scholars and experts helped make this book better. Imelda Maher, Uwe Puetter and Martin Westlake provided invaluable feedback on early drafts. Jasmine Bhatia, Simon Brain, Ali Güven, Emma Haddad, László Horváth, Conor Kelly, Deborah Mabbett, Barry Maydom, Antonella Patteri, Sabine Saurugger, David Styan, Zbigniew Truchlewski, Matthijs van den Bos, Thijs Vandenbussche,

ACKNOWLEDGEMENTS

Sarah Wolff and Ben Worthy shared their expertise on specific chapters. Erik Jones, Director of the Robert Schuman Centre for Advanced Studies at the European University Institute in Florence, invited me to present the book to a prestigious group of economists, historians and political scientists. I would like to thank him and Veronica Anghel, Jelena Džankić, Heather Grabbe, Simon Hix, Manuela Moschella, Waltraud Schelkle, Philipp Ther and Glenda Sluga for their invaluable comments. Any errors that remain are mine alone.

Aidan, Paula and other family members in Dublin and London provided so much support during the writing of this book, even when a global pandemic intervened. My sister Deirdre, fellow European voyager, had a considerable impact on this work, as did her husband, Simon, and their children, Roísín, Samuel and Aidan. My parents, Kevin and Noreen, deserve heartfelt thanks, not only for their unfailing encouragement, but also for serving as my very own two-person Conference on the Future of Europe since long before citizens' conventions were in vogue.

This book is dedicated to my wife, Emma, and sons, William and Hugh. It is customary to apologise to loved ones for absences and absent-mindedness during the writing of a book, but such declarations surely belong to an earlier era. Thank you for being there with me.

London, April 2023

Endnotes

Prologue: Hopes and Fears

1. H. Von der Groeben (1998) 'Walter Hallstein as President of the Commission' in W. Loth, W. Wallace and W. Wessels (eds) *Walter Hallstein: The Forgotten European?* (Basingstoke: Palgrave Macmillan): 109.
2. Council of Ministers (1985) 'European Council – 28–29 June, Milan 1985' SN 2740/1/1985.
3. European Commission (1988) 'Europe 1992 – The Overall Challenge', Sec (88)524 Final.
4. J. Delors (1993) 'Address by Jacques Delors to the European Parliament (On the Occasion of the Investiture Debate Following Appointment of the New Commission)', 10 February, SPEECH/93/8 (Brussels: European Commission).
5. J. Goldsmith (1993) *Le Piège* (Paris: Fixot).
6. See, for example, Goldsmith v Pressdram Ltd, [1984] EWCA Civ J0921-8.
7. Goldsmith (1993) 158.
8. J. Goldsmith (1994) *The Trap* (New York: Carroll & Graf): 68.
9. Goldsmith (1994): 68–70.
10. On the idea of thin-centred ideologies, see M. Freeden (1998) *Ideologies and Political Theory: A Conceptual Approach* (Oxford: Clarendon Press). On its application to Europe, see C. Mudde (2007) *Populist Radical Right Parties in Europe* (Cambridge: Cambridge University Press); M. Freeden (2016) 'After the Brexit Referendum: Revisiting Populism as an Ideology' *Journal of Political Ideologies*, 22(1): 1–11; B. Stanley (2008) 'The Thin Ideology of Populism' *Journal of Political Ideologies*, 13(1): 95–110.
11. M. Thatcher (1988) 'Speech to the College of Europe', 20 September, Thatcher Archive.
12. Goldsmith (1994): 75.
13. Preamble, Treaty on European Union (1992).
14. Source: 'European Commission: 1992 Staff Budget', HL Deb 28 January 1992, vol. 534 cc46-7WA.
15. Preamble, Treaty on European Union (1992).
16. M. Matthijs (2020) 'The Right Way to Fix the EU' *Foreign Affairs*, 99(3): 160–64.
17. There is a large political science literature on the negotiation of the Maastricht Treaty. Seminal contributions include A. Moravcsik (1998) *The Choice for Europe: Social Purpose and State Power from Messina to Maastricht* (Abingdon: Routledge) and K. Dyson and K. Featherstone (1999) *The Road to Maastricht: Negotiating Economic and Monetary Union* (Oxford: Oxford University Press).
18. F. Mitterrand (1981) '110 propositions pour la France', *Le Poing et la Rose*, February 1981.

19. K. Dyson (1999) 'EMU, Political Discourse and the Fifth French Republic: Historical institutionalism, path dependency and "craftsmen" of discourse' *Modern & Contemporary France*, 7(2): 181.
20. Moravcsik (1998): 387.
21. 'Helmut Kohl's Ten-Point Plan for German Unity', November 28, 1989. CVCE Archive, University of Luxembourg.
22. Moravcsik (1998): 402.
23. J. Major (1992) 'Europe and the World after 1992', Queen Elizabeth II Conference Centre, 7 September (London: John Major Archive).
24. 'Intervention de M. Jacques Delors lors de la cérémonie de signature du traité', Maastricht, 7 February 1992. Jacques Delors Archive, JD-323, Historical Archives of the European Union.
25. Delors (1993).
26. J. Goldsmith (1990) 'Europe: Why and How?' The Institute of Directors Annual Lecture, 12 June. Sir James Goldsmith Archive. http://www.sirjamesgoldsmith. com/wp-content/uploads/2015/01/Europe-Why-and-How-12_06_1990.pdf
27. Goldsmith (1993): 45; Goldsmith (1994): 80 and Goldsmith (1990). James Goldsmith (1984) 'Soviet Active Measures and the Western Media', 22 May. Sir James Goldsmith Archive. http://www.sirjamesgoldsmith.com/wp-content/ uploads/2015/01/Soviet-Active-Measures-and-the-Western-Media-CCVol1-22_ 05_1984.pdf
28. On deliberation and consensus-seeking, see U. Puetter (2012) 'Europe's Deliberative Intergovernmentalism: The role of the Council and European Council in EU economic governance' *Journal of European Public Policy*, 19(2): 161–78.
29. J. Goldsmith (1985) *Counter Culture*, privately published.
30. 'Europe's St George in a War on Free Trade' *Observer*, 21 November 1993.
31. On 12 October 1993, the German Federal Constitutional Court ruled that Maastricht was compatible with the country's Basic Law and the principle of democracy more generally. This allowed the German government to deposit the country's instrument of ratification with the Italian Ministry of Foreign Affairs in Rome, the last member state to do so.
32. J. Palmer (1993) 'A Shift in Common Ground as European Union Comes of Age' *Guardian*, 1 November.
33. Palmer (1993).
34. At the European Council in Brussels in December 1993, the Heads of State or Government mainly used 'European Union' when referring to the common foreign and security policy. European Council (1993) 'European Council – Brussels, 10–11 December 1993' (Brussels: Council of Ministers). By the time they met in Essen twelve months later, national leaders employed the term much more freely to include plans for economic and monetary union and other areas of economic policy cooperation. European Council (1994) 'European Council – Essen, 9–10 December 1994' (Brussels: Council of Ministers).
35. European Commission (1994) 'Growth, Competitiveness, Employment: The challenges and ways forward into the 21st century: White paper' (Luxembourg: Office for the Official Publications of the European Communities): 9.
36. European Commission (1994): 13.
37. European Commission (1994): 13.
38. In 2019, for example, the right-wing populist group Identity and Democracy won seventy-three seats, making them the fifth-largest group in the European Parliament.
39. European Council (1994).
40. European Commission (1994): 32. See also J. Vignon (2014) 'The Rich Legacy of the White Paper on "Growth, Competitiveness and Employment"', Brief, 13 February

(Paris: Institut Jacques Delors): 4. The European Currency Unit was a synthetic currency used by the EU as a unit of account prior to the introduction of the euro.

41. Reuters (1994) 'Delors Candidacy Urged' *Independent*, 20 July.
42. Sir James Goldsmith (2015) 'Breakfast with Frost: The Maastricht Treaty' *YouTube*, 23 January. https://www.youtube.com/watch?v=wITbD8NRzGw.
43. David Smith 6510 (2017) 'Election 97: James Goldsmith describes the Referendum Party' *YouTube*, 4 September. https://www.youtube.com/watch?v=PvWzjweDE8g
44. Delors (1993): 32.
45. Delors (1993).
46. Goldsmith (1994): 72.
47. See the Further Reading section at the end of this volume for a list of books which deal with the history of European integration.
48. A. Milward (2000) *The European Rescue of the Nation State*, 2nd edn (Abingdon: Routledge): 318.
49. While most EU member states are represented in the European Council by their Head of Government, Cyprus, France, Lithuania and Romania are represented by their Heads of State.
50. With a heraldic description 'On an azure field a circle of 12 golden mullets, their points not touching', the European flag was adopted by the Council of Europe in 1955. The European Community did not have a single emblem until the Heads of State or Government agreed in 1985 to adopt the European flag, which the EU continues to share with the Council of Europe. The Council of the European Union denotes the official symbolism of the circle of stars as 'Unity, solidarity and harmony among the people of Europe'. Council of the European Union (2020) 'The European Flag' (Brussels: Council of Ministers). For alternative interpretations of the European flag, see J. Fornäs (2012) *Signifying Europe* (Bristol: Intellect): 115–48.

Chapter 1 Maastricht to Amsterdam

1. S. Averill and S. McGrath (2016) 'Offset 2016'. https://www.iloveoffset.com/stephen-averill/
2. U2, 'Zoo Station', 1991. New York: Island Records.
3. N. McCormick (2006) 'U2 by U2' (New York: HarperCollins): 247, 252.
4. McCormick (2006): 248.
5. U2, *Zooropa*, 1993. New York: Island Records.
6. K.K. Patel (2020) *Project Europe: A History* (Cambridge: Cambridge University Press).
7. Council of Ministers (1989) 'Presidency Conclusions, European Council, Madrid, 26–27 June', SN 254/2/89.
8. Patel (2020): 72.
9. Articles J.1 and J.4, Treaty on European Union (1992).
10. Heads of State or Government (1972) 'Statement from the Paris Summit (19 to 21 October 1972)' *Bulletin of the European Communities*. October 1972, No 10. Luxembourg: Office for Official Publications of the European Communities: 14–26. The court is referred to in this book by its informal name, the European Court of Justice, rather than its formal name at the time of writing, the Court of Justice.
11. P.N. Ludlow (1999) 'Challenging French Leadership in Europe: Germany, Italy, the Netherlands and the outbreak of the empty chair crisis of 1965–1966' *Contemporary European History*, 8(2): 231–48.
12. The referendum also concerned the question of whether the UK, Ireland, Denmark and Norway should be allowed to join the European Community. Norway voted 'no' to accession in a referendum of its own and never joined.

13. Heads of State or Government (1972) 'Statement from the Paris Summit (19 to 21 October 1972)' *Bulletin of the European Communities*. October 1972, No 10. Luxembourg: Office for official publications of the European Communities: 14–26. CVC.EU Archive, University of Luxembourg.

14. Heads of State or Government (1974) 'Final communiqué of the Paris Summit (9 and 10 December 1974)' *Bulletin of the European Communities*. December, No. 12. Luxembourg: Office for Official Publications of the European Communities.

15. L. Tindemans (1976) 'European Union: Report by Mr Leo Tindemans, Prime Minister of Belgium, to the European Council', *Bulletin of the European Communities*. Supplement 1/76. Luxembourg: Office for Official Publications of the European Communities.

16. M. Gilbert (2020) *European Integration: A Political History* (London: Rowman & Littlefield): 188.

17. M. Leigh (1977) 'Giscard and the European Community' *The World Today*, 33(2): 73–80.

18. L. Vigogne (2019) '6 décembre 1978: Chirac lance l'appel de Cochin contre le "parti de l'étranger"' *l'Opinion*, 26 September.

19. 'Interview de Leo Tindemans / Leo Tindemans, Étienne Deschamps, prise de vue: François Fabert. Bruxelles: CVCE [Prod.], 24.02.2006; CVCE, Sanem. video (00:13:33, Couleur, Son original)'. CVCE.eu Archive, University of Luxembourg.

20. C. Schweiger (2016) *Exploring the EU's Legitimacy Crisis: The Dark Heart of Europe* (Cheltenham: Edward Elgar): 5–6.

21. European Commission (1996) 'Standard Eurobarometer 35' (Brussels: European Commission).

22. European Commission (1996) 'Standard Eurobarometer 45' (Brussels: European Commission).

23. Source: European Commission AMECO database.

24. K. Siune (1993) 'The Danes Said NO to the Maastricht Treaty: The Danish EC referendum of June 1992' *Scandinavian Political Studies*, 16(1): 98.

25. J. Nundy (1992) 'French Referendum: Mitterrand loses political gamble' *Independent*, 20 September.

26. A. Marshall (1992) 'Mitterrand Endures Maastricht Grilling' *Independent*, 3 September.

27. See M. Lorimer (2019) 'Europe from the Far Right: Europe in the ideology of the Front National and Movimento Sociale Italiano/Alleanza Nazionale (1978–2017)', D.Phil thesis, European Institute of the London School of Economics: 62–5.

28. On the post-Maastricht period, see C.J. Bickerton, D. Hodson and U. Puetter (eds) *The New Intergovernmentalism: States and Supranational Actors in the Post-Maastricht Era* (Oxford: Oxford University Press).

29. J. Goldsmith (1994) 'Speech to the European Foundation Meeting at the Conservative Party Conference', 11 October. Sir James Goldsmith Archive. http://www.sirjamesgoldsmith.com/wp-content/uploads/2015/01/The-Bournemouth-Speech-11_10_1994.pdf

30. Article B, Article J.4(5), Article N. Declaration 16, Treaty on European Union (1992).

31. 'Mr Major's Commons Statement on Qualified Majority Voting – 29 March 1994'. John Major Archive. https://johnmajorarchive.org.uk/1994/03/29/mr-majors-commons-statement-on-qualified-majority-voting-29-march-1994/

32. 'Interview du ministre délégué aux Affaires européennes, M. Michel Barnier au "Figaro" (Paris, 10 juillet 1995)'. CVCE.eu Archive, University of Luxembourg.

33. 'Intergovernmental Conference' Hansard, HC Deb 10 January 1996, vol 269 cc203-4. https://api.parliament.uk/historic-hansard/commons/1996/jan/10/intergovernmental-conference-2

34. Tindemans group (1995) *Europe: Your Choice* (London: Harvill Press).
35. B. McDonagh (1998) *Original Sin in a Brave World: An Account of the Negotiation of the Treaty of Amsterdam* (Dublin: Institute of European Affairs): 201.
36. Treaty of Amsterdam (1997), OJ C 340, 10.11.1997, 11997D/TXT.
37. R. Dahl (1999) 'Can International Organizations Be Democratic? A Skeptic's View' in G.W. Brown and D. Held (eds) *The Cosmopolitanism Reader* (Cambridge: Polity Press): 30.
38. Quoted in B. Laffan (1997) 'From Policy Entrepreneur to Policy Manager: The challenge facing the European Commission' *Journal of European Public Policy*, 4(3): 426.
39. J. Peterson (1999) 'The Santer Era: The European Commission in normative, historical and theoretical perspective' *Journal of European Public Policy*, 6(1): 46–65.
40. Judgment of the Court (Full Court) of 11 July 2006. Commission of the European Communities v Édith Cresson, Case C-432/04, EU:C:2006:455, paragraphs 138–9 and 146.
41. 'The Schreiber Affair – Scandal that rocked the government of Helmut Kohl' *DW-Deutsche Welle*, 18 January 2010. https://www.dw.com/en/the-scandal-that-rocked-the-government-of-helmut-kohl/a-5137950?maca=en-rss-en-all-1573-rdf
42. Council of the European Union (1999) 'Presidency Conclusions. Helsinki European Council', 10–11 December. https://www.consilium.europa.eu/media/21046/helsinki-european-council-presidency-conclusions.pdf

Chapter 2 Return to Europe

1. M. Kundera (1984) 'The Tragedy of Central Europe' *New York Review of Books*, 31(7). This essay originally appeared in French as M. Kundera (1983) 'Un Occident kidnappé: ou la tragédie de l'Europe centrale', *Le Débat*, 5(27): 3–23.
2. S. Whitefield and G. Evans (2001) 'Attitudes towards the West, Democracy, and the Market' in J. Zielonka and A. Pravda (eds) *Democratic Consolidation in Eastern Europe*, Volume 2: *International and Transnational Factors* (Oxford: Oxford University Press).
3. See H. Sjursen (2002) 'Why Expand? The question of legitimacy and justification in the EU's enlargement policy' *Journal of Common Market Studies*, 40(3): 491–513.
4. L. Wałęsa (1987) *A Way of Hope: An autobiography* (New York: Henry Holt and Company): 164– 66.
5. Speech by V. Orbán, *BBC Summary of World Broadcasts*, 20 June 1989. The movement was initially known as Alliance of Young Democrats (FIDESZ) but eventually changed its name to the Hungarian Civic Alliance (Fidesz – Magyar Polgári Szövetség).
6. V. Havel (1989) 'The Declaration of the Civic Forum by Representative Vaclav Havel on Wenceslas Square', 23 November.
7. V. Havel (1990) 'Speech Made to the Parliamentary Assembly of the Council of Europe', 10 May.
8. Havel (1990).
9. 'Allocution de M. François Mitterrand, Président de la République, à l'occasion de la présentation de ses voeux, Paris, dimanche 31 décembre 1989'.
10. 'Political Resolution of The Hague Congress (7–10 May 1948)'. CVCE.eu Archive, University of Luxembourg.
11. G. Lysen (1989) 'The Joint Declaration by the EEC and the CMEA' *North Carolina Journal of International Law and Commercial Regulation*, 14(3): 369–90.
12. European Commission (1991) 'European Agreements with Czechoslovakia, Hungary, and Poland', Press Release, 22 November.

13. F. Breuss (1995) 'Cost and Benefits of EU's Eastern European Enlargement', Austrian Institute of Economic Research (WIFO) Working Papers No. 78: 7.
14. Source: WITS (World Integrated Trade Solution), World Bank DataBank.
15. E. Zamrazilová (2000) 'External Imbalance: The Czech case' *Eastern European Economics*, 38(3): 82–94.
16. United Nations Economic Commission for Europe (1997) 'Main Developments in the ECE Economies in 1997 and the Outlook for 1998' (Geneva: UNECE).
17. V. Havel (1994) 'Speech to the European Parliament', Strasbourg, 8 March. Reprinted in M. Segers and Y. Albrecht (eds) (2016) *Re:Thinking Europe: Thoughts on Europe: Past, Present and Future* (Amsterdam: Amsterdam University Press).
18. H. Field (2002) 'Awkward States: EU enlargement and Slovakia, Croatia and Serbia' in Cameron Ross (ed.) *Perspectives on the Enlargement of the European Union* (Leiden: Brill): 215–38.
19. See M. Cini (2008) 'Political Leadership in the European Commission: The Santer and Prodi Commissions, 1995–2005' in J. Hayward (ed.) *Leaderless Europe* (Oxford: Oxford University Press): 113–30.
20. 'Address given by Jacques Delors to the European Parliament' *Bulletin of the European Communities*. 17 January 1989, Supplement 1/89. Luxembourg: Office for Official Publications of the European Communities.
21. H. Binnendijk (1991) 'The Emerging European Security Order' *Washington Quarterly*, 14(4): 67–81.
22. J. Santer (1995) 'Statement Made by Jacques Santer to the European Parliament on EU Enlargement', Debates of the European Parliament. Report of proceedings. 02.03.1995, No 4-458. *Official Journal of the European Communities*, CVCE.eu Archive, University of Luxembourg.
23. R. Prodi (1999) 'Speech by Romano Prodi President-designate of the European Commission to the European Parliament Strasbourg', 14 September, Press Release, SPEECH/99/114 (Brussels: European Commission).
24. H. Kohl (1990) 'Ten-Point Plan to Overcome the Division of Germany and Europe (28 November 1989)'. CVCE.eu Archive, University of Luxembourg.
25. S. Wood (2003) 'Is Eastern Enlargement of the European Union a Beneficial Investment for Germany?' *Political Science Quarterly*, 118(2): 294.
26. A. Lücke (1992) 'German Foreign Investment in Poland: Problems and perspectives' *The Polish Review*, 37(4): 455–9.
27. European Council (1993) 'Conclusions of the Presidency', Copenhagen, 21–22 June, SN 180/1/93 REV 1 (Brussels: Council of the European Union).
28. European Council (1993).
29. Prodi (1999).
30. J. O'Brennan (2006) *The Eastern Enlargement of the European Union* (Abingdon: Routledge): 82.
31. I. Traynor (1999) 'Schröder Faces Dual Challenge' *Guardian*, 19 March.
32. T. Blair (2000) 'Address given by Tony Blair to the Polish Stock Exchange (Warsaw, 6 October 2000)'. CVCE.eu Archive, University of Luxembourg.
33. H. Grabbe (2006) *The EU's Transformative Power* (Basingstoke: Palgrave Macmillan): 26.
34. 'Leszek Miller, Poland's Wily Man of the Future' *The Economist*, 19 April 2001.
35. European Commission (1997) 'Agenda 2000 – Commission Opinion on Slovakia's Application for Membership of the European', 15 July DOC/97/20 (Brussels: European Commission).
36. European Council (2002) 'Presidency Conclusions, 12 and 13 December' 15917/02, POLGEN 84 (Brussels: Council of the European Union).

37. S. Coates (2003) 'Marathon Success Leaves Campbell in a Spin' *The Times*, 14 April.
38. C. Adebahr (2013) 'If Yugoslavia Were an EU Member' *Carnegie Europe*, 13 December.
39. European Commission (1990) 'EEC–Yugoslavia Cooperation Council (1990)', Memo 90-64, 17 December.
40. European Commission (1990).
41. See B. Crawford (1996) 'Explaining Defection from International Cooperation: Germany's unilateral recognition of Croatia' *World Politics*, 48(4): 482–521.
42. In 2020, Serbia's Gini coefficient – a measure of income inequality – was 6.1 per cent. This was second only to Turkey's among candidate countries. Source: Eurostat (2022) 'Enlargement Countries – Statistics on living conditions' (Luxembourg: Eurostat).
43. Nikolic quit the party after winning the presidency and governed as an independent.
44. C. Adebahr (2013). The EU referred to Macedonia as the former Yugoslav Republic of Macedonia between 1991 and 2019 in view of a name dispute with Greece, which feared irredentism and revisionism because of perceived ambiguity over this country's name, the Greek region of Macedonia and Macedon, a kingdom of ancient Greece. After this protracted dispute was resolved, the country changed its name to North Macedonia, clearing the way for it to begin accession negotiations with the EU in 2022.
45. European Council (2003) 'Presidency Conclusions', D/03/3 (Brussels: Council of the European Union).
46. For a discussion of Turkish constitutional reforms during this period, see E. Özbudun (2015) 'Europeanization and Turkey's Constitutional Reform Process' in A. Tekin and A. Güney (eds) *The Europeanization of Turkey: Polity and Politics* (Abingdon: Routledge): 33–50.
47. 'Fortuyn Murder Case: "Confession" ' CNN, 23 November 2022.
48. I. Bickerton (2004) 'Wilder Shores' *Financial Times*, 6 September.
49. J. Quatremer (1995) 'Les Quinze font une petite place à Ankara. L'union douanière avec la Turquie entrera en vigueur à partir du 1er janvier' *Libération*, 14 December.
50. 'Sarkozy et la Turquie' *Le Monde*, 28 August 2007. 'Les grandes lignes du programme de Nicolas Sarkozy 2007' *RFI*, 20 April 2007.
51. S. Marthaler (2008) 'Nicolas Sarkozy and the Politics of French Immigration Policy' *Journal of European Public Policy*, 15(3): 382–97; K. Willsher (2005) 'French Celebrities Desert Sarkozy in Wake of Attack on Urban Poor' *Guardian*, 23 December.
52. R.T. Erdoğan (2004) 'Why the EU Needs Turkey' *Insight Turkey*, 6(3): 7–15.
53. T. Snyder (2002) *The Reconstruction of Nations: Poland, Ukraine, Lithuania, Belarus, 1569–1999* (New Haven and London: Yale University Press): 290–1.
54. Council of the EU (2003) 'Presidency Conclusions – 16–17 October', Press Release 15188/03 (Brussels: Council of the European Union).
55. S. Gänzle (2009) 'EU Governance and the European Neighbourhood Policy: A framework for analysis' *Europe–Asia Studies*, 61(10): 1716.
56. K. Gorchinskaya (2020) 'A Brief History of Corruption in Ukraine: The Kuchma era' *Eurasianet*, 20 May.
57. 'Georgiy Gongadze Murder Tied to Late Ukrainian Minister' *BBC News*, 14 September 2010.
58. E. Korosteleva (2009) 'The Limits of EU Governance: Belarus's response to the European neighbourhood policy' *Contemporary Politics*, 15(2): 230. Over time, the EU focused this aid on civil society groups but it was unclear how much difference

it made. See European Commission (2020) 'EU Strengthens Its Direct Support to the People of Belarus', Press Release, 11 December IP/20/2309 (Brussels: European Commission).

59. 'Belarus: "Don't Use the Blue Flag": Protesters argue about using EU flags in demos', *Ruptly* 19 August 2020.

60. European Union External Action Services (2020) 'The EU Continues to Stand with the People of Belarus', Press Release, 12 December (Brussels: EEAS).

Chapter 3 Nice to Lisbon

1. 'Analysis: What do the protesters want?', *NCC*, 7 December 2001.

2. C. Schweiger (2014) 'The "Reluctant Hegemon": Germany in the EU's post-crisis constellation', in K.N. Demetriou (ed.) *The European Union in Crisis: Explorations in Representation and Democratic Legitimacy* (Cham: Springer): 18.

3. 'So That's All Agreed, Then' *The Economist*, 14 December 2002.

4. J. Fischer (2000) 'Speech by Joschka Fischer on the Ultimate Objective of European Integration (Berlin, 12 May)'. CVCE.eu Archive, University of Luxembourg.

5. '"Mit Verlaub, Sie sind ein Arschloch"' *Süddeutsche Zeitung*, 26 March 2009.

6. 'Address given by Jacques Chirac to the Bundestag entitled "Our Europe" (Berlin, 27 June 2000)'. CVCE.eu Archive, University of Luxembourg.

7. T. Blair (2000) 'Address given by Tony Blair to the Polish Stock Exchange (Warsaw, 6 October 2000)'. CVCE.eu Archive, University of Luxembourg.

8. Declaration (23) on the Future of the Union, Treaty of Nice (2001), OJ C 80, 10.3.2001, 12001C/TXT.

9. Declaration (23) on the Future of the Union, Treaty of Nice (2001), OJ C 80, 10.3.2001, 12001C/TXT.

10. D. Hodson and I. Maher (2018) *The Transformation of EU Treaty Making: The rise of parliaments, referendums and courts since 1950* (Cambridge: Cambridge University Press): 148.

11. See, for example, A. Coughlan (2000) 'The Economics and Politics of Ireland's Boom' *Journal of the European Foundation*, 7(8): 17–18; A. Coughlan (2000) 'Moves to European Superstate Demand Debate' *Irish Times*, 21 September; A. Coughlan (1998) 'Treaty Would Give Brussels Huge New Powers over Rights', *Irish Times*, 11 May.

12. See J. Barrett (1998) *National Way Forward* (Granard, Co. Longford: The Guild Press) and A. Beesley (2003) 'Book Rails against "Whole Rotten Cabal of the Left"' *Irish Times*, 17 May.

13. Council of the European Union (2002) 'Presidency Conclusions', Brussels, 24 October, 13463/02, POLGEN 52 (Brussels: Council of the European Union).

14. K. Hayward (2003) '"If at First You Don't Succeed . . .": The second referendum on the Treaty of Nice, 2002' *Irish Political Studies*, 18(1): 120–32.

15. See G. De Búrca (2009) 'If at First You Don't Succeed: Vote, Vote Again: Analyzing the second referendum phenomenon in EU treaty change' *Fordham International Law Journal*, 33(5): 1472–89.

16. M.E. Synon (2009) 'Brussels Is Buying a Yes in the Irish "Neverendum" . . . and It Doesn't Care How Much of Your Cash It Costs' *Daily Mail*, 27 September.

17. T. Sims (2003) 'ECB Chief Wins Fans on Eve of Departure' *Wall Street Journal*, 2 October.

18. 'Candidates Who Deserve the Eurosceptic Vote' *The Times*, 1 May 1997. 'Tories Flaunt the Flag of Prejudice' *Independent*, 8 March 1997.

19. T. Blair (2011) *A Life* (London: Arrow): 320.

20. One issue that Stuart exerted influence over, she later claimed, was the creation of an exit clause through which a member state could give notice to leave the EU. See

'Gisela Stuart – Brexit Witness Archive' *UK in a Changing Europe*, 2 November 2020. https://ukandeu.ac.uk/brexit-witness-archive/gisela-stuart/

21. 'Contribution présentée par M. Jens-Peter Bonde, membre de la Convention', 1 October 2002, CONV 277/02 (Brussels: Convention on the Future of Europe).

22. 'Prodi Document Leak Causes Dismay among Commissioners' *Politico Europe*, 11 December 2002.

23. 'M. Giscard d'Estaing ironise sur la "Constitution Pénélope" de M. Prodi' *Le Monde*, 7 December 2002.

24. 'Laeken Declaration on the Future of the European Union (15 December 2001)'. CVCE.eu Archive, University of Luxembourg.

25. J. Graff (2002) 'How to Build a More Perfect Union' *Time*, 4 March.

26. The Intergovernmental Conference in which this agreement was struck was not plain sailing. In December 2003, it came close to collapse, but national delegations worked through their differences over qualified majority voting and other contentious issues in six months of intensive negotiations chaired by Ireland, as the country occupying the EU's six-month rotating presidency. For a first-hand account, see B. McDonagh (2007) 'The Intergovernmental Conference: How the deal was done' in G. Amato, H. Bribosia and B. De Witte (eds) *Genesis and Destiny of the European Constitution* (Brussels: Bruylant): 87–136.

27. 'Draft Treaty Establishing a Constitution for Europe', Brussels, 18 July 2003, CONV 850/03 (Brussels: Convention on the Future of Europe).

28. 'Address by the President of the European Council, José M. Aznar, at the Inaugural Meeting of the Convention on the Future of Europe', Brussels, 28 February 2002, CONV 4/02 (Brussels: Convention on the Future of Europe); H. Mahony (2004) 'Aznar Criticises EU Constitution' *EU Observer*, 6 July.

29. M. Berezin (2006) 'Appropriating the "No": The French National Front, the vote on the constitution, and the "new" April 21' *PS: Political Science and Politics*, 39(2): 279.

30. J.M. Aznar (2002) 'Open Remarks', The Convention on the Future of Europe, Brussels, 28 February.

31. J. Lichfield (2005) 'EU Constitution Can Be Rewritten, Delors Admits' *Independent*, 14 May.

32. 'Contribution by Mr Frans Timmermans, member of the Convention: "The Future of the European Statistical System"', 17 January 2003 CONV 491/03 (Brussels: Convention on the Future of Europe).

33. S. Hollander (2019) *The Politics of Referendum Use in European Democracies* (Basingstoke: Palgrave Macmillan): 234.

34. M. Simons (2005) 'Tired of Hiding, 2 Dutch Legislators Emerge' *International Herald Tribune*, 4 March.

35. S. Castle (2005) 'In the Footsteps of Fortuyn: Geert Wilders, the scourge of Dutch liberalism, is determined to make race the key issue in the EU referendum campaign' *Independent*, 20 May.

36. A. Barker and P. Spiegel (2015) 'Frans Timmermans, the Man Standing Between Brussels and Brexit' *Financial Times*, 19 May.

37. European Council (2005) 'Declaration by the Heads of State or Government of the Member States of the European Union on the Ratification of the Treaty Establishing a Constitution for Europe' (European Council, 16 and 17 June).

38. European Commission (2006) 'Debate Europe! The Future of Europe internet forum has reached one million hits' 13 July IP/06/989 (Brussels: European Commission).

39. 'Record of the Proceedings of the Conference "The Sound of Europe" on the Future of Europe (Salzburg, 27 and 28 January 2006)'. CVCE.eu Archive, University of Luxembourg.

40. M. Beunderman (2006) 'EU Leaders Seek Legitimacy through Action at "Elitist" Event' *EU Observer*, 30 January.
41. 'Exit Schröder, Enter Merkel? Surprise: voters don't like pain without gain' *The Economist*, 26 May 2005.
42. 'Merkel Vows to Seek European Constitution' *Irish Times*, 11 May 2006.
43. 'Declaration on the Occasion of the 50th Anniversary of the Signature of the Treaties of Rome', 25 March 2007 (Brussels: Council of the European Union).
44. S. Mulvey (2007) 'Poles in War of Words over Voting' *BBC News*, 21 June.
45. 'European Leaders Sign Landmark Lisbon Treaty' *Malta Independent*, 14 December 2007.
46. H. McGee (2008) 'The Anti-Lisbon Lion' *Irish Times*, 12 January.
47. D. de Breadun (2007) 'A Sad Day for Europe, Says Ganley' *Irish Times*, 14 December.
48. H. McDonald (2008) 'I Have Witnessed How Inherently Undemocratic Socialism Was, and That is Why I Don't Want an Overweening EU' *Guardian*, 13 June.
49. H. McGee (2008) 'Ganley Defends Comments on Detention of Young Children' *Irish Times*, 30 May; 'Anti-Lisbon Leader Urged to Retract Abortion Comments' *Belfast Telegraph*, 19 May 2008.
50. 'Sarkozy "Plans to Make Irish Vote Again on Rejected EU Treaty"' *Daily Mail*, 15 July 2008.
51. F. Sheahan (2009) 'Ryanair Boss Backs "Yes" Vote for Lisbon' *Irish Independent*, 27 August.
52. The proposed opt-out was neither concluded nor ratified by the time it was eventually withdrawn by the Czech government in 2014.
53. M.A. Pollack (2006) 'Rational Choice and EU Politics' in K.E Jørgensen, M.A. Pollack and B. Rosamond (eds) *The SAGE Handbook of European Union Politics* (London: SAGE Publications): 31–56.
54. M. Weaver, L. Radnofsky and agencies (2007) 'Brown Flies to Lisbon for Belated EU Treaty Signing' *Guardian*, 13 December.
55. E. Macron (2017) 'Speech by the President of the French Republic in Greece', Athens, 7 September (New York: Consulate General of France).

Chapter 4 Fundamental Values

1. 'Haider in Context: Nazi Employment Policies' *BBC News*, 11 February 2000; 'Jörg Haider, an Austrian Conundrum' *The Economist*, 10 February 2000.
2. I. Black (2000) 'Europe Issues Haider Ultimatum to Austria', *Guardian*, 1 February.
3. Black (2000).
4. 'Statement by the Portuguese Presidency of the EU on behalf of 14 Member States (31 January 2000)'. CVCE.eu Archive, University of Luxembourg.
5. D.G. McNeil Jr (2000) 'A Threat by Austria on Sanctions' *New York Times*, 4 July.
6. A. Osborn and K. Connolly (2000) 'Austria is Winning EU Sanctions Battle' *Guardian*, 13 July.
7. P. Smyth (2000) 'Austria Warned by EU States on Haider' *Irish Times*, 1 February.
8. M. Ahtisaari, J. Frowein and M. Oreja (2000) 'Report Adopted in Paris on 8 September 2000' (Strasbourg: Council of Europe): 27.
9. Ahtisaari, Frowein and Oreja (2000): 27.
10. Ahtisaari, Frowein and Oreja (2000): 33.
11. D. Staunton (2000) 'Resignation of Haider Widely Seen as Tactical' *Irish Times*, 1 March.
12. Article F, Treaty on European Union (1992).
13. 'The Charter of Fundamental Rights of the European Union'. CVCE.eu Archive, University of Luxembourg.

14. B. Blagoev (2011) 'Expulsion of a Member State from the EU after Lisbon: Political threat or legal reality?' *Tilburg Law Review* 16(2): 191–237.
15. J. Thornhill and M. Vipotnik (1998) 'Adamkus Pledges to Rule by Example: President of Lithuania says country must shake off its past' *Financial Times*, 19 February.
16. S. Brittan (2000) 'Lithuania's Tough Test for Toleration: Newly emerged into independence, the Baltic state is struggling to recover from its often tragic past' *Financial Times*, 2 September.
17. Source: World Bank DataBank.
18. P. Ignazi (1996) 'From Neo-fascists to Post-fascists? The transformation of the MSI into the AN' *West European Politics*, 19(4): 693–714.
19. M. Sznajder (1995) 'Italy's Right-Wing Government: Legitimacy and criticism' *International Affairs*, 71(1): 99.
20. W. Marten (2006) *Europe: I Struggle, I Overcome* (Berlin: Springer): 140.
21. L. Davies (2013) 'Silvio Berlusconi Ousted from Italian Parliament after Tax Fraud Conviction' *Guardian*, 27 November.
22. 'Berlusconi Urges EPP to Ally with Right-Wing Populists against Left' *Euractiv*, 2 April 2019.
23. S. Fella (2018) 'The New Italian Government', House of Commons Briefing Paper No. 8357, 29 June.
24. S. Kirchgaessner (2018) 'Matteo Salvini: A political chameleon thriving on fears' *Guardian*, 22 June.
25. L. Davies (2014) 'Beppe Grillo Sparks Controversy with Image of Blacked-up Politician' *Guardian*, 3 September; 'Beppe Grillo: Profile' *BBC News*, 26 February 2013; T. Mueller (2008) 'Beppe's Inferno: A comedian's war on crooked politics' *New Yorker*, 27 January.
26. M. Rose and G. Jones (2018) 'France's Macron Warns of Populism "Leprosy", Italy Hits Back' *Reuters*, 21 June.
27. L. Montalto Monella and S. Amiel (2019) 'Salvini Claims He Is Saving Europe from Islam, What Are the Facts?' *Euronews*, 6 May.
28. R. Saviano (2022) 'Giorgia Meloni Is a Danger to Italy and the Rest of Europe' *Guardian*, 24 September.
29. 'Justice or Revenge? The human rights implications of lustration in Poland' (Warsaw: Humanity in Action Polska).
30. H. Suchocka (2007) 'Lustration: Experience of Poland', CDL-PI(2015)029 (Strasbourg: European Commission For Democracy Through Law).
31. R. Wright (2001) 'Prodi in Warning to Budapest on EU Accession' *Financial Times*, 6 April.
32. E. Vucheva (2008) 'Polish Parliament Approves EU Treaty' *EU Observer*, 1 April.
33. Komorowski governed as an independent, but he retained the support of Civic Platform.
34. Quoted in A.L. Pap (2018) *Democratic Decline in Hungary: Law and Society in an Illiberal Democracy* (Abingdon: Routledge).
35. S. Auer (2022) *European Disunion: Democracy, Sovereignty and the Politics of Emergency* (London: Hurst): 54.
36. On the concept of challenger parties, see C.E. De Vries and S.B. Hobolt (2020) *Political Entrepreneurs: The Rise of Challenger Parties in Europe* (Princeton, NJ: Princeton University Press). On the idea of challenger governments, see D. Hodson and U. Puetter (2019) 'The European Union in Disequilibrium: New intergovernmentalism, postfunctionalism and integration theory in the post-Maastricht Period' *Journal of European Public Policy*, 26(8): 1153–71.
37. In 2006, 73 per cent of Polish respondents suggested that their country had benefited from being an EU member state. This figure was only 41 per cent in Hungary, but it steadily increased after Orbán regained the premiership. By 2022, 69 per cent

of Hungarians had a positive view of the EU. Eurobarometer (2006) 'Standard Eurobarometer 66 – Autumn 2006 (Brussels: Eurobarometer). M. Fagan and S. Gubbala (2022) 'Positive Views of European Union Reach New Highs in Many Countries', *Pew Research*, 13 October.

38. 'Opinion on the Fourth Amendment to the Fundamental Law of Hungary' Adopted by the Venice Commission at its 95th Plenary Session, Venice, CDL-AD(2013)012-e, 14–15 June 2013.

39. J.M. Magone (2005) 'José Manuel Durão Barroso: A political scientist in the world of European Union politics' *International Journal*, 60(2): 544–52.

40. T. Barber (2010) 'Clouds of Nationalism Gather over Hungary's EU Presidency' *Financial Times*, 4 June.

41. L. Phillips (2010) 'Sarkozy to Reding: 'You will pay consequences for insulting France' *EU Observer*, 28 October.

42. 'Hungary – Infringements: Commission takes further legal steps on measures affecting the judiciary and the independence of the data protection authority, notes some progress on central bank independence, but further evidence and clarification needed', Press Release, 7 March 2012, MEMO/12/165 (Brussels: European Commission).

43. 'Full Text of Viktor Orbán's Speech at Băile Tuşnad (Tusnádfürdő) of 26 July' *Budapest Beacon*, 26 July 2014.

44. V. Reding (2013) 'Speech: The EU and the rule of law – what next?' SPEECH/13/677 (Brussels: European Commission).

45. Euronews (2015) '"Here comes the dictator": Juncker's cheeky welcome for Hungarian PM' *YouTube*, 22 May. https://www.youtube.com/watch?v=1hl83Jpd_OI

46. W. Sadurski (2019) 'Polish Constitutional Tribunal under PiS: From an activist court, to a paralysed tribunal, to a governmental enabler' *Hague Journal on the Rule of Law*, 11(1): 63–84.

47. European Commission for Democracy Through Law, Opinion No. 904 / 2017, CDL-AD(2017)031, Strasbourg, 11 December 2017.

48. G. Gotev (2015) 'Poland Demands Apology after Schulz Calls Judicial Changes "Coup"' *Euractiv*, 15 December.

49. 'Full Text of Viktor Orbán's Speech at Băile Tuşnad' (Tusnádfürdő) of 26 July' *Budapest Beacon*, 26 July 2014.

50. E. Zalan (2017) 'Anti-Soros University Bill Sparks Protest in Budapest' *EU Observer*, 5 April.

51. 'Orbán Names Soros and EU Among Those "Attacking" Hungary' *Euractiv*, 13 February 2017.

52. C. Barbière (2015) 'Daul: 'Orbán Is the "Enfant Terrible" of the EPP Family, but I Like Him', *Euractiv*, 3 July.

53. Manfred Weber (2017) 'Freedom of thinking, research and speech are essential for our European identity. @EPPGroup will defend this at any cost. #CEU', *Twitter*, 5 April. https://twitter.com/ManfredWeber/status/849666581391183872

54. Manfred Weber (2018) 'Extremely disappointed by the refusal of the Hungarian government to agree with @ceuhungaryn on their double degree program. It is unacceptable that a university in EU today is forced to move elsewhere with their curriculum. #CEU', *Twitter*, 3 December. https://twitter.com/manfredweber/status/1069596131087327233

55. M. De La Baume (2021) 'Orbán Walkout Shakes Up European (Political) Family Drama' *Politico Europe*, 3 March.

56. H. Grabbe and S. Lehne (2019) 'The EU's Values Crisis: Past and future responses to threats to the rule of law and democratic principles' in P. Bevelander and R. Wodak (eds) *Europe at the Crossroads: Confronting Populist, Nationalist and Global Challenges* (Oslo: Nordic Academic Press): 49–62.

57. E. Schultz (2021) 'The Rise and Fall of Heinz-Christian Strache, Austria's Far-Right Firebrand' *Politico Europe*, 7 July.
58. E. Turner-Graham (2008) 'Austria First: HC Strache, Austrian identity and the current politics of Austria's Freedom Party' *Studies in Language & Capitalism*, 3(4): 181–98; N. Beret (2006) 'The Politics of Austrian Hip-Hop: HC Strache's xenophobia gets dissed' *Colloquia Germanica*, 39(2): 209–30.
59. A. Bodlos and C. Plescia (2018) 'The 2017 Austrian Snap Election: A shift rightward' *West European Politics*, 41(6): 1354–63.
60. R. Atkins (2017) 'Austria's Sebastian Kurz Leans Towards Tougher Line on Migrants' *Financial Times*, 18 October.
61. 'PM Orbán Congratulates Sebastian Kurz on Austrian Election Win' *About Hungary*, 17 October 2017. http://abouthungary.hu/news-in-brief/pm-orban-congratulates-sebastian-kurz-on-austrian-election-win/
62. L. Varadkar (2017) 'Contacted @sebastiankurz today to congrat him on becoming Chancellor of Austria. One more @EPP Prime Minister. Am no longer the youngest of the bunch!' *Twitter*, 16 December. https://twitter.com/LeoVaradkar/status/942045990474977282

Chapter 5 European Culture

1. M. Ball, R. Oulds and L. Rotherham (2002) 'Federalist Thought Control: The Brussels propaganda machine' The Bruges Group Paper No. 45.
2. G. Delanty (1995) *Inventing Europe: Idea, Identity, Reality* (Basingstoke: Macmillan): 128.
3. C. Shore (2013) *Building Europe: The Cultural Politics of European Integration* (Abingdon: Routledge): 54 and 225.
4. European Broadcasting Union (2015) '60th Eurovision Song Contest Seen by Nearly 200 Million Viewers', Press Release, 3 June.
5. A. Rettman (2021) 'EU's First-Ever "Eurovision" Song Stirs Controversy' *EU Observer*, 1 April.
6. 'Countdown to 1993 and the United States of Europe – Are You Prepared? Everything you need to know about the European Commission and the Maastricht Treaty' *Art Newspaper*, 1 April 1992.
7. E. Tretter (2011) 'The "Value" of Europe: The political economy of culture in the European community' *Geopolitics*, 16(4): 926–48.
8. L. Bekemans (1990) 'European Integration and Cultural Policies: Analysis of a dialectic polarity', European University Institute Working Paper ECS No. 90/1.
9. Article 128, Treaty on European Union (1992), OJ C 191, 29.7.1992, 11992M/TXT.
10. A. Scott (2004) 'Hollywood and the World: The geography of motion-picture distribution and marketing' *Review of International Political Economy*, 11(1): 33–61.
11. 'Council Decision of 21 December 1990 concerning the implementation of an action programme to promote the development of the European audiovisual industry (Media)', 90/685/EEC, OJ L 380, 31.12.1990, 37–44.
12. European Commission (2000) 'Statistics on Audiovisual Services – Data 1980–1998' (Brussels: European Commission): 8.
13. Quoted in M.K. Nelson (1996) '"Television Without Frontiers": The EC Broadcasting Directive' in R. Folsom, R.B. Lake and V.P. Nanda (eds) *European Union Law after Maastricht: Practical Guide for Lawyers Outside the Common Market* (Dordrecht: Kluwer): 636.
14. European Commission (2000): 35.
15. S. Roxborough (2016) 'European Films Still Struggle to Cross Borders' *Hollywood Reporter*, 23 June.

16. European Audiovisual Observatory (2020) 'Focus World Film Market 2020' (Strasbourg: European Audiovisual Observatory): 17; European Audiovisual Observatory (2020) 'Focus World Film Market 2003' (Strasbourg: European Audiovisual Observatory): 21.
17. European Audiovisual Observatory (2020): 21.
18. European Audiovisual Observatory (2020): 24.
19. M. Bächler (2014) 'The Christmas Truce of 1914 – Remembered in 2005. The staging of European similarities in the movie *Merry Christmas – Joyeux Noël*' *European Network Remembrance and Solidarity*, 20 August.
20. M. Robinson (2013) '"Squirmingly Embarrassing, Atrocious and Fabulously Awful": "Excruciating" new Diana film panned in series of one-star reviews' *Daily Mail*, 6 September.
21. Kermodeandmayo (2015) 'Mark Kermode Reviews *The Lobster*' *YouTube*, 16 October. https://www.youtube.com/watch?v=e1VyXx7GiAo
22. P. Hoeg (1993) *Miss Smilla's Feeling for Snow* (London: Harvill Press).
23. Source: Human Development Index (HDI) Composite indices. https://hdr.undp.org/en/indicators/137506#
24. M. Booth (2014) *The Almost Nearly Perfect People: Behind the Myth of the Scandinavian Utopia* (New York: Random House).
25. T. Modini (2019) 'As Nordic Noir Phenomenon "The Bridge" and its Adaptations Launch at SBS On-Demand, We Look at What Makes the Concept So Remarkable' *SBS*, 26 December.
26. See L. Block (2012) 'EU Joint Investigation Teams: Political ambitions and police practices' in S. Hufnagel, C. Harfield and S. Bronitt (eds) *Cross Border Law Enforcement: Cross-Border Law Enforcement Regional Law Enforcement Cooperation – European, Australian and Asia-Pacific Perspectives* (Abingdon: Routledge): 87–108.
27. I. Bondebjerg (2020) 'Bridging Cultures: Transnational cultural encounters in the reception of *The Bridge*' in A. Marit Waade, E. Novrup Redvall and P. Majbritt Jensen (eds) *Danish Television Drama* (Basingstoke: Palgrave): 209–30.
28. S. Broughton Micova (2013) 'Content Quotas: What and whom are they protecting?' in K. Donders, C. Pauwels and J. Loisen (eds) (2013) *Private Television in Western Europe: Content, Markets, Policies* (Basingstoke: Palgrave Macmillan): 245–59.
29. Directive 2010/13/EU and Directive 89/552/EEC.
30. 'Study on the Application of Measures Concerning the Promotion of the Distribution and Production of European Works in Audiovisual Media Services (i.e. Including Television Programmes and Non-Linear Services)' Final Study Report, 28 May 2009 (Brussels: European Commission): 375.
31. European Commission (2010) 'Report from the Commission to the European Parliament, the Council, the European Economic and Social Committee and the Committee of the Regions. First Report on the Application of Articles 13, 16 and 17 of Directive 2010/13/EU for the period 2009–2010, Promotion of European Works in EU Scheduled and On-Demand Audiovisual Media Services' COM/2012/0522 final (Brussels: European Commission).
32. L. van Middelaar (2013) *The Passage to Europe: How a Continent Became a Union* (New Haven and London: Yale University Press): 231–32.
33. L. Ene and C. Grece (2015) 'Origin of Films in VOD Catalogues in the EU', Note 4 (Strasbourg: European Audiovisual Observatory).
34. Associated Press (2015) 'Fictional Russian Invasion Sparks Row with Moscow' *Guardian*, 30 August.
35. J.E. Roos (1988) 'Television and the Integration of Europe in the Era of Satellite Communications', PhD thesis, Old Dominion University. https://digitalcommons.odu.edu/cgi/viewcontent.cgi?article=1110&context=gpis_etds

36. Roos (1988).
37. European Commission (2003) 'Euronews: Contribution by the Commission', Communication by the President and Mr Vitorino, SEC(2003)792 (Brussels: European Commission).
38. I. Garcia-Blanco and S. Cushion (2010) 'A Partial Europe Without Citizens or EU-Level Political Institutions: How far can Euronews contribute to a European public sphere?' *Journalism Studies*, 11(3): 393–411.
39. S. Stolton and L. Bayer (2021) 'Euronews Defends Independence after Buyout by Hungary-linked Firm' *Politico Europe*, 21 December.
40. S. Stolton and L. Bayer (2021). On Orbán's grip on Hungarian media, see K. Lane Scheppele (2022) 'How Viktor Orbán Wins' *Journal of Democracy*, 33(3): 45–61.
41. A. Hujic (1999) 'MTV Europe: An analysis of the channel's attempt to design a programming strategy for a pan-European youth audience', PhD thesis, Goldsmiths, University of London.
42. A. Higgs (1994) 'New Law Now Makes MTV Technically Illegal in Turkey' *Billboard*, 11 June.
43. See J. Banks (1997) 'MTV and the Globalization of Popular Culture' *Gazette* 59(1): 43–60.
44. Creative Practice (2019) 'Brent Hansen – Media Professional' *Creative Practice Podcast*, 11 April. https://creative-practice.net/2019/04/22/brent-hansen-media-professional/
45. 'MTV's X-Ray Vision Live from Hamburg (9 May 1996)' *YouTube*. https://www.youtube.com/watch?v=_V5iBjAYsrk
46. A. Szemere and K.M. Nagy (2017) 'Setting Up a Tent in the "New Europe": The Sziget festival of Budapest' in E. Barna and T. Tófalvy (eds) *Made in Hungary: Studies in Popular Music* (Abingdon: Routledge): 27–38.
47. Z. Győri (2019) 'Between Utopia and the Marketplace: The case of the Sziget festival' in E. Mazierska and Z. Győri (eds) *Eastern European Popular Music in a Transnational Context: Beyong the Borders* (Cham: Palgrave Macmillan): 191–211.
48. M. Pronczuk (2018) 'Polish Judges Face the Music as State Tightens Grip', *Financial Times*, 4 October; A. Charlish and A. Wlodarczak-Semczuk (2019) 'Poland's Rights Commissioner on Fault Lines of Divided Country' *Reuters*, 13 August.
49. A. Hochschild (2020) 'The Fight to Decolonize the Museum' *Atlantic*, January/February.
50. B. Rogan (2003) 'The Emerging Museums of Europe' *Ethnologia Europaea*, 33(1): 51–60.
51. C. De Cesari (2017) 'Museums of Europe: Tangles of memory, borders, and race' *Museum Anthropology*, 40(1): 18–35.
52. A. Giuffrida (2022) 'Italy Returns Parthenon Fragment to Greece Amid UK Row Over Marbles' *Guardian*, 5 January; 'Le pape François restitue trois fragments du Parthénon à l'archevêque d'Athènes' *Le Figaro*, 16 December 2022.
53. H.G. Pöttering (2007) 'Pöttering: Priority is dialogue for partnership and tolerance', Press Release, 13 February.
54. H.G. Pöttering (2007) 'Inaugural Address by the President of the European Parliament' 13 February, Strasbourg.
55. J. Panichi (2015) 'House of European History Gets Cash and a Lot of Flak' *Politico Europe*, 30 December.
56. H.G. Pöttering (2016) *United for the Better: My European Way* (London: John Harper): 452.
57. D. Bilde (2016) 'Motion for a European Parliament Resolution on the House of European History', 7.9.2016, PE589.571v01-00, B8-0984/2016 (Strasbourg: European Parliament).

58. C. Cadot (2010) 'Can Museums Help Build a European Memory? The example of the Musée de l'Europe in Brussels in the light of "new world" museums' experience' *International Journal of Politics, Culture, and Society*, 23(2): 127–36.
59. W. Kaiser (2017) 'Limits of Cultural Engineering: Actors and narratives in the European Parliament's House of European History project' *Journal of Common Market Studies*, 55(3): 520.
60. Interpret Europe (2019) 'Taja Vovk van Gaal: Keynote address' *YouTube*, 5 July. https://www.youtube.com/watch?v=zEPJMfUXKOg
61. Kaiser (2017).
62. Prague Declaration on European Conscience and Communism, 3 June 2008 (Prague: Senate of the Parliament of the Czech Republic).
63. 'European Parliament resolution of 2 April 2009 on European conscience and totalitarianism', P6TA(2009)0213, RC-B6-0165/2009.
64. European Parliament (2017) 'European Parliament opens the House of European History on 6 May 2017', Press Release, 4 May.
65. J. Rankin (2018) 'Brexit through the Gift Shop: Museum of European History divides critics' *Guardian*, 12 August.
66. C. Garbowski (2020) 'The Polish Debate on the House of European History in Brussels' *Polish Review*, 65(4): 60–70.
67. Garbowski (2020).
68. D. Sally (2018) 'Poland Denies New Law Will Hinder Debate about Nazi Era' *Irish Times*, 1 February.
69. Quoted in B. Fox (2013) 'The EU in Exile – A cautionary tale' *EU Observer*, 24 September.
70. Vovk van Gaal (2019).

Chapter 6 The Frankenstein Directive

1. J. Tozer (2008) 'Man Gets a £31,500 Bill for TV Show on Laptop' *This is Money*, 4 July.
2. A Commission Green Paper published in 1987 foresaw the rise of mobile telephony, albeit it alongside telex, paging and other short-lived technologies. European Commission (1987) 'Towards A Competitive Community-Wide Telecommunications Market in 1992: Implementing the Green Paper on the development of the common market for telecommunications services and equipment' COM(87) 290 (Brussels: European Commission).
3. 'Robbery by Telephone' *The Economist*, 26 September 1992.
4. A.A. Huurdeman (2003) *The Worldwide History of Telecommunications* (Hoboken, NJ: John Wiley & Sons): 575.
5. L. Manigrassi, E. Ocello and V. Staykova (2016) 'Recent Developments in Telecoms' *Competition Merger Brief* 3/2016 (Brussels: European Commission).
6. Manigrassi, Ocello and Staykova (2016).
7. Eurostat (2011) 'Telecommunication Statistics', 29 November (Luxembourg: Eurostat).
8. E. Baranes and M. Bourreauc (2005) 'An Economist's Guide to Local Loop Unbundling' *Communications & Strategies*, 57: 13–31.
9. Source: World Bank DataBank.
10. World Bank DataBank.
11. European Commission (2002) EU Cordis 'eEurope Benchmarking Report Says EU Internet Penetration Reaching Plateau' Article 17965, 8 February (Brussels: European Commission).
12. Source: World Bank DataBank.

13. Regulation (EC) No 717/2007 of the European Parliament and of the Council of 27 June 2007 on roaming on public mobile telephone networks within the Community and amending Directive 2002/21/EC (Text with EEA relevance).
14. European Commission (2013) 'What Did the EU Ever Do for the Mobile Industry and Consumers?' MEMO 13-139 (Brussels: European Commission).
15. M. Cini and M. Šuplata (2017) 'Policy Leadership in the European Commission: The regulation of EU mobile roaming charges' *Journal of European Integration*, 39(2): 143–56.
16. A. Barker and J. Brunsden (2018) 'Close Juncker Aide Martin Selmayr Named Brussels' Top Civil Servant' *Financial Times*, 21 February.
17. S. Roberts, S. Christie and G. Harrison (2017) 'Roam Sweet Roam: What does the end of EU roaming charges mean, and where in Europe can you send texts and calls at UK rates?' *Sun*, 1 September.
18. J. Gorst Williams (2015) 'I've Been Charged Roaming Fees Because I Live on the Coast' *Telegraph*, 23 February.
19. European Commission (2015) 'A Digital Single Market Strategy for Europe' COM/2015/0192 final (Brussels: European Commission).
20. 'EFADs Speaks Out on Geo-Blocking Regulation', *Cineuropa*, 22 March 2017.
21. J. Poort and G. van Til (2020) 'The Role of Territorial Licenses and Public Support Schemes in Financing European Films' *International Journal of Cultural Policy*, 26(5): 597–616.
22. Directive (EU) 2019/790 of the European Parliament and of the Council of 17 April 2019 on copyright and related rights in the Digital Single Market and amending Directives 96/9/EC and 2001/29/EC (Text with EEA relevance) PE/51/2019/REV/1.
23. K. Walker (2019) 'EU Copyright Directive: One step forward, two steps back' *Blog. Google*, 3 March.
24. P. McCartney (2018) 'An Open Letter to the European Parliament', 3 July. See @IFPI_org (2018) 'EU set to vote on 2 years of work on EU copyright directive. Over 1,000 recording artists - inc @PlacidoDomingo, @JamesBlunt, @cabrelfrancis, @Vienna_Phil, @udolindenberg & now the legend Sir @PaulMcCartney have called on their MEPs.Vote YES (Tomorrow, 12pm CET) #ValueGap EU' *Twitter*, 4 July. https://twitter.com/IFPI_org/status/1014429611176972288
25. G. Leali and M. Scott (2022) 'France Accepts Google's Truce with Publishers' *Politico Europe*, 21 June.
26. J.N. Bhagwati (1984) 'Splintering and Disembodiment of Services and Developing Nations' *World Economy*, 7(2): 133–44.
27. M.E. Porter (2011) *Competitive Advantage of Nations: Creating and Sustaining Superior Performance* (New York: Simon and Schuster): 250–3.
28. European Commission (1994) 'Growth, Competitiveness, Employment: The challenges and ways forward into the 21st century: White Paper' (Luxembourg: Office for the Official Publications of the European Communities): 9.
29. M.P. Smith (2001) 'In Pursuit of Selective Liberalization: Single market competition and its limits' *Journal of European Public Policy*, 8(4): 519–40.
30. European Council (2000) 'Presidency Conclusions', Lisbon, 23–24 March.
31. R. Prodi (2002) 'Public Services: A role for Europe', Université Paris IX Dauphine Paris, 18 October, Speech 02-498 (Brussels: European Commission).
32. F. Bolkestein (ed.) (1982) *Modern Liberalism: Conversations with Liberal Politicians* (The Hague: Elsevier).
33. C. Mortished (2003) 'EU's Bids Directive has Bite Removed' *The Times*, 28 November.
34. Copenhagen Economics (2005) *Economic Assessment of the Barriers to the Internal Market for Services* (Copenhagen: Copenhagen Economics).

35. B. Hoekman (1995) 'Tentative First Steps: An assessment of the Uruguay Round agreement on services', World Bank Policy Research Working Paper 1455.
36. European Commission (2002) 'Proposal for a Directive of the European Parliament and of the Council on Services in the Internal Market', COM/2004/0002 (Brussels: European Commission).
37. European Commission (2004) 'Commission Staff Working Paper Extended Impact Assessment of Proposal for a Directive on Services in the Internal Market' 31 January, COM(2004)2 (Brussels: European Commission): 36.
38. G. Van Gyes (2004) 'Unions Protest against Draft EU Services Directive' *Eurofound*, 27 June.
39. F. Bolkestein (2001) 'Speech at the Ambrosetti Annual Forum', 7 September Speech 01-373 (Brussels: European Commission).
40. J. Böröcz and M. Sarkar (2017) 'The Unbearable Whiteness of the Polish Plumber and the Hungarian Peacock Dance around "Race"' *Slavic Review*, 76(2): 308.
41. P. de Villiers (2005) 'La grande triche du oui' *Le Figaro*, 15 March.
42. L. Jeanneau and H. Nathan (2005) 'Bolkestein prêche sa bonne parole' *Libération*, 7 April.
43. 'Bolkestein Blows a French Fuse' *Financial Times*, 14 April.
44. Eurobarometer (2005) 'The European Constitution: Post-referendum in France' *Flash Eurobarometer* 171 (Brussels: European Commission).
45. M. Monti (2010) 'Report by Mario Monti to the President of the European Commission: A new strategy for the single market', 9 June (Brussels: European Commission).
46. G. Galindo (2018) '"F**k how I hate this!" Says Commissioner at the Parliament' *Politico Europe*, 9 May.
47. H. Kassim and H. Stevens (2010) *Air Transport and the European Union: Europeanization and Its Limits* (Basingstoke: Palgrave Macmillan): 28.
48. European Commission (2017) 'EU Aviation: 25 years of reaching new heights' (Brussels: DG Mobility and Transport).
49. European Commission (2017).
50. T. Anderson (2014). *easyLand: How easyJet Conquered Europe* (London: Grosvenor House Publishing). See in particular Chapter 2.
51. R.I. Jobs (2017) *Backpack Ambassadors: How Youth Travel Integrated Europe* (Chicago, IL: University of Chicago Press): 161.
52. M. Van der Klis and C.H. Mulder (2008) 'Beyond the Trailing Spouse: The commuter partnership as an alternative to family migration' *Journal of Housing and the Built Environment*, 23(1): 6.
53. Joseph O'Connor (2008) *Cowboys and Indians* (New York: Random House).
54. Title IV, Treaty Establishing the European Economy Community (1957).
55. Kassim and Stevens (2009).
56. P. Donovan (1990) 'Transport Issues Need a Rethink: Political rivalry blocks the road to 1992' *Guardian*, 9 July.
57. European Commission (1989) 'Community Airlines: No nationality discrimination between Community citizens', Press Release, IP-89-628, 2 August (Brussels: European Commission).
58. 'The Irritating Commissioner' *The Economist*, 31 January 1998.
59. R. Travis (2001) 'Air Transport Liberalisation in the European Community 1987–1992: A case of integration' PhD thesis, Uppsala Universitet: Acta Universitatis Upsaliensis: 35.
60. P. Uittenbogaart (1997) 'Airline Competition on the Route between Amsterdam and London' *Journal of Air Transport Management*, 3(4): 217–25.

61. P. Hanlon (1996) *Global Airlines: Competition in a Transnational Age* (Oxford: Butterworth-Heinemann): 148.

62. B.J. Graham (1992) 'A Conflict of Interests: The European Commission's proposals for competition in the scheduled airline industry' *Area*, 24(3): 251.

63. H. Bruch and T. Sattelberger (2000) 'The Turnaround at Lufthansa: Learning from the change process' *Journal of Change Management*, 1(4): 349.

64. European Commission (1996) 'Communication from the Commission to the Council and the European Parliament Impact of the Third Package of Air Transport Liberalization Measures', COM(96) 514 final (Brussels: European Commission): 16.

65. H. Hauser (2000) 'Entrepreneurship in Europe' *Business Strategy Review*, 11(1): 1–9.

66. M. Cooper (2018) *Michael O'Leary: Turbulent Times for the Man Who Made Ryanair* (London: Penguin): 83.

67. S. Field (2016) 'Southwest Airlines and the Impact of Low-Cost Carriers on Airline Ticket Prices' *Bentley Undergraduate Research Journal*, 36–58.

68. C. Lucier (2004) 'Herb Kelleher: The thought leader interview' *Strategy + Business*, 1 June.

69. S.D. Barrett (2004) 'The Sustainability of the Ryanair Model' *International Journal of Transport Management*, 2: 90.

70. Charlemagne (2000) 'Low-cost Founding Fathers' *The Economist*, 27 January.

71. S. Ison (2017) *Low Cost Carriers: Emergence, Expansion and Evolution* (Abingdon: Routledge).

72. L. Budd, G. Francis, I. Humphreys and S. Ison (2014) 'Grounded: Characterising the market exit of European low cost airlines' *Journal of Air Transport Management*, 34: 78.

73. 'Ryanair's 117 Million Pax in 2016 Tops European Airline Groups' *Centre for Aviation*, 17 January 2017.

74. M. Staniland (2008) *A Europe of the Air? The Airline Industry and European Integration* (Lanham, MD: Rowman & Littlefield): 211; C. Keena (2001) 'O'Leary Claims Ryanair's Belgian Base is "a Direct Loss to Dublin and Ireland"' *Irish Times*, 1 March.

75. Cooper (2018).

76. Cooper (2018): Chapter 13.

77. Created under the Single European Act to ease the burden on the European Court of Justice, the Court of First Instance heard cases by individuals against the EU institutions. Under the Lisbon Treaty, it was renamed the General Court and incorporated into the Court of Justice of the EU.

78. 'Ryanair Attacks EU over Subsidy for Aer Lingus' *The Times*, 22 April 1995.

79. G. Percival and G. Deegan (2020) 'Ryanair Seeks Government Sweetener to Restore Cork Airport Base' *Irish Examiner*, 23 December; G.E. Folch (2022) 'Ryanair Calls on Authorities for Incentives to Expand Flight Operations in Catalonia' *Catalan News*, 8 September.

80. 'Court Ruling Postpones Ryanair Hamburg-base Plans' *Irish Examiner*, 13 September 2005.

81. Judgment of the Court (Grand Chamber) of 21 December 2016, European Commission v Hansestadt Lübeck, ECLI:EU:C:2016:971; Richard Maslen (2016) 'Wizz Air Makes Hamburg Airport Switch' *Routes Online*, 18 March.

82. M. Juul (2016) 'Employment and Working Conditions in EU Civil Aviation' *European Parliament Research Service*, PE 580.915.

83. 'Passengers See Our Ryanair Uniforms and Think We are Out to Screw Them' *Irish Times*, 26 September 2017.

84. 'Should Aircrew be Declared Posted?' Van Olmen & Wynant Report, Action in the Framework of the EU Commission's Support for Social Dialogue, VP/2018/001/0064 (Brussels: European Commission): 56.

85. Cooper (2018): 145.
86. N. Lancefield (2018) 'Ryanair Boss Michael O'Leary Says Staff Strikes Necessary to Keep Fares Low' *Irish News*, 13 September; 'Ryanair Boss Threatens to Move Jobs to Poland in Face of Walkouts' *Guardian*, 31 July 2018.
87. P. Hollinger and M. Kahn (2017) 'Ryanair Loses Legal Battle on Cabin Crew Contracts' *Financial Times*, 14 September.
88. G. Ross (1992) 'Confronting the New Europe' *New Left Review*, 191: 49.
89. S. Saeed (2019) 'The Popular Revolt against Flying' *Politico Europe*, 11 June.
90. 'Ryanair One of Europe's Top Polluters, EU Data Suggests' *BBC News*, 2 April 2019.
91. S. Morgan (2019) 'EU Citizens Insist Jet Fuel Must Be Taxed' *Euractiv*, 30 April.
92. J. Spero and R. Toplensky (2019) 'Leaked EU Report Boosts Case for Jet Fuel Tax' *Financial Times*, 13 May.
93. J. Lapeyre (2018) *The European Social Dialogue: The History of a Social Innovation (1985–2003)* (Brussels: ETUI): 134.
94. 'Emilio Gabaglio: Hard act to follow' *European Voice*, 1 April 1998.
95. European Commission (1986) 'Commission President Calls for Continued Efforts to Adjust European Economic Structures Without Abandoning the "European Model"', Press Release IP 88-281, 5 June (Brussels: European Commission).
96. M. Thatcher (1992) 'Speech to Conservative Candidates Conference', 22 March. https://www.margaretthatcher.org/document/108294
97. Article 2(4), Protocol on Social Policy and an Agreement, annexed to the Protocol, between 11 Member States, with the exception of the UK (which benefited from an opt-out), also on Social Treaty on European Union (1992).
98. Lapeyre (2018): 132–34.
99. Lapeyre (2018): 133.
100. 'Hoover Gets £5m Grant Aid for Jobs: Funding deal one of Scotland's biggest' *Herald Scotland*, 26 January 1993.
101. 'Big Name in UNICE' *European Voice*, 10 December 1997.
102. C. Adams (2002) 'TUC Chief Eyes Top Union Job in Europe' *Financial Times*, 27 March.
103. 'John Monks Says Barroso Initiative Could Put Debate on Social Europe at Risk' *Agence Europe*, 15 September 2005.
104. J.M. Magone (2005) 'José Manuel Durão Barroso: A political scientist in the world of European Union politics' *International Journal*, 60(2): 545.
105. P. Stuart (2004) 'Portugal's Prime Minister Barroso Nominated as European Commission President' *World Socialist Website*, 21 July.
106. J.M. Barroso (2004) 'Speech to the European Parliament', 26 October, SPEECH 04/474 (Brussels: European Commission).
107. R. Carter (2005) 'Lisbon "Relaunch" Sparks Fierce Debate' *EU Observer*, 2 February.
108. 'Barroso Declares Aim of Creating "Social Europe"' *European Voice*, 15 September.
109. B. Ségol (2015) 'Social Europe: Yesterday, today and tomorrow' Lowry Lecture, 16 March (Brussels: ETUC).
110. D. Gow (2002) 'Glasgow Cleans Up in Hoover's War with Dyson' *Guardian*, April 11.
111. Gow (2002).
112. D. Gow (2003) 'Hoover Shifts Production to China' *Guardian*, 9 October.

Chapter 7 The Third Way

1. C-SPAN (1999) 'Progressive Governance for the 21st Century', 25 April. https://www.c-span.org/video/?122788-1/progressive-governance-21st-century

2. P. Wintour (2002) 'Political Route Map That Led to Dead End' *Guardian*, 27 April.
3. R. Tiersky (1995) 'Mitterrand's Legacies' *Foreign Affairs*, January/February: 115.
4. T. Levitt (1983) 'The Globalization of Markets' *Harvard Business Review*, May.
5. Source: StatBank Denmark and European Commission AMECO database.
6. Source: European Commission, AMECO database.
7. For earlier uses of the Third Way, see A. Giordano (2018) 'The Making of the "Third Way": Wilhelm Röpke, Luigi Einaudi, and the identity of neoliberalism' in P. Commun and S. Kolev (eds) *Wilhelm Röpke (1899–1966)* (Basingstoke: Palgrave): 41–64.
8. A. Giddens (1998) *The Third Way: The Renewal of Social Democracy* (Cambridge: Polity Press).
9. Giddens (1998): 7–8.
10. Although the Third Way distanced itself from traditional Keynesian policies, it was influenced by so-called New Keynesian thinking. For more on this New Keynesian paradigm, see D. Hodson and D. Mabbett (2009) 'UK Economic Policy and the Global Financial Crisis: Paradigm lost?' *Journal of Common Market Studies* 47(5): 1041–61.
11. Giddens (1998): 7–8.
12. Giddens (1998): 64.
13. Giddens (1998): 30–31.
14. Giddens (1998): 65.
15. T. Blair and G. Schröder (1998) 'Europe: The Third Way/Die Neue Mitte' (Johannesburg: Friedrich Ebert Foundation): 5.
16. Blair and Schröder (1998): 4.
17. Blair and Schröder (1998): 12.
18. Giddens (1998): 54.
19. Giddens (1998): 147.
20. Giddens (1998): 142.
21. Giddens offered a more in-depth account of European integration in his later work. See, for example, A. Giddens (2013) *Turbulent and Mighty Continent: What Future for Europe?* (Cambridge: Polity Press).
22. J. Farrell (2020) 'Brexit: What image best sums up our departure?' *Sky News*, 1 February.
23. Resolution on Growth and Employment, Amsterdam, 16 June, OJ C 236, 2.8.1997, 3–4.
24. European Council (1998) 'Presidency Conclusions, 15–16 June', SN 150/1/98 REV 1 (Brussels: Council of the European Union).
25. Source: European Commission AMECO database.
26. Source: European Commission AMECO database.
27. T. Andersson (2000) 'Seizing the Opportunities of a New Economy: Challenges for the European Union' (Paris: OECD): 28.
28. Anderson (2000): 9.
29. A. Guterres (1999) 'Placing Human Beings at the Centre of Our Concerns' *Socialist Affairs*, 48(3–4): 5. The event included Microsoft's Bill Gates as a keynote speaker and was the first World Exhibition to stream events live on the internet.
30. M.J. Rodrigues (2002) 'For a European Strategy at the Turn of the Century' in M.J. Rodrigues (ed.) *The New Knowledge Economy in Europe: A Strategy for International Competitiveness and Social Cohesion* (Cheltenham: Edward Elgar): 1–27.
31. European Council (2000) 'Presidency Conclusions, 23–24 March 2000' (Brussels: European Council).

32. European Council (2000).
33. European Council (2000).
34. European Council (2000).
35. The European Currency Union (ECU) was the EU's unit of account until being replaced by the euro in 1999.
36. European Council (2000).
37. G. Esping-Andersen (2002) 'A New European Social Model for the Twenty-first Century?' in M.J. Rodrigues (ed.) *The New Knowledge Economy in Europe: A Strategy for International Competitiveness and Social Cohesion* (Cheltenham: Edward Elgar): 55.
38. D. Hodson and I. Maher (2001) 'The Open Method as a New Mode of Governance: The case of soft economic policy co-ordination' *Journal of Common Market Studies*, 39(4): 719–46.
39. S. Deroose, D. Hodson and J. Kuhlmann (2008) 'The Broad Economic Policy Guidelines: Before and after the re-launch of the Lisbon strategy' *Journal of Common Market Studies*, 46(4): 827–48.
40. R. Welscheke (2004) 'Only by Accepting Shared Responsibility Can Lisbon Succeed' *Politico Europe*, 15 December.
41. Esping-Andersen (2002).
42. European Council (2000).
43. European Monitoring Centre on Change (2008) 'Perceptions of Globalisation: Attitudes and responses in the EU' (Loughlinstown: Eurofound).
44. European Monitoring Centre on Change (2008).
45. European Council (1997) 'Presidency Conclusions, 12–13 December' (Brussels: Council of the European Union).
46. 'Programme de M. Jean-Marie Le Pen, président du Front national et candidat à l'élection présidentielle 2002, intitulé : "Pour un avenir français", avril 2002'. Full text: https://www.vie-publique.fr/discours/129981-programme-de-m-jean-marie-le-pen-president-du-front-national-et-candid
47. Eurobarometer (2005) 'Flash Eurobarometer 171: The European Constitution: Post-referendum in France' Flash Eurobarometer 171 (Brussels: European Commission).
48. Eurobarometer (2005).
49. Hansard HL European Union (Amendment) Bill, volume 702, col. 185, 18 June 2008.
50. A. Gani (2015) 'Clause IV: A brief history' *Guardian*, 9 August; M. Kenny and M.J. Smith (1997) 'Discourses of Modernization: Gaitskell, Blair and the reform of Clause IV' *British Elections & Parties Review*, 7(1): 110–26.
51. 'Blair's Statement in Full Tuesday' *BBC News*, 11 September 2001.
52. T. Blair (2005a) 'Speech to the European Parliament' *Guardian*, 23 June.
53. T. Blair (2005b) 'Letter of Invitation: Informal meeting of EU Heads of State or Government to the Hampton Court Summit 27 October', Downing Street, 10 October.
54. Blair (2005b).
55. A. Seldon (2007) *Blair Unbound* (London: Simon and Schuster): 405.
56. Q. Peel (2005) 'Time for the Big Three to Shut Up' *Financial Times*, 19 October.
57. A. Sapir (2006) 'Globalization and the Reform of European Social Models' *Journal of Common Market Studies*, 44(2): 369.
58. Blair (2005b).
59. M. Ferrera (2005) 'The Caring Dimension of Europe: How to make it more visible and more vigorous', Discussion paper prepared for the UK Presidency (London: Cabinet Office).

60. L. Tsoukalis (2005) 'Why We Need a Globalization Adjustment Fund', Discussion paper prepared for the UK Presidency (London: HM Cabinet Office): 5.

61. Seldon (2007): 407 reports that a ' "very distinguished" French Bordeaux' was consumed over lunch.

62. Regulation (EC) No 1927/2006 of the European Parliament and of the Council of 20 December 2006 establishing the European Globalisation Adjustment Fund.

63. European Commission (2014) 'European Globalisation Adjustment Fund Solidarity in the Face of Change' (Brussels: DG Employment and Social Inclusion).

64. European Commission (2022) 'Summary of EGF Applications' (Brussels: DG Employment and Social Inclusion).

65. G. Claeys and A. Sapir (2018) 'The European Globalisation Adjustment Fund: Easing the pain from trade?' Bruegel Policy Contribution, Issue No 05.

66. Source: European Commission AMECO database.

67. Source: European Commission AMECO database.

68. European Commission (1994).

69. 'Italy's Poll Rivals End Campaigns' *CNN.com*, 11 May 2001.

70. Source: European Commission AMECO database.

71. A. Greenspan (1997) 'Testimony of Chairman Alan Greenspan: The Federal Reserve's semiannual monetary policy report before the Committee on Banking, Housing, and Urban Affairs, U.S. Senate' 22 July, Washington DC: Federal Reserve Board.

72. Source: World Bank Open Data.

73. Source: U.S. Census Bureau and U.S. Department of Housing and Urban Development, Median Sales Price of Houses Sold for the United States [MSPUS], retrieved from FRED, Federal Reserve Bank of St. Louis. https://fred.stlouisfed.org/series/MSPUS, 4 March 2023.

74. Mortgage Bankers Association (2008) 'National Delinquency Survey Q4/07' (Washington DC: Mortgage Bankers Association): 10

75. Mortgage Bankers Association (2008): 10.

76. European Central Bank (2007) 'Financial Stability Review – June 2007' (Frankfurt A.M.: ECB).

77. S. Kar-Gupta and Y. Le Guernigou (2007) 'BNP Freezes $2.2 bln of Funds Over Subprime' *Reuters*, 9 August.

78. European Central Bank (2007) 'Monthly Bulletin' September (Frankfurt A.M.: ECB): 30–1.

79. G. Brown (2005) 'How to Lighten the Regulatory Burden on UK Business' *Financial Times*, 23 May.

80. Council of the European Union (2008) 'Presidency Conclusions' Brussels, 17, 11018/1/08 REV 1.

81. C. Taylor (2008) 'Darling Intervened on Bank Guarantee Plan – Report' *Irish Times*, 2 October.

82. D. Charter (2008) 'Spain Goes it Alone as Europe Squabbles over Unity' *The Times*, 8 October. Merkel's criticisms were not only levelled at the uncoordinated character of the Irish bank guarantee, but also at its being at odds with the single market by applying, initially at least, to domestic banks. Rallying Call, *DW-Deutsche Welle*, 7 October 2008.

83. I. Black and P. Wintour (2003) 'Learn from Me, Brown Tells EU Finance Ministers' *Guardian*, 5 November.

84. L. Quaglia, R. Eastwood and P. Holmes (2009) 'The Financial Turmoil and EU Policy Co-operation in 2008' *Journal of Common Market Studies*, 47(1): 63–87.

85. The European Commission (2009: 31n) estimated that half of EU member states had already embarked on fiscal consolidation efforts by autumn 2009, in some cases

alongside stimulus measures. European Commission (2009) 'European Economic Forecast – Autumn 2009' European Economy 10/2009 (Brussels: European Commission).

86. H. Morris (2008) 'Sarkozy Pressed for Capitalism Summit' *Financial Times*, 24 September.
87. Irish Times (2008) 'Bush Calls World Leaders to Financial Crisis Summit' *Irish Times*, 19 October.
88. G-20 Leaders (2009) 'London Summit – Leaders' Statement' 2 April (Washington DC: International Monetary Fund).
89. Council of the European Union (2009) 'Brussels European Council', 15265/1/09 REV 1 (Brussels: Council of the European Union).

Chapter 8 The Euro Crisis

1. M. Draghi (2012) 'Speech by Mario Draghi, President of the European Central Bank at the Global Investment Conference in London' 26 July (Frankfurt A.M.: ECB).
2. J. Blitz (1997) 'The Driving Force behind Privatisation: Treasury chief is leading the sell off of state companies and the opening up of boardrooms' *Financial Times*, 10 December; M. Atkinson (1999) 'Italians Ready to Fill Vacancy at IMF' *Guardian*, 18 December.
3. F. Kempe (2005) 'La Dolce Vita' *Wall Street Journal*, 12 December.
4. G. Jones (2010) 'Mario Draghi: The rise of "Mr Somewhere Else"' *Reuters*, 10 November.
5. 'Goldman Sachs Details 2001 Greek Derivative Trades' *Reuters*, 22 February 2001.
6. Draghi (2012).
7. Draghi (2012).
8. N. Barkin (2008) 'U.S. will Lose Financial Superpower Status: Germany' *Reuters*, 25 September.
9. P. Garnham (2009) 'Euro at Three-Month Dollar Low' *Financial Times*, 20 February.
10. B. Benoit and T. Barber (2009) 'Germany Ready to Help Eurozone Members' *Financial Times*, 18 February.
11. European Commission (2010) 'Report on Greek Government Deficit and Debt Statistics' (Brussels: European Commission): 3.
12. European Commission (2010) 'Report on Greek Government Deficit and Debt Statistics' 8 January, COM(2010) 1 final: 22 (Brussels: European Commission).
13. W. Schäuble (2010) 'Why Europe's Monetary Union Faces Its Biggest Crisis' *Financial Times*, 11 March.
14. A. Crawford and T. Czuczka (2013) *Angela Merkel: A Chancellorship Forged in Crisis* (Hoboken, NJ: John Wiley & Sons).
15. S. Kornelius (2013) *Angela Merkel: The Authorized Biography* (London: Alma Books): Chapter 15; 'German Finance Ministry Dismisses Speculation Schaeuble to Resign' *Reuters*, 18 July 2015.
16. D. Hodson (2015) 'The IMF as a De Facto Institution of the EU: A multiple supervisor approach' *Review of International Political Economy*, 22(3): 570–98.
17. Heads of State or Government of the European Union, Statement 11 February 2010 (Brussels: Council of the European Union).
18. A. Willis (2010) 'Merkel Says European Fund Would Require Treaty Change' *EU Observer*, 9 March.
19. A. Tooze (2018) *Crashed: How a Decade of Financial Crises Changed the World* (New York: Allen Lane): 329–33.
20. Tooze (2018): 332–3.
21. H. Smith (2010) 'Fury in Greece over IMF Intervention' *Guardian*, 16 April.

22. F.W. Scharpf (2011) 'Monetary Union, Fiscal Crisis and the Preemption of Democracy' LSE Europe in Question Discussion Paper Series 36/2011.
23. European Commission (2009) 'European Economic Forecast – Autumn 2009' European Economy 10 (Brussels: European Commission): 92.
24. European Commission (2010) 'European Economic Forecast – Spring 2010' European Economy 2 (Brussels: European Commission): 90.
25. Source: European Commission AMECO database.
26. European Commission (2010): 90.
27. 'Marfin Bank Firebombing Case Reopens', ekathimerini.com, 31 March 2021.
28. WSJ Staff (2010) 'Papandreou Addresses Cabinet on Bailout' Wall Street Journal, 2 May.
29. WSJ Staff (2010).
30. WSJ Staff (2010).
31. T. Catan and I. Talley (2013) 'Past Rifts over Greece Cloud Talks on Rescue' Wall Street Journal, 7 October.
32. International Monetary Fund (2010) 'Greece: Staff Report on Request for Stand-By Arrangement' IMF Country Report No. 10/110 (Washington DC: IMF): 18.
33. See, for example, M. Buti (2020) 'Economic Policy in the Rough: A European journey' Centre for European Policy Research Policy Insight No. 98.
34. T. Barber (2010) 'Saving the Euro: Dinner on the edge of the abyss', Financial Times, 22 October.
35. Barber (2010).
36. See M. Salines, G. Glöckler and Z. Truchlewski (2012) 'Existential Crisis, Incremental Response: The eurozone's dual institutional evolution 2007–2011' Journal of European Public Policy, 19(5): 665–81. See also L. van Middelaar (2019) Alarums and Excursions: Improvising Politics on the European Stage (Newcastle upon Tyne: Agenda Publishing).
37. A. Weber (2009) 'Reflections on the Financial Crisis', Cass Business School, 13 May (Frankfurt A.M.: Bundesbank).
38. J. Stark (2009) 'Monetary Policy Before, During and After the Financial Crisis', University Tübingen, 9 November (Frankfurt A.M.: ECB).
39. P. Williams (2013) 'Inside Anglo: The secret recordings' Independent, 24 June.
40. V. Browne (2006) 'No Hard Questions Asked of Charlie Haughey, Then or Now' Magill, 13 December.
41. The Moriarty Tribunal (2011) Report of the Tribunal into Payments to Politicians and Related Matters Part II, Volume 2 (Dublin: Tribunal Office): 1156.
42. J. Brennan (2018) 'Accountant Had Meteoric Rise and Fall as Anglo Chief: Bank's loan book trebled to €73bn during four years he was in charge' Irish Times, 7 June.
43. 'Former Bank Boss Guilty of Multi-Billion Euro Fraud' BBC News, 6 June 2018.
44. Source: European Commission AMECO database.
45. J.C. Trichet (2010) 'Letter of the ECB President to the Irish Minister for Finance dated 19/11/2010 on the Large Provision of Liquidity by the Eurosystem and the Central Bank of Ireland to Irish Banks and the Need for Ireland to Agree to an Adjustment Programme' LC/JCT/10/1444 (Frankfurt A.M.: ECB).
46. Cardiff (2016): 184–90.
47. J. Kollewe and L. O'Carroll (2010) 'Ireland Bailout Worth "Tens of Billions" of Euros, Says Central Bank Governor' Guardian, 18 November.
48. RTE Prime Time (2010) 'We All Partied' YouTube, 25 November. https://www.youtube.com/watch?v=YK7w6fXoYxo
49. W. Buiter and E. Rahbari (2010) 'Greece and the Fiscal Crisis in the Eurozone' CEPR Policy Insight 51.

50. W. Schäuble (2011) 'A Comprehensive Strategy for the Stabilization of the Economic and Monetary Union' Brussels Economic Forum, 18 May.
51. J. Edwards (2015) 'Schäuble Reportedly Told Greece: "How Much Money Do You Want to Leave the Euro?"' *Business Insider*, July 10.
52. P. Spiegel (2014) 'How the Euro Was Saved' *Financial Times*, 11 May.
53. D. Scally (2012) 'Schäuble Concedes Third Greek Bailout on the Cards' *Irish Times*, 25 February.
54. Spiegel (2014).
55. E. Conway (2009) 'Germany's Angela Merkel Attacks Bank of England's Move to Pump Money into UK Economy' *Telegraph*, 3 June.
56. R. Atkins, Q. Peel and J. Wilson (2011) 'Bundesbank Chief Throws ECB Race into Confusion' *Financial Times*, 10 February.
57. S. O'Grady (2011) 'EU Ministers Meet to Restore Faith in Flagging Eurozone' *Independent*, 23 October.
58. R. Atkins and Q. Peel (2011) 'Merkel Backs Draghi for ECB' *Financial Times*, 12 May.
59. M. Draghi (2011) 'Hearing before the Plenary of the European Parliament on the Occasion of the Adoption of the Resolution on the ECB's 2010 Annual Report', 1 December (Frankfurt A.M.: ECB).
60. European Council (2011) 'European Council Conclusions 16–17 December', EUCO 30/1/10.
61. European Council (2010) 'European Council 16–17 December, 17 December', Press Release D/10/5.
62. T. Fairless (2012) 'Merkel, Hollande Vow to Support Euro' *Wall Street Journal*, 27 July.
63. 'Schäuble Defends ECB's Bond-Buying Program', *DW-Deutsche Welle*, 8 September 2012.
64. Source: European Commission AMECO database.
65. S. Constantinos (2011) 'The Banking System in Cyprus: Time to rethink the business model' *Cyprus Economic Policy Review*, 5(2): 123–30.
66. SYRIZA (2014) 'The Thessaloniki Programme'. Full text: https://www.syriza.gr/article/SYRIZA---THE-THESSALONIKI-PROGRAMME.html
67. 'Greece's Election Syriza Wins: An anti-austerity party claims a big victory' *The Economist*, 25 January 2015.
68. European Council (2015) 'President Donald Tusk Congratulates Alexis Tsipras on his Appointment as Prime Minister of Greece', Press Release, 26 January.
69. A. Tsipras (2015) 'Greece Can Balance Its Books Without Killing Democracy' *Financial Times*, 21 January.
70. Y. Varoufakis (2013) 'The Dirty War for Europe's Integrity and Soul', inaugural Europe Public Lecture, State Library of New South Wales, 25 October. Full text: https://www.yanisvaroufakis.eu/2013/10/25/the-dirty-war-for-europes-integrity-and-soul-europe-inaugural-public-lecture-uws-state-library-of-new/
71. Varoufakis (2013).
72. Varoufakis (2017) *Adults in the Room: My Battle with Europe's Deep Establishment* (New York: Vintage Books): 259–371.
73. Y. Varoufakis and S. Holland (2010) 'A Modest Proposal for Europe', November 2010. Full text and later versions: https://www.yanisvaroufakis.eu/modest-proposal/
74. Euronews Business (2015) 'Greece Rejects Austerity in Tense Meeting with Eurozone's Bailout Chief' *Youtube*, 30 January. https://www.youtube.com/watch?v=hOucRMHI_tk
75. See also Varoufakis (2017): 170.
76. Varoufakis (2017): 210.

77. Varoufakis (2017): 213.
78. L. Alderman and J. Kanter (2015) 'Eurozone Officials Reach Accord with Greece to Extend Bailout' *New York Times*, 20 February.
79. S. Ferro (2015) 'Greece's Finance Minister Is Showing Off his Fancy Athens House in a Glossy French Magazine' *Business Insider*, 13 March.
80. Varoufakis (2017): 213.
81. 'Varoufakis Admits Plans for Parallel Payment System, Denies Grexit Goal' *ekathimerini.com*, 27 July 2015.
82. European Commission, European Central Bank and the International Monetary Fund (2015) 'Reforms for the Completion of the Current Programme and Beyond'. Full text: https://online.wsj.com/public/resources/documents/reform.pdf
83. Press Association (2015) 'Greece Calls Snap Referendum over Eurozone Bailout' *Guardian*, 27 June.
84. I. Jurado, N. Konstantinidis and S. Walter (2015) 'Why Greeks Voted the Way They Did in the Bailout Referendum' *LSE European Politics and Policy Blog*, 20 July.
85. Varoufakis (2017): 468.
86. G. Steinhauser (2015) 'German Document Floats Five-Year Greek Exit from Eurozone' *Wall Street Journal*, 11 July.
87. A. Macdonald and J. Strupczewski (2015) '"Kindergarten" as Weary Euro Ministers Divide over Greece' *Reuters*, 12 July.
88. Donald Tusk (2019) 'Keynote Speech by President Donald Tusk at the Opening Ceremony of the 2019/2020 Academic Year at the College of Europe' Speech /2019/11/13 (Brussels: European Council).
89. Euro Summit Statement 12 July 2015 SN 47/15 (Brussels: Council of the European Union).
90. Source: European Commission AMECO database.
91. European Anti-Poverty Network (2020) 'Poverty Watch: Greece – 2019' (Brussels: European Anti-Poverty Network).
92. J. Doran (2017) 'An Antidote to Pasokification' in M. Perryman (ed.) *The Corbyn Effect: And Labour's Existential Crisis* (Dagenham: Lawrence & Wishart): 214–26.
93. A. Chrisafis (2013) 'François Hollande Becomes Most Unpopular French President Ever' *Guardian*, 29 October.
94. S. Haugbolle (2019) 'Did the Left Really Win in Denmark?' *Foreign Policy*, 7 June.
95. Source: European Commission AMECO database; C. Moury, E. De Giorgi and P. Pita Barros (2020) 'How to Combine Public Spending with Fiscal Rigour? "Austerity by stealth" in post-bailout Portugal (2015–2019)' *South European Society and Politics*, 25(2): 151–78.
96. R. Naumann (2018) 'The Fourth Way' *IPS Journal*, 28 March.
97. B. Carreño (2020) 'With Once-Radical Podemos Tamed, Spain's New Coalition is Happy – For Now' *Reuters*, 24 February.
98. R. Minder (2019) 'Gaining Strength in Spain, Sánchez Emerges as Beacon for Socialism in Europe' *New York Times*, 28 May.
99. D.M. Herszenhorn (2017) 'EU Leaders Promise "People First" at Summit on Social Rights' *Politico Europe*, 17 November.
100. L. Gehrke (2021) 'New German Chancellor Scholz Vows Continuity with Merkel' *Politico Europe*, 8 December.

Chapter 9 Global Europe

1. J. Delors (1993) 'Address by Jacques Delors to the European Parliament (On the Occasion of the Investiture Debate Following Appointment of the New Commission)', 10 February, SPEECH/93/8 (Brussels: European Commission).

2. See J. Armatta, (2010) *Twilight of Impunity: The War Crimes Trial of Slobodan Milosevic* (Durham, NC: Duke University Press); Foreign and Commonwealth Office of the United Kingdom (1998) 'Joint Declaration on European Defence. Joint Declaration issued at the British-French Summit, Saint-Malo' (London: FCO).

3. R. Jaura (1999) 'A Step Towards Political and Military Autonomy' Inter Press Service, 4 June. https://www.ipsnews.net/1999/06/politics-europe-a-step-towards-political-and-military-autonomy/

4. G. Tremlett (1995) 'Solana: Ex-NATO opponent is converted' UPI Archives, 1 December.

5. R.C. Hendrickson (2002) 'NATO's Secretary General Javier Solana and the Kosovo Crisis' *Journal of International Relations and Development*, 5(3) (September): 240–57.

6. S. Everts (2008) 'Mission Impossible? Managing the growing divide between Europe and the US' *International Spectator* 37(3): 31–41. See also I. Black (2002) 'EU Plays Down its Role in Brokering Siege Deal' *Guardian*, 10 May.

7. 'Clinton Meets with Guy with Tie' *The Onion*, 25 August 1999.

8. 'Peace Talks Just an Excuse to Visit Scenic Mideast' *The Onion*, 5 May 2004.

9. J. Dempsey (2003) 'Solana Laments Rift Between Europe and "Religious" US: Foreign policy chief believes stark White House world view is widening gulf' *Financial Times*, 8 January.

10. T. Blair (2010) *A Journey: My Political Life* (New York: Vintage): 78.

11. 'Full Transcript of Tony Blair's Statement' *Guardian*, 11 September 2011.

12. J. Chirac (2003) 'Full Transcript of Interview with Jacques Chirac' *New York Times*, 21 September.

13. T. Forsberg (2005) 'German Foreign Policy and the War on Iraq: Anti-Americanism, pacifism or emancipation?' *Security Dialogue*, 36(2): 213–31.

14. J. Hooper and I. Black (2003) 'Anger at Rumsfeld Attack on "Old Europe"' *Guardian*, 24 January.

15. 'Leaders' Statement on Iraq' *BBC News*, 30 January 2003.

16. Council of the European Union (2003) 'European Security Strategy', Brussels, 8 December, 15895/03 PESC 787 (Brussels: Council of the European Union).

17. R. Alcaro (2018) 'Europe and Iran's Nuclear Crisis (Basingstoke: Palgrave): 60.

18. 'Text of President Bush's 2002 State of the Union Address' *Washington Post*, 29 January 2002.

19. Council of the European Union (2003) 'Summary of the Statement of Javier Solana, EU High Representative for CFSP at a Press Conference in Tehran', Tehran, 30 August S0167/032003 (Brussels: Council of the European Union). https://www.consilium.europa.eu/uedocs/cms_data/docs/pressdata/en/declarations/77051.pdf

20. A. Pierce (2010) 'Who Earns More, Hillary Clinton or Baroness Nobody? Cathy Ashton . . . even though she's the laughing stock of the EU' *Mail on Sunday*, 9 March.

21. Alcaro (2018): 267.

22. Alcaro (2018): 67.

23. T. Vogel (2009) 'Javier Solana: Ten years is enough' *Politico Europe*, 6 July.

24. C. Nünlist (2015) 'EU Foreign Policy: Mogherini takes over' *CSS Analyses in Security Policy* 167.

25. S. Ahmari (2014) 'Have Passport, Will Appease' *Wall Street Journal*, 15 July.

26. L. Davies (2014) 'A Portrait of Federica Mogherini, the EU's Next Foreign Policy Chief' *Guardian*, 30 August.

27. 'EU Foreign Policy, Libya & Ukraine Discussed during Federica Mogherini's Iberian Visit', Press Release, 18 February 2015 (Brussels: EEAS).

28. P. Lewis (2015) 'John Kerry "Walked Away Three Times" from Nuclear Talks with Iran' *Guardian*, 21 July.

29. Joint Comprehensive Plan of Action, Vienna, 14 July 2015 (Washington DC: State Department).
30. K. Robinson (2022) 'What Is the Iran Nuclear Deal?' Council of Foreign Relations Backgrounder, 28 April.
31. E. Yeranian (2015) 'EU's Mogherini Visits Iran, Vows to Implement Nuclear Deal' *Voice of America News*, 28 July.
32. 'Read the Full Transcript of Trump's Speech on the Iran Nuclear Deal' *New York Times*, 8 May 2018.
33. 'Remarks by Federica Mogherini on the Statement by US President Trump Regarding the Iran Nuclear Deal (JCPOA)', EU in Serbia, 8 May 2018 (Brussels: EEAS).
34. R. Heath (2018) 'Federica Mogherini: Iran nuclear deal will hold' *Politico Europe*, 11 May.
35. 'Mike Pompeo Speech: What are the 12 demands given to Iran?' *Al Jazeera*, 21 May.
36. R. Alcaro (2021) 'Europe's Defence of the Iran Nuclear Deal: Less than a success, more than a failure' *International Spectator*, 56(1): 55–72.
37. Source: TrumpTweets. https://gist.github.com/zzzev/b47a19c4e108c756157513de0aa3c8da
38. J. Flanagan (1987) 'Pan Am Crisis: Desperate but not hopeless' *Los Angeles Times*, 12 August.
39. T. Moore (1987) 'How the 12 Top Raiders Rate: Soaring stocks and a public backlash have revolutionized takeovers' *Fortune Magazine*, 28 September.
40. K. Balls (2016) 'Marine Le Pen Causes a Stir on Marr' *Spectator*, 13 November.
41. 'France's Marine Le Pen Seen in Trump Tower' *BBC News*, 12 January 2017.
42. C. Giacomo (2016) 'Angela Merkel's Message to Trump' *New York Times*, 9 November.
43. D. Trump (1987) 'There's Nothing Wrong with America's Foreign Defense Policy That a Little Backbone Can't Cure' *Washington Post [New York Times] [Boston Globe]*, 19 November.
44. 'Donald Trump: European Union is a foe on trade' *BBC News*, 15 July 2018.
45. Z. Sheftalovich (2018) 'Sealed with a Juncker Kiss, Trump Says EU and US "Love Each Other"' *Politico Europe*, 26 July.
46. A. Macdonald and J. Strupczewski (2018) 'It Started with a Kiss: How Juncker Wooed Trump' *Reuters*, 26 July.
47. A. Walker (2021) 'Ursula von der Leyen Hits Out at Donald Trump for Past Jibes at NATO' *Politico Europe*, 19 November.
48. High Representative of the Union for Foreign Affairs and Security Policy (2016) 'Shared Vision, Common Action: A Stronger Europe: A global strategy for the European Union's foreign and security policy' (Brussels: European External Action Service).
49. High Representative of the Union for Foreign Affairs and Security Policy (2016).
50. G. Paravicini (2017) 'Angela Merkel: Europe must take "our fate" into own hands' *Politico Europe*, 28 May.
51. 'Emmanuel Macron Warns Europe: NATO is becoming brain-dead' *The Economist*, 7 November 2019.
52. V. Putin (2001) 'Speech in the Bundestag of the Federal Republic of Germany', 25 September. Text: http://en.kremlin.ru/events/president/transcripts/21340
53. V. Putin (2007) 'Speech and the Following Discussion at the Munich Conference on Security Policy', 10 February.
54. J. O'Loughlin, G. O'Tuathail and V. Kolossov (2004) 'A "Risky Westward Turn"? Putin's 9/11 script and ordinary Russians' *Europe–Asia Studies*, 56(1): 3–34.

55. J. Mearsheimer (2014) 'Why the Ukraine Crisis Is the West's Fault: The liberal delusions that provoked Putin' *Foreign Affairs*, 93 (September/October): 77–89.
56. A. Rettman (2009) 'Ukraine Revolutionary Hosts Valedictory EU Summit' *EU Observer*, 4 December.
57. C. Grant (2008) 'Poland's Bold New Foreign Policy', *Council for European Reform Insight*, 17 January.
58. J. Stern (2006) 'The Russian-Ukrainian Gas Crisis of January 2006' Oxford Institute for Energy Studies, 16(1).
59. A. Rettman (2005) 'Ukraine Gets Enlargement Wink' *EU Observer*, 6 October.
60. A. Åslund (2013) 'Ukraine's Choice: European association agreement or Eurasian union?' Peterson Institute for International Economics, Number PB13-22.
61. 'Barroso Reminds Ukraine that Customs Union and Free Trade with EU Are Incompatible' *Ukrimform*, 25 February 2013.
62. 'Ukraine Ratifies EU Association Agreement' *DW-Deutsche Welle*, 16 September 2014.
63. M. Bělín and J. Hanousek (2019) 'Making Sanctions Bite: The EU–Russian sanctions of 2014' *Vox EU*, 29 April.
64. 'Putin Criticises Estonia over War Memorial' *BBC News*, 9 May 2006; 'Government Split over Bronze Soldier' *Baltic Times*, 8 September 2006.
65. '"E-stonia" Accuses Russia of Computer Attacks' *New York Times*, 18 May 2007.
66. J. Cañas (2019) Priority question for written answer P-003967/2019 to the Commission Rule 138 (Renew) Parliamentary questions, 21 November (Strasbourg: European Parliament).
67. A. Roth (2021) 'Russia Issues List of Demands It Says Must Be Met to Lower Tensions in Europe' *Guardian*, 17 December.
68. M. Baldwin (2006) 'EU Trade Politics – Heaven or hell?' *Journal of European Public Policy*, 13(6): 926–42.
69. Under the Marrakesh Agreement, 123 countries had agreed to cut tariffs on industrial goods, phase out quotas on textiles, introduce new rules on services, trade-related investment measures and intellectual property rights and continue negotiations on contentious issues such as agriculture services.
70. G. Ross (1994) 'Inside the Delors Cabinet' *Journal of the Common Market Studies*, 32(4): 499–524.
71. G. de Jonquieres, M. Suzman and F. Williams (1999) 'Protesters Throw WTO Meeting into Disarray: Opening ceremony is cancelled as clashes paralyse Seattle city centre' *Financial Times*, 1 December.
72. World Trade Organization (2008) DG Press Conference, 29 July (Geneva: WTO).
73. 'Commission Staff Working Document – Annex to the Communication from the Commission to the Council, the European Parliament, the European Economic and Social Committee and the Committee of the Regions – Global Europe: competing in the world – Contribution to the EU's Growth and Jobs Strategy COM(2006) 567 final.
74. T. Heron (2007). 'European Trade Diplomacy and the Politics of Global Development: Reflections on the EU–China 'bra wars' dispute' *Government and Opposition*, 42(2): 190–214.
75. 'Greece Completes Transfer of 16% Stake in Piraeus Port to COSCO' *Reuters*, 7 October 2021.
76. D. Stroikos (2022) '"Head of the Dragon" or "Trojan Horse"? Reassessing China–Greece relations' *Journal of Contemporary China*, published online (April): 1–18.
77. M. Tsimitakis (2021) 'China's Cosco Under Fire after Fatal Accident in Piraeus Port' *Euractiv*, 27 October.

78. R. Emmott and A. Koutantou (2017) 'Greece Blocks EU Statement on China Human Rights at UN' *Politico Europe*, 18 July.
79. 'Chinese Firms Now Hold Stakes in Over a Dozen European Ports' *NPR*, 9 October 2018.
80. A. Delfs and J. Fokuhl (2022) 'Hamburg Port to Sell Stake to China's Cosco after Scholz's Push' *Bloomberg*, 26 October.
81. G. Chazan and Y. Yang (2022) 'German Coalition Divided over Sale of Port Terminal Stake to China's Cosco' *Financial Times*, 20 October.
82. Delfs and Fokuhl (2022).
83. M. Frese (2019) 'Italy Takes China's New Silk Road to the Heart of Europe' *EU Observer*, 22 March.
84. D. Boffey (2021) 'Open Sesame: Alibaba's push into Europe a mixed blessing for Liège' *Guardian*, 14 February.
85. 'Alibaba in Liège: It's official!', Press Release, undated. Text: http://www.investin-wallonia.be/news-1/news-2/alibaba-in-liege-it-s-official
86. 'Chinese Company Buys Ailing Frankfurt Hahn Airport' *DW-Deutsche Welle*, 6 June 2016.
87. S. Wilmès, E. Macron, K. Mitsotakis, L. Varadkar, G. Conte, X. Bettel, A. Costa, J. Janša and P. Sánchez (2020) 'Letter to President of the European Council Charles Michel', 25 March (Rome: Presidenza del Consiglio dei Ministri).
88. Regulation (EU) 2019/452 of the European Parliament and of the Council of 19 March 2019 establishing a framework for the screening of foreign direct investments into the Union.
89. 'An Overview of the China/EU Comprehensive Agreement on Investment', Norton Rose Fulbright, February 2021.
90. 'Borrell Complains to China about Uighur Abuse' *EU Observer*, 9 February 2021.
91. European Parliament (2021) 'MEPs Refuse Any Agreement with China Whilst Sanctions Are in Place', Press Release, 20 May (Strasbourg: European Parliament).
92. S. Lau (2022) 'China Direct: EU-China in 2022 – Lithuania's infighting – Xi'an COVID outbreak' *Politico Europe*, 6 January.
93. Council of the European Union (2000) 'Africa-Europe Summit under the Aegis of the OAU and the EU Cairo', 3–4 April PRES7 April, Conseil/00/901 (Brussels: Council of the European Union).
94. F. Stender, A. Berger, C. Brandi and J. Schwab (2021) 'The Trade Effects of the Economic Partnership Agreements Between the European Union and the African, Caribbean and Pacific Group of States: Early empirical insights from panel data' *Journal of Common Market Studies*, 59(6): 1495–515.
95. In 1992 alone, the European Development Fund allocated more than ECU 91 million to Rwanda, a former Belgian colony, under the fourth Lomé Convention, an ambitious trade and development agreement linking the EU and associated countries and overseas territories in Africa, the Caribbean and the Pacific.
96. Z. Marriage (2016) 'Aid to Rwanda: Unstoppable rock, immovable post' in T. Hagmann and F. Reyntjens (eds) *Aid and Authoritarianism in Africa: Development Without Democracy* (Uppsala: Nordiska Afrikainstitutet): 44–66.
97. D. Styan (2012) 'EU Power and Armed Humanitarianism in Africa: Evaluating ESDP in Chad' *Cambridge Review of International Affairs*, 25(4): 651–68.
98. European External Action Service (2009) 'EU Military Operation in Eastern Chad and North Eastern Central African Republic (EUFOR Tchad/RCA)' March Tchad-RCA/9 (Brussels: EEAS).
99. Source: World Bank Open Data.
100. Source: World Bank Open Data.

101. 'EU Suspends Ethiopian Budget Support over Tigray Crisis' *Reuters*, 15 January 2021.
102. Source: Freedom House (2022) 'Freedom in the World 2022: The global expansion of authoritarian rule' (Washington DC: Freedom House).
103. A. Kanko (2022) 'EU–Africa: Let's end EU's "nanny diplomacy" and commit to building a real partnership with Africa, argues Assita Kanko' *Parliament Magazine*, 22 February.
104. G. Okemuo (2013) 'The EU or France? The CSDP mission in Mali the consistency of the EU Africa policy' *Liverpool Law Review* 34(3): 217–40.
105. 'The European Union–African Union Summit: A Joint Vision for 2030', 17–18 February 2022 (Brussels: Council of the European Union).
106. 'EU Ends Part of Mali Training Mission, Fearing Russian Interference, Borrell Says' *Reuters*, 12 April 2022.
107. Source: https://peacekeeping.un.org/en/troop-and-police-contributors
108. D. Styan (2020) 'China's Maritime Silk Road and Small States: Lessons from the case of Djibouti' *Journal of Contemporary China*, 29(122): 191–206.
109. Council of the EU (2021) 'Mozambique: EU sets up a military training mission to help address the crisis in Cabo Delgado', Press Release, 12 July (Brussels: Council of the European Union).
110. A. Schipani (2021) 'Rwanda Flexes Muscles in Fight against Terror in Mozambique' *Financial Times*, 3 October.
111. European Council (2022) 'Sixth European Union–African Union Summit: A Joint Vision for 2030', Press Release, 18 February (Brussels: European Council).
112. European Council (2022).

Chapter 10 Ecological Europe

1. M.J. Lasky (1993) 'The Pacifist and the General' *National Interest*, 34 (Winter): 66–78.
2. R.A. Bevan (2001) 'Petra Kelly: The other green' *New Political Science*, 23(2): 181–202.
3. S. Milder (2010) 'Thinking Globally, Acting (trans-)Locally: Petra Kelly and the transnational roots of West German green politics' *Central European History*, 43(2): 318–19.
4. On the history of European green parties, see E. van Haute (ed.) (2016) *Green Parties in Europe* (Abingdon: Routledge).
5. Quoted in W. Rüdig (2002) 'Green Parties and the European Union' in J. Gaffney (ed.) *Political Parties and the European Union* (London: Routledge): 256.
6. S. Milder (2017) *Greening Democracy: The Anti-Nuclear Movement and Political Environmentalism in West Germany and Beyond, 1968–1983* (Cambridge: Cambridge University Press).
7. P. Kelly (1991) 'Green Politics in New Europe: Hope for change?', Tenth Annual Ava Helen Pauling Memorial Lecture for World Peace, 30 October, Oregon State University.
8. European Commission (2020) 'New Eurobarometer Survey: Protecting the environment and climate is important for over 90% of European citizens', 3 March, IP_20_331 (Brussels: European Commission).
9. Articles 2 and 130r, Treaty of Maastricht (1992).
10. R.K. Wurzel (2010) 'Environmental, Climate and Energy Policies: Path-dependent incrementalism or quantum leap?' *German Politics*, 19(3–4): 463.
11. M. Thatcher (1988) 'Speech to the College of Europe', 20 September (London: Margaret Thatcher Foundation); M. Thatcher (1988) 'Speech to the Royal Society', 27 September (London: Margaret Thatcher Foundation).

12. G. Sainteny (2003) 'François Mitterrand and Nature' *Environment and History*, 9(1): 77–100.
13. 'Last Words: Carlo Ripa di Meana and Anthony Lejeune' *Sunday Times*, 1 April 2018.
14. M.T. Hatch (1993) 'Domestic Politics and International Negotiations: The politics of global warming in the United States' *Journal of Environment & Development*, 2(2): 29.
15. L.R. Cass (2012) *The Failures of American and European Climate Policy: International Norms, Domestic Politics, and Unachievable Commitments* (Albany, NY: SUNY Press): 72.
16. D. Nicholson-Lord (1992) 'What Will We Do Without Carlo? Politicians may welcome his departure, but David Nicholson-Lord says our environment needed Carlo Ripa di Meana's protection' *Independent*, 30 June.
17. K. Bäckstrand and O. Elgström (2013) 'The EU's Role in Climate Change Negotiations: From leader to "leadiator"' *Journal of European Public Policy*, 20(10): 1376
18. Council of the European Union (1997) 'Environment Council – 3 March 1997', Press Release, 6 March (Brussels: Council of the European Union).
19. L. Ringius (1999) 'Differentiation, Leaders, and Fairness: Negotiating climate commitments in the European Community' *International Negotiation*, 4(2): 133–66.
20. S. Oberthür and K. Roche (2008) 'EU Leadership in International Climate Policy: Achievements and challenges' *International Spectator*, 43(3): 35–50.
21. Bureau of Oceans and International Environmental and Scientific Affairs (1998) 'United States Signs the Kyoto Protocol', 13 November (Washington DC: U.S. Department of State).
22. Office of the Press Secretary (2001) 'President Bush Discusses Global Climate Change', 11 June (Washington DC: White House).
23. J. Borger (2001) 'Bush Kills Global Warming Treaty' *Guardian*, 29 March.
24. J. Frankel (2005) 'Climate and Trade: Links between the Kyoto Protocol and WTO' *Environment: Science and Policy for Sustainable Development*, 47(7): 12.
25. M. Tempest (2007) 'Climate Change Bill Is Revolutionary, Says Blair' *Guardian*, 13 March.
26. As chancellor, Schröder spoke favourably about oil and gas as a catalyst for cooperation between Russia and Germany. See, for example, G. Schröder (2004) 'Russia and Germany: The core tenet of cooperation' *Russia in Global Affairs*, 2(4): 76–83. Shortly after he stepped down as chancellor, Schröder became chair of Nord Stream AG's shareholder committee. See 'Schroeder Attacked over Gas Post' *BBC News*, 10 December 2005.
27. L. Éloi (2010) 'The French Carbon Tax: Autopsy of an ambition' *French Politics, Culture & Society*, 28(3): 121.
28. Eurobarometer (2008) 'Eurobarometer 69' (Brussels: European Commission): 61.
29. W. Woodward (2007) 'Cameron's Global Vision for Europe' *Guardian*, 6 March.
30. L. Van Schaik and S. Schunz (2012) 'Explaining EU Activism and Impact in Global Climate Politics: Is the Union a norm- or interest-driven actor?' *Journal of Common Market Studies*, 50(1): 169–86.
31. International Atomic Energy Agency (2004) 'Poland' Country Profile, December (Vienna: IEEA).
32. 'Council of the European Union (2007) 'Brussels European Council 8/9 March', 2 May, 7224/1/07 REV 1 CONCL 1 (Brussels: Council of the European Union).
33. Decision No 406/2009/EC of the European Parliament and of the Council of 23 April 2009 on the effort of Member States to reduce their greenhouse gas emissions to meet the Community's greenhouse gas emission reduction commitments up to 2020.

34. D. Helm (2009) 'EU Climate-Change Policy – A critique' in D. Helm and C. Hepburn (eds) *The Economics and Politics of Climate Change* (Oxford: Oxford University): 222–44.
35. D. Buchan (2010) 'Eastern Europe's Energy Challenge: Meeting its EU climate commitments' Oxford Institute for Energy Studies Paper EV55: 8–11.
36. 'Copenhagen "the World's Last Chance" – Dimas', *Edie Newsroom*, 8 May 2009.
37. 'Ban Voices Cautious Optimism Ahead of Copenhagen Climate Conference' *UN News*, 28 October 2009.
38. 'President Barack Obama's Inaugural Address', Obama Whitehouse Archives, 21 January 2009. Text: https://obamawhitehouse.archives.gov/blog/2009/01/21/president-Barack-obamas-inaugural-address
39. J. Vidal (2009) 'Miliband: China tried to hijack Copenhagen climate deal' *Guardian*, 20 December; 'China Doesn't Want to Lead, and the US Cannot' *Spiegel International*, 28 December 2009.
40. 'Winners and Losers in Copenhagen' *The Economist*, 21 December 2009.
41. J. Kanter (2009) 'Europe Stews as its Clout Diminishes On Climate' *New York Times*, 3 December.
42. Bäckstrand and Elgström (2013).
43. C.F. Parker and C. Karlsson (2010) 'Climate Change and the European Union's Leadership Moment: An inconvenient truth?' *Journal of Common Market Studies* 48(4): 923–43.
44. European Council (2014) 'European Council Conclusions 23/24 October 2014', EUCO 169/14 CO EUR 13 CONCL 5 (Brussels: European Council).
45. European Council (2014) 'Agreed Headline Targets 2030 Framework for Climate and Energy' Brussels, 24 October EUCO 169/14 (Brussels: European Council).
46. D. Keating (2014) 'MEPs Say Cañete's Family Still Has Ties to Oil Industry' *Politico Europe*, 25 September.
47. 'A "Petrolhead" as the Next Climate Commissioner?' *Avaaz: World in Action*, 2 October 2014. Text: https://secure.avaaz.org/campaign/en/canete_climate_pa_eugen/
48. S. Yeo (2015) 'The Carbon Brief Interview: Tony deBrum' *Carbon Brief*, 15 May.
49. E. King (2015) 'Tony deBrum: The emerging climate champion at COP21' *Climate Change News*, 10 December.
50. J. Crisp (2015) 'China Pours Cold Water on EU's Ambition Coalition at COP21' *Euractiv*, 11 December.
51. EUClimateAction (2015) 'High Ambition Coalition Walking Together to the Plenary at COP21' *YouTube*, 12 December. https://www.youtube.com/watch?v=82WKVOgGsLg
52. Paris Agreement, 12 December 2015 UN Treaties, 4 November 2016, No. 54113.
53. Office of the Press Secretary (2014) 'U.S.–China Joint Announcement on Climate Change', 11 November (Washington DC: White House).
54. 'Ceremony to Mark the Expiry of the ECSC Treaty (Brussels, 23 July 2002)'. CVCE Archive, University of Luxembourg.
55. P. Barnes (2007) 'Going Forward into the Past: The resurrection of the EURATOM Treaty', paper presented at the European Union Studies Association (EUSA) Tenth Biennial International Conference, Le Centre Sheraton, Montreal, Canada, 17–19 March: 11.
56. Federal Ministry of Economics and Technology and Federal Ministry for the Environment, Nature Conservation and Nuclear Safety (2010) 'Energy Concept for an Environmentally Sound, Reliable and Affordable Energy Supply' (Berlin: Bundesregierung).
57. B. Wehrmann (2022) 'German Offshore Wind Power – Output, business and perspectives' *Clean Energy Wire*, 27 January.

58. Source: Eurostat, Renewable Energy Statistics.
59. Source: U.S. Energy Information Administration, International Data.
60. T. Vandenbussche (2021) 'A Just Energy Transition for Workers: Tapping into a century of ideas', European Policy Centre Discussion Paper 30 (Brussels: EPC).
61. D. Bellamy (2020) 'Environmentalists in Dismay as Europe's Newest Coal-Powered Plant Opens in Germany – Access to the comments' *Euronews*, 30 May.
62. C. Lankowski (2022) 'The Merkel Era' in K. Larres, H. Moroff and R. Wittlinger (eds) *The Oxford Handbook of German Politics* (Oxford: Oxford University Press): 339.
63. A. Bros, T. Mitrova and K. Westphal (2017) 'German–Russian Gas Relations: A special relationship in troubled waters', Stiftung Wissenschaft und Politik Working Paper: 17.
64. D. Tusk (2014) 'A United Europe Can End Russia's Energy Strangle Hold' *Financial Times*, 21 April.
65. European Council (2015) 'European Council Meeting (19 and 20 March 2015)' EUCO 11/15 CO EUR 1 CONCL 1 (Brussels: European Council).
66. E. Barclay and B. Resnick (2019) 'How Big was the Global Climate Strike? 4 million people, activists estimate' *Vox*, 22 September.
67. G. Thunberg (2019a) *No One Is Too Small to Make a Difference* (New York: Penguin): 8.
68. Thunberg (2019a): 7
69. A. de Carbonnel (2018) 'EU's Climate Chief Calls for Net-Zero Emissions by 2050' *Reuters*, 27 November.
70. G. Thunberg (2019b) '"You're Acting Like Spoiled Irresponsible Children"', 21 February (Brussels: European Economic and Social Committee).
71. 'Greta Thunberg Changes Twitter Bio after Trump Dig' *BBC News*, 12 December 2019.
72. Thunberg (2019a).
73. A. Sabherwal, M.T. Ballew, S. van Der Linden, A. Gustafson, M.H. Goldberg, E.W. Maibach, John E. Kotcher, J.K. Swim, S.A. Rosenthal and A. Leiserowitz (2021) 'The Greta Thunberg Effect: Familiarity with Greta Thunberg predicts intentions to engage in climate activism in the United States' *Journal of Applied Social Psychology*, 51(4): 321–33.
74. D. Boffey (2019) 'Belgian Minister Resigns over School-Strike Conspiracy Claims' *Guardian*, 5 February.
75. G. Liston (2020) 'Enhancing the Efficacy of Climate Change Litigation: How to resolve the "fair share question" in the context of international human rights law' *Cambridge International Law Journal*, 9(2): 241–63.
76. B. Butterworth (2019) 'Extinction Rebellion London Protest: 91-year-old man arrested for demonstrating outside Cabinet Office' *The I*, 9 October.
77. Greens/EFA Group (2019) 'Greens/EFA Group Voted against Ursula von der Leyen', Press Release, 16 July (Strasbourg: European Parliament).
78. M. Siddi (2020) 'The European Green Deal: Assessing its current state and future implementation', Finnish Institute of International Affairs Working Paper 114.
79. A. Hernández-Morales (2021) 'Poland and Spain Show Two Faces of the Energy Transition at Biden's Climate Summit' *Politico Europe*, 23 April.
80. European Council (2020) 'European Council Meeting' Brussels, 11 December 2020, EUCO 22/20 CO EUR 17. The target was later enshrined in Regulation (EU) 2021/1119.
81. K. Abnett (2020) 'EU Unveils Climate Law, Thunberg Calls It "Surrender"' *Reuters*, 4 March.
82. 'Greta Thunberg Urges EU to Do "as Much as Possible" on Climate' *Euractiv*, 15 October.

Chapter 11 Borders

1. 'EU Drops Border Controls 1995' *RTÉ*, 3 November 2020. https://www.rte.ie/archives/2020/0311/1121659-schengen-agreement/
2. R. Zaiotti (2008) *Cultures of Border Control: Schengen and the Evolution of Europe's Frontiers* (Toronto: University of Toronto): 70.
3. 'The Schengen acquis – Agreement between the Governments of the States of the Benelux Economic Union, the Federal Republic of Germany and the French Republic on the gradual abolition of checks at their common borders', OJ L 239, 22.9.2000, 13–18.
4. 'Mr Major's Speech to Conservative Central Council – 23 March 1991'. https://johnmajorarchive.org.uk/1991/03/23/mr-majors-speech-to-conservative-central-council-23-march-1991/
5. B. Vaughan (2007) 'Cooperation on Justice under the Third Pillar: Propping up a shaky consensus' in M. Callanan (ed.) *Foundations of an Ever Closer Union: An Irish Perspective on the Fifty Years since the Treaty of Rome* (Dublin: Department for Foreign Affairs): 148.
6. P. Hersh (1991) 'Killy Would Be at Home Skiing Olympus' *Chicago Tribune*, 31 March.
7. M. Kolomayets (1995) 'Ukraine: Chernobyl to close by 2000' *UPI Archives*, 13 April 1995.
8. M. Barnier (1995) 'Statement on the Application of the Schengen Agreements', Paris, 7 October 1995. CVCE Archive, University of Luxembourg.
9. R.D. Hutchins and D. Halikiopoulou (2020) 'Enemies of Liberty? Nationalism, immigration, and the framing of terrorism in the agenda of the Front National' *Nations and Nationalism*, 26(1): 67–84.
10. Barnier (1995).
11. M. Turner (1997) 'Peace Pipe on Offer in Drugs Policy Conflict' *European Voice*, 8 January.
12. See I. Schwarz (2016) 'Racializing Freedom of Movement in Europe: Experiences of racial profiling at European borders and beyond' *Movements: Journal for Critical Migration and Border Regime Studies*, 2(1): 253–65.
13. D.G. Home (2022) 'Member States' Notifications of the Temporary Reintroduction of Border Control at Internal Borders Pursuant to Article 25 and 28 et seq. of the Schengen Borders Code' (Brussels: European Commission).
14. I. Traynor (2011) 'EU Warns Denmark over Border Controls' *Guardian*, 13 May.
15. 'Fight over Schengen' *DW-Deutsche Welle*, 14 March 2012.
16. C. Caulcutt (2021) 'Barnier Seeks Limelight with Pledge to Shut Borders' *Politico Europe*, 11 May.
17. J. Barigazzi (2019) 'Croatian PM's European Ambitions' *Politico Europe*, 8 May; 'Croatia Can Join Border-Free Schengen Area, EU Governments Say' *Euractiv*, 9 December 2021.
18. J. Christou (2021) 'EU Says Cyprus Not Ready to Join Schengen Area' *Cyprus Mail*, 2 June.
19. 'EU Delays Schengen Decision for Bulgaria, Romania' *EUbusiness*, 2 March.
20. 'Eastern Europe Berates Wilders over Anti-East Website' *DW-Deutsche Welle*, 14 February 2012.
21. Neither Bulgaria nor Romania was in a position to join Schengen at this point, but they continued to face opposition from Austria as of late 2022.
22. Article 8, Treaty Establishing the European Community (1992).
23. See, for example, J. Rees-Mogg (2012) 'Debate on EU Citizenship in the House of Commons, European Committee B', Hansard, 5 March. https://publications.parliament.uk/pa/cm201012/cmgeneral/euro/120305/120305s01.htm

24. E. Balibar (2009) *We, the People of Europe?* (Princeton, NJ: Princeton University Press).
25. Article 49, Treaty Establishing the European Community (1992).
26. Eurobarometer (1997) 'Eurobarometer – Report Number 47' (Brussels: European Commission): 57.
27. A. Pellegata (2018) 'Rising Support for Free Movement Stops at EU Migration' *EU Visions*, 25 April.
28. J. Moses (2016) *International Migration: Globalization's Last Frontier* (London: Zed Books): 171.
29. High Level Panel on the Free Movement of Persons Chaired by Mrs Simone Veil (1997) 'Executive Summary of the Report Presented to the European Commission', 18 March (Brussels: European Commission).
30. S. Royo (2007) 'Lessons from the Integration of Spain and Portugal to the EU' *PS: Political Science & Politics*, 40(4): 692.
31. Source: European Commission AMECO database.
32. 'Blair's Migration Speech' *Guardian*, 27 April 2004.
33. N. Doyle, G. Hughes and E. Wadensjö (2006) 'Freedom of Movement for Workers from Central and Eastern Europe Experiences in Ireland and Sweden' SIEPS 2006:5 (Stockholm: Swedish Institute for European Policy Studies): 8.
34. 'Dail Row over "Socialist" Ahern' *Irish Times*, 16 November.
35. M. Ruhs and E. Quinn (2009) 'Ireland: From rapid immigration to recession', 1 September (Washington DC: Migration Policy Institute).
36. J. Humphreys (2002) 'Coughlan Says Worker Movement Policy Not Relevant to Nice Treaty' *Irish Times*, 20 August.
37. C. Dustmann, M. Casanova, M. Fertig, I. Preston and C.M. Schmidt (2003) 'The Impact of EU Enlargement on Migration Flow' Home Office Online Report 25/03 (London: Home Office).
38. J. Salt (2015) 'International Migration and the United Kingdom Report of the United Kingdom SOPEMI Correspondent to the OECD, 2015' (London: UCL): 19.
39. Eurostat (2005) 'GDP per capita in 2004: GDP per capita varied by one to five across the EU25 Member States', Press Release, 3 June (Luxembourg: Eurostat).
40. O. Doyle and J. Fidrmuc (2006) 'Who Favors Enlargement? Determinants of support for EU membership in the candidate countries' referenda' *European Journal of Political Economy*, 22(2): 520–43.
41. Eurobarometer (2004) 'Public Opinion in the European Union – Eurobarometer 62', Autumn 2004 (Brussels: European Commission).
42. T. Helm (1998) 'Germany Will Not Pay for EU Expansion Says Schroder' *Independent*, 27 November.
43. S. Longhi and M. Rokicka (2012) 'European Immigrants in the UK Before and After the 2004 Enlargement: Is there a change in immigrant self-selection?' Institute for Social and Economic Research Working Paper Series No. 2012-22.
44. D. Ingham (2010) 'Polish Immigration and the UK', *Mancunian Matters*, 1 June.
45. See S. Blinder and L. Richards (2020) 'UK Public Opinion toward Immigration: Overall attitudes and level of concern' (Oxford: The Migration Observatory).
46. S. Brook (2008) '*Daily Mail* Gives Platform to Polish Community Spokesman' *Guardian*, 5 August.
47. Brook (2008).
48. 'Nigel Farage Attacked over Romanians "Slur"' *BBC News*, 18 May 2014.
49. P. Worrall (2014) 'Is There a Romanian Crimewave?' *Channel 4 News*, 19 May.
50. Source: IPSOS Mori (1997) 'Issues Index: Trends 1988–1997' (London: IPSOS Mori). https://www.ipsos.com/en-uk/issues-index-trends-1988-1997

51. 'Economist / Ipsos May 2016 Issues Index' IPSOS Mori, 31 May 2016 (London: IPSOS Mori).
52. A. Barrett (2010) 'EU Enlargement and Ireland's Labor Market' in M. Kahanec and K.F. Zimmermann (eds) *EU Labor Markets after Post-Enlargement Migration* (Berlin: Springer): 145–61.
53. Barrett (2010)
54. B. Fanning, W. Kloc-Nowak and Ma. Lesińska (2021) 'Polish Migrant Settlement Without Political Integration in the United Kingdom and Ireland: A comparative analysis in the context of Brexit and thin European citizenship' *International Migration* 59(1): 263–80; C. Lynch (2010) 'Racism is on the Increase in Europe and Ireland Is No Exception' (Dublin: Irish Network Against Racism).
55. H. McDonald (2006) 'Dublin Heralds a New Era in Publishing for Immigrants' *Guardian*, 12 March.
56. D. Holland, T. Fic, A. Rincon-Aznar, L. Stokes and P. Paluchowski (2011) 'Labour Mobility within the EU: The impact of enlargement and the functioning of the transitional arrangements' (London: National Institute Economic and Social Research): 3.
57. Holland et al. (2011): 4.
58. P. Healey (2015) 'Up to 10,000 Polish Fans Seeking Tickets for Sunday's Showdown' *Independent*, 26 March.
59. S. Cockroft (2021) 'Twitter Reminds Nigel Farage about His Remarks on Romanians after He Hails Emma Raducanu as a "Megastar"' *Indy100*, 13 September.
60. Cockroft (2021).
61. M. Ryan (2010) 'Sounding Different Notes: Approaching the other through music in John Carney's film *Once*' *Otherness: Essays and Studies*, 1 (2010): 1–16.
62. M. Hermann (2010) 'Immigrants, Stereotypes and the New Ireland: Czech identity in and in response to the film *Once*' in B. Korte, E.U. Pirker and S. Helff (eds) *Facing the East in the West: Images of Eastern Europe in British Literature, Film and Culture* (Leiden: Brill Rodopi).
63. 'Kohl Calls for EC Quota on Refugees from Former Yugoslavia' UPI Archives, 24 July 1992.
64. Archives, 24 July 1992.
65. R. Carroll (2000) '"They Were God-Fearing People Like Us, and God Knows We Needed Them"' *Guardian*, 22 March.
66. J. Tagliabue (1998) 'More Kurds Reach Italy: Northern Europe upset' *New York Times*, 2 January.
67. 'Schengen Members Get Cold Feet' *European Voice*, 11 February.
68. 'EU: Kurds, smuggling' *Migration News*, February 1998.
69. 'Under Fire at Europe's Border' *Observer*, 2 October 2005.
70. 'Canaries Migrant Death Toll Soars' *BBC News*, 28 December 2006.
71. Frontex (2006) 'Longest FRONTEX Coordinated Operation – HERA, the Canary Islands', Press Release 19 (Warsaw: Frontex).
72. Committee on Migration, Refugees and Population, Ad Hoc Sub-Committee on the large-scale arrival of irregular migrants, asylum seekers and refugees on Europe's southern shores (2011) 'Report on the Visit to Lampedusa (Italy)', AS/MIG/AHLARG (2011) 03 REV 2 (Strasbourg: Parliamentary Assembly of the Council of Europe).
73. UNHCR (2016) 'Global Trends: Forced displacement in 2015' (Geneva: UNHCR).
74. Source: UNHCR Refugee Data Finder.
75. Pew Research (2016) 'Number of Refugees to Europe Surges to Record 1.3 Million in 2015', 2 August.
76. Pew Research (2016).

77. For a critical analysis of the European migration crisis as an asylum policy crisis, see P. Castelli Gattinara and L. Zamponi (2020) 'Politicizing Support and Opposition to Migration in France: The EU asylum policy crisis and direct social activism' *Journal of European Integration*, 42(5): 625–41.

78. UNHCR (2016) 'Greece: Lesvos Island snapshot (31 Dec 2015)' (Geneva: UNHCR).

79. 'Inside Moria, Greece's 1st "hotspot" refugee camp' *DW-Deutsche Welle*, 11 November 2015.

80. Pew Research (2016).

81. J. Delcker (2015) 'Merkel's Migrant Problem' *Politico Europe*, 26 August.

82. J. Delcker (2016) 'The Phrase That Haunts Angela Merkel' *Politico Europe*, 19 August.

83. J. Elgot (2016) 'How David Cameron's Language on Refugees Has Provoked Anger' *Guardian*, 27 January.

84. F. Gülzau (2021) 'A "New Normal" for the Schengen Area: When, where and why member states reintroduce temporary border controls?' *Journal of Borderlands Studies*, published online: 14n.

85. T. Kurdi (2018) *The Boy on the Beach: My Family's Escape from Syria and Our Hope for a New Home* (New York: Simon and Schuster).

86. 'France's Hollande Says Binding System Needed to Take in Refugees', *Reuters*, 3 September 2015.

87. 'The Jobbik Party in Hungary: History and background' *Human Rights First*, 13 July 2015.

88. L. Cendrowicz (2015) 'Refugee Crisis: EU faultlines revealed as Hungary's PM warns of risk to "Christian" culture' *Independent*, 3 September.

89. D. Hodson and I. Maher (2022) 'Single Issue EU Referendums: Tying hands, domestic effects and the challenge of consentification' *Journal of European Public Policy*, published online: 1–19.

90. P. Connor (2018) 'A Majority of Europeans Favor Taking in Refugees, But Most Disapprove of EU's Handling of the Issue' Pew Research, 19 September.

91. J. Poushter (2016) 'European Opinions of the Refugee Crisis in 5 Charts' Pew Research, 16 September.

92. S. Ardittis (2017) 'Live and Let Die? The end of the EU migrant relocation programme' *Open Democracy*, 26 September.

93. A. Fantz and C.E. Shoichet (2015) 'Syrian Toddler's Dad: "Everything I was dreaming of is gone"' *CNN*, 4 September.

94. European Council (2016) 'EU–Turkey Statement', Press Release, 18 March (Brussels: Council of the European Union).

95. K. Terry (2021) 'The EU–Turkey Deal, Five Years On: A frayed and controversial but enduring blueprint' (Washington DC: Migration Policy Institute).

96. Terry (2021).

97. Terry (2021).

98. A. Chapman (2020) 'A Doctor's Story: Inside the 'living hell' of Moria refugee camp' *Observer*, 9 February.

99. D. Murray (2017) *The Strange Death of Europe: Immigration, Identity, Islam* (London: Bloomsbury).

100. In 2022, the UNHCR recorded 26.7 million refugees worldwide, more than twice the population of a midsized EU member state. Source: Refugee Data Finder, UNHCR.

101. Eurostat (2021) 'Statistics on Countries Responsible for Asylum Applications (Dublin Regulation), July 2021' (Luxembourg: Eurostat).

102. M. Stierl (2021) 'The Mediterranean as a Carceral Seascape' *Political Geography*, 88 (2021): 1–10; M. Gkliati (2022) 'The Next Phase of The European Border and Coast Guard: Responsibility for returns and push-backs in Hungary and Greece' *European Papers: A Journal on Law and Integration*, 1: 171–93.

103. Council of the European Union (2015) 'Political Declaration', Valletta Summit on Migration, 11–12 November (Brussels: Council of the European Union). Figure comes from Oxfam (2020) 'The EU Trust Fund for Africa: Trapped between aid policy and migration' (London: Oxfam).

104. Oxfam (2020).

105. 'Migrants Reach Spain's Ceuta Enclave in Record Numbers', *BBC News*, 18 May.

Chapter 12 Terror

1. M. Van der Hulst (2016) 'Investigation Committee – Terrorist Attacks. 22 March 2016. Summary of the Activities and Recommendations' (Brussels: Department of the House of Representatives).

2. 'Nigel Farage on EU Migration Rules and Brussels Attacks' *BBC News*, 23 March.

3. S. Erlanger (2016) 'Brussels Attacks Fuel Debate Over Migrants in a Fractured Europe' *New York Times*, 22 March; Leon de Winter (2016) 'Europe's Muslims Hate the West' *Politico Europe*, 29 March.

4. M. de Fougières and H. El Karoui (2021) 'Bataclan 6 Years On: The attacks that changed 18 November' (Paris: Institute Montaigne).

5. J. Dwivedi (2020) 'Fact Check: Does this Belgian city with terror links have 100% Muslim population?' *India Today*, 19 September.

6. I. Traynor (2015) 'Molenbeek: The Brussels borough becoming known as Europe's jihadi central' *Guardian*, 15 November.

7. R. Cohen (2016) 'The Islamic State of Molenbeek' *New York Times*, 11 April.

8. A. M'Kele and A. Jamieson (2016) 'Brussels Attacks: El Bakraoui brothers were jailed for carjackings, shootout' *NBC News*, 24 March.

9. T. Renard and R. Coolsaet (eds) (2018) 'From the Kingdom to the Caliphate and Back: Returnees to Belgium' in T. Renard and R. Coolsaet (eds) 'Returnees: Who are they, why are they (not) coming back and how should we deal with them? Assessing policies on returning foreign terrorist fighters in Belgium, Germany and the Netherlands', Egmont Paper 101: 19.

10. C. Kroet (2016) 'Donald Trump: Brussels is "like a hellhole"' *Politico Europe*, 27 January.

11. L. Dearden (2016) ' "I'm in a Rush, I Don't Know What to Do": Brussels attackers' will found in bin reveals panic after Abdeslam caught' *Independent*, 23 March.

12. Source: European Commission AMECO database.

13. IBSA (2016) 'Molenbeek-Saint-Jean, Zoom sur les communes, Édition 2016 20-22 (Brussels: IBSA).

14. K.F. Zimmermann, M. Kahanec, A. Constant and D. Devoretz (2008) 'Study on the Social and Labour Market Integration of Ethnic Minorities', IZA Research Report No. 16 (Bonn: IZA): 15.

15. 'Swede Held over Attacks ID'd as Palestinian "Brainwashed" by Jihadis' *Times of Israel*, 10 April 2016.

16. 'Osama Krayem Caught Thanks to Facebook Wall, DNA and CCTV' *VRT NWS Flandersnews.be*, 9 April.

17. D. Bilefsky (2016) 'A Dual Citizen of Belgium and Italy, With a Cosmopolitan Spirit' *New York Times*, 26 March.

18. European Council (1995) 'La Gomera Declaration, Annex to the Madrid European Council', 15 and 16 December (Brussels: Council of the European Union).

19. M. White and P. Wintour (2001) 'Blair Calls for World Fight against Terror' *Guardian*, 12 September.
20. European Council (2001) 'Conclusions and Plan of Action of the Extraordinary European Council Meeting on 21 September 2001', SN 140/01 (Brussels: Council of the European Union).
21. S. Westall (2007) 'Germany Applies Lessons from Hamburg 9/11 Trauma' *Reuters*, 10 September.
22. O. Bures (2008) 'Europol's Fledgling Counterterrorism Role' *Terrorism and Political Violence*, 20(4): 498–517.
23. D. Cronin (2005) 'Member States' Failure to Share Intelligence Saps Europol Work' *Politico Europe*, 16 March.
24. Cronin (2005).
25. R. Bosilca (2021) 'Europol and Counter Terrorism Intelligence Sharing' *Europolity: Continuity and Change in European Governance*, 7(1): 11. See also C. Andreeva (2021) 'The Evolution of Information-Sharing in EU Counter-Terrorism Post-2015: A paradigm shift?' *Global Affairs*, 7(5): 751–76.
26. A. Macdonald (2016). 'The Race against Time That Belgium Lost' *Reuters*, 27 March.
27. Dearden (2016).
28. McCrary Institute (2018) 'Europol Executive Director Rob Wainwright' *YouTube*, 12 April. https://www.youtube.com/watch?v=wNfBz2DJ3Ls&t=1928
29. Europol (2014) 'Organised Crime Networks Targeted in Huge Law Enforcement Operation in Europe', Press Release, 24 September.
30. Europol (2017) 'Europol Rob Wainwright – @DOJ Press Conference – Takedown of AlphaBay & Hansa marketplaces' *YouTube*, 21 July. https://www.youtube.com/watch?v=k2FI45hdlXs&t=28s
31. M. Cauldron (2018) 'How Europol Became the Centre Point for the FBI' *Medium*, 27 April.
32. McCrary Institute (2018).
33. J. Rankin (2016) 'FBI Tipped Off Dutch Police about Bakraoui Brothers' *Guardian*, 29 March.
34. 'FBI Warned Dutch about El Bakraoui Brothers Week Before Brussels Attacks' *Reuters*, 29 March.
35. 'Europol Chief: Further terrorist attacks in Europe "Very Probable"' *Parliament Magazine*, 28 November.
36. Europol (2015) 'Annual Review' (The Hague: Europol).
37. Europol (2018) 'Islamic State Propaganda Machine Hit by Law Enforcement in Coordinated Takedown Action', Press Release, 27 April (The Hague: Europol); Europol (2021) 'Spanish Police Arrests 5 Jihadists on Suspicion of Preparing a Terrorist Attack', Press Release, 14 October (The Hague: Europol).
38. 'Attack on Nice: Who was Mohamed Lahouaiej-Bouhlel?' *BBC News*, 19 August; 'Berlin Truck Attack: Tunisian perpetrator Anis Amri', *BBC News*, 23 December.
39. E. Assoudeh and L. Weinberg (2021) 'In Western Europe, Right-Wing Terrorism Is on the Rise' *Open Democracy*, 7 January 2021.
40. K. Rawlinson (2018) 'Darren Osborne Jailed for Life for Finsbury Park Terrorist Attack' *Guardian*, 2 February.
41. P. Oltermann (2020) 'Hanau Attack Gunman Railed against Ethnic Minorities Online' *Guardian*, 20 February.
42. C. Kaunert (2007) ' "Without the Power of Purse or Sword": The European arrest warrant and the role of the Commission' *Journal of European Integration*, 29(4): 396.
43. European Council (2001) 'Conclusions and Plan of Action of the Extraordinary European Council Meeting on 21 September 2001', 21 September (Brussels: European Council).

44. Kaunert (2007): 399.
45. Kaunert (2007): 400–1.
46. M. Mackarel (2007) ' "Surrendering" the Fugitive: The European arrest warrant and the United Kingdom' *Journal of Criminal Law*, 71(4): 362–81.
47. House of Lords European Union Committee (2003) 'EU Police and Criminal Justice Measures: The UK's 2014 opt-out decision', 13th Report of Session 2012–13, HL Paper 159 (London: House of Lords).
48. E. Rigby and C. Binham (2014) 'Tory and Ukip Team Up to Fight EU Arrest Warrant' *Financial Times*, 15 October.
49. 'Jacob Rees-Mogg on European Arrest Warrant Vote' *BBC News*, 10 November 2014.
50. 'Commissioner Vitorino and Counter-Terrorism Coordinator De Vries are in United States this Week for High Level Meetings', Press Release, Agence Europe, 11 May 2004.
51. K. Karstens (2003) 'Europe Agrees Passenger Data Deal with US' *Politico Europe*, 17 December.
52. European Council (1995).
53. European Parliament (2004) 'European Parliament Resolution on the Draft Commission Decision Noting the Adequate Level of Protection Provided for Personal Data Contained in the Passenger Name Records (PNRs) Transferred to the US Bureau of Customs and Border Protection' 2004/2011(INI) (Strasbourg: European Parliament).
54. E. Fahey (2013) 'Law and Governance as Checks and Balances in Transatlantic Security: Rights, redress, and remedies in EU–US passenger name records and the terrorist finance tracking program' *Yearbook of European Law* 32(1): 368–88.
55. ALDE (2007) 'Sophie in 't Veld on PNR Agreement with the United States' *YouTube*, 11 July. https://www.youtube.com/watch?v=d9z2lZB8P1M
56. 'Examination of Witnesses (Questions 70–79)', Select Committee on European Union Minutes of Evidence, 2 April 2008. Session 2007-08, European Union Committee Publications (London: House of Lords).
57. J. Kanter and R. Minder (2010) 'Air Travelers Lead European Privacy Concerns' *New York Times*, 28 April.
58. 'EP Rapporteur In 't Veld set to reject new EU–US Passenger Name Records Agreement (PNR)', Euractiv Press Release, 1 February 2022.
59. J. Kanter (2012) 'Official Assails Sharing of Passenger Data' *New York Times*, 31 January.
60. C. Brand (2012) 'MEPs Back Passenger Data Deal with US' *Politico Europe*, 27 March.
61. European Commission (2011) 'Proposal for a Directive of the European Parliament and of the Council on the use of Passenger Name Record Data for the Prevention, Detection, Investigation and Prosecution of Terrorist Offences and Serious Crime', COM/2011/0032 final (Brussels: European Commission).
62. European Parliament Civil Liberties Committee (2013) 'Civil Liberties Committee Rejects EU Passenger Name Record Proposal', Press Release LIBE 24-04-2013 - 14:12 (Strasbourg: European Parliament).
63. Renew Europe (2016) 'Sophia in 't Veld 13 Apr 2016 Plenary Speech on EU PNR' *YouTube*, 13 April. https://www.youtube.com/watch?v=WT3ZXe2K-ak
64. S. Pogatchnik (2021) 'Ryanair CEO Calls Belarus Landing a "State-Sponsored Hijacking" ' *Politico Europe*, 24 May.
65. Amnesty International (2021) 'Belarus: Roman Protasevich placed under house arrest in "cynical ploy" ', Press Release, 25 June.
66. 'Was Passenger Name Record Data Exploited to Kidnap Belarusian Journalist? Access Now calls for EU investigation' *Access Now*, 6 October.

67. C. Allen and J.S. Nielsen (2002) 'Summary Report on Islamophobia in the EU after 11 September 2001' (Vienna: EU Monitoring Centre on Racism and Xenophobia).
68. R. Ivandic, T. Kirchmaier and S. Machin (2019) 'Amplifying Islamophobic Hate Crime: UK media in the wake of terror attacks' *LSE British Politics and Policy Blog*, 9 May.
69. A. Milošević (2018) 'Historicizing the Present: Brussels attacks and heritagization of spontaneous memorials' *International Journal of Heritage Studies*, 24(1): 53–65.
70. 'Molenbeek: The Moroccan artist Mustapha Zoufri realizes a monument against terrorism', *Council of the Moroccan Community News*, 22 September 2016.

Chapter 13 Brexit

1. N. Farage (2015) *The Purple Revolution: The Year That Changed Everything* (London: Biteback Publishing): 102. Justin Adams, the plane's pilot, later took his own life.
2. S. Jeffries (2014) 'Ukip Founder Alan Sked: "The party has become a Frankenstein's monster"' *Guardian*, 26 May.
3. Jeffries (2014).
4. O. Gibson (2004) 'BBC Pulls Kilroy-Silk Show after Anti-Arab Comments' *Guardian*, 9 January.
5. D. Gow (2004) 'Ukip Stokes Row over Barroso Deputy' *Guardian*, 20 November.
6. 'Ukip's Nigel Farage Tells Van Rompuy: You have the charisma of a damp rag' *Guardian*, 25 February.
7. A. Brown (2019) 'Nigel Farage Drinks Beer "To Be Seen With It" and Actually "Prefers Wine"' *Daily Star*, 7 May.
8. 'Michael Howard's Speech on Europe' *Guardian*, 12 February.
9. M. Tempest (2003) 'Blair: EU constitution rules out superstate' *Guardian*, 23 June.
10. Publicae (2018) 'BREXIT: Nigel Farage vs Tony Blair, the most furious and greatest debate ever at EU Parliament' *YouTube*, 20 December. https://www.youtube.com/watch?v=zupuJkLWwfM
11. D. Cameron (2005) 'Speech to Launch Leadership Bid', 20 November. Text: https://www.ukpol.co.uk/david-cameron-2005-speech-to-launch-leadership-bid/
12. 'Full Text of David Cameron's Speech on the NHS' *Guardian*, 4 January 2006.
13. D. Cameron (2006) 'Conservative Party Conference Speech', 20 November. Text: https://www.ukpol.co.uk/david-cameron-2006-conservative-party-conference-speech/ In his regular column for the *Guardian*, Cameron wrote of 'the dreaded European issue, which has side-tracked the Conservative party for so long': D. Cameron (2003) 'Reasons To Be Cheerful: For the first time since 1997, the future seems to look rosy for the Conservatives' *Guardian*, 15 May.
14. P. Lynch and R. Whitaker (2008) 'A Loveless Marriage: The Conservatives and the European People's Party' *Parliamentary Affairs*, 61(1): 31–51.
15. D. Cameron (2009) 'Fixing Broken Politics', 26 May. Text: https://conservative-speeches.sayit.mysociety.org/speech/601355
16. N. Watt (2009) 'Tragic, Unwise: Conservative grandees turn on David Cameron over plans for European Union' *Guardian*, 29 May.
17. Z. Wood (2010) 'Alistair Darling Rules Out British Support for Euro' *Guardian*, 9 May.
18. M. Wells (2010) 'David Cameron Rules Out Transfer of Powers to Strengthen Eurozone' *Guardian*, 21 May.
19. D. Cameron (2007) 'Speech on the European Union', European Reform Conference, Brussels, 6 March.
20. T. Castle (2011) 'Cameron Resists Rebel Anger over Europe' *Reuters*, 6 December.

21. 'Is Brussels Really about to Force Britain to Admit Benefit Tourists?' *The Economist*, 30 September 2011.
22. G. Parker and A. Barker (2011) 'Cameron Urges Liberal Reform on EU' *Financial Times*, 23 March.
23. N. Watt (2011) 'David Cameron Rocked by Record Rebellion as Europe Splits Tories Again' *Guardian*, 25 October.
24. L. Davies (2012) 'Ukip Says No Tory Election Deal without EU Referendum Pledge' *Guardian*, 21 September.
25. R. Taylor (2006) 'Cameron Refuses to Apologise to Ukip' *Guardian*, 4 April.
26. T. Helm, D. Boffey, H. Stewart and P. Beaumont (2011) 'After David Cameron's EU Treaty Veto: Seven key questions Britain must face' *Guardian*, 10 December.
27. T. Shipman (2015) 'Keen Not to Be Yesterday's Man, Cameron Gears Up to Be Radical Tomorrow' *Sunday Times*, 16 August.
28. D. Cameron (2019) *For the Record* (New York: HarperCollins): 622–3.
29. H.E. Marshall (2008) *Our Island Story* (London: Hachette).
30. 'Full Text of Cameron's Speech' *Financial Times*, 23 January 2013.
31. 'David Cameron's EU Speech – Our experts react' *LSE European Politics and Policy Blog*, 23 January 2013.
32. 'YouGov/The Sun', 2–3 January 2013 (London: Yougov); 'YouGov/Sunday Times', 10–11 January 2013 (London YouGov); 'Survation/Mail on Sunday, New Years Issues Poll Prepared on Behalf of the Mail on Sunday' 5 January 2013 (London: Survation).
33. EU member states had already agreed on small-scale treaty revision in March 2011. The aim was to provide the European Stability Mechanism, a euro crisis fund, with a more clear-cut basis in EU law, something which German Chancellor Angela Merkel had called for in her speech to the College of Europe in November 2010: A. Merkel (2010) 'Speech by Federal Chancellor Angela Merkel at the Opening Ceremony of the 61st Academic Year of the College of Europe in Bruges' 2 November (Bruges: College of Europe).
34. D. Cameron (2015) 'EU Reform: PM's letter to president of the European Council Donald Tusk', 10 November (London: 10 Downing Street).
35. V. Miller (2015) ' "Ever Closer Union" in the EU Treaties and Court of Justice Case Law' Research Briefing, Number 07230 (London: House of Commons).
36. D. Tusk (2015) 'Letter by President Donald Tusk to the European Council on the Issue of a UK In/Out Referendum', Press Release, 7 December (Brussels: European Council).
37. M. Tempest (2015) 'Poland Disagrees with UK on "Brexit" Welfare Restrictions' *Euractiv*, 10 December.
38. E. Pineau and K. MacLellan (2016) 'Hollande Tells Cameron Still Work to be Done on EU Deal' *Reuters*, 15 February.
39. R. Boyle (2016) 'Merkel Pops Out for Belgian Chips at Maison Antoine' *Bulletin*, 23 February.
40. C. Boyle (2016) 'Leaders Reach Deal Aimed at Keeping Britain from Bolting European Union' *LA Times*, 19 February.
41. 'EU Deal Gives UK Special Status, Says David Cameron' *BBC News*, 20 February 2016.
42. P. Dallison (2016) 'Boris Johnson's 11 Best Europe Moments' *Politico Europe*, 23 February.
43. B. Quinn (2012) 'Boris Johnson Rejects Necessity for In/Out Referendum Vote on EU' *Guardian*, 25 November.
44. B. Johnson (2013) 'We Must Be Ready to Leave the EU If We Don't Get What We Want: There are pros and cons to staying in Europe – and it's time to talk about them' *Daily Telegraph*, 13 May.

45. T. McTague (2021) 'The Minister for Chaos' *Atlantic*, July/August.
46. G. Hinsliff (2004) 'Boris Johnson Sacked by Tories over Private Life' *Guardian*, 14 November.
47. D. Lawson (2019) 'Boris Johnson's Manifesto: I want it! I want it! I want it!' *Sunday Times*, 26 May.
48. J. McDevitt (2019) 'Dominic Cummings Honed Strategy in 2004 Vote, Video Reveals' *Guardian*, 12 November.
49. N. Watt, A. Travis and R. Mason (2016) 'David Cameron Ridicules Boris Johnson's Second EU Referendum Idea' *Guardian*, 22 February.
50. J. Grierson (2017) 'Britons' Trust in Government, Media and Business Falls Sharply' *Guardian*, 16 January.
51. E. Williams (2016) 'A Tale of Two Britains – Trust Eurobarometer', 22 January (London: Edelman).
52. 'Witnesses: Lord Rose, Chairman, Britain Stronger in Europe, and Will Straw, Executive Director, Britain Stronger in Europe', Treasury Committee, Wednesday 2 March 2016. https://www.parliamentlive.tv/Event/Index/b2e04db8-1dd2-4846-a765-010993724210
53. 'Full Text of Cameron's Speech' *Financial Times*, 23 January.
54. C. Oliver (2018) *Unleashing Demons: The Inside Story of Brexit* (London: Hodder & Stoughton).
55. B. Glaze and D. Bloom (2016) '"Brexit" Could Trigger World War Three, Warns David Cameron' *Mirror*, 9 May.
56. HM Treasury (2013) 'Unfunded Commitments in "Scotland's Future"' (London: HM Treasury).
57. HM Treasury (2016) 'HM Treasury Analysis Shows Leaving EU Would Cost British Households £4,300 Per Year', Press Release, 18 April (London: HM Treasury).
58. J. Stone (2016) 'The Campaign to Stay in the EU is "Project Fear", Says Boris Johnson' *Independent*, 29 February.
59. J. Cox and N. Coyle (2016) 'We Nominated Jeremy Corbyn for the Leadership. Now We Regret It' *Guardian*, 6 May.
60. HC Deb 13 January 1993 vol 216 cc935-1011. http://hansard.millbanksystems.com/commons/1993/jan/13/treaty-on-european-union-1
61. C. Mortimer (2016) 'Jeremy Corbyn on *The Last Leg*: Enthusiastic about staying in the EU but won't share a platform with Cameron' *Independent*, 10 June.
62. S. Cunningham (2016) 'Theresa Villiers: Irish border concerns over Brexit are just "scaremongering"' *Irish News*, 18 April.
63. See G. Stuart (2003) *The Making of Europe's Constitution* (London: Fabian Society).
64. T. McTague (2016) 'EU Referendum: Backing Brexit does not make you a "bad" person, says Vote Leave head Gisela Stuart' *Independent*, 12 March.
65. 'Forecast: Brexit could hit UK–Ireland trade by a fifth' *Belfast Telegraph*, 23 June.
66. I. Cobain (2016) 'Jo Cox Murder Trial: MP told assistants to flee to safety after she was shot' *Guardian*, 16 November.
67. Cox and Coyle (2016).
68. R. Booth, V. Dodd, K. Rawlinson and N. Slawson (2016) 'Jo Cox Murder Suspect Tells Court His Name Is "Death to Traitors, Freedom for Britain"' *Guardian*, 18 June.
69. B. Beaumont-Thomas (2016) 'Jeff Mitchell's Best Photograph: "These people have been betrayed by Ukip"' *Guardian*, 22 June.
70. H. Stewart and R. Mason (2016) 'Nigel Farage's Anti-Migrant Poster Reported to Police' *Guardian*, 16 June.
71. TV Live News (2016) 'EU Referendum: The Great Debate – 21st June 2016' *YouTube*, 22 June. https://www.youtube.com/watch?v=30ijwPbjzns

72. J. Moore (2016) 'Nigel Farage Says "Looks Like Remain Will Edge It" as Polls Close' *Newsweek*, 23 June.
73. A. Withnall (2016) 'EU Referendum: Nigel Farage's 4am victory speech' *Independent*, 24 June.
74. 'Pro-Brexit Leader Johnson Says Nothing Will Change in Short Term' *Reuters*, 24 June 2016.
75. 'Text of David Cameron's Speech After "Brexit" Vote' *New York Times*, 24 June.
76. T. Helm and R. Mason (2016) 'Leadsom Told to Apologise for Claim Children "Make Her a Better PM"' *Guardian*, 9 July.
77. R. Partos (2016) 'Campaigning in Poetry, Governing in Prose? The development of Conservative Party immigration policy in government and in opposition since 1945', PhD thesis, University of Sussex: 225.
78. T. May (2016) 'Theresa May – 2016 Speech to Launch Leadership Campaign', 11 July. Full text: https://www.ukpol.co.uk/theresa-may-2016-speech-to-launch-leadership-campaign/
79. European Council (2016) 'Press Statement by President Donald Tusk on the Outcome of the Referendum in the UK', 24 June.
80. May (2016).
81. D. Davis (2016) 'Trade Deals. Tax cuts. and taking time before triggering Article 50. A Brexit economic strategy for Britain' *Conservative Home*, 14 July.
82. N. Dooley (2022) 'Frustrating Brexit? Ireland and the UK's conflicting approaches to Brexit negotiations' *Journal of European Public Policy*, published online.
83. B. Laffan (2019) 'How the EU27 Came to Be' *Journal of Common Market Studies*, 57(s1): 13–27.
84. B. Johnson (2016) 'I Cannot Stress Too Much That Britain Is Part of Europe – And always will be' *Telegraph*, 26 June.
85. R. Tuck (2020) *The Left Case for Brexit: Reflections on the Current Crisis* (Cambridge: Polity Press): 112.
86. 'UK Ambassador to US Meets May after Trump Backs Farage for Job' *Sky News*, 23 November 2016; N. Woolf and J. Elgot (2016) 'Nigel Farage Would Be Great UK Ambassador to US, Says Donald Trump' *Guardian*, 22 November.
87. 'Border Between Republic and Northern Ireland Difficult Issue Says UK's Brexit Minister' *Irish Examiner*, 17 July 2016.
88. T. May (2017) 'The Government's Negotiating Objectives for Exiting the EU: PM speech', 17 January (London: Prime Minister's Office).
89. S. Coates (2017) 'May to EU: Give us a fair deal or you'll be crushed' *The Times*, 18 June; J. Slack (2017) 'Steel of the New Iron Lady' *Daily Mail*, 18 January.
90. N. Farage (2017) 'I can hardly believe that the PM is now using the phrases and words that I've been mocked for using for years. Real progress' *Twitter*, 17 January. https://twitter.com/nigel_farage/status/821336404257017856
91. A. Seldon (2020) *May at 10: The Verdict* (London: Biteback Publishing): 302.
92. T. May (2016) 'EU and Our Place in the World', 25 April (London: Home Office).
93. 'Brussels Draft Brexit Plans "Unacceptable" – Arlene Foster' *News Letter*, 28 February 2018.
94. 'May Insists UK Will Leave EU Customs Union and Single Market' *RTÉ*, 2 July 2018.
95. T. Shipman and C. Wheeler (2018) 'David Davis Brands PM "Dishonest" Over his Brexit Alternative' *Sunday Times*, 15 July.
96. H. Stewart, P. Crerar and D. Sabbagh (2018) 'May's Plan "Sticks in the Throat", Says Boris Johnson as He Resigns over Brexit' *Guardian*, 9 July.
97. P. Dallison and J. Barigazzi (2018) 'Emmanuel Macron Says Leading Brexiteers Are "Liars"' *Politico*, 20 September.

98. T. May (2018) 'PM Statement on Brexit Negotiations', 15 November 2018 (London: Prime Minister's Office).
99. J. McCormack (2018) 'Brexit: Arlene Foster to reaffirm opposition to backstop at conference' *BBC News*, 24 November.
100. 'Boris Johnson Says Brexit Deal Will Make Britain an EU Colony' *Reuters*, 13 November 2018.
101. 'British Prime Minister Theresa May Announces her Resignation' *Reuters*, 24 May 2019.
102. *Telegraph* (2019) 'Boris Johnson Smashes "Gridlock" Wall with "Get Brexit Done" JCB | General Election 2019' *YouTube*, 10 December. https://www.youtube.com/watch?v=tzKFpeEUl0k
103. The UK only participated in the 2019 European Parliament elections because of delays over negotiating its withdrawal from the EU. Perhaps for this reason, it was a keenly fought contest in which overall turnout increased slightly on the 2014 election.
104. J. Rankin and R. Mason (2019) 'Boris Johnson Gets his Deal and a Slap on the Back in Brussels' *Guardian*, 17 October.
105. A. Quinn (2019) 'Watch Boris Johnson Tell the DUP in 2018 He Would Never Put Border in the Irish Sea – Today He Put a Border in the Irish Sea' *News Letter*, 17 October.
106. Revised text of the Political Declaration setting out the framework for the future relationship between the European Union and the United Kingdom as agreed at negotiators' level on 17 October 2019, to replace the one published in OJ C 66I of 19.2.2019, TF50 (2019) 65 – Commission to EU 27.
107. S. van Kessel (2020) 'Populist Radical Right Parties across Europe Not Eager to Leave the EU' *UK in a Changing Europe*, 4 March.
108. B. Johnson (2019) 'PM Statement in the House of Commons', 21 October 2019 (London: House of Commons).
109. 'The UK Celebrates Brexit Day 2020, In Pictures' *Telegraph*, 31 January.
110. R. Merrick (2021) 'Brexit: Tariffs paid on £9.5bn of UK exports to EU despite Boris Johnson's claim of "tariff-free" deal' *Independent*, 15 November.
111. F. Ghouri (2021) 'Brexit Hit: City of London suffers £2.3 trillion derivatives loss in a single month' *City AM*, 11 May.
112. S. Brush (2021) 'New York Wins from Brexit's $3.3 Trillion Hit to One Key Market' *Bloomberg*, 11 May.
113. S. Sleigh (2021) ' "A New Dawn": Boris Johnson hails UK–Australia trade deal' *Evening Standard*, 15 June.
114. Office for Budget Responsibility (2021) 'Economic and Fiscal Outlook – October 2021' (London: OBR): 58.
115. 'Opinion Panel Poll Finds Majority Now View the Protocol as Positive for Northern Ireland' Queens University Belfast, 28 October 2021.
116. J.R. Gillingham (2018) *The EU: An Obituary* (London: Verso): xiv.
117. M. Savage and L. O'Carroll (2021) 'Majority of Northern Irish Voters Want Vote on Staying in UK' *Guardian*, 29 August.
118. T. Emin RA, 'I Want My Time With You', terrace wires, St Pancras International.
119. Patel (2020): 2–3.
120. K. Keener (2019) 'Banksy Comments on the Removal of 2017 Brexit Mural' *Art Critique*, 12 September.
121. Savanta (2021) 'EU Referendum Polling', 12 November 2021.
122. Savanta (2023) 'Brexit Poll – Independent', 1 January 2023.
123. R. Sayal (2021) 'Record Number of People Cross Channel to UK in Small Boats' *Guardian*, 5 November.
124. 'Channel Migrants: Emmanuel Macron and Boris Johnson clash over crisis' *BBC News*, 26 November.

Chapter 14 Next Generation EU

1. Rotterdam Philharmonic Orchestra (2020) 'From Us, for You: Beethoven Symphony No. 9' *YouTube*, 20 March. https://www.youtube.com/watch?v=3eXT60rbBVk
2. AFP (2020) 'Epidemic Infects Europe with "Germ of Division"' *France 24*, 28 March.
3. A. Malara (2020) 'Diagnosing the First COVID-19 Patient in Italy – Codogno, Italy' *European Society of Cardiology*, 25 March.
4. As Luuk van Middelaar notes in his account of the pandemic, France had recorded three Covid-19 cases by this point. Unlike Mattia Maestri, the individuals concerned had recently visited China: L. van Middelaar (2021) *Pandemonium: Saving Europe* (Newcastle upon Tyne: Agenda Publishing). Some studies suggest that the virus was circulating in Europe even earlier: A. Cerqua and R. Di Stefano (2022) 'When Did Coronavirus Arrive in Europe?' *Statistical Methods & Applications*, 31(1): 181–95.
5. World Health Organization (2020) 'HIV/AIDS Surveillance in Europe 2020: 2019' (Geneva: WHO): 6.
6. J. Rentoul (1996) 'Beef War a Fiasco, PM Admits' *Independent*, 11 September.
7. Council of the European Union (2009) 'Extraordinary Council meeting Employment, Social Policy, Health and Consumer Affairs', Luxembourg 30 April, 9347/09 (Presse 111) (Brussels: Council of the European Union).
8. M. Rivasi (2010) 'Report on the Evaluation of the Management of H1N1 Influenza in 2009–2010 in the EU' European Parliament Committee on the Environment, Public Health and Food Safety (2010) (2010/2153(INI)) (Strasbourg: European Parliament).
9. European Centre for Disease Prevention and Control (2020a) 'Threat Assessment Brief: Pneumonia cases possibly associated with a novel coronavirus in Wuhan, China', 9 January (Solna: ECDC).
10. The countries in question were San Marino, Monaco, Switzerland and the UK. European Centre for Disease Prevention and Control (2020b) 'ECDC Assessment of the COVID-19 Situation in Europe as of 2 March 2020', 2 March 2020 (Solna: ECDC).
11. 'Coronavirus Disease 2019 (COVID-19) in the EU/EEA and the UK – eighth update', Rapid Risk Assessment, 8 April 2020 (Solna: ECDC).
12. These lockdowns varied in their severity. In Sweden, younger children continued to attend school, while their Spanish counterparts were not even allowed to play outside.
13. 'Ryanair Boss Condemns "Lunacy" and "Hysteria" over Coronavirus' *This Week*, 4 March 2020.
14. Ryanair (2020) 'Ryanair Full Year Profits Up 13% to €1bn Due to Stronger Revenue and 4% Traffic Growth Pre-Covid', 18 May, https://corporate.ryanair.com/news/ryanair-full-year-profits-up-13-to-e1bn-due-stronger-revenue-4-traffic-growth-pre-covid/; Ryanair (2022) 'Ryanair Reports Full Year Loss of €355m', 16 May, https://investor.ryanair.com/wp-content/uploads/2022/05/FY22-Ryanair-Results.pdf.
15. J. Maarten De Vet, D. Nigohosyan, J. Núñez Ferrer, A.-K. Gross, S. Kuehl and M. Flickenschild (2021) 'Impacts of the COVID-19 Pandemic on EU Industries', Study requested by the IRTE Department, European Parliament, PE 662.903 (Strasbourg: European Council).
16. European Commission (2019) 'Economic Forecast – Autumn 2019' European Economy (Brussels: DG ECFIN).
17. European Commission (2020) 'Economic Forecast – Summer 2020' (Interim) European Economy (Brussels: DG ECFIN).
18. S. Carrera and N. Chun Luk (2020) 'In the Name of COVID-19: An assessment of the Schengen internal border controls and travel restrictions in the EU', Study requested by the LIBE Committee, PE 659.506 (Strasbourg: European Parliament).

19. 'Child Dies in Fire in Greek Migrant Camp on Lesbos' *Al Jazeera*, 16 March 2020.
20. L. Marlowe (2020) 'Coronavirus: European solidarity sidelined as French interests take priority. Row over face masks exposes threat to EU principles of free trade and collaboration' *Irish Times*, 30 March.
21. 'The Fight against COVID-19 and EU and US Export Controls' *Reed Smith Client Alerts*, 23 March 2020.
22. U. von der Leyen (2020) 'Speech by President von der Leyen at the European Parliament Plenary on the European Coordinated Response to the COVID-19 Outbreak', Speech 20/532 (Brussels, European Commission).
23. D.M. Herszenhorn, J. Barigazzi and R. Momtaz (2020) 'Virtual Summit, Real Acrimony: EU leaders clash over "corona bonds"' *Politico Europe*, 27 March.
24. 'Italy's PM Conte: "Mr Nobody" who found his voice' *France 24*, 20 August 2019.
25. J. Follain, A. Speciale and T. Ebhardt (2019) 'Democrats, Five Star Back Conte to Lead New Government' *Bloomberg*, 28 August.
26. 'Italy's M5S "Minibot" Proposal Illegal: Economy Minister' *teleSUR*, 8 June 2019.
27. M. Duncan (2018) 'Italy Allows Migrant Ship to Dock' *Politico Europe*, 16 July.
28. 'Prime Minister Conte Calls Out Salvini on Roma Register' *CDE News*, 20 June 2018.
29. R. Mason (2020) 'Boris Johnson Boasted of Shaking Hands on Day Sage Warned Not To' *Guardian*, 5 May.
30. D. Ghiglione, S. Jones and B. Hall (2020) 'Italy Faces Its "Darkest Hour" with Coronavirus, Says Prime Minister' *Financial Times*, 9 March.
31. 'Italy Shuts Down All Shops and Restaurants as Coronavirus Cases Rise' *Time*, 11 March.
32. 'Italy Set to Ease Coronavirus Lockdown Beginning May 4, Prime Minister Conte Says' *CNBC*, 21 April 2020.
33. Van Middelaar (2021): 80.
34. European Central Bank (2020) 'ECB Announces €750 billion Pandemic Emergency Purchase Programme (PEPP)', Press Release, 18 March.
35. Report on the Comprehensive Policy Response to the COVID-19 Pandemic, Eurogroup, 9 April 2020.
36. J. Strupczewski and G. Jones (2019) 'Italy's Alarm over Reform of Eurozone Bailout Fund May Be Overblown' *Reuters*, 20 November.
37. Herszenhorn, Barigazzi and Momtaz (2020).
38. J. Henley (2020) 'Merkel Among Winners as Europeans Give Verdict on Anti-Covid Battles' *Guardian*, 6 June.
39. U. Krotz and L. Schramm (2022) 'Embedded Bilateralism, Integration Theory, and European Crisis Politics: France, Germany, and the birth of the EU corona recovery fund' *Journal of Common Market Studies*, 60(3): 536.
40. H. Von Der Burchard, I. Oliveira and E. Schaart (2020) 'Dutch Try to Calm North–South Economic Storm over Coronavirus' *Politico Europe*, 27 March.
41. R. Emmott and B.H. Meijer (2020) 'EU Delays Strict Rule-of-Law Conditions for Recovery Fund' *Reuters*, 21 July.
42. D.M. Herszenhorn and L. Bayer (2020) 'EU Leaders Agree on €1.82T Budget and Coronavirus Recovery Package' *Politico Europe*, 21 July.
43. U. von der Leyen (2021) 'Statement by President von der Leyen on Italy's Recovery and Resilience Plan' Statement 21/358 (Brussels: European Commission).
44. L. Zanotti (2021) 'What Mario Draghi's Invitation to Form a Government Tells Us about Italian Democracy' *LSE European Politics and Policy Blog*, 2 March.
45. O. Blanchard (2020) 'Italy, the ECB, and the Need to Avoid Another Euro Crisis' in R. Baldwin and B. Weder di Mauro (eds) *Mitigating the COVID Economic Crisis: Act Fast and Do Whatever It Takes* (London: CEPR): 49–50.

46. International Monetary Fund (2021) 'Italy: 2021 Article IV Consultation-Press Release; Staff Report and Statement by the Executive Director for Italy', 2 June (Washington DC: IMF).

47. European Commission (2022) Economic Forecast – Winter 2022, European Economy Institutional Papers 169 (Brussels: DG ECFIN).

48. European Commission (2022).

49. Source: European Central Bank (2022) 'Economic Bulletin – Issue 5' (Frankfurt A.M.: ECB).

50. Z. Eda (2020) 'Germany Lifts Covid-19 Prompted Export Ban for Personal Protective Equipment', 19 March.

51. S. Morgan (2020) 'Keep on Trucking: EU deploys "green lanes" to unclog freight' *Euractiv*, 23 March.

52. J. Scott Marcus, N. Frederic Poitiers, L. Guetta-Jeanrenaud, M. Grzegorczyk, N. Röhner, S. Buckingham, F. Hortal Foronda and J. Pelkmans (2021) 'The Impact of Covid-19 on the Internal Market', Study requested by the European Parliament's Imco Committee, PE 658.219 (Strasbourg: European Parliament).

53. Decision No. 1082/2013/EU of the European Parliament and of the Council of 22 October 2013 on serious cross-border threats to health and repealing Decision No 2119/98/EC.

54. Commission Decision of 18.6.2020 approving the agreement with Member States on procuring Covid-19 vaccines on behalf of the Member States and related procedures, Brussels, 18.6.2020 C(2020) 4192 final (Brussels: European Commission).

55. European Investment Bank (2020) 'Commission and EIB Provide Curevac with a €75 Million Financing for Vaccine Development and Expansion of Manufacturing', Press Release, 6 July; C. Knight (2020) 'BioNTech moves to head of pack in fight against coronavirus', PressRelease, 17 November 2020 (Luxembourg EIB).

56. A. Hernández-Morales (2020) 'Germany Confirms That Trump Tried to Buy Firm Working on Coronavirus Vaccine' *Politico Europe*, 15 March.

57. Hernández-Morales (2020).

58. 'Italy Rallies Round Nurse Abused over Covid Vaccination' *The Times*, 31 December 2020.

59. E. Schaart (2020) 'Rutte Says Dutch Government is Doing Enough to Fight Coronavirus' *Politico Europe*, 18 March.

60. J. Barigazzi (2020) 'Italy's Matteo Salvini Makes U-turn on Face Masks' *Politico Europe*, 3 August.

61. OECD (2020) 'COVID-19 Deaths on the Rise Again in the European Union', OECD Data Insights, 19 November.

62. Eurobarometer (2021) 'The EU and the Coronavirus Pandemic', Standard Eurobarometer 94, Winter 2020–21 (Brussels: European Commission).

63. J. de Vries (2021) 'How Covid Derailed the Great Hope of the Dutch Far Right' *Guardian*, 4 May.

64. AFP (2021) 'Twitter Marks Dutch Populist's Vaccine Tweet "Misleading"' *France 24*, 9 March.

65. M. Potters (2021) 'Bokito in Blijdorp besmet met corona, ook andere gorilla's en leeuwen hebben het virus' *AD.nl*, 19 November 2021.

66. C. Vergnano (2023) 'Italian Uprising from Covid Skepticism to Societal Polarization' in M. Butler and P. Knight (eds) *COVID Conspiracies in Global Perspective* (Abingdon: Routledge): 247; Daniele Lettig (2021) 'Salvini's Lega Joins Protests against COVID Certificate' *Euractiv*, 29 July.

67. T. Stickings (2021) 'Anti-Vax German Politician Dies of Coronavirus' *National News*, 22 December.

68. A. Condomines (2021) 'Covid-19 : La fondation de Bill Gates "se doutait-elle de quelque chose" comme l'affirme Philippe de Villiers?' *Libération*, 18 April; 'French Presidential Hopeful Zemmour Says COVID Fears are Overblown' *Reuters*, 22 November 2021.
69. Source: https://www.politico.eu/article/coronavirus-vaccination-europe-live-data-tracker-coverage/
70. P. Paunova, D. Veleva and T. Wesolowsky (2022) ' "I'll Kill You!": COVID anti-vaxxer attacks doctor in Bulgaria' *Radio Free Europe / Radio Liberty*, 19 January.
71. 'Diana Sosoaca Says 75% of Teenagers and Young Adults at Risk Because of Vaccine in Romania, Bucharest' *Newsflare*, 2 October 2021; Antenna 3 CNN (2021) 'Dosar penal, după circul făcut de Şoşoacă la un centru de vaccinare' *YouTube* 7 December. https://www.youtube.com/watch?v=oZzNN-Z_gzo
72. D. Stefan, G. Oana, V. Raiu Catalin, A. Doina, D. Popovici Emilian and A. Cristian (2021) 'COVID-19 in Romania: What went wrong?' *Frontiers in Public Health*, 17 December.
73. F. Guarascio and L. Burger (2021) 'AstraZeneca to Supply 31 Million COVID-19 Shots to EU in First Quarter, a 60% Cut – EU Source' *Reuters*, 22 January.
74. J. Deutsch (2021) 'Breton: No AstraZeneca jabs exported from the Netherlands after EU export controls' *Politico Europe*, 3 March.
75. 'Timeline: How the EU provoked anger in Ireland and the UK with plans for a hard border for vaccines' *Journal*, 1 February 2021.
76. 'UK's Johnson Tells EU's Von Der Leyen of "Grave" Vaccine Concerns' *Reuters*, 29 January 2021; D. Frost (2021) 'Observations on the Present State of the Nation' 12 October (London: Cabinet Office).
77. J. Holder (2022) 'Tracking Coronavirus Vaccinations around the World' *New York Times*, 22 April.
78. As of May 2022, the EU exported 2.4 billion vaccines. Of these, it exported 156 million to Africa compared to 1.5 billion to Europe. Source: WTO-IMF COVID-19 Vaccine Trade Tracker, June 2022 update.
79. Source: 'Who Are We?' *Europeans United*. https://www.europeansunited.eu/europeansunited-2/
80. 'Tens of Thousands Protest against Coronavirus Measures' *VRT*, 23 January 2022; S. Molloy (2021) 'Far-Right Extremists Hijacked Tradie Covid Anger to Fuel Chaos and Groom New Recruits, Expert Claims' *News.com.au*, 22 September 2022.
81. A. Hope (2022) 'Brussels Covid Demonstrations Turn Violent as Police Clash with Protesters', *Brussels Times*, 23 January.

Chapter 15 Ukraine

1. *Al Jazeera* (2022) ' "No Other Option": Excerpts of Putin's speech declaring war', 24 February. Full text: https://www.aljazeera.com/news/2022/2/24/putins-speech-declaring-war-on-ukraine-translated-excerpts
2. *Al Jazeera* (2022).
3. Z. Wojnowski (2022) 'Putin's "History" of Ukraine Has an All-Too Soviet Legacy' *Open Democracy*, 25 February.
4. R. Mellen (2022) 'The Human Toll of the Russian–Ukraine Conflict since 2014', *Washington Post*, 22 January.
5. See: L.J. Trautman (2019) 'Impeachment, Donald Trump and the Attempted Extortion of Ukraine' *Pace Law Review*, 40(2): 141–224.
6. 'Energy Security Dominates EU–Ukraine Summit, as Prices Continue to Surge' *Euronews*, 13 October 2021.
7. 'Ukraine Conflict Death Toll: What we know' *France24.com*, 13 April 2022.

8. *USA Today* (2020) 'Ukrainian President Volodymyr Zelenskyy Shares a Message from Kyiv' *YouTube*, 25 February. https://www.youtube.com/watch?v=tLv9IqcoNe8
9. N. Saad (2022) 'Netflix is Bringing Back "Servant of the People", the TV Show That Made Ukraine's President Famous' *Press Herald*, 16 March.
10. A. Guterres (2022) 'Secretary-General's Remarks to Press on the War in Ukraine', Office of the UN Secretary, 22 March.
11. 'Ukraine: Civilian casualty update', Office of the UN High Commissioner for Human Rights, 3 January 2023.
12. Ukrainian Institute (2022) 'Donetsk Academic Regional Drama Theatre'. Full text: https://ui.org.ua/en/sectors-en/donetsk-academic-regional-drama-theatre/
13. Council of the European Union (2022) 'EU Adopts Package of Sanctions in Response to Russian Recognition of the Non-Government Controlled Areas of the Donetsk and Luhansk Oblasts of Ukraine and Sending of Troops into the Region', Press Release, 23 February (Brussels: Council of the European Union).
14. Council of the European Union (2022).
15. Council of the European Union (2022) 'Fourth Package of Sanctions in View of Russia's Military Aggression against Ukraine', Press Release, 15 March.
16. A. Åslud (2022) 'Fortress Russia Crumbles' *Project Syndicate*, 9 March.
17. A. Frangos (2022) 'S&P Hits Russia with Default Rating on Foreign Debt' *Wall Street Journal*, 9 April.
18. Source: Imports of Natural Gas by Partner Country (NRG_TI_GAS), Eurostat.
19. L. Gehrke and H. Von Der Burchard (2022) 'Scholz: Russian energy ban would mean European recession' *Politico Europe*, 23 March.
20. M. Arnold, A. Kazmin and E. Solomon (2022) 'Can Europe Wean Itself Off Its Dependence on Russian Fossil Fuels?' *Financial Times*, 21 March.
21. @GitanasNauseda (2022) 'From this month on – no more Russian gas in Lithuania. Years ago my country made decisions that today allow us with no pain to break energy ties with the agressor [*sic*]. If we can do it, the rest of Europe can do it too!' *Twitter*, 2 April. https://twitter.com/GitanasNauseda/status/1510277034357968898
22. M. Petkova (2022) 'Europe's Dependence on Gas Is Growing, Not Slowing', *Energy Monitor*, 28 February.
23. Council of the EU Press (2022) 'Member States Commit to Reducing Gas Demand by 15% Next Winter', Press Release, 26 July (Brussels: Council of the European Union).
24. Source: Council of the European Union (undated) 'Infographic – Where Does the EU's Gas Come From?' (Brussels: Council of the European Union).
25. C. Cooper and A. Zimmermann (2022) 'Qatar Scandal Gives Europe a Big Gas Headache' *Politico Europe*, 19 December.
26. M. Stothard (2018) 'Spanish Foreign Minister Sanctioned by Securities Regulator' *Financial Times*, 10 October.
27. D.M. Herszenhorn (2021) 'Realpolitik Prevails as EU Takes No Action for Navalny' *Politico Europe*, 25 January.
28. D.M. Herszenhorn and J. Barigazzi (2021) 'Borrell Stands By as Lavrov Calls EU "Unreliable Partner"' *Politico Europe*, 5 February.
29. P. Oltermann (2022) '"German Thinkers" War of Words over Ukraine Exposes Generational Divide', *Guardian*, 6 May; D. Janjevic (2022) 'Ukraine: German lawmakers overwhelmingly approve heavy weapons deliveries' *DW-Deutsche Welle*, 28 April.
30. E. Macron (2017) 'Initiative for Europe: Speech by M. Emmanuel Macron President of the French Republic', 26 September. Full text: http://international.blogs.ouest-france.fr/archive/2017/09/29/macron-sorbonne-verbatim-europe-18583.html
31. J. Dempsey (2022) 'The War in Ukraine Could Change Poland' *Carnegie Europe*, 15 March. https://carnegieeurope.eu/strategiceurope/86636

32. i24NEWS–AFP (2022) 'Borrell: EU countries to send "fighter jets" to Ukraine', *i24NEWS*, 27 February.

33. G. de Briganti (2022) 'The Almost Comical Saga of Polish MiG-29 Fighters for Ukraine' *Defense-Aerospace.com*, 9 March.

34. K. Griffith, J. Gordon and B. Patel (2022) 'US Gives Poland the "Green Light" to Give Ukraine MIG Fighter Jets as Russia Warns It Is at WAR with ANY Country Hosting Kyiv's Aircraft' *Daily Mail*, 6 March.

35. 'US Rejects Poland's Offer to Send Mig-29 Fighter Jets to Ukraine', *Al Jazeera*, 9 March.

36. RadioRomania Iasi (2022) 'EU Foreign-Policy Chief Josep Borrell, on the Subject of Fighter Jets to Ukraine' *Youtube*, 4 March. https://www.youtube.com/watch?v=DJ_Ax5bQQks

37. S. Auer (2022) *European Disunion* (London: Hurst): 254.

38. G. Leali (2022) 'EU's Borrell Makes Premature Pledge of €500M More Military Aid to Ukraine' *Politico Europe*, 12 March.

39. H. Maurer, R.Whitman and N. Wright (2023) 'The EU and the Invasion of Ukraine: A collective responsibility to act?' *International Affairs*, 99(1): 219–38.

40. S. Pogatchnik (2022) 'Poll: More Irish want to join NATO in wake of Ukraine invasion' *Politico Europe*, 27 March.

41. 'Russia Warns of Nuclear Deployment if Sweden, Finland Join NATO' *Al Jazeera*, 14 April 2022.

42. UNHCR (2022) 'Ukraine Refugee Situation Operational Update – Poland, 25 April 2022' (Geneva: UNHCR). By the end of 2022, nearly 8 million individual refugees from Ukraine had been recorded, with 1.5 million claiming temporary protection in Poland. UNHCR (2023) 'Ukraine Situation Flash Update #39 (27 January 2023)' (Geneva: UNHCR); UNHRC (2023) 'Ukraine Situation Regional Refugee Response Plan (January–December 2023): Poland' (Geneva: UNHCR).

43. K. Ferral (2022) '"Now We Are Like One Family": Despite tense past, Poles open homes to Ukrainians in wake of war' *Milwaukee Journal Sentinel*, 4 April.

44. L. Drazanova (2022) 'Why Are Ukrainian Refugees Welcomed in Central and Eastern Europe?' 23 March, *EUI MPC Blog*; L. Tondo and E. Akinwotu (2022) 'People of Colour Fleeing Ukraine Attacked by Polish Nationalists' *Guardian*, 2 March.

45. United Nations (2021) 'Uphold safety, Human Rights on Belarus–Poland Border, UN Agencies Urge', Press Release, 9 November (New York: UN).

46. European Commission (2022) 'Poland: Survey finds majority of Poles would welcome refugees from Ukraine', Press Release, 3 March (Brussels: European Commission).

47. E. Nicholson (2022) 'Ukrainians Fleeing War, and Volunteers to Help Them, Fill a Berlin Train Station' *NPR*, 4 March.

48. G. Topham (2022) 'Ryanair Will Be "First Airline to Return to Ukraine"' *Guardian*, 2 March.

49. B. Futàk-Campbell (2020) 'Political Synergy: How the European far-right and Russia have joined forces against Brussels' *Atlantisch Perspectief*, 44(1): 30–5; AP (2022a) '"Your Friend Putin": Salvini confronted during border visit' *Independent*, 8 March.

50. AP (2022b) '"See What Your Friend Putin Has Done": Italy's Matteo Salvini confronted in Poland' *Guardian*, 9 March.

51. V. Zelenskyy (2022) 'Speech by President of Ukraine Volodymyr Zelenskyy at a Meeting of the European Council', 25 March 2022. Full text: https://www.president.gov.ua/en/news/promova-prezidenta-ukrayini-volodimira-zelenskogo-na-zasidan-73809

52. European Council (2014) 'Conclusions on Ukraine', Brussels, 20 March 2014 (Brussels: European Council).
53. Zelenskyy (2022).
54. @ZelenskyyUa (2022) 'Sincerely commend EU leaders' decision at #EUCO to grant UA a candidate status. It's a unique and historical moment in UA-EU relations. Grateful to @CharlesMichel', @vonderleyen, and EU leaders for support. Ukraine's future is within the EU. #EmbraceUkraine' 23 June. https://twitter.com/ZelenskyyUa/status/1540038995178037249

Chapter 16 'To the People of Europe'

1. Bono (2018) 'A Thought That Needs to Become a Feeling' *Frankfurter Allgemeine Zeitung*, 27 August.
2. M. Le Pen (2022) 'Mon Projet Présidentiel': 19.
3. 'Programme de M. Jean-Marie Le Pen, président du Front national et candidat à l'élection présidentielle 2002'. https://www.vie-publique.fr/discours/129981-programme-de-m-jean-marie-le-pen-president-du-front-national-et-candid
4. 'Court Upholds Jean-Marie Le Pen Fine for Holocaust Comment' *France 24*, 27 March 2018.
5. É. Zemmour (2022) 'Pour que la France reste la France: Mon Programme'; J.L. Mélenchon (2022) 'L'Avenir en commun: Le programme pour l'Union Populaire'.
6. M. Le Pen (2022).
7. The movement was initially known as En Marche but it later changed its name to La République En Marche. In May 2022 it changed its name once more to Renaissance.
8. For a discussion of Macron as a technopopulist, see C.J. Bickerton and I. Accetti (2022) *Technopopulism: The New Logic of Democratic Politics* (Oxford: Oxford University Press).
9. M.-P. Bourgeois (2021) '27 Ans après son refus de se présenter en 1995, Jacques Delors se pose encore des questions' *BFM.tv*, 4 April.
10. N. Barré (2018) 'Macron à Davos: Il faut redonner un sens à la mondialisation' *Les Echos*, 24 January.
11. K. Willsher (2022) 'French Far-Right Leader Marine Le Pen Forced to Defend Putin Links' *Guardian*, 2 March.
12. J. Henley (2002) 'Le Pen Vote Shocks France' *Guardian*, 22 April.
13. J.F. Arnaud (2022) 'Maxime, électeur mélenchoniste, après le débat: "Macron-Le Pen, c'est la peste et le choléra"' *Challenges*, 21 April.
14. Franceinfo (2022) 'Revoir le débat entre Marine Le Pen et Emmanuel Macron' *YouTube*, 20 April. https://www.youtube.com/watch?v=v6g0u6yrDGc&t=1930s
15. Y. Serhan (2022) 'Italy Is Getting Its First Female Leader – A polished far-right firebrand' *Time*, 26 September.
16. A. Mingardi and N. Rossi (2022) 'Giorgia Meloni Is No Fascist, But Can She Revive Italy's Economy?' *Wall Street Journal*, 26 September.
17. G. Orsina (2022) 'Meloni Unlikely To Pick a Fight With Brussels' *Politico Europe*, 6 October.
18. L. Scazzieri (2022) 'What Meloni's Victory Means for Europe' *UK in a Changing Europe Blog*, 27 September.
19. J. Horowitz (2022), 'Giorgia Meloni May Lead Italy, and Europe Is Worried' *New York Times*, 15 September.
20. A. Kaval and P. Jacqué (2022) 'Italy's Meloni Appeals to Brussels While Drawing Criticism Back Home' *Le Monde*, 4 November.
21. European Commission (2021) 'Conference on the Future of Europe' *YouTube*, 9 May. https://www.youtube.com/watch?v=np1nkgAALag&t=330s

22. G. Gotev (2017) 'Macron, Merkel: EU treaty change is not taboo' *Euractiv*, 27 June.
23. E. Macron (2017) 'Speech by the President of the French Republic in Greece', Athens, 7 September. https://newyork.consulfrance.org/Speech-by-the-President-of-the-French-Republic-in-Greece
24. E. Macron (2019) 'Dear Europe, Brexit is a Lesson for All of Us: It's time for renewal' *Guardian*, 4 March.
25. M. Banks (2019) 'Italian Socialist David Sassoli Elected as New European Parliament President' *Parliament Magazine*, 3 July.
26. 'Conference on the Future of Europe Franco-German Non-Paper on Key Questions and Guidelines'. Text: https://www.politico.eu/wp-content/uploads/2019/11/Conference-on-the-Future-of-Europe.pdf
27. The plenary also included representatives of the European Parliament, the Council, the Commission, member states, regional and local government and civil society.
28. 'Joint Declaration of the European Parliament, the Council and the European Commission on the Conference on the Future of Europe Engaging with Citizens for Democracy – Building a More Resilient Europe' 2021/C 91 I/01, OJ C 91I, 18.3.2021, 1–4.
29. T. Nguyen (2021) 'Time to Be Honest: The future will not be decided by the Conference on the Future of Europe' *Notre Europe Policy Position*, 1 April.
30. P. Taylor (2021) 'Hijack the Conference on the Future of Europe!' *Politico Europe*, 7 May.
31. European Commission (2022) 'Special Eurobarometer on the Future of Europe (Jan 2022)' (Brussels: Eurobarometer).
32. M. Reuchamps and J. Suiter (2016) *Constitutional Deliberative Democracy in Europe* (Colchester: ECPR).
33. European Parliament (2021) 'Live Conference on the Future of Europe Citizens', ID: I-210432, Parliament – EbS contribution, 24/09/2021. https://audiovisual.ec.europa.eu/en/video/I-210432
34. Conference on the Future of Europe (2022) 'European Citizens Panel 1 – "Stronger economy, social justice, jobs, education, culture, sport, digital transformation" – Recommendations' (Strasbourg: Conference on the Future of Europe); (Strasbourg: Conference on the Future of Europe) 'European Citizens Panel 2 – "EU democracy, values, rights, rule of law, security" – Recommendations' (Strasbourg: Conference on the Future of Europe); 'European Citizens Panel 3 – "Climate change, environment, health" – Recommendations' (Strasbourg: Conference on the Future of Europe); 'European Citizens Panel 4 – "EU in the world, migration" – Recommendations' (Strasbourg: Conference on the Future of Europe).
35. A. Alemanno (2022) 'Over the last 6 months, 800 randomly-selected EU citizens came up with 178 recommendations addressed to EU leaders. How many of them require Treaty change to become a reality?' Twitter, 1 April. https://twitter.com/alemannoEU/status/1509819879410515970
36. Conference on the Future of Europe (2022) 'European Citizens Panel 2'.
37. European Parliament (2022) 'Live: Closing event of the Conference on the Future of Europe' *YouTube*, 9 May. https://www.youtube.com/watch?v=KtjH1ix0CHE
38. Preamble, Treaty on European Union (1992).
39. J. Delors (1993) 'Address by Jacques Delors to the European Parliament (On the Occasion of the Investiture Debate Following Appointment of the New Commission)' 10 February, SPEECH/93/8 (Brussels: European Commission).
40. J. Goldsmith (1994) *The Trap* (New York: Carroll & Graff).
41. D. Hodson (2016) 'Jacques Delors: Vision, revisionism, and the design of EMU' in D. Kenneth and M. Ivo (eds) *Architects of the Euro: Intellectuals in the Making of European Monetary Union* (Oxford: Oxford University Press): 212–32.

42. Delors (1993).
43. J.R. Gillingham (2018) *The EU: An Obituary* (London: Verso): 245.
44. Gillingham (2018): vii.
45. L. van Middelaar (2021) *Pandemonium: Saving Europe* (Newcastle upon Tyne: Agenda Publishing).
46. Eurobarometer (2022) 'Standard Eurobarometer 96 – Winter 2020–2021 (Brussels: European Commission).
47. Goldsmith (1994): 19.
48. 'Donald Trump: European Union is a foe on trade' *BBC News*, 15 July 2018.
49. Goldsmith (1994): 68.
50. Associated Press in Rome (2021) 'Matteo Salvini to Face Trial over Standoff with Migrant Rescue Ship' *Guardian*, 17 April.
51. N. Farage, 'Preparation for the European Council Meeting (23 October 2011) (debate)', 12 October 2011, Brussels; G. Wilders (2017) 'Our population is being replaced and the European Commission is proud of it' *Twitter*, 28 September. https://twitter.com/geertwilderspvv/status/913479487832170497
52. Source: 'European Commission: 1992 Staff Budget', HL Deb 28 January 1992 vol 534 cc46-7WA; European Commission (2022) 'HR key figures 2022' (Brussels: European Commission); 'Luxembourg 28,000 State Employees Struggle to Keep Up with Demand' *Luxembourg Times*, 22 October 2019.
53. Eurobarometer (2022) 'Standard Eurobarometer 97 – Summer 2022' (Brussels: European Commission): 41.
54. A. Sparrow (2016) 'EU Referendum: Michael Gove questioned on Sky News – live' *Guardian*, 3 June.
55. A. Moravcsik (2008) 'The Myth of Europe's Democratic Deficit' *Intereconomics*, 43(6): 331–40.
56. N. Tocci (2022) *A Green and Global Europe* (Cambridge: Polity).
57. K. Byrne (2022) 'U.K. Cools Off after Record-Breaking Heat Wave' *UPI*, 20 July.
58. P. Weston and J. Watts (2021) 'Highest Recorded Temperature of 48.8C in Europe Apparently Logged in Sicily' *Guardian*, 11 August.
59. S. Hudak (2022) 'Mariupol Theatre's Actors Interpret the Cry of a Nation' *Institute for War and Peace Reporting*, 21 July.

Further Reading

There are numerous insightful books on European integration. Here are a few that readers may wish to consult in the first instance.

History

Perry Anderson (2009) *The New Old World* (London: Verso)

Marie-Thérèse Bitsch (2004) *Histoire de la construction européenne de 1945 à nos jours* (Brussels: Éditions complexe)

Mark Gilbert (2020) *European Integration: A Political History* (London: Rowman & Littlefield)

John R. Gillingham (2018) *The EU: An Obituary* (London: Verso)

Brigitte Leucht, Katja Seidel and Laurent Warlouzet (eds) (2023) *Reinventing Europe: The History of the European Union, 1945 to the Present* (London: Bloomsbury)

Klaus Kiran Patel (2020) *Project Europe: A History* (Cambridge: Cambridge University Press)

Luuk van Middelaar (2013) *The Passage to Europe: How a Continent Became a Union* (New Haven and London: Yale University Press)

Philipp Ther (2016) *Europe since 1989: A History* (Princeton, NJ: Princeton University Press)

Integration

Philipp Genschel and Markus Jachtenfuchs (eds) (2013) *Beyond the Regulatory Polity? The European Integration of Core State Powers* (Oxford: Oxford University Press)

Andrew Moravcsik (1998) *The Choice for Europe: Social Purpose and State Power from Messina to Maastricht* (Abingdon: Routledge)

Sabine Saurugger (2020) *Théories et concepts de l'intégration européenne* (Paris: Presses de Sciences Po)

Alex Stone Sweet and Wayne Sandholtz (eds) (1998) European Integration and Supranational Governance (Oxford: Oxford University Press)

Institutions

Frédéric Mérand (2015) *The Political Commissioner: A European Ethnography* (Oxford: Oxford University Press)

Tommaso Pavone (2022) *The Ghostwriters: Lawyers and the Politics Behind the Judicial Construction of Europe* (Cambridge: Cambridge University Press)

Uwe Puetter (2014) *The European Council and the Council: New Intergovernmentalism and Institutional Change* (Oxford: Oxford University Press)

Ariadna Ripoll Servent (2017) *The European Parliament* (Basingstoke: Palgrave)

FURTHER READING

Politics and Governance

Michelle Cini and Nieves Pérez-Solórzano Borragán (2022) *European Union Politics* (Oxford: Oxford University Press)

Simon Hix and Bjørn Høyland (2022) *The Political System of the European Union* (London: Bloomsbury)

Erik Jones, Anand Menon and Stephen Weatherill (eds) (2012) *The Oxford Handbook of the European Union* (Oxford: Oxford University Press)

Helen Wallace, Mark A. Pollack, Christilla Roederer-Rynning and Alasdair R. Young (eds) (2020) *Policy-Making in the European Union* (Oxford: Oxford University Press)

Policies

Michelle Egan (2015) *Single Markets: Economic Integration in Europe and the United States* (Oxford: Oxford University Press)

Andrew Geddes, Leila Hadj-Abdou and Leiza Brumat (2020) *Migration and Mobility in the European Union* (London: Red Globe Press)

Sarah Léonard and Christian Kaunert (eds) (2018) *Searching for a Strategy for the European Union's Area of Freedom, Security and Justice* (Abingdon: Routledge)

Waltraud Schelkle (2017) *The Political Economy of Monetary Solidarity: Understanding the Euro Experiment* (Oxford: Oxford University Press)

Nathalie Tocci (2022) *A Green and Global Europe* (Cambridge: Polity)

Crises

Stefan Auer (2022) *European Disunion: Democracy, Sovereignty and the Politics of Emergency* (London: Hurst)

Fintan O'Toole (2018) *Heroic Failure: Brexit and the Politics of Pain* (New York: Apollo)

Adam Tooze (2018) *Crashed: How a Decade of Financial Crises Changed the World* (London: Penguin)

Luuk van Middelaar (2021) *Pandemonium: Saving Europe* (Newcastle upon Tyne: Agenda)

Leadership

Helen Drake (2002) *Jacques Delors: Perspectives on a European Leader* (Abingdon: Routledge)

Henriette Müller and Ingeborg Tömmel (eds) (2022) *Women and Leadership in the European Union* (Oxford: Oxford University Press)

Matthew Qvortrup (2014) *Angela Merkel: Europe's Most Influential Leader* (New Haven: Yale University Press)

Parties

Cas Mudde (2007) *Populist Radical Right Parties in Europe* (Cambridge: Cambridge University Press)

Peter Mair (2013) *Ruling the Void: The Hollowing of Western Democracy* (London: Verso)

Catherine E. De Vries and Sara B. Hobolt (2020) *Political Entrepreneurs: The Rise of Challenger Parties in Europe* (Princeton, NJ: Princeton University Press)

Emilie van Haute (ed.) (2016) *Green Parties in Europe* (Abingdon: Routledge)

Index

INDEX